SOCIAL MEDIA MADE ME RICH

SOCIAL MEDIA

—— MADE ME ——

RICH

Here's How it Can do the Same for You

MATTHEW LOOP

New York

SOCIAL MEDIA MADE ME RICH

Here's How it Can do the Same for You

Published in New York, New York, by Morgan James Publishing. Morgan James and The Entrepreneurial Publisher are trademarks of Morgan James, LLC.
www.MorganJamesPublishing.com

The Morgan James Speakers Group can bring authors to your live event. For more information or to book an event visit The Morgan James Speakers Group at
www.TheMorganJamesSpeakersGroup.com.

The information, ideas and suggestions in this book do not guarantee the reader will make the type of income the author has made, or any income at all. Everyone's ability to follow instructions and implement the action steps are different.

Neither the author nor the publisher shall be liable or responsible for any loss or damage allegedly arising as a consequence of your use or application of any information or suggestions in this book.

Limit of Liability / Disclaimer of Warranty: While the publisher and author have used their best efforts in preparing this book, they make no representations or warranties regarding the accuracy or completeness of the contents of this book. The publisher and author specifically disclaim any implied warranties of merchantability or fitness for a particular purpose, and make no guarantees whatsoever that you will achieve any particular result. Any case studies that are presented herein do not necessarily represent what you should expect to achieve, since business success depends on a variety of factors. We believe all case studies and results presented herein are true and accurate, but we have not audited the results. The advice and strategies contained in this book may not even be suitable for your situation, and you should consult your own advisors as appropriate. The publisher and the author shall not be held liable for any loss of profit or any other commercial damages, including but not limited to special, incidental, consequential, or other damages. The fact that an organization or website is referred to in this work as a citation and/or a potential source of information does not mean that the publisher or author endorses the information the organization or website may provide or the recommendations it may make. Further, readers should be aware that Internet websites listed in this work may have changed or disappeared after this work was written.

Earnings Disclaimer: We don't believe in get-rich programs—all human progress and accomplishment takes hard work. As stipulated by law, we cannot and do not make any guarantees about your ability to get results or earn any money with our ideas, information, tools or strategies. After all, it takes hard work to succeed in any type of business. In fact, it takes hard work to succeed at ANYTHING in life—try learning to play the guitar without putting in any work, and see how that goes! Your results in life are up to you and the amount of effort and resources that you are willing to put into succeeding. Nothing in this book or any of our websites is a promise or guarantee of results or future earnings, and we do not offer any legal, medical, tax or other professional advice. Any financial numbers referenced here, or on any of our sites, are simply estimates or projections, and should not be considered exact, actual or as a promise of potential earnings—all numbers are illustrative only. In fact, the average person who purchases this book and other programs never finishes the book, never puts the work into implementing the strategies taught, and therefore achieves little to no results.

Shelfie

A free eBook edition is available with the purchase of this print book.

CLEARLY PRINT YOUR NAME ABOVE IN UPPER CASE

Instructions to claim your free eBook edition:
1. Download the Shelfie app for Android or iOS
2. Write your name in **UPPER CASE** above
3. Use the Shelfie app to submit a photo
4. Download your eBook to any device

ISBN 978-1-63047-793-6 paperback
ISBN 978-1-63047-794-3 eBook
ISBN 978-1-63047-795-0 hardcover
Library of Congress Control Number:
2015914991

Cover Design by:
Brittany Bondar

In an effort to support local communities and raise awareness and funds, Morgan James Publishing donates a percentage of all book sales for the life of each book to Habitat for Humanity Peninsula and Greater Williamsburg.

Get involved today, visit
www.MorganJamesBuilds.com

CONTENTS

ACKNOWLEDGEMENTS

This book is dedicated to anyone that's ever been the underdog in life. It's for those that have encountered tremendous adversity and constant rejection, those that never had a silver spoon, the right connections, or odds stacked in their favor.

People have been telling me "you can't" for over thirty years. But you know what? They couldn't step into my mind and see the grand vision I held. They didn't have the passion, work ethic, and determination I had.

The voice inside me was stronger than all the limiting voices on the outside. This work you're holding in your hands represents opportunity, freedom, and abundance. It's your golden ticket to the life of prosperity you've always imagined for yourself.

This is a movement started to empower the average person, giving them the tools and resources to build a wildly profitable online business around what they love. With this powerful knowledge and by implementing what's revealed, you have the potential to finally live life on your terms, to start and grow a business around your ideal lifestyle.

As you'll soon see, I held nothing back in this work. It's not a pitch-fest.

This book is a tactical blueprint that shares the common denominators of the world's highest-paid Internet entrepreneurs, coaches, marketers, and information product developers.

I'd like to acknowledge my wife and Colombian princess, Tadser. She's everything I've ever wanted in a woman, my best friend, and an amazing mother. I'd also like to acknowledge my little man, Ethan. He makes my day, every day. He's destined for greatness. Family comes first.

I also want to extend my gratitude to the following life mentors. The truth is, anyone that's ever done great things in the world has had a coach. Here are the most notable ones in my life in regards to personal growth and business.

- Anthony Robbins
- Sylvester Stallone
- Robert Kiyosaki
- Frank Kern
- Richard Branson
- Yanik Silver
- Bob Proctor
- Joe Polish

INTRODUCTION

Be careful who you get advice from.
I get advice from people who are where I want to be.
—Robert Kiyosaki

My intention for writing this book is to create a quick, practical, easy-to-understand, comprehensive reference guide for those serious about learning how to generate life-changing, recurring income from the Internet.

This time-tested blueprint is meant to empower you and give you the strategies, tools, and resources you need to not only make your first dollar online, but to build a legitimate Internet-based business that can make you six or seven figures per year doing what you love.

I'm not into BS filler, hype, or theory, so you're going to discover what I've personally used to build my own Internet empire consisting of e-books, online courses, DVD trainings, membership sites, consulting and coaching programs, software, iPhone apps, and more.

I'm a VERY big advocate of finding those individuals who are successful, or who are where you want to be in any given area of life, then modeling exactly what they do. Why? These people have already spent enormous amounts of time, energy, effort, and money figuring out a formula that works. There's no need to reinvent the wheel, as associating with experienced mentors can provide a shortcut to your success, reduce your "hard knocks," and save you time—along with vast sums of cash.

Here's a great example of what I mean.

Let's say you want to prepare an absolutely delicious plate of lasagna, but you don't have the slightest clue how to cook. You have a couple options at your disposal.

You can go to culinary school for a year with the best chefs in the world. In this scenario, you'll spend the time and money to learn about food, combining spices, preparations, presentation, and a whole host of other things in the culinary arts.

The other option you have is this.

Maybe you know a relative or friend who actually prepares that incredible lasagna you're thinking about right now. So you pick up the phone, grab a pen and some paper, then proceed to write the valuable recipe you're given so you can make the perfect lasagna.

Now, even as far-fetched as this may sound, both scenarios above are things you could do. Which way is the easiest and fastest though? Which one costs you the least amount of time, money, and effort? Obviously, getting your hands on the exact recipe would be a no-brainer.

In this book, I offer you the recipe that has given my family and me the freedom and flexibility to do whatever we want when we choose. Knowing and applying this information has allowed us to live a fulfilling life on our terms.

This book contains the shortcut I wish I would've had starting out.

The large sums of income I've generated from the Internet are secondary to being able to have real freedom. Money is only a means to an end. It's geared to make you comfortable while enabling you to provide service beyond your physical means.

There has never been a better time in history for you to cash in on your passion.

The World Wide Web is the ultimate equalizer. It doesn't care if you're poor or rich. Everyone has the same incredible opportunity to better their circumstances.

Imagine waking up in the morning when you want and really being excited about your work. Imagine getting paid for doing what you love each day and feeling like you're fulfilling your life's purpose. Lastly, picture getting out of bed, powering up your laptop, checking your bank account, and noticing you had actually made money while you slept.

This will sound like a pipe dream or a fairy tale to some, but as you'll soon see, there's absolutely no reason that you cannot create this type of life for yourself.

Never let anyone tell you otherwise.

Those that love you the most (like your family and friends) will tend to criticize you the most because this is completely different from what they know. We'll talk more about attitudes, values, and beliefs later because you cannot succeed if you don't have the appropriate mindset.

I didn't come from a wealthy family, nor did I have any unfair advantage when I started in 2005. I was a beginner and didn't have a clue where to start. So if you're reading this right now and haven't made any money online, know that I was in the same exact position.

I made a lot of costly mistakes initially and throughout my time on the Internet. You get the benefit of shaving years off your learning curve while reading this book. Even if you're an intermediate or advanced marketer online, you'll save time and money. Frankly, I know what works and what doesn't.

"My pain, your gain," as they say.

My aim is to provide the strategies, tools, encouragement, and recipe to help empower you toward a new and extraordinary life. I'm going to show you how to take the specialized knowledge you possess and package it into information products and/or services that can be marketed and sold online. In the process, you have the potential to make a small fortune.

The choice in how you receive this information, and how you decide to apply it to your own life, is ultimately yours. This stuff works, but only if you do.

Have fun learning this highly sought-after skill set that will pay you well for the rest of your life. This is the MOST valuable and useful set of skills I've ever discovered. Don't be surprised if you feel the same after you start generating real passive income from the Internet.

PART I
THE FOUNDATION

Chapter 1

FOR THE SKEPTICS – FAQ

---

*People who say it cannot be done shouldn't
interrupt those who are doing it.*
—George Bernard Shaw

I felt it necessary to add this chapter because undoubtedly there will be many skeptics who claim that you cannot start a lucrative business (from scratch) using the Internet without having the right "connections." Some might even believe the myth that opportunity has been monopolized and the great gold rush is over.

Other people just have fears and doubts because this is so far removed from their current reality and comfort zone. Here are some of the most commonly asked questions I wanted to address:

Can anyone make money online with something they're passionate about?
The real truth is yes, as long as you have access to an Internet connection and can read and write at a third-grade level. Of course, there is work involved, so if

you're not a consistent action taker and have trouble following instructions, you won't make any money.

This book provides you with the tools, resources, and strategies that the world's highest-paid Internet entrepreneurs are using right now.

Do I have to leave my current job?

Absolutely not. In fact, when I started my online career, I was still in practice. I worked part-time on my new Internet-based business at first.

Then, as this online "secondary" source of income grew to surpass my primary, I decided to devote more time to it. Initially, I would allocate a small percentage of my existing income to building my Internet business.

Start first by devoting an hour or two per day. Either turn the time you'd normally be on the computer into productive time or turn the TV off for a couple hours each night so you can do more.

Do I have to be in my twenties or thirties to do this?

No. You're never too old to learn the skill set of Internet and social media marketing to start, manage, and grow an online business. Age is irrelevant in determining your success here.

Do I have to travel to make it work?

Not at all. You can work on your business from home in your spare time. Or, if you're like me, you can run your business from any place you travel anywhere in the world. It's your call. You just need an Internet connection.

Does it cost a lot of money to start an online business?

No, it doesn't. You can spend as little or as much as you want or have in your budget. I'm going to show you how to begin even if you have only a few dollars to your name. It's called "bootstrapping," and it's what I initially did.

Do I need to have a formal, university-based education?

Heck no. It's probably better if you don't have one (I'm smiling as I say that). Look, I went through eight years of formal education after high school, and it taught me NOTHING about real-world marketing, entrepreneurship, and creating a multimillion-dollar business.

There's a time and place for undergraduate or graduate university training, but it teaches you to be an employee, not an entrepreneur. This book is all about you taking control of your future once and for all and not leaving it in the hands of someone else.

Let me tell you something you already know at a subconscious level: You'll never get rich working for someone else. You need your own venture.

Do I have to "recruit" anyone?

No! Let's be clear. This is not MLM or network marketing. No downlines are involved or needed. You'll no longer be the outcast at the family Christmas party because you're trying to enroll them on a monthly auto-ship program.

Are there any physical products to ship? Do I have to stock inventory?

No. Since you'll be making money promoting digital information products that can be instantly downloaded, you don't have to worry about stocking any inventory or dealing with shipping hassles.

Is it hard work to start a four-, five-, or six-figure monthly online business?

The answer is no—if you seek out and follow a mentor that's already successfully done it. By investing in this book, you've gotten your hands on a blueprint and recipe that has been proven to work, regardless of background or upbringing.

Let's be clear though.

It does take work and commitment. However, what you'll learn in this book is how to become more resourceful. You'll be privy to one of the most important lessons I've ever learned about delegating and outsourcing so you can ALWAYS be doing what you love and do best!

On the opposite side of the coin, if you try to figure everything out on your own, making an income from the Internet is very difficult. In fact, it's damn near impossible because there is so much out there—not to mention you'd be operating without a road map. It's easy to get overwhelmed if you don't have an experienced coach.

―――――――――― *Chapter 2* ――――――――――

WHO AM I AND
WHY YOU NEED THIS BOOK

*The only thing keeping you from getting what you want is
the story you keep telling yourself about why you can't have it.*
—Anthony Robbins

S o, why should you listen to me as someone who's an authority on making
money from the Internet? Truthfully, I don't really like these "about me"
discussions as they're usually filled with hype and ego stroking. (I think we
all could live without that crap.)

It would be very easy to Google me so you could see any accolades,
accomplishments, testimonials, and how I became a respected thought leader.

However, I understand that building a strong foundation with you is
extremely important because you're my valued reader. I want you to take action
with what you discover here and succeed beyond your wildest expectations.

In fact, a big reason why I wanted to put this in book form is that people who
pay for information are typically 1,000 times more likely to apply what they've

learned because they have "skin in the game." The last thing I want is to give away my best marketing strategies and resources only to have a low percentage of people actually put them to use.

As I write this, I'm thirty-six years old. I graduated from Logan College in 2004. I'm the president and founder of several prominent companies such as DCincome, The Social Media Revenue Summit™, and *Automated Social Networking*.

Since 2005, I've been teaching regular people, fellow entrepreneurs, brands, doctors, and professionals how to rapidly build businesses using the Internet while at the same time showing them how to create multiple sources of passive income from social media. This is right when the next-generation communication movement really began to charge full-steam ahead like a rhino. Some called it web 2.0 and others called it social media.

That was when Facebook's predecessor Myspace was starting to completely take the web by storm and change the landscape forever. Facebook, at that time, was only for college students. Since then, it's evolved into an enormous new customer-acquisition powerhouse that can transform your business overnight. We'll touch on this in depth later in this book.

I didn't realize it at the time, but I was one of the fortunate few that didn't listen to all the mainstream negativity regarding social media. In fact, I still remember the strong criticism I experienced from colleagues. They thought these platforms were unprofessional. "Silly kids' stuff," I kept hearing.

I was spending eight to ten hours a day on these networks, learning and mastering all I could. (It's important to note that there weren't any social media outreach training videos online or comprehensive blueprints at that time.) A lot of trial and error went into figuring out the best way to harness social networks to build relationships, create enormous impact, and to profitably grow my business.

There seemed to be a big communication shift going on, which I really wanted to take advantage of. The goal at the time was to put myself in the best position to capitalize for my chiropractic practice.

Things weren't always good though. Not by a long shot.

Let me backtrack a little.

Before I discovered the power of Internet marketing and social media, I was desperately struggling in business and juggling over $135,000 of loan debt. My personal and business credit cards were maxed because of all the ineffective advertising gimmicks I tried.

I even went to Bank of America one day and attempted to cash a convenience check. If you're not familiar with what that is, it's a preprinted check that's linked to your credit card. When you cash it, they jack up your interest rate and charge you fees up the wazoo. As I stood at the counter, the bank teller came back from talking with her manager. My palms were sweating and I felt terrible. She politely said they couldn't cash the check.

My heart sank. I felt crushed. I was quickly running out of options.

I still remember being on the verge of collapse, having more and more anxiety daily. My stomach was constantly knotted up. I was scared because I knew if I didn't make something happen fast, I'd have to close my doors and take a job waiting tables. That sure wasn't what I signed up for when I went to grad school.

I felt like a total failure because I could not make the promotion and advertising work. By this time, I could hardly afford rent in my small one-bedroom apartment.

Probably the worst part was when my ex-girlfriend's dad took me out to lunch one day at Bahama Breeze. After we ate, he presented me with a $2,000 check because he had gotten wind of my financial circumstances. I had no idea this was coming.

You might say, "Why was that so bad?"

Well, whatever I had left of my ego was totally squashed that day. I was humiliated, and it was a very humbling experience. To say I felt less than a man would be an understatement. However, I had no choice at the time but to accept the loan from Mr. S. Now, the pressure was really on.

I had to make things work in a major way. There was just no other option. It's one thing to let yourself down. It's another thing to let someone else down—especially when they invest in you. It turns out this situation was the kick in the ass I needed to get laser-focused and motivated to start making things happen.

Right after that hardship experience, I began to take an interest in social media and human behavior. I became fascinated with why people make the decisions they make when it comes to purchasing. I started asking myself questions like: Why would someone that clearly needs my service not invest in their health? What psychological factors influenced buying habits?

I devoured books on the subject. Probably one of the most powerful books I ever read on the subject was called *Influence: The Psychology of Persuasion* by Robert Cialdini. It was like a fog had lifted. I finally understood how valuable marketing was in the grand scheme of things.

Marketing is simply the ability to effectively communicate (1) what you do (2) to the perfect audience (3) at the right time and (4) in such a way that enables a prospective customer to take necessary action so you can help them. It's about ethically influencing an individual so they can achieve the result they're already seeking at a much faster pace. We'll talk more about influence and psychology later.

The rest is, as they say, history.

As I began to grow my brick-and-mortar business quickly using the Internet, a friend asked me to show him what I was doing because he was having problems getting the word out about his practice.

He was completely blown away by what I was doing on Myspace and YouTube. After all, everyone I spoke with thought it was just for kids. A short time later, he began to see brag-worthy results in his own practice by cloning the same social media marketing process I developed.

Right around that time I started to realize the power of connecting people who were faced with real problems to effective solutions. If you can successfully do this, others will gladly pay you for your expertise, coaching, and advice.

In the mentioned example, my chiropractic colleague had a problem he needed solved. Chiropractors, like most professionals, aren't trained to market in school, so acquiring new patients when they get out is very difficult for many.

However, it's not difficult for the reason you might think.

There's no shortage of people looking for wellness, holistic health providers, alternatives to medicine, and natural solutions for pain. With that said, why aren't many chiropractic practices booming like crazy?

It's because these professionals (like most other businesses) don't know how to properly market and communicate to the people that actually need their services. Marketing is EVERYTHING online and offline, no matter what type of company you have or are thinking about starting!

According to the Small Business Association (SBA), a whopping eight out of ten businesses fail within their first year. The main reason for their failure is that they don't know how to effectively market their product or service.

You, reading this book, are about to unlock the keys to the kingdom! You're about to join the 1 percent club of people that start an online business and thrive. The main reason you'll succeed is that you'll have a firm grasp of how to market and grow your business using the power of the Internet!

So after I had my little epiphany in 2006, I decided to put my Internet marketing expertise in DVD format so I could reach the masses of other chiropractors worldwide. That was my initial big taste at harnessing the Internet to help others with my specialized knowledge. It was also my first real information product.

I still get regular testimonials sent in from doctors that have applied the concepts, letting me know how it's changed their practices and lives for the better. I cannot even describe to you what an amazing feeling it is to serve others doing what you love—while getting paid ridiculously well for it.

The crazy thing was that my "secondary" source of income eventually overtook my primary practice income. I was totally shocked. The demand increased so much that I had accidentally stumbled upon a career in consulting.

I loved helping patients in the office, but I figured that if I was able to show doctors how to reach and serve more with social media, I could directly and indirectly impact millions of people in need. Being able to leave a positive legacy like that really excited me.

Throughout the last several years, I've been fortunate to have trained several thousand ordinary people, business owners, brands, consultants, authors, entrepreneurs, and famous public figures.

I've spoken from stages at world-class events and also run a popular blog at MatthewLoop.com. It's the source for fresh social media profit strategies that help you create more awareness, attract a bigger audience, increase website traffic, maximize your impact, and multiply your new customers and sales numbers.

I built a culture from scratch and a celebrity-like following in a few different industries. You'll learn how to replicate that process in the following chapters.

I'm going to share the exact methods I've discovered and used that position your brand anywhere and everywhere a prospective customer searches within a given topic or niche online. You'll be able to find people with problems who are seeking your advice, and then turn those individuals into raving fans (and customers!) if you follow what I teach.

As I became more visible to my target markets, people began to pay attention to what I had to say and got to know me well. This built trust and rapport because I gave away so much valuable information that helped others get the results they were seeking. We're going to cover this process extensively.

Over the years, I've invested well over $125,000 in "me" (including seminars, private mastermind groups, and courses). I ambitiously did this so I could develop my expertise in order to help people like YOU financially prosper, experience more flexibility, and have a better quality of life by strategically using the internet to start or further scale a business.

I'm extremely passionate about helping aspiring entrepreneurs and business owners set up sustainable mini ATM's online that generate passive recurring paychecks for years to come.

You see, social media, such as Facebook, Instagram, YouTube, Pinterest, and Twitter, aren't just some hobby for me like they are for most others. I've actually built a successful brick-and-mortar business—a chiropractic practice—using it.

Then, I took that advanced knowledge, applied it to online commerce, and established two highly profitable seven-figure companies from scratch. The Internet has allowed me to sell millions of dollars' worth of services and products over the years.

Very few, if any, social media "gurus" you might already know have actually built a physical, brick-and-mortar business using social media. Yet they peddle course after course about growing companies with Facebook. I never understood how certain people could possibly teach real-world, moneymaking social media marketing tactics without ever having experienced the true business-building power of it for themselves.

This is another huge reason why this book is different from 99 percent of the other social media business books out there. My journey didn't start as a consultant. I also didn't have a million-dollar business or the luxury of a big bank roll when I began.

The overwhelming majority of people are in the same boat I was. They don't have a comfortable financial cushion or rich parents. Maybe you, reading this right now, know what I mean and can identify. Scaling a business from a couple million to tens of millions is MUCH easier than starting from zero and going to seven figures.

The bottom line is this.

The new social era of communication has completely transformed my life! It's given me a voice, a global platform to share my message, a way to impact the masses, a path to prosperity, and the ability for my family to do what we want when we want. In this book, I'm going to pull back the curtain on how social media can dramatically change your life for the better, too!

As you'll see, this is not a pitch-fest.

It's simply what I've used to build my brand, gain mass exposure, and generate income hand over fist consistently from the Internet. The formula is reliable, and it works if you do!

This book needs to be in as many hands as possible because it can fuel a REAL economic stimulus by showing millions how to turn their life experience, passion, and ideas in their head into valuable products and services they can sell online.

When you execute this plan, the end result will be you multiplying the amount of money coming in, having the freedom you seek, spending more time with the family, having less stress, giving more back to your favorite causes, and just experiencing more fun.

My hope is that after applying this information, you'll finally get to live the life you've always imagined for yourself. Get ready for an amazing journey!

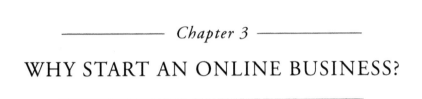

Chapter 3

WHY START AN ONLINE BUSINESS?

Find something you love to do and you'll never work a day in your life
—Harvey Mackay

I could list a hundred reasons why you should start an online business around a hobby you're in love with. However, I've narrowed it down to the top ten. These reasons below showcase the most powerful benefits.

By the time you finish this chapter, I hope you start to see the big picture and why starting an Internet business is one of the best things you could ever do for yourself and family.

1. Your office can be anywhere you want.

The cool thing about selling digital products on the World Wide Web is that you can run your business from home, the local coffee shop, or Costa Rica. It doesn't matter where in the world you are as long as you have access to a laptop and an Internet connection.

Actually, a tablet or smart phone will even do nowadays. The feeling of freedom this provides is immeasurable. No more working in a cubicle for forty to sixty hours per week. No more going to a job you're only minimally enthusiastic about.

2. You set your own hours.

You decide how many hours you will work today. Don't like Mondays? No problem. Take them off! When you do decide to "work," it doesn't feel like work in many cases.

Why? It's because you're focused on developing great ideas, creating high-value content, and publishing products around stuff that excites you.

3. You are your own boss.

No more annoying boss looking over your shoulder, telling you what to do and how to do it. You have total creative control because this is your business. You call the shots and make the final decisions.

This is an adjustment at first, but you get used to it. You will still want to have accountability partners and deadlines to ensure you follow through; however, the dynamic is different.

4. There's no inventory to stock.

When you offer and sell digital products, everything is downloadable and hassle-free! You don't have to store and handle bulky inventory.

Should you choose to create a physical product like a DVD training (or anything that needs shipping), I provide my drop-ship company in the resources section of this book.

5. You get to work with whom you choose.

This is priceless. You don't have to deal with rude customers—just fire the ones that aren't right for your business. You get to hire contractors or employees as your business grows. No more playing office politics or being around weird coworkers as you have to do in some jobs.

6. Your work is based on what you're passionate about.

How many people do what they love for a living? I'm talking about those that cannot wait to wake up in the morning and start working. Ask around and you'll find not too many people feel this way.

When you start an online business around your passion, you join the 1 percent club, folks that have careers, not jobs. There is a huge difference between the two.

Famed comedian Chris Rock said it best. I'm not going to spoil it though. When you get a second, go to YouTube and search "Chris Rock on Careers." What he says is hilarious and true.

The great thing is you get to share your knowledge, expertise, and life experience with the world on a daily basis. Others come to you for solutions to their problems. They're seeking your expert advice and will pay you to learn from your life experience.

7. You're paid by the value you deliver, not by the hour.

Exchanging time for money is an unfulfilling trap most people fall into because that's what they've been taught since birth. I fell into this hamster wheel, too.

You know the routine: go to school, get good grades, graduate, go to college, get good grades, graduate, get a job, get promoted, and so on.

You WILL NOT be able to live the life you've always imagined for yourself if you exchange time for dollars. Even the best paying jobs in corporate America require you to be behind a desk thirty or more hours per week.

Let's take a CEO, for example. They usually don't just take a month off. They can't, even though they make millions of dollars per year. Their lifestyle is not as flexible and glamorous as you might think.

From coaching thousands, I can tell you that the overwhelming majority of entrepreneurs value freedom over money. It's the freedom to spend time with their family and to do what they want while having the ability to come and go at will.

Money is simply a tool, and a necessary one at that. It's a means to an end. When you deliver enough value to your audience online, they'll pay you more than you ever dreamed.

A big chunk of this book is devoted to showing you how to create sustainable, life-changing, PASSIVE income that pours into your bank account 24/7. We do this by forming relationships with our audience and creating ten times the value than the price we charge.

I want to inspire you and provide you with the success tools, not just create another "job" for you. When the fruits of your labor start rushing in fast and furious, you need to be in a position to enjoy them fully.

8. You don't need a big team.

I've personally sold millions of dollars' worth of products and services online and networked with other Internet millionaires, and you know what? Industry influencers and A-players typically employ teams of five or fewer people.

9. The tools for success are relatively inexpensive.

The start-up cost and barrier to entry are very low in this type of business model as compared to risky stocks or expensive real estate. You can bootstrap your way to profitability like many entrepreneurs do initially. It's easy to start a business for less than $500.

Your biggest up-front investment will be a professional website. However, with just a few mouse clicks, you can have an interactive social community (Facebook), a video broadcast channel (YouTube), a public relations outlet (Twitter), and an online storefront to accept money (PayPal).

Most people I speak with have a home computer, laptop, tablet, or smart phone. You can strategically use any of these devices to record video, publish, and effectively distribute the content if you know what you're doing. We'll get into this later.

10. The amount of money you can make is arguably more than any other industry.

You have the opportunity to "create your own economy," as I like to say. I remember early on in my online business when I made a total of $6,400 in just four days from a few emails I sent! My list had only 1,000 people on it too. This was one of those monumental moments.

Can you imagine making in a few days what most people make in a month? Imagine turning your annual income into your monthly income! This has happened to me and countless others. It's absolutely life changing. (Since that time, I've actually made five figures in a single day on numerous occasions.)

With the right guidance, this is something you are FULLY capable of. It doesn't matter what your background is. You don't have to be born under a lucky star either.

Let me share a quick story with you.

I grew up in a lower-middle-class family in the small town of Monroe, Michigan. We lived in a 700-square-foot duplex on West 8th Street with my mother, father, and sister at one point.

If you're not familiar with what a duplex is, picture a one-story house with a dividing wall in the center. You essentially take a single-family house and split it in half so two families can live there. It can get a little tight.

On one specific occasion, I remember that the church we belonged to would take up collections and conduct a food drive once per month. Well, my papaw (who was deacon at the time) stood up in front of the congregation and mentioned they would be visiting a family in need that evening.

I had no idea what was going on at the time with my parent's finances. When you're young, that's usually not your concern. I know I was mostly preoccupied with playing with friends and just being a kid. Yeah, I was a little insecure about how incredibly small my house was compared to my friends' houses, but none of them seemed to care.

So we got home from church that evening and were watching television. Then I hear this unexpected knock at the back door. I went to see who it was, and when I opened the door, my papaw was there with a big smile.

He had his arms FULL of groceries, and I was a little confused. Then I saw he was with a couple other church deacons, and they were also carrying food. They kept piling it in. Bag after bag after bag.

I'll never forget that day.

One, because it was such an incredible act of kindness. And two, because I didn't know how bad our financial situation really was. This life event had a big impact on me, and it's why I try to pay it forward so much.

I've come a long way since those days. My wife and I now live in one of the most exclusive country clubs in the southern United States. I remain grateful every single day for the abundant life we're presently living.

I mention this personal story of hardship to help inspire you.

Regardless of where you came from (or where you are presently), you can start a profitable online business from scratch, sell millions, and make a HUGE impact on the world.

Tell me your current situation and why you "can't" duplicate my Internet success, and I'll show you countless others that have been in far worse situations that have become multimillionaires.

Tony Robbins said it brilliantly, "The only thing keeping you from having what you want is the story you tell about why you can't have it."

If you deliver enough value to your community and follow my advice, the Internet will enable you to generate more revenue than you ever dreamed possible. This book gives you all the tools and resources you need to start and grow a business around what you love in order to have the freedom and prosperity you deserve.

Chapter 4

THE #1 WAY MOST BEGINNERS SABOTAGE THEMSELVES

To think what you want is to think truth regardless of appearances.
—Wallace Wattles

It would be impossible to write a book about starting, managing, and growing an Internet-based business into the six- to seven-figure annual mark without touching on the topic of mindset and programming.

Programming basically happens when we uncritically accept attitudes, values, ideas, and beliefs. These "paradigms" get passed down from the time we're children by those closest to us. They are the truths we live by. Some are empowering while others stealthily fly under the radar and sabotage our best success efforts.

Oftentimes these paradigms are inherited from our parents without our conscious awareness. Family, friends, and the media always play a large part in shaping our beliefs as well as how we think.

Additional factors that influence how our beliefs are created include personal life experience, what others say about you, and what you say and feel about yourself. The truth is, we're limited by our beliefs more than our actual present circumstances. In most instances, we create our own reality, and our beliefs have no bearing on what we're capable of.

Frankly, if you don't "think" you can create a real business online that generates a healthy income each month, you probably won't have success doing it.

Here's what I mean.

When the Wright brothers built the world's first controlled, powered, and sustained heavier-than-air human flight in 1903, they first had to have the idea it was absolutely possible, unlike generations of people before. They didn't just automatically discard the notion and think it was impossible like the masses did. The word "can't" wasn't in their vocabulary. You'd be wise to exclude it from yours too. "Can't" is a cancer.

So what did the Wright brothers do? They began to ask the very important question that eludes so many: "HOW can it be done?"

We can easily relate this to income too. I heard Bob Proctor once say, "The person that makes $50,000 per year doesn't make that because he wants to. He makes that amount of money because he doesn't know how to make $100,000 per year."

Does this make sense?

Albert Einstein even mentioned, "Current reality is merely an illusion, albeit a persistent one." Instead of immediately thinking you can't do something, start thinking about HOW it can be accomplished—regardless of how big or out of reach it may appear on the surface.

The friend factor

Best-selling author Robert Kiyosaki discusses taking an inventory of your closest friends and those with whom you spend most of your time. He says your income and lifestyle will be proportional to those with whom you hang out. Most wealthy people will tell you the same thing.

People that make $35,000 per year do not think like those that make over a million dollars per year. If they did, they'd be at the same income level. That's why it becomes critically important to spend most of your time surrounded by those who empower you and are where you want to be. These successful people think and act differently from your family or friends.

This isn't good or bad … it just is.

I love my parents very much, but I recognized early on they did the best with the information that they had available to them. They were in the lower-middle-class bracket and had no experience generating the income that I wanted to make. They were of a different mindset that was based on their life experiences and programming. Therefore, I had to make a decision not to listen to them regarding what I should or shouldn't be doing in my business.

Where you are right now in life is the result of how you've been conditioned to think and act. If you don't like where you are, you MUST change the way you think and act! You have to control the internal and external programming factors.

Several ways you can control external programming

1. Turn off the TV and radio.

Mass media is notorious for its ability to influence and control the population. Psychological manipulation and propaganda dissemination is a science, and you must break away from the control. The masses think and act predictably, hence the reason most people are stuck in jobs they hate while complaining to no end.

Most people really don't think for themselves either. The tell-LIE-vision and radio tell them how to think. This is very dangerous and detrimental to your success in life and business. It's crucial to unplug from the consistent conditioning that occurs daily.

In the car, instead of turning on the radio, listen to an empowering CD about personal growth or something by a successful entrepreneur that's getting the results you want in business.

Instead of sitting down to watch TV, use that time to build your Internet business and be productive. You'll be amazed how many more hours open up when you detach from the plug-in drug.

2. Spend less time with those that consistently push negativity your way.

Too frequently, family and friends will be the first to criticize when you begin to think bigger and start your online business. Why? This stuff is way out of their comfort zone, that's why. It's not the reality they know, and they cannot see how it can be accomplished. They've never entertained the question, "How?"

Spend large amounts of time only with those that create empowering relationships for you. It will mean less resistance and will help you fast-track your development and growth. You may be forced to make a tough decision, but ultimately it's your life and you need to be happy living your dream. Guard your time very carefully.

Several ways you can control internal programming

1. Start using and repeating positive affirmations.

This is so basic but it works because of the consistent repetition. I want you to think about this: how many times daily do you think your family, friends, and the radio and/or TV reinforce those core beliefs that may not be beneficial to you living the life you want? It's a constant barrage and assault on both your conscious and subconscious mind.

Of all the times you can remember this happening, now just think about how many you cannot remember. This is where just having the TV and radio playing in the background gets dangerous. Even if you're not consciously paying attention, the information is still going into your subconscious mind, which further indoctrinates you into the same patterns and belief systems you've been guided by since infancy.

Several times per day, you need to retrain your mind to focus on those things that will help you get closer to your big goal. One of the easiest things to do is to carry a card on you that contains a positive affirmation. Carry it in your wallet or by your keys. Every time you reach for your keys, train yourself to look at and read the card.

Your affirmation may say something like, "I'm very happy and grateful now that I have a successful business netting $30,000 per month that allows me freedom to be with my family anytime I want" (or fill in the blank for your strongest desires BUT be specific).

This might sound stupid to some, but it works to recondition your brain. My affirmation when I was just starting out was, "I'm so happy and grateful that money comes to me easily and effortlessly. I'm a magnet for success and prosperity."

You see, before money ever came to me easily and effortlessly, I had the idea in my mind, and I knew my thoughts and strategic action would eventually help to manifest the reality I wanted.

The bottom line is that the more you repeat positive affirmations like this, the more you start to believe them. Also, it just feels good to say the words. What you think about causes certain feelings inside that inspire you to ultimately take action consistently toward the goals that you set.

2. Start using your imagination to focus on your ideal life.

Why is it that as children, we're encouraged to use our imagination, and when we're adults, it seems to be frowned upon? Many employees working for companies they hate have lost sight of their imagination and lifelong dreams.

It's important to do whatever you can to get a clear picture of the life that you want for yourself. I'm talking about the life that you REALLY want, not what you just think you can get.

Create a vision board with magazine cutouts of everything you want in life (family goals, material or otherwise) and look at it daily. Really imagine how you'll feel once you've accomplished everything you've set out to do. Close your eyes and get into the moment until your heart starts racing fast.

This is such a powerful exercise.

Long before I ever drove one, I went to the Ferrari dealership in Roswell, Georgia, and sat behind the wheel of an F430. Why? So I could smell the leather, grip the steering wheel, and get a view of the car from inside.

Doing this cemented the vision in my mind. Always do what it takes to paint the clearest picture possible of the life you want. I'd be willing to bet that only a tiny fraction of people that really want a Ferrari actually go to the dealership. Why? It can be a little intimidating or maybe they just don't think they could ever acquire one.

Don't ever let fear stop you! Fate favors the bold.

This is just one example, and by no means am I trying to sound materialistic. You just want to surround your space with things that keep you focused on WHY you must succeed in starting a business online.

The "why factor" is different for everyone. Maybe it's to be able to spend more time with your children. Maybe you just want to never have to worry about being behind on your house payment again. Maybe you want to take more vacations with loved ones and experience an abundant life.

You need to be very clear on why you're starting the business you are. This is your driving factor and will push you through no matter how many times you feel like giving up. A strong "why factor" also helps you be more accountable because you have others depending on you. Success is the only option.

I personally just wanted to help other chiropractors do what I had been able to do when I initially started out. I knew the countless frustrations other doctors were going through. That was what primarily fueled me.

I liked seeing someone who had no presence online go from struggling to flooding their offices with new patients because of the Internet. I liked knowing they'll be able to help serve more people and be rewarded with an awesome quality of life.

More on mindset

From the time we're children it seems like we're taught to go to school, get good grades, get a college degree, then find a job in the workforce working forty hours per week. This is touted as the gold standard to start your success journey. What a joke. This is nothing more than mass conditioning.

While I'm grateful for my formal university education, did it teach me to be an entrepreneur so that I could control my own financial future in any economy?

No.

Your success in starting a business online has nothing to do with whether or not you have a college degree. The Internet does not discriminate. Never let anyone ever tell you otherwise.

Your mindset on how you approach this business will greatly determine whether you succeed or not. Your thoughts dictate how you feel inside, which determines the action you take or whether you remain stationary.

The big distinction here is that you have a choice as to what you believe is possible and what you don't. You can choose your truth knowing you have a level playing field starting out. You can follow those that have already been successful and soak up their time-tested strategies like a sponge.

Having the appropriate winner's mindset is foundational and critical to your success as an Internet entrepreneur. Every millionaire I've spoken with always cites mindset as one of the most important reasons why they've achieved the great success they have.

Instead of thinking that building a six- to seven-figure business online cannot be done, start asking the question, "How can it be done?" You don't always need to know the "how" right away, but asking yourself the question allows you to begin thinking in a way that most of the population doesn't.

Here's what to do next:

1. Set a BIG clear goal. Go for what you really want and NOT what you just think you can get. Maybe you want to set a goal to make an extra $15,000 per month passively from your new Internet business.

2. Reverse engineer how much money per month it takes to live your ideal dream life. You might be surprised; it's probably less than you think. You have to get very specific here. What kind of house do you want? What type of car? Clothes? How many vacations per year? Club memberships? Real estate, etc.? (See the example below and complete this exercise on a separate she et of paper.)

What I want	How much per month	Why I want it
Ferrari F430	$2,700	It's my favorite sports car
5,000-sq-ft home	$3,500	Comfortable living for family
Housekeeper	$850	I don't like to clean
Private schooling	$2,083	My children deserve the best
NetJets membership	$4,166	Commercial air travel sucks
7 Vacations / Year	$14,000	Vacations make me happy
Personal assistant	$3,333	I tend to be very unorganized

A-list charity events	$2,000	To give back and meet celebs
Real estate investing	$5,000	My preferred way to invest
Jewelry collection	$3,000	Watches are my kryptonite
Total	**$40,632**	

Okay … in this example to live my dream life, I need to make $40,632 per month, which breaks down to $1,354 per day. So what I need to do now is to start, market, manage, and grow my online business/portfolio so that it sells enough to reach my daily goals.

Remember, I have several types of products I could use to accomplish this, such as e-books, instruction manuals, online courses, DVD trainings, membership sites, one-on-one coaching programs, webinar systems, iPhone apps, live masterminds, etc.

Alright, let's just say I created a digitally delivered, downloadable instruction manual about underwater basket weaving. How many manuals would I need to sell per day to reach my goal of $1,354?

If my manual was priced at $19.97, I would need to sell right around sixty-eight units per day to hit the magic mark. You follow?

Okay, let's say I created a DVD video training series about how to do this, and I sold the system of tutorials for $39.97. Everyone knows that DVDs command more of a premium than a PDF download in the example above.

I would need to move about thirty-four DVD units per day to reach my daily income goal. The next logical question becomes, "How can I move thirty-four units per day?" This comes down to traffic, exposure, and conversion, which we'll discuss heavily later on.

Now whether or not underwater basket weaving is a commercially viable industry and niche is another thing. We'll go more in depth on that later in this book when I speak about how to conduct proper market research.

I think you get the idea though.

Mind you, this is just taking into account having one product. You can always develop a valuable product and repackage it to sell in another medium. Some people prefer to watch DVD trainings as opposed to reading books.

To recap:

Everything starts with your belief as to whether or not it can be done. It's not necessarily what you do that determines your success, but how you do it. Two ways you can change your current limiting beliefs are by constant repetition and by having an experience that elicits a strong emotional impact.

You must control your internal and external programming and have the mindset of a champion, or you'll inadvertently sabotage your own success efforts. This takes a conscious daily effort to master. However, soon enough a new habit will be created that positively impacts and serves you for years to come.

Hopefully, after reading this chapter and doing the exercise above, you're already starting to think bigger and you will have painted a clear image of the life you really want.

Chapter 5

THE 5 SUCCESS PILLARS FOR INTERNET ENTREPRENEURS

If you don't design your own life plan, chances are you'll fall into someone else's plan. And guess what they have planned for you? Not much.
—Jim Rohn

Over the years I've discovered there are five key pillars to starting and growing a profitable business online. Success is predictable when all of these foundational factors align. At the same time, failure is inevitable when even just one of these pillars is missing.

Here they are in order:

1. Vision

Do you know why most people don't get what they want in life? It's because they have no freakin' idea what they really want! Seriously, ask your friends or family what their grand plan in life is. Or ask them what specifically (down to the number) they want in all areas of life, including health, finances, relationships, spiritually, etc.

Have you ever written it down on a piece of paper and spent an afternoon imagining your ideal future? If not, I'm going to STRONGLY encourage you to do this immediately.

When you're clear, you're 90% of the way there.

Just saying "I want to make more money" is not specific at all. It cannot be reverse engineered. "More" is not a specific goal. It's a moving target.

Now, if you say, "I want to make $100,000 per year selling my products, advice, expertise, and/or services online," that's a specific goal. We can do the math and figure out just how many information products (e-books, DVD trainings, coaching programs, iPhone apps, etc.) we need to sell per year to make this a reality.

If you take nothing else away from this, know that there's power in specificity and getting crystal clear on what you want in life.

2. Your "why"

Why do you wake up in the morning? Why do you do what you do? What fuels your innermost desires? What is your purpose (a.k.a. your "why")?

Why do you want to be successful?

This is an important concept to grasp because life hits very hard sometimes. Obstacles will surface. You're going to get knocked down many times. The only thing that will keep you getting up and moving forward is a strong "why." You must be focused and on purpose.

Why must you be successful? Why is failure not an option? Do you have children? Do you want them to have a better life? Do you believe you deserve better in life?

Everyone's "why" will be different … and that's okay. The most important part is to connect with the real reason that motivates you. Money alone is not a sufficient motivator. That's a by-product of providing massive value and helping others get what they want.

3. Getting the best tools and resources

Let's face it: you could have a clear vision and a strong why, but you still need to acquire the right tools and resources that will help you start a six- or seven-figure business online.

There are a couple options available to you in this regard.

You can learn from the school of hard knocks like I did. You might stumble your way to profitability in a couple years and eventually zigzag your way to some degree of success. This way is really not sustainable for the overwhelming majority of business owners though. Why? It's because there's usually no proven, concrete plan to take you on an upward.

A big reason why most fail online is that they choose to go at it alone.

Which brings me to your second (and smarter) option: find a mentor/coach that's already achieved the level of success you want. Then, simply model them. Learn from their wisdom.

I'm sure you'd agree there's no sense in reinventing the wheel. It's no accident you're reading this right now. I believe you've attracted this book into your life because you know you're capable of more prosperity and abundance.

This work was written, in large part, to give you the tools and resources that most aspiring entrepreneurs never get. I've taken the hard knocks for you. I know what works and what doesn't. I've spent the money and made the mistakes so you don't have to.

What you ultimately choose to do with this information is entirely up to you, though. If you're truly serious about starting a wildly profitable online business around doing what you love, you'll heed my advice and apply the tools and resource you learn here.

4. Taking massive action

Nothing happens without action. In fact, if you look at the word "attraction," you'll notice the last six letters are A-C-T-I-O-N! If you want to draw abundance and prosperity into your life, you'll need to get off your butt and be unstoppable.

Consistent daily action is the key to success when starting your business online. It doesn't have to be a lot; it just needs to be regular. Develop a habit of acting.

Many people fail here—just totally miss the bus. They think that just visualizing their new life and getting emotionally engaged is all it takes. Then magically they'll manifest a seven-figure business.

I'm here to tell you that visualization, affirmations, and feelings do not work to attract abundance in your life UNLESS you're going to back them up with massive action. This should be obvious, but I need to point it out anyway.

The crazy thing is, there always seems to be reciprocity in the universe. Meaning, the harder and smarter you work, the more opportunities and money come your way. I'd like to stress the word "smarter." You don't need to personally do everything as you'll discover in this book.

I'm reminded of a quote by hip-hop mogul and entrepreneur Russell Simmons when he says, "I've been blessed to find people who are smarter than I am, and they help me to execute the vision I have."

Once I discovered and internalized the fact I didn't need to do everything myself to have a life of prosperity and abundance, it was such an awakening. Almost instantly, I stopped being a control freak and saw the big picture.

Many times we, as business owners, get stuck on "How is it going to get done?" instead of focusing on bringing key, intelligent players aboard to handle stuff we're not good at. It's important to strengthen your strengths and delegate your weaknesses, not the other way around. Piggyback on the specialized knowledge of others in order to fast-track your growth and dramatically improve your results.

Here's another favorite quote of mine by Tony Robbins that resonates as truth: "It's not the lack of resources, it's your lack of resourcefulness that stops you."

I'm going to give you specific action steps to take in this book and also show you how to be as resourceful as possible. Your life will never be the same again when you implement these strategies consistently.

5. Measuring and fine-tuning

After we achieve a certain degree of success in our business online, it's important to evaluate where we are. We need to measure and track the progress, then make minor adjustments to maximize our global impact, traffic, conversion, and profits.

Sometimes it's those minor tweaks that can make the biggest difference on your bottom line. I see this all the time with private coaching clients. Many already have solid five- to six-figure businesses going from the web, so we'll adjust and fine-tune one simple strategy and BOOM! Another six figures are added to their bank account. The small details are critically important as you'll find out soon.

----------- *Chapter 6* -----------

HOW TO POSITION
YOURSELF AS A LEADER

*There is no passion to be found in playing small—in settling
for a life that is less than the one you are capable of living.*
—Nelson Mandela

Positioning simply refers to how you're perceived in your prospective
customers' minds from their initial interaction with you. It's easily
one of the most important (and overlooked) aspects when starting an
online business.

If you don't position yourself strategically from the beginning, your business
is doomed to fail because you won't appear original, unique, or special. People
will look at you like a commodity of sorts. You won't be able to stand out from
the crowd.

In a sense, positioning is what a person's first impression is of you or your
company when they first encounter your website, a video you produced, an

advertisement online, a TV commercial, a consumer review, a blog post you wrote, etc.

This also applies offline when a person meets you at a live event for the first time, hears you speak, sees how you dress, observes your network, checks out your business card, and so on.

Here are some questions you need to think strongly about:

- What do you want your marketplace to think about you?
- Do you have a personal story of hardship, tragedy, or triumph?
- Do you appear professional and elegant?
- Does your brand appear cheap or premium?
- Does your website look like it was designed by a second grader?
- Do you appear likeable and trustworthy?
- Have you earned (or engineered) celebrity status in your industry?
- Do you seem popular and well networked?
- Do you appear genuine, as if you actually give a damn about your audience?
- Does your website give the impression you're in demand?
- How many positive reviews do you, your company, and/or product have online?
- Does your site make it seem like you're a large company?
- Do you come across as knowledgeable and enthusiastic?
- Do you have a mission/purpose as to why you do what you do?

If you currently have an Internet business, you must ask these thirteen questions immediately. See if friends, family, or random strangers can give you feedback here so you can really get an objective opinion.

If you're getting ready to start a business online around something you're passionate about, then keep these questions in mind when you have your website built.

Your goal should always be to position yourself as THE leader in the marketplace. You want to be known as the go-to person in your field—or, as I like to say, "a center of influence." Another way to phrase it is you must manufacture celebrity in your industry. Make it easy for others to get to know, like, and trust you.

Even if you're just starting out online, when you follow my instructions, you can be perceived as an industry authority right from the start. You'll establish instant credibility. Here's what you need to do.

1. Tell your personal story.

Stories are very powerful and connect us to the rest of the world. They also tend to be very sticky in our minds, kind of like that catchy song you can't seem to get out your head. Do you remember the bedtime stories your parents used to read to you? I know I do and can still recite most of them verbatim!

A personal story of adversity to triumph makes you memorable and RELATABLE. Maybe you had some type of tragedy or hardship in your life that you overcame. Talk about this on your website, in live presentations, and in some of the online content you create. Our past life experiences (good and bad) have shaped the person we've become.

Ask most people and they'll tell you that life isn't all sunshine and roses. Everyone has setbacks and obstacles they have to overcome on their journey. If you come across as empathetic, people will bond with you faster because you'll appear more believable.

Really get specific and think about how you want to present your story. The more detailed and revealing you can be, the more real you seem. You might initially be embarrassed to talk about these intimate life experiences, but I assure you it's well worth it. It's actually therapeutic to get it out in the open, and it helps to inspire others who are facing their own challenges.

For the longest time, it was really hard for me to talk about being in debt over $135,000 and having my credit cards maxed due to poor choices. It was humiliating to be rejected by a bank teller for trying to cash a convenience check. I was devastated when I had to accept a $2,000 check from my ex-girlfriend's father while sitting at Bahama Breeze. It really sucked living in a tiny apartment, barely skating by week after week.

I thought I didn't measure up because I came from a lower-middle-class family. I had no connections. I wasn't a member of the old boys' club.

With all of this, at the end of the day, I had to stop letting my past define who I was. I knew if I wanted to improve my circumstances, I needed to improve myself and make better choices.

Stories can act like rocket fuel and empower you to seize your dreams, or they can keep you from achieving greatness. You are not your past. Every day is a new day.

My recommendation is to study The Hero's Journey by Joseph Campbell and to use the outline as a guide when crafting your story. Hollywood does this well with many of their movies. The epic Rocky series with Sylvester Stallone is a great example of the hero's journey in cinema.

If you Google "the hero's journey," you'll see basic outlines and graphics that do a great job detailing the steps in this process. It's the foundation of some of the most successful stories ever told in print or on the big screen.

Action Step: Get your story and personal journey down on paper. Chart the highs and lows, your struggle through adversity, and how you overcame challenges. Remember, you need to tailor this to the market you service. Your prospective customers need to be able to relate to you, in that you've faced similar problems. Humanize yourself so people hear your story and think, "He/She is like me."

2. Create a custom category where you can be #1.

This is not a new technique at all, but it's incredibly powerful in terms of how others perceive your business. The first time I heard about this method was from legendary marketer Dan Kennedy.

Let me give you an example.

Let's say Mary Jane has an underwater basket-weaving business, but she doesn't have a lot of customers. She's thinking about a tagline that can position her as a respected authority though. She's pretty confidant she's the only one doing underwater basket weaving. Let's face it—it's a specific technique.

Mary Jane decides on this tag-line:

"The Largest Underwater Basket-Weaving Retailer in the World"

And ... you know what? For all means and purposes, this is true in her case. In reality, if there was another underwater basket-weaving company that had more customers than her, we could make a slight modification to that title and it would still be true. Let's say her competitor was in Europe and she lived here in the United States. She could go with:

"The Largest Underwater Basket-Weaving Retailer in North America"

You see how that works?

Action Step: Your goal is to create a category where you can be the LARGEST. Take a few minutes and do it now. Grab a pen and paper and start jotting down ideas.

We are managing perception here. When most people think of the "largest" business in any space, they assume it must be good. In the example above, Mary Jane essentially created a custom category where she was number one.

Once you've solidified your position and have this catalyzing statement, you will use this on your business card, website, promotional materials, bio, etc.

3. Get a professionally designed website.

You're going to have to spend money here. There's no getting around it. This is typically the largest start-up expense for many Internet entrepreneurs.

There's good news though. You can find affordable, experienced professionals all over the world in a few minutes. I recall when I want to have my blog created, the programmer I found here in the US was going to charge me $3,000.

After I received that quote, I decided to go to Upwork.com and get more quotes from seasoned freelance website designers around the world. I needed a WordPress specialist at the time.

The cool thing about Upwork is that when someone bids on your project, you can check out their portfolio to see their previous work completed. You can also view their user feedback (1–5 star average). Finally, you can see the amount they've earned.

These stats are very helpful because you can feel confident about the provider you choose, regardless of where in the world they live. It just so happened, the most qualified provider I found was in India.

He wasn't the cheapest, but he offered to do the site for $1,500. That's 50 percent less than what I was originally quoted! I was thrilled! Not to mention, he had nothing but great feedback from over seventy websites he built.

There is a time and place to save money; however, don't just select the cheapest bid. Experience trumps price any day. Remember, we are looking for a high-quality, elegant, professional website design.

This programmer I found was a great fit, and his turnaround time was less than two weeks. Once I selected his bid, we agreed on the terms. I would fund the Upwork escrow account then release half the funds once the project was 50 percent completed.

The final half was due upon my approval of the website and project completion. During this whole process, I (as the buyer) was protected by Upwork as well.

Now, do you have to spend $1,500 on a new website with all the bells and whistles? Absolutely not. You can easily get something professional outsourced for under $600. Then you can add to the site over time. Just make sure it's build on the WordPress framework.

Even if you go for a more basic site, your website should still have a WOW factor to it. You want to make the best first impression possible, yet you also want to be strategic in the way you set it up. Remember those questions I wanted you to think about a few moments ago? Use them to your advantage in this stage.

I would STRONGLY recommend visiting about a dozen high-end luxury brands online to see how they've positioned themselves as better and/ or different from everyone else in the same space. Check out the appearance of their site. Observe what type of descriptive language they use. View the image quality. Immerse yourself in their experience. Also, depending on what niche or industry you're going into, view the websites of the famous brands in the space.

Action Step: If you don't have a professional, elegant website, it's time to set one up. This is your home online—your central hub, so to speak. I suggest finding a programmer from Upwork.com to do this for you.

As I've already mentioned, I recommend building your site upon the WordPress platform. This is because of its simplicity and ease of use. Plus, Google and other search engines love these sites, and it's easier to rank them well. Your web developer will actually install WordPress on your hosting account.

SIDE NOTE: Every business online MUST have a website address and hosting. This is your cornerstone on the web. The overwhelming majority of my websites are hosted on Bluehost. Their platform is reliable and ridiculously cheap, and they offer 24/7 customer support, too.

Bluehost is easy to use even if you aren't a computer geek. They also offer a free domain with hosting and one-click automatic WordPress installation. I STRONGLY RECOMMEND Bluehost for your website hosting. I negotiated a very low rate for readers of this book at:

DCincome.com/blog/Bluehost

4. Add credibility-boosting social signals to your website at the top.

If you look at my blog at MatthewLoop.com, you'll notice that I've included the Facebook "like" and Google+ buttons at the very top right.

Why?

The first reason was to create social proof and manage perception. When a new visitor comes to this site, one of the first things they see is 1,300 people clicked the Facebook "like" button. This is important because it tells the prospective customer that a lot of other people were here and find the content valuable. You might hear me say this over and over again, but the web is a big popularity contest.

When you have more social signals such as Facebook "likes," Tweets, Google+'s, etc., you seem more popular. This keeps the visitor on the page longer to look around. They become curious as to why so many have liked the website. Essentially, what we're trying to do is calm skepticism and break through the wall of distrust most people have when searching online.

The #1 reason people don't use your product or service is that they don't believe you or they still remain skeptical. Positioning yourself, brand, or product in the way I'm showing you helps knock down those mental barriers consumers have.

Now, the second reason we have social signals on our website is to allow others to share our site/content with their friends on social media. I call this "earned exposure."

When someone clicks the Facebook "share" or "like" button, the action is posted on Facebook for their friends to see. It's an indirect referral and a simple way to get more traffic to your current website. Our goal is to make it as simple as possible for people to share our content with their friends. In order for this to occur, you must have your social share buttons in easily visible places.

The last reason to have social signals on your website is to help your search engine optimization (SEO). This is basically how your site ranks on Google or Bing for any given keyword phrase.

The search engines use Facebook shares, likes, Twitter tweets, Pinterest pins, etc. in their ranking algorithms. You absolutely MUST have these buttons on your home page and blog posts if you want to rank well on search engines.

<u>Action Step</u>: Talk with your programmer or webmaster today to make sure you have the social signals installed on your website. Use my blog at MatthewLoop. com as an example of where you should have them.

5. Have pictures of celebrities or recognized industry leaders on your homepage.

Celebrity = credibility.

You can have pictures with industry-specific public figures or international celebrities. If you go to my blog at MatthewLoop.com, you'll see rotating pictures with quite a few mainstream celebs, such as Usher, Def Leppard, David Copperfield, Charlie Sheen, Rob Schneider, Michael Gerber, Bob Proctor, and more.

Why? It all goes back to positioning and shaping public perception. When a visitor comes to your website and sees pictures of you with famous individuals, it's an instant credibility booster and positions you above other businesses in your market.

It's credibility by association, and you look important and cool.

Now, if you can't get pictures with globally famous people, then go for the movers and shakers in your current market. For example, let's say you're selling information products in the personal development and/or self-help space. You might be a fan of best-selling author Dr. Wayne Dyer, who's widely recognized in this industry.

Why not find out where he's speaking and purchase the highest ticket package available? In many situations, there will be opportunities for a meet and greet. Other times, you can catch best-selling authors like him (for free) at book signings.

Imagine if you had pictures with other public figures in your industry featured on your blog. What do you think other prospective customers and website visitors would think? You gain instant authority by association.

<u>Action Step</u>: Do your research and find out who the top industry influencers are in your market. Then identify their public appearance schedules, tour dates, book signings, etc. Try at least once per month to get a photo op with someone famous. These pictures can then be placed on your website.

The money you invest to meet them will be nothing compared to the top positioning you'll gain in the marketplace. Your new customers and sales depend on how well you position yourself.

Here's an important note: Don't claim a celebrity has used or endorses your product if they really haven't. That can land you in hot water very quickly.

6. Define your mission and feature the global impact you want to make by giving back.

If you have a look at my website, one of the first things you see highlighted in blue above the fold are the words "Earn More – Experience More – Give Back." The purpose of my site and products is to help people do those three things.

You'll also see that I have a "giving back" tab in the navigation bar of the site. Why? It's because each "for-profit" training I have is tied to a nonprofit initiative. I want prospective customers to know this early in our relationship.

When you invest in your success through our products and programs, you're not only helping yourself, but you're also helping support wounded soldiers, entrepreneurs in developing nations, and more.

A simple act like this positions you as a conscious capitalist. It lets the visitor know you're committed to leaving a legacy that makes a positive difference in the world through contribution and philanthropy. How many other competing brands or companies do this in your industry?

I can already tell you ... NOT MANY.

This can be a great way to position and differentiate your business far above everyone that sells similar products in your field.

Action Step: I've included a powerful article in the back of this book titled, "Is Philanthropy Part of Your Social Media Strategy." You'll want to read it ASAP. The action steps are included within that article.

7. Manage your reputation.

Let me tell you a quick story about a client of mine named Joe. This cautionary tale is applicable to any type of business online and offline. It should drive home the importance of regularly checking what's being said about you and your company on the Internet.

Joe was a dentist out in Arizona, and he had a fairly busy practice. Then, one week he started to notice a drop-off in business. He chalked it up to the fact that it was summer and maybe people were out of town. Most of Joe's new business came from referrals, and he really didn't do much advertising or marketing.

Well, four months went by and he observed he was still much slower than he had been before. So he began to look at other avenues to market his practice. That's when we connected through a mutual friend.

One of the very first things I did was reverse engineer his presence online in order to see what people were saying about the business. As it turns out, when you Googled his practice name, there was a big fat ONE-STAR review sticking out like a sore thumb on Yelp and Google Maps. It was pretty scathing, and this previous patient went on to discuss her wait time in the office as well as billing issues.

I immediately confronted Joe about it, and he remembered the patient. However, Joe had never actually Googled his name or practice name so he had no idea what was being said about the office. As you can imagine, he was saddened and felt a bit betrayed.

As it turns out, the problem occurred on the day when his assistant quit without notice and didn't bother showing up in the morning. That basically caused a traffic jam in the clinic, and patients were waiting much longer than usual.

To top it all off, there was an error in the billing because the assistant that normally handled collections was gone. So this patient was accidentally charged $20 more than she should've been. It was an honest mistake, but it didn't matter.

The patient had a bad experience that day and was intent on letting the world know, so she went to Google and Yelp to vent her frustration.

Let's face it. Sometimes shit just happens. Sooner or later even the best products and services will get a negative review online. You've got to plan for it. Some factors are within your control while others are not.

This was all new to Joe, and he didn't plan ahead for it. So anytime a prospective patient searched his name, that ugly review would surface. We wouldn't know how much money this was costing him until we initiated a campaign to get positive feedback from existing patients, which is exactly what we did. I gave him a proven script to follow with specific instructions so people would feel compelled to rate him on Google and Yelp.

Here's what happened.

Within three weeks, twenty-three reviews were added to his Google listing and twelve reviews were added to Yelp! In essence, the negative review was now buried. You might be wondering how that impacted his practice.

Almost instantly, he started to get an increase in the volume of calls from people searching on the web. We tracked it out over six months so we could get a feel for how much business he lost.

With the positive reviews as they were, he was averaging fifteen new clients per month from the Internet. His average case value per client was $2,500. That amounts to $37,500 in collections per month just from the patients that found him online! Now, let's compare that to before when the negative review was front and center.

Joe told me that during his "slump" he was averaging three new clients per month from the Internet. Honestly, I was surprised anyone was calling him based on how terrible the rating was. It was one of those that made you cringe and tightly grip the seat of your chair.

If we do the math, he averaged $7,500 per month during the slow-down period. $37,500 - $7,500 = $30,000! That's how much he was losing.

Can you see how JUST ONE bad review can impact your brand or business?

This is very serious stuff. You should be conducting a Google search at least once per week in regards to your brand or name, then going through the first five pages to see if anything has been said.

If you discover a negative rating, it's important to respond professionally. Do not attack the reviewer. As you can imagine, this is an extremely delicate situation; however, you always want to respond because it shows you're not hiding from anything.

When I consult private clients who are in "damage control" mode, I help them craft the perfect response and stack social proof in their favor.

Reputation is currency. It can either make or break you online.

Furthermore—and I cannot stress this enough—you must be proactive and stack the chips in your favor early on! If you don't have any feedback online at the moment, you don't appear review-worthy! That's certainly not a good position to be in.

Our mission is to stand out from the crowd so that we're the no-brainer obvious choice when a prospective customer searches a service or product in the industry we serve. Whoever has the most testimonials wins the social-proof game.

Depending on if you're an Internet entrepreneur, information product developer, or a local business owner, the review sites at your disposal will vary. All you need to do to find review networks that cater to your industry is to Google the top competitor in your market and see which websites surface on the first five pages of the search.

For a local business, these are top review websites you must have a strong presence on. If you want to reap the lion's share of new customers searching for (insert your specialty), you should have at least three times the number of reviews that your highest-rated local competitor has.

- Google Local (also called Google Maps)
- Yelp

- TripAdvisor
- Expedia
- AngiesList
- HealthGrades
- Bing Places
- Yahoo Local
- Better Business Bureau (BBB)
- Oyster.com
- Travelocity
- Orbitz
- Judy's Book
- Home Advisor
- Trivago
- Booking.com

If you're a brand and sell products to a global marketplace, here are some sample review engines you'll want to monitor and initiate campaigns for. Again, based on your product or service type, there might be other networks out there that are more relevant. Do a Google search to find them.

- Amazon
- Consumer Reports
- iTunes
- cNet
- Engadget
- GoodReads
- ConsumerAffairs
- PissedConsumer
- RipOffReport

This brings me to another important point. You can never have too many testimonials. Collecting them is an ongoing process and should be a top priority. The #1 reason people won't buy from you is that they're skeptical and don't believe you. The more people sing your praises, the more growth your business will experience.

Don't be afraid to ask happy clients for their honest feedback. As the old saying goes, "Ask and ye shall receive." Make this a standard operating protocol. Trust me, it will increase your conversions and pay huge dividends in the long term.

<u>Action Step</u>: Google your name, company, and individual product name on a weekly basis. Also, Google these keywords with "reviews" afterward. An example would be "Jane Smith reviews" or "(your product name) reviews."

You can also set up a Google Alert or SocialMention to automatically notify you when someone posts anything about a keyword you're tracking. See the following sites: www.Google.com/alerts and www.SocialMention.com.

Monitor your reputation and proactively get positive feedback on the sites mentioned or in video testimonial format. We want to be the only logical choice when a prospective customer sees this listing and compares us to anyone else.

If you're a local professional with a brick-and-mortar business, DO NOT get reviews from the same computer in your office or they'll get filtered. Google and Yelp track IP addresses. Have clients either do them at home and/or with their smart phone in your office. They'll need to download the Google Maps application, which is free. Then they can search your business from their phone and post a review.

Lastly, it's important to monitor our reputation on forums and social media websites. I'm referring to popular platforms such as Facebook, LinkedIn, Twitter, Pinterest, YouTube, Google+, and Instagram. Check each site individually, and use their search function to see if there are conversations going on regarding your name, brand, or product. Topsy.com and SocialMention are good investigative tools that can be used to search targeted keywords on social outlets.

8. Other important psychological triggers that position you as the leader
Professional photos

Spend the money and get a set of professional photos taken. One of them should go front and center on your website's homepage. This is important to present your best foot forward when meeting prospective customers online.

Television logos on your website

If you've been featured on major media (FOX, NBC, CNN, ABC, and CBS), display the logos above the fold on your blog. People automatically give you more credibility if you've been showcased on mainstream media outlets.

If you haven't been on TV, have a press release written about an announcement in your business. Then go to PRweb.com and purchase their $250 package. Why? When you do this, PRweb.com will distribute your press release into the major news outlets. Many times you'll get picked up on local NBC, CBS, FOX, and ABC affiliates. You can link to those websites from your blog and legitimately say you've been featured on these mainstream channels, adding yet another important layer of credibility.

Remember, people are incredibly skeptical these days. We're just trying to get them to let their guard down so we can actual help transform their lives for the better. Use the TV logos on your site.

Facebook fan page widget

To see what this looks like, visit MatthewLoop.com and look right below the rotating images on the right-hand side.

This serves as a social-proof builder simply because visitors can now see the thousands upon thousands of other real people that have liked your Facebook fan page. (This is not the same as the social share buttons I spoke about earlier.)

Remember what I said earlier: the Internet is a big popularity contest. If you're perceivably more popular than competitors, you'll reap the lion's share of the customers and sales.

NEVER let social proof work against you. Always try to stack it in your favor, whether it's fans on Facebook, followers on Twitter, reviews on Google, etc. You want to dwarf your competitor

Twitter live stream plug-in

To see an example of this, go to my blog, scroll down a little, then look below the Facebook fan page widget on the right side.

You'll want to have your Twitter stream feature on your website or blog because it's real-time conversation. It shows you're active and consistently engaging with your audience. It helps encourage questions and makes you appear easily approachable, too.

With one simple click, website visitors can talk with you or ask a question. It gets them involved and starts your relationship off on a good foot. As you probably already know, people tend to do business with those they feel comfortable with. This WordPress Twitter plug-in helps them with this.

How others perceive you and your brand online or offline is critically important. It has a direct impact on the amount of influence you'll have in the marketplace and income you'll generate. You MUST come across as intelligent, honest, believable, and trustworthy.

One of the best books I've ever read on this subject is called The Credibility Code by Cara Hale Alter. Get your hands on this gem. It will improve your overall verbal and nonverbal communication by leaps and bounds.

Action Step: Get these psychological triggers up and running on your website ASAP.

Chapter 7

HOW TO MANUFACTURE CELEBRITY

Destiny is no matter of chance. It is a matter of choice.
It is not a thing to be waited for, it is a thing to be achieved.
—William Jennings Bryan

This is really an important continuation of the last chapter. The truth is, your positioning and pre-framing efforts have more effect on your actual conversion than anything else! By conversion, I'm referring to those that elect to subscribe to your email list and/or buy your product.

Remember that our goal is to strategically engineer you as a celebrity in your space. Why? It's quite simple. You'll be paid the MOST for your position in the marketplace.

Let me break it down in terms of everyday life. We'll use medicine as an example. A general practitioner makes a lot less money than a neurosurgeon. Why is this? It really comes down to perceived value.

A neurosurgeon has about eight to ten years of extra education and hands-on experience. Also, this type of medical doctor is a specialist! He is not a jack-of-all-trades and doesn't pretend to be. He can do what the GP can do, but he has extensive knowledge of the spine and nervous system and performs surgical procedures.

Now, let's take it a step further.

At the top of the ladder, you have the specialist who's a celebrity. Cardiothoracic surgeon Dr. Mehmet Oz falls into this category. All around the world he's known as an authority when it comes to health. I read in a publication that Dr. Oz banks about $4 million per year. I don't believe this includes endorsements either. He's been featured on hit TV shows like Oprah and Larry King, not to mention he's authored a few NY Times best sellers.

As you can see, a typical neurosurgeon earning a respectable $550,000 per year doesn't even come close to what Dr. Oz makes. Notoriety definitely has it perks! When you're famous in an industry, you become a money magnet.

Here's something really cool though. Even if you're a beginner online, we can strategically engineer celebrity through a series of planned events. In the last chapter, I gave you several proven, effective methods to implement.

So, how do you further position yourself to reap the benefits in your marketing?

I'm going to let you in on one of the most powerful secrets I ever discovered. I learned this from the highest-paid direct-response copywriter in the Internet marketing industry, Frank Kern. In fact, most of the concepts talked about in this chapter come from his work, Convert. You want to get your hands on that one. Heck, I'd recommend picking up a copy of all his products. (I don't get compensated for saying that either. They're just that damn good.) Frank's trainings have helped me turn my annual income into my monthly income. I don't say that lightly either.

Phase 1: Determine your desired position.

This is what you want everyone in your industry to think about you. Let's look at it like this. Imagine you're about to get on stage and speak to over 1,000 prospective customers. These people are directly in your target market. Knowing that there's a HUGE opportunity to help a lot of people and generate a tremendous amount of sales, how would you want to be introduced by the event host?

Thinking about this scenario is a powerful way to get specific on what you want your global desired position or public perception to be. You also want to answer these four questions:

1. What's your magic power in the market you serve?

   You might be really good at finding real estate foreclosure deals. Or maybe you're highly skilled at saving people money when it comes to taxes. Maybe you're good at reversing chronic diseases through nutrition and lifestyle. I want you to zero in on what your special ability is.

   I'm known as the highest-paid social media revenue strategist in North America. When I do interviews, it's common for hosts to refer to me as the king of social media. This is because they see me all over the place, and I've positioned and pre-framed myself well.

2. What is your superhero identity?

   This is the character you want to be known as, e.g., a presidential figure, the athletic pro, relaxed beach guy, etc.

   Remember this: How your market perceives you will directly affect your conversion, profitability, and how in demand you are. We're obviously looking to increase all three of these.

3. What do you stand for?

   This is pretty self-explanatory. If answered correctly, you can create goodwill in your community and build a strong character. People will identify with you on a deeper, more meaningful level.

   If we go back to our stage example above, we could use a sentence like this. Fill in the blanks with your information.

   "(your name) is known as the most sought after (insert magic power or superhero identity) in the marketplace."

   That would be the first sentence of your introduction. You might follow it up with something like this.

   "He/She is famous for (fill in this blank with the application of your magic power applied to what you stand for)."

4. What do you stand against?

You'll want to finish that last sentence with what you stand against. The reason this is so important is that one of the most classic and effective headline formulas in the world is something that Frank Kern calls, "how to yay without boo." In other words, how to get an awesome result without bad stuff. When people know what you stand against, it helps build up your desired marketplace perception.

Let me give you a personal example. If I was going to be introduced from stage, this is what it would sound like:

> *Dr. Matthew Loop is an author, speaker, and the most sought after social media revenue strategist in North America.*
>
> *He's famous for showing celebrities, entrepreneurs, and small business owners how to create wildly profitable five-figure monthly passive income streams by harnessing the power of the Internet ... WITHOUT appearing unprofessional, salesy, or desperate.*

Do you see how I used the templates above to create this introduction? Make sure you understand how to do this; you need to get clear on these things.

Now I want to discuss pre-framing and the power it holds.

Pre-framing is simply the marketing we use to control public opinion and feeling about you (or your brand) before people read your sales message or interact with you in any way. It's akin to the speaker's introduction example I gave previously.

Remember that everything discussed in this section occurs before they become subscribers to your email list and get placed in your funnel. When done correctly, prospective customers in your market will love you before they actually opt-in to receive more information. This means you've already scaled a big wall in their mind and most of the uphill fight is won.

The overall process is not terribly difficult, but there are several moving parts of the machine. Here are several ways you can pre-frame before you actually interact with anyone.

1. Online Video – A few things to consider here are how you're introduced in the video (either by someone speaking or a professional video intro), your appearance on camera, how easily you speak about the subject matter, and the value you deliver.

2. Pay Per Click (PPC) ad copy – What you say in the advertisement obviously affects the way a prospective customer perceives you. Choose your words wisely, and refer to the previous four questions we asked. You can even include some of that text in the ad copy.

3. Press Releases – This is simply news outlets that distribute announcements. The content of the press release directly affects your positioning and how you appear within the marketplace. This content also gets ranked on Google for certain words you target.

4. Blog Posts – These are great for pre-framing because it's easy to deliver value with a simple post. We can even promote blogs on Facebook and other media to distribute the content quickly to our target market.

5. Guest Interviews – Who interviews you and who you interview can make a very large difference in how you're perceived in your industry.

6. Articles – Writing or submitting a guest post for a major industry publication can boost your credibility fast if it gets picked up and published.

7. Once I started to make a name for myself in the health space, I was approached by a few publications to write for them. This gets you credibility by association because famous influencers normally grace the cover of these magazines.

8. Forum Contribution – Answering questions and being regarded as a problem solver is one of the most effective ways to pre-frame in today's time.

9. Syndicated Content – This can be two things: valuable content you've created that others feel compelled to share or (potentially) content you've created for other people's products.

So, let's say someone buys a product in your market from a known guru and you're a contributor. Psychologically speaking, this puts you on par with that expert they just purchased from. It makes it much more likely they will do business with you.

The above methods, if done right, are VERY effective for pre-framing. Remember, we are not using a sales pitch at all here. We're inundating the market with our core message.

Phase 2: Indoctrination

Once a prospective client has come into our funnel and circle of influence as a result of our pre-framing efforts, the next step deals with indoctrination. This is where we firmly implant our positioning in the marketplace to magnetically attract our ideal customer.

Let's be clear. Your indoctrination materials are what people see AFTER they have been conditioned to already think you're awesome. This is where so many business owners and entrepreneurs totally drop the ball. They don't follow up correctly, and sometimes not at all.

They try to get the sale immediately rather than focusing on creating a strong relationship with the potential customer. Remember, we need to deliver value, build social proof, and get people to know, like, and trust us before they will do business with us. When this is done the right way, your demand increases, and you can charge whatever you want for your product or service.

Indoctrination and the ability to convert is everything from the time the prospect gives you their name and email, to after they've purchased from you, to ongoing contact. These conditioning materials are what people see after they've been pre-framed by your ads and such. The end goal of this process is to establish trust and desire, which ultimately ends in conversion.

Here are some examples of indoctrination materials:

Blog posts – My blog at MatthewLoop.com is FULL of practical content that helps business owners turn social media into a 24/7 revenue-generating machine. There are hundreds of videos and articles that create value and establish goodwill in my respective markets.

Some of those blog posts are sent to my large email lists, and others act as powerful lead-generation mechanisms. This helps greatly with pre-framing and indoctrination.

<u>Launch videos</u> – Some marketers use these types of videos to educate and sell prospects after they opt-in to receive your ethical bribe.

<u>Webinars</u> – These can be educational, or you can actually sell your products and services with them. I have an entire training course about them called The Ultimate Webinar Marketing Blueprint.

<u>Free PDF reports</u> – My flagship free report is my Ultimate Blogging Success Blueprint. It's been downloaded over 53,000 times. The document is packed with forty-four pages of solid business-building content and shows you how to create a high-traffic blog that makes you money.

<u>Teleseminars</u> – I like to conduct teleseminars for my lists periodically to deliver even more valuable information and to sell products. They work well because you actually get to touch your list with your voice. Everyone has a phone, too. They're relatively simple to host.

So remember, the purpose of an indoctrination campaign is not to make the sale. It's to strengthen your relationship with the consumer so that, when it's time to make your irresistible offer, the sale becomes almost effortless. We're also trying to further position ourselves as the celebrity authority in the marketplace.

Through the types of content above, you can earn the trust of your audience and they will come to like you. The by-product of this is that your conversion process (your ability to turn your subscribers into paying customers) will be more efficient.

Establishing goodwill like this also allows you to also increase your price, and this basically leads us into really the only couple ways to increase your business profits. You can either optimize your entire conversion process or simply charge more for your product or service. Increasing your volume of new customers and increasing the number of repeat purchases fall under the conversion optimization aspect.

I spoke about trust briefly above, too. It's very important and affects your ability to influence.

With this in mind, consider that there are only two reasons people don't buy from you. One, they just don't want what you have. Truthfully, there's not much you can do about these folks. If your market research and targeting is accurate, unqualified individuals will be few and far between.

The second reason people don't buy is that they just don't trust or believe you. This factor is within our control. We can strategically use indoctrination materials plus client testimonials to establish trust.

Other things to consider when manufacturing celebrity

Associate and be seen with other celebrities. We touched on this before. Their credibility rubs off on you, and you will stick out like a sore thumb in your market. Very few businesses do this.

Charge a premium price for your quality products (think Louis Vuitton here). If something is priced through the roof, we natural assume it's better in every way compared to competitors.

Observe how mainstream celebrities are presented to the public. Copy this.

Go beyond what's expected of you. Always over-deliver. That should speak for itself.

Have an application-based program and waiting list. If you are selective about who you accept for your products and programs, you appear in demand. This makes people want you more.

If you do seminars or events, have an exclusive, higher-priced package for attendees. For example, you might guarantee them a seat in the first two rows, early access to the event, a picture with you, and a signed copy of your book.

Attend the top events in your industry each year—those where you can see and be seen.

Action Step: Go through and complete the exercises in this chapter and think of how you can use these valuable tips to create a celebrity brand in your space. We'll get heavier into the tactical aspect later on in this book.

Chapter 8

THE SIMPLE PRODUCT CREATION FORMULA

You can have everything in life you want,
if you'll just help other people get what they want.
—Zig Ziglar

Creating your very first product online doesn't have to be complicated at all. In fact, as you'll soon see, you can develop something of value in five easy steps. This is really the fun part because now is your opportunity to package your expertise, advice, and life experience into a product that will transform lives.

You have wisdom and a solution that other people desperately need. This is your chance to really make a difference, to leave a positive legacy that thrives long after you're gone!

The following are just a few of the areas you can choose from to create your products and services.

Lifestyle:
- Recreation: boats, cars, planes
- Travel
- Hobbies
- Sports: peak performance, coaching, how to play
- Home: buying your first home, renovations, investment properties, moving
- Pets
- Protecting the environment

Health:
- Fitness
- Weight loss
- Nutrition
- Healing
- Energy + living healthier
- Quitting smoking
- Breaking addictions
- How to deal with illness
- Eating disorders

Mindset & Spirituality:
- Personal development
- Meditation
- Spiritual growth
- Pursuing your dreams
- Writing a book
- Living a more balanced life
- Religion

Business & Education:
- Starting a new business or home-based business
- Finding (and getting) your ideal first job

- Managing others, leadership
- Outsourcing strategies
- Retirement
- Marketing strategies: social media, video marketing, online marketing
- Sales training
- Negotiation strategies
- Communication strategies
- Time management
- Project management
- Skill training: writing, copywriting, design, video production, etc.
- Getting into college
- Getting an MBA
- Going back to school
- Pedagogy

Family:
- Getting pregnant, managing pregnancy
- Adopting a child
- Parenting
- Empty-nest syndrome
- Caring for aging parents
- Death of a loved one (parent, child, spouse, etc.)
- Domestic violence
- Communication strategies
- Special events: planning a wedding, honeymoon, bar mitzvah, birthday

Intimate Relationships:
- A new relationship
- Getting engaged
- A breakup
- Marriage
- Divorce
- Passion, intimacy, sex

- Discovering your spouse is having an affair
- Moving in, living together
- Coming out of the closet
- Counseling
- Communication strategies

Finances:
- Taking control of your money
- Reading a balance sheet
- Managing your business finances
- Inheritance
- Estate planning: wills, trusts, living wills, etc.
- Getting out of debt
- Going bankrupt
- Being sued
- Tax strategies
- Investing strategies

Now, for the good stuff. Here's how to develop your million-dollar idea in five simple steps. We're going to start with one product idea then eventually evolve that into other powerful training programs.

Remember, downloadable information products can be things such as e-books, audio courses, video tutorials, teleseminars, webinar trainings, membership sites, software programs, iPhone apps, coaching programs, etc.

Take out a separate pen and paper and write the answers to all the questions below to gain clarity. Really immerse yourself in this process.

Step 1: Brainstorm an Idea.
1. What do you absolutely love to do?
2. What is your passion? What would you do for free if you could?
3. What are you really good at (personally and professionally)?
4. How do you spend your free time?
5. What do others consistently ask you to help them with?

6. Who do you know who has a special skill or expertise that you can leverage?

7. Who do you like to work with? What group or type of people do you want to help?

Step 2: Adjust and Narrow Your Focus.

1. Ask for feedback from those you trust.

2. Get as much information as possible on your concept, idea, or opportunity.

3. Brainstorm outrageous solutions.

4. Ask better questions:
   - ✓ "What if?" Challenge your thoughts by imagining alternative solutions.
   - ✓ "How would they do that?" See things through the eyes of someone you admire.

5. Consider combinations. Many new ideas are the fusion of other ideas. Look for ways to combine something you love (or hate) with a product/service/concept that will make it easier, more efficient, or more fun.
   - ✓ What new product/concept/service can you generate by matching together ones that already exist?
   - ✓ What individuals or companies can you PARTNER with to create a new business venture?
   - ✓ How can you combine your personal skill set with that of someone else to develop a niche market?
   - ✓ How can combining products make it easier for the end consumer?
   - ✓ Decide on the best direction—not the perfect idea, but an idea that can help you develop and produce.

Step 3: Decide on a Course of Action.

1. What types of products can you create out of your idea?
   - ✓ How-to training (step-by-step how-to)
   - ✓ Provide done-for-you resources that make things easier
   - ✓ Case studies, examples, and stories

✓ Automated systems that save people time and money

✓ Live events and experiences

2. How can you create escalation (higher-end product offerings) with this idea?

✓ What are some related products and services you can create to enhance your product portfolio?

3. Who can you model?

✓ Who is doing something similar—successfully—in your target market?

4. How will the marketplace respond to your product idea?

✓ In what way is this not currently being marketed or maximized?

✓ What segment of an established market is currently being ignored?

✓ What can you give away to get people excited about your topic/product?

5. Who is the ideal market and customer you're committed to serving?

✓ Overall group (entrepreneurs, golfers, diabetes sufferers, moms, etc.)?

✓ Gender?

✓ Education, profession?

✓ Annual income?

✓ Geographic location (if applicable)?

✓ Where can you find these people online?

✓ What is their biggest problem or fear?

✓ If they could make three changes in their life, what would it be?

✓ Which celebrities do they trust in this market?

Step 4: Know Your Purpose and Why You Do What You Do.

1. Why do you want to create and promote your own products and services?

✓ What lifestyle do you want to create for you or your family?

✓ What impact can you have on people's lives as a result?

2. Reasons to create your own product or service

3. Add massive value and make a difference for your customers.

✓ Create healthy competition in the marketplace, advancing your industry.

✓ Provide an ongoing source of revenue that pours in 24/7.

✓ Build a sustainable revenue strategy to grow your business through time.

✓ Provide a creative outlet for your ideas in a tangible way.

✓ Create an environment that necessitates personal learning and growth.

✓ Connect you to customers and people in new ways, deepening your relationships with others in the process.

✓ Leave a positive legacy and personal brand that lives long after you're gone.

Step 5: Get it done!

1. Imperfect action beats perfect planning—every time.
2. Get to work and turn your idea in reality.
3. Pick what product or service you want to create first.
4. Decide on an irresistible marketing offer that will get your ideal customer to buy.
5. Reverse engineer your product development.
6. Design your product so that it delivers on your offer and will help solve your customers' biggest problems.
7. Model what works. Find the proven strategies for getting your product to market, and save yourself time and money by not reinventing the wheel.

When you follow the product creation outline above, you're practically guaranteed a winner. This formula has worked for thousands of aspiring entrepreneurs, and it WILL work for you. Developing your own information product allows you leverage, the ability to make money while you sleep, and a way to make a difference impacting the masses.

In the end, there are three things that matter in the big picture: (1) What exactly are you selling? (2) Who specifically are you selling it to? (3) What will it take to get them to buy?

When you make your offer on your sales page, the product must solve a big problem people face, it must make a bold promise, it must have proof it works, and you must show them the process.

In its simplest form you're telling prospective customers what you have, what it will do for them, and what you want them to do next. We'll get much more in depth on this sales process in the chapter titled "The Art of Copywriting and Sales."

Consumers are really paying for your unique perspective, the experience they believe the product will deliver, and your ability to structure and/or simplify the info so they can use it.

To close this chapter, I'd like to give you some of the most common product formats and ways to monetize your expertise. If you look at the list of products and services I offer at MatthewLoop.com, you'll see that I've incorporated virtually all of them.

You should as well. Start with one product, follow my instructions in this book (and in my blog trainings), and you'll eventually have your own online empire.

1. E-books, Instruction Guides
2. Teleclasses, Audio Courses
3. Webinars, Webcasts
4. Membership Sites
5. Video training programs
6. Multimedia Products, Training Courses (DVD trainings)
7. Software
8. Mobile Applications (Apps)
9. Coaching Programs
10. Professional Speaking
11. Live Events and Seminars
12. Private Masterminds (Retreats)

13. Done-for-You Service (if applicable)

14. Selling Private-Label Products on Amazon

What you ideally want to do is give a prospective client something for free in exchange for a name and email address. We call that an "ethical bribe." Understand that this is the point of entry in your funnel. Your giveaway can be a free report, free video training series, etc.

Because your email list is your number one asset online, you should always be trying to build it. To do so effectively, you must have your offer on your ethical bribe on your website and above the fold, as well as on a separate squeeze page that is solely about your giveaway. Sometimes this is also referred to as a landing page.

The following screenshot shows a quick example of what a squeeze page looks like. You can see the full page at http://DCincome.com/go/bloggingsuccess/.

For two more squeeze page examples with slightly different styles, check these pages:

http://DCincome.com/go/headlines

http://DCincome.com/go/reviews

The "secret sauce" of a high-converting squeeze page is quite simply this:

1. You must have a big, bad, bold promise in the title headline (you've got to know exactly what your market wants). Make the text red—it jumps out.

2. You must have four to five bullet points that tell the reader "what's in it for me." They might be formatted like "Avoid the BIGGEST mistakes when _____" or "Discover the #1 secret to _____."

3. You must have an email capture form (opt-in box) to the right with an arrow pointing to it. There should be no mistake about what you want visitors to do.

A good squeeze page will convert at least 30 percent of the people that come to it. Meaning, if you get 100 visitors, then thirty should give you their name and email to get your free report. Shoot for numbers like those. I've even had squeeze pages convert at 60 percent before! This gives you an idea of what's possible.

As people get to know, like, and trust you, we can escalate them up the product funnel. If they find immense use-value from your free report, then the next step is to offer them what's called a "low barrier" offer, one that is very affordable, typically under $10.

For example, let's say you're a personal trainer in the fitness market and you already have your website finished. You decide to offer a free report on the homepage as your ethical bribe. The report is titled, "5 Mistakes MOST People Make When Hiring a Personal Trainer." It's formatted like a consumer awareness guide and answers the most frequent questions as well as addresses the most common mistakes most people make when trying to get in shape.

Let's say this report is packed full of great content that will help the end consumer make the best decisions, lose weight safely, get toned, save money, and look better. Well, the prospective customer tries it, and they begin to see improvement in their own life. They're happy, have more energy, and are more confident. So naturally their skepticism and distrust start fading away.

Important side note: The number one reason people don't buy from you online is that they don't believe you. Always remember this. It's rarely about the money. Internet users are very skeptical these days. You must do your best to remove the conscious and unconscious mental walls of distrust they have.

Not long after they opt-in for your ethical bribe, you send an email offering a thirty-five–page e-book on "How to Sculpt a Hollywood Beach Body in 30 Days or Less." You then offer a proven workout training schedule and a strict meal plan as a bonus.

The e-book costs $7, and they get access to the two awesome fast-action bonuses. You even have a sixty-day money-back guarantee because you believe in the product so much because it works. Case studies and testimonials are also featured all over your site to prove the product works.

What you've essentially done now is remove ALL risk associated with making this very inexpensive investment. The goal is to get your product into the hands of a customer because you know it will transform their life for the better.

To do this, the consumer has to feel compelled to take the credit card out of their wallet and make the purchase. Statistics show that if a customer spends money with you once, they're MUCH more likely to do so again. It's easier to sell happy customers that have already bought something from you than it is to sell someone that's never invested in your products.

In this example, we gave them a free report then "graduated" them up to a low-barrier e-book that has even more value and practical strategies that will change their life for the better.

The next step might be to introduce them to an audio program, then on to a video training series, then on to a monthly membership site, then on to private coaching, etc. We're continuously delivering more value and escalating the customer up to our highest-level trainings. We're earning their trust then giving them more of what they want, which includes private access to you.

If we tried to immediately pitch an interested lead that comes into our funnel on a $2,000 coaching program or a $997 live weekend seminar, it would be incredibly difficult. We haven't built a relationship with them.

Make sense?

We'll get heavily into the "list building" and Internet marketing strategies in later chapters. I'll show you how to create an absolute avalanche of traffic to your website that you couldn't turn off even if you wanted to.

In my opinion, traffic is the easy part of building a highly profitable business online. We'll discuss powerful mediums such as Facebook, YouTube, Google AdWords, Facebook advertising, blogging, SEO, joint ventures, affiliate programs, retargeting, and more.

Converting the traffic, your website visitors, into sales is the part that can take testing and tweaking. Once you nail it though, get ready to see the sales pour in fast and furiously!

Alright, after answering all the above questions in this chapter, and after doing extensive market research online, you should have a clear idea of where you want to go with your first product. You should know if it's going to be an e-book, video training, membership site, etc. Also, you should have a firm understanding of who your perfect customer is.

How to easily create digital products:

1. E-books, Instruction Guides

    You can write the free report, e-book, or guide yourself or just have a ghostwriter do it. For a list of freelance writing professionals, see the "Tools and Resources" section of this book. Once the e-book is written, you'll need an e-cover to put on your squeeze page, sales page, or regular website.

    You'll find e-cover designers in the "Tools and Resources" section as well. Enable a shopping cart and PayPal to collect payments. See "Tools and Resources" section for the shopping cart I use.

2. Teleclasses, Audio Courses

    Use FreeConferenceCall.com for teleclasses and to record them. Prepare an outline of what you want to discuss. See my program The Ultimate Webinar Marketing Blueprint for how to script the perfect call. This training was originally created for doctors, but it is applicable to any business.

Once the call is over, get it transcribed; that way you can offer the audio and transcription together. Get an e-cover for the product. Create a sales page—or have one created—to sell the program. Enable a shopping cart and PayPal to collect payments. See the "Tools and Resources" section for the shopping cart I use.

3. Webinars, Webcasts

See the webinar platform I use and recommend at StealthSeminarDiscount.com. Use Camtasia Studio or an inexpensive equivalent to record the screen and audio while doing the presentation. See the chapter on webinars for how to script the perfect webinar.

Once the webinar is over, get it transcribed; that way you can offer the transcription together. You can even have the audio stripped out to offer a separate MP3 as added value. Get an e-cover for the product. Create a sales page—or have one created—to sell the program. Enable a shopping cart and PayPal to collect payments. See the "Tools and Resources" section for the shopping cart I use.

4. Membership Sites

Find a programmer from Upwork.com (formerly Elance and Odesk) to build a membership site or integrate WordPress plug-ins like OptimizePress and WishList member. Create videos, articles, or MP3 content for your membership site. Get an e-cover for the product. Create a sales page—or have one created—to sell the program. Enable a shopping cart and PayPal to collect payments. See the "Tools and Resources" section for the shopping cart I use.

5. Video Training Programs

Use Camtasia Studio or an inexpensive equivalent to record the screen and audio while doing the presentation. Create video tutorials on "how to _____." Get the videos transcribed; that way you can offer the transcription together. You can have the audio stripped out to offer a separate MP3 as added value. Get an e-cover for the product. Create a sales page—or have one created—to sell the program.

If you intend to have an actual physical product where you're shipping something to a client, use Disk.com. They drop-ship and store everything to make it seamless for you as orders come in. If you intend to host the video content online, you can use a simple storage platform like DropBox. Enable a shopping cart and PayPal to collect payments. See the "Tools and Resources" section for the shopping cart I use.

6. Multimedia Products, Training Courses (DVD trainings)

    See previous protocol. It's the same as #5.

7. Software

    Once you have your idea, go to either vWorker.com, ScriptLance.com, or Upwork.com to find a programmer. Communicate your idea clearly to them. They will create the software.

    Get an e-cover for the product. Create a sales page—or have one created—to sell the program. Enable a shopping cart and PayPal to collect payments. See the "Tools and Resources" section for the shopping cart I use.

8. Mobile Applications (Apps)

    Once you have your app idea, go to Upwork.com to find a mobile app developer. Communicate your idea clearly to them. They will create the app and upload it to iTunes.

    Get an e-cover for the app. Some choose to have a one-page website for the app, but it's not really necessary. Next, sign up for the Apple Developer program. Read my free report titled, How to Easily Create an iPhone App

9. Coaching Programs

10. Professional Speaking

11. Live Events and Seminars

12. Private Masterminds (Retreats)

13. Done-for-You Service (if applicable)

14. Selling Private-Label Products on Amazon

Numbers 9–13 above are more advanced and not really for the average beginner. I normally work one-on-one with entrepreneurs looking to create any of those high-level products. I have two programs available for this. Both are application based. Visit the pages below to see if you qualify.

http://DCincome.com/blog/coaching (private phone coaching)
http://DCincome.com/blog/total-immersion-day (we meet in person)

For number 14, I've dedicated an entire section in this book to selling private-label products on Amazon. There's such a massive opportunity right now if you set up the business and market your product correctly. Refer to chapter 31 for all the specifics on making big money with Amazon.

Once you've created your product, it's time to get your sales funnel up and running. We discuss this in the next chapter. From there, you're ready to launch the product for all the world to see! This is where the fun really begins.

Part II of this book is dedicated to that entire process. Traffic generation is covered in depth. You can have the best product in the world; however, if no one knows it exists, then it really doesn't matter.

You're going to discover which strategies the world's highest-paid entrepreneurs are using to stand out above the crowd while creating an unstoppable FLOOD of traffic that couldn't be turned off—even if you wanted to.

Chapter 9

THE ART OF COPYWRITING
AND SALES FUNNELS

The written word is the strongest source of power in the universe.
—Gary Halbert

I f you truly want to be successful online and create a seven-figure business that pays you effortlessly over and over again, you absolutely MUST master the art of writing sales copy. This is what gets you paid. In fact, most top-level Internet marketers will tell that copywriting is the most valuable skill set you could ever learn when it comes to starting an online business.

I completely agree.

In the words of the late Gary Halbert, "You are one sales letter away from being rich."

You can have all the qualified, targeted traffic pouring into your website all day long, but if you cannot convert those visitors into actual sales, it doesn't matter. You must be able to ethically influence and persuade interested prospects to buy your product or service.

Notice I said "ethically." Yes, there is a right way and a wrong way to do this.

"Selling" is not evil nor does it have to be sleazy. Joe Polish said it best when he stated, "People love to be sold; they hate to be pressured."

A BIG reason why many entrepreneurs fail online is that they don't know how to effectively sell their product to those that are already interested in buying. Those that fail miserably don't know how to communicate the VALUE of their product in a way that compels the visitor to pull out their credit card and pay for what is being offered.

I look at selling like this: if you honestly believe in your product and it transforms people's lives for the better, it's your obligation to get it in their hands. The only way you can effectively do this is to master copywriting, sales, and communication.

Within your marketing funnel, what you write (and the precise words you choose) is responsible for the interested lead taking action. Everything from advertisements, website headlines, sales letters, squeeze pages, email subject lines, etc., relies on compelling headlines to get the prospective customer to act.

Do yourself a favor. Begin to search out and find "direct response" sales letters in your specific industry to get an idea of how they're formatted and how other entrepreneurs are using them to sell products. When I refer to direct response, I'm referring to marketing and sales methods that get prospective customers to take action now. The most successful online entrepreneurs ALWAYS combine traditional Internet marketing methods and branding with direct-response strategies. If you don't merge the three, you're simply wasting your time and money.

You can view a couple sales letters I wrote at the following links. This will give you an idea of their typical structure and format.

http://DCincome.com/go/webinars
http://DCincome.com/go

Sales letters can also be in video form. Meaning, you can basically sell using a PowerPoint presentation on a page where the written sales letter would normally be. There's a specific way to do this though.

The outline below will help you greatly. Each of these points should ALWAYS be addressed in any sales copy you write or have created. I got this powerful guide from Internet entrepreneur and sales master Perry Belcher.

The Perfect Sales Letter Outline (in 21 Steps)
1. Call out your audience.
2. Use an attention-grabbing headline.
3. Back it up with a sub-headline.
4. Identify the problem.
5. Provide the solution.
6. Show the pain and cost of development.
7. Explain the ease of use.
8. Show the speed and result.
9. Futurecast for them.
10. Show your credentials.
11. Detail the benefits of the service.
12. Get and show social proof.
13. Make your offer.
14. Add the bonus.
15. Build up your value.
16. Reveal your price point.
17. Inject scarcity if there is any.
18. Give a money-back guarantee.
19. Make a call to action.
20. Give a warning.
21. Finally, close with a reminder.

The 8-Part Copy Test after Finishing the Sales Piece:
1. Did you grab your readers by the throat with your headline?
2. Did you clearly explain that you understand the problem?
3. Did you show them so much proof that they can't possibly doubt what you had to say?

4. Did you show features and benefits to your offer that included the word "so" in each line?

5. Did you assure your prospects that your product will be very, very easy to use?

6. Did you assure your prospects that your product would work very quickly to solve the problem?

7. Did you clearly explain the pain of the experience by not accepting your offer?

8. Did you demonstrate incredible value in your offer—so much so that your prospect would feel stupid for not buying your product?

The art of the sales funnel

A sales funnel is just what it sounds like. Circulating just above the funnel, you should have swarms of traffic. Nothing happens online without good qualified visitors to your website, products, or services. The marketing funnel "captures" the traffic from many sources as you'll discover throughout this book.

The first layer of the funnel at the top (and the widest part) is your ethical bribe, which is a free gift in exchange for a name and email. We use this like bait to attract our ideal customer. Some examples of ethical bribes include free cheat sheets, free PDF reports, video trainings, software demos, audio interviews, etc.

Another strategic way to compel prospective customers is to create an irresistible quiz that your market identifies with. You've probably observed these floating around on Facebook or other social media.

For example, maybe you've seen a post in your newsfeed asking the question, "Will you survive a zombie attack? Take this quiz to find out!"

Then what happens?

You click the link out of curiosity and answer four quick multiple-choice questions. After you've answered the last one and are mentally invested in the outcome, you're prompted to enter your name and email so they can send you the results.

I've got news for you. These quizzes are from marketers, entrepreneurs, and business owners trying to build an email list so that they can sell you something related later on. It's a highly effective engagement strategy that gets an interested person into your funnel.

Two powerful, simple quiz software programs are the following:

Viral Quiz Builder – http://DCincome.com/blog/quiz
Survey Funnel Software – http://DCincome.com/blog/survey

After this prospective customer takes the quiz or receives the ethical bribe, we move them to the next layer of the funnel called the low-barrier offer. This is a product of ours that typically costs under $10. The goal here is to deliver more value to the subscriber and make this "upsell" an impulse purchase.

We want them to take their credit card out of their wallet—the sooner the better too. If someone buys a product from you, they're a hundred times more likely to buy something else from you in the future, assuming you deliver on what you promise.

Now, if you sold a higher ticket item right out of the gate and skipped the low-barrier offer, your volume of purchases would be much less because you haven't built liking, trust, or rapport with this new individual that came into your funnel. Because of this, I recommend that one of your products be under $10 so we can distinguish buyers from non-buyers early on. Next—and this is critically important too—the offer has to be available for this ONE TIME ONLY. In other words, the prospective customer will never see it again.

That should be literally written in big letters so they can't miss it. When a "one-time offer" is immediately placed on the thank-you page (the page an individual is immediately directed to after they give you their name and email), it creates urgency and scarcity!

Let me be clear.

On the thank-you page, you always give what you promise first. So if you're giving away a free report, the download link should be one of the first things they see. Or if you're emailing the report to the subscriber, let them know either with written text or video.

As you might guess, not everyone will take us up on our low-barrier offer, but that's okay. We have them on our email list! We can communicate with them a few times per week, deliver value, establish trust, and make them more offers down the road.

If we would've never built an email list, we would've never been able to follow up, create a relationship, and eventually make that person a customer.

Neglecting to build an email list is the #1 cardinal sin for any Internet-based business! Don't learn the hard and stupid way. I can tell you from personal experience, every time we run a promotion, at least 40 percent of the buyers have been on the email list for a year or more!

Your email list is the LIFEBLOOD of your online business. If set up correctly, it allows you to generate customers and sales while you sleep. You can also make money on demand.

In order to build a large email list, you need a reliable email management system. Some call this an autoresponder, but it functions as so much more. I've always used Aweber to house my database, and I recommend you do as well.

It's consistently rated one of the best email follow-up programs in the business, and it's pretty simple to figure out—not to mention their phone support is awesome. If you decide to go with them, I negotiated a dollar trial for you at MyProResponse.com.

Let me explain why you need an autoresponder like this.

Aweber serves many different purposes. One of the primary functions is that it allows you to create a web form on your site. This is also referred to as an email capture box.

For example, if you go to my blog at MatthewLoop.com, you'll notice that below the three bullet points in the header banner on the right, you'll see two white rectangular boxes. One is for a name, and the other is for an email.

When an individual types their name and email and then clicks the orange "Get Access" button, they are instantly populated in my Aweber email database. Then the first prewritten autoresponder email automatically goes out to them, delivering the free report as promised.

The reason I have this form on my blog home page, and on multiple pages throughout my website, is to generate interested leads that will eventually convert into paying customers. I'm also building a huge email list so that readers can get to know, like, and trust me.

<u>The money is in the email list!</u>

Some folks will click the orange RSS feed to subscribe to my blog, but that's not guaranteed. Email list building is one of my top priorities, and it should be yours too. It's a foundational pillar for any successful Internet business.

When you don't have an automated follow-up system and are not building an email list, you're gambling haphazardly. You're essentially "hoping" a prospective client, patient, or customer will return to your website and do business with you.

This rarely happens.

I don't like to gamble or leave anything to chance. I prefer to stack the odds in my favor. I'd recommend you adopt the same mentality.

When you build a targeted email list and have a reliable management system like Aweber, you're setting your business up for success. Your programmer can install this script quickly for you too. (We'll discuss how to find a programmer in the outsourcing chapter of this book.)

So we have prospective customers who have opted in for our ethical bribe and provided us their name and email. For those that do decide to purchase our low-barrier offer, we can immediately make another offer after they've bought it and while their credit card is still in their hand. This item might be in the $100–$500 range. We call this the middle layer of our funnel.

This product can be an extension of the low-barrier offer or something that's the perfect complement. This might also be your flagship training that you become primarily known for. For me, Social Media Elite falls into this range. It's what gained me notoriety in the small-business sector.

Even if the individual does not buy the middle-range offer or the low-barrier upsell, no problem. They're on our email list, and we'll establish more liking and trust over time. As you make offers later on and show your subscribers more testimonials, many will eventually opt for your flagship product.

Something I'd like to point out here is that we're also trying to identify hyperactive buyers. If a prospect purchases your low-barrier e-book then invests in your middle-range offer during the same transaction, they've demonstrated they're in greater need of a solution. This person is experiencing more pain, and there's a sense of urgency to get it fixed.

Let me give you a personal example. When I was nineteen years old, a few of my buddies and I went to the driving range to hit golf balls. One of my friends had been playing for three months and thought he was going to show off his skills.

We were all playing with his dad's clubs that were about twenty years old. As we started hitting, everyone was shanking the balls left and right—even my friend that started playing golf a few months prior.

Well, I've always been the type of person that can learn a sport really quickly. So after fifteen minutes or so, I started to annihilate ball after ball with this rusted, prehistoric driver! Not all my drives were straight, but I was destroying my friends in terms of distance. I was laughing in disbelief and talking to my friends about a couple hacks I discovered that might help them hit longer and straighter too.

I still remember my buddy's face, the one that had been playing for three months prior. He was getting so mad. I mean livid! He did have a jump start advantage on all of us. Who was I to tell him how to play better? The crazy thing is that he was so furious it started to affect his game even more. He began to chunk everything like he was digging a hole in the ground.

After another thirty minutes we called it quits.

A few days later, I got a call from him and to my surprise he invited me back to the range. As soon as we got there, he whipped out this brand-new set of clubs, a leather glove to enhance his grip, and new golf shoes with spikes to prevent slipping.

I was blown away. He was really serious about improving and kicking the crap out of me. Needless to say, I still smoked him that day. I crushed his irons farther and with more accuracy than he did.

This brings me to my point. He was a little embarrassed after we played the first time, so he went home, got on the computer, did his research, and then visited the store to make several purchases in an attempt to get better and beat me.

My friend in this example was a classic hyperactive buyer. There was a small window of opportunity for a golf retailer to get his business—and they did—

because he was experiencing the pain of humiliation. He spent just over $500 in an instant.

The faster we can identify hyperactive buyers, the better.

So you need to be thinking about what you can offer as an upsell to customers after their initial low-barrier purchase. If you don't give them additional options, they'll most likely go to a competitor and spend their money.

As we age the relationship, our goal is to escalate them into one of our "high ticket" products, services, or programs. We call this the back end of the funnel. Our most expensive trainings are usually found here.

With the consulting side of my business, I have several high-ticket items that range from *The Social Media Revenue Summit, Caribbean Adventure Mastermind*, private phone coaching, a one-on-one *Total Immersion Day* where we meet in person, and *The Private Jet Mastermind*.

The interesting thing about many high-ticket purchases is that many previous customers and prospects usually want to speak to someone live first. Even in my business when dealing with an affluent client, it's rare that they will just click a $15,000 "buy-it-now" button and purchase. (We have an application process anyway.)

My assistant or I will then get on the phone with them to answer any questions they have and to further qualify the individual or company. So for the back end of your funnel, we're going to need an application and a way to talk to them offline before they invest. (A great book on the science of funnels and how to most effectively utilize them for sales is DotComSecrets: The Underground Playbook by Russell Brunson.)

Action Step: My advice to you is to read at least three sales letters per week in and out of your current industry. This will give you great insight regarding all the moving parts of an effective script. Also, pay attention to the power words that are used in the copy. By "power words" I mean words that evoke strong emotion and get people to take action. You can view a comprehensive list of 317 power words at this great blog post:

http://boostblogtraffic.com/power-words/.

Besides the plain text, also observe the color of the initial headline at the top, the bullet points found throughout the copy, the clean white background, how testimonials are used throughout, the call to action, and how easy the reading is on the eyes.

You see, some people will want the CliffsNotes version of what you're offering, so they'll skim the titles on the sales page. Others will want to read the whole sales letter in its entirety. You need to appeal to both types of readers.

Remember: sales letters are formatted and written to get consumers to take action immediately.

If you're serious about starting and growing a highly profitable business around your passion, you must master the art of copywriting. If you want the best shortcut I've ever seen, check out Yanik Silver's course below:

http://www.DCincome.com/blog/Copywriting

If you're interested in done-for-you sales letters that can be created almost instantly, you'll want to get your hands on this:

http://www.DCincome.com/blog/InstantSales

In terms of sales funnels, you need to take a comprehensive approach to monetization as I mentioned in this chapter. This is arguably one of the biggest factors that separate Internet businesses that do five, six, seven, or even eight figures per year!

All successful funnels should have traffic, an ethical bribe, a front-end, low-barrier offer, a mid-range offer, and a back-end high-ticket product. More importantly, they should convert well.

You have a couple options at your disposal. Either hire a freelance programmer to build your sales funnel pages for you or go with a done-for-you solution like ClickFunnels. See the following link.

http://DCincome.com/blog/clickfunnels

Pay attention the next time you purchase something from the Internet and observe what takes place after the purchase. This can give you more insight into many other aspects of the funnel you may choose to integrate.

Chapter 10

6 ETHICAL PERSUASION SECRETS THAT BRING YOU MONEY

*The greatest good you can do for another is not just
to share your riches but to reveal to him his own.*
—Benjamin Disraeli

In this chapter, you'll discover six universal principles of persuasion that make you more effective in life and MULTIPLY your business revenue almost immediately! These are powerful, proven influence factors that make people say "yes." As you'll soon see, there is an exact science to this process.

As a business owner who's looking to make a greater impact, this is one of the most valuable lessons you can ever learn. This comes directly from Dr. Robert Cialdini's work in regards to the science of persuasion. Researchers have been studying the factors that influence us to say "yes" to others' requests for over sixty years. There's no doubt there's a science to how we are persuaded.

A lot of this is surprising, too.

When making a decision, it would be nice to think that people consider all the available information in order to guide their thinking. But the reality is very often different. In the increasingly overloaded lives we lead, we need shortcuts (or rules of thumb) to guide our decision making.

Cialdini's own research has uncovered six of these shortcuts as universals that guide human behavior. They are:

1. Reciprocity
2. Scarcity
3. Authority
4. Consistency
5. Liking
6. Consensus

Understanding these shortcuts and employing them in an ethical manner can substantially increase the chances that someone will be persuaded by you request. Now let's dig a little deeper into each one.

Reciprocity

Simply put, reciprocity refers to people feeling obliged to give back to others in the form of a behavior, gift, or service they have received first. If a friend invites you to their party, there's an obligation for you to invite them to a future party you are hosting. If a colleague does you a favor, then you owe that colleague a favor. In the context of a social obligation, people are more likely to say "yes" to those that they owe.

One of the best demonstrations of the principle of reciprocation comes from a series of studies conducted in restaurants. Think about this: the last time you visited a restaurant there's a good chance the waiter gave you a gift, maybe a mint—probably about the same time they brought your check.

Here's the question though: does the giving of a mint have any influence over how much of a tip you're going to leave them? Most people will say no. However, that mint can make a surprising difference.

In the study, giving customers a single mint at the end of their meal typically increased tips by 3 percent. Interestingly, if the gift is doubled and two mints are provided, tips don't double.

They quadruple!

Here's what's most interesting of all though. If the waiter provides one mint, starts to walk away from the table, pauses, walks back, and then says, "For you nice people, here's an extra mint," tips go through the roof! A 23 percent increase is noted, influenced by not by what was given but HOW it was given.

So the key to using the principle of reciprocation is to be the first to give and to ensure what you give is personalized and unexpected.

Scarcity

This refers to the fact that people want more of those things they can have less of. Let me give you a great example.

In 2003, when British Airways announced they would no longer be operating the Concord flight because it had become uneconomical, sales the very next day skyrocketed! Notice, nothing had changed about the Concord itself. It certainly didn't fly any faster. The service didn't suddenly get better. The airfare didn't drop. It had simply become a scarce resource, and as a result, people wanted it more.

So when it comes to effectively persuading others using the scarcity principle, the science is clear. It's not enough to just tell people about the benefits they gain if they choose your product and/or service. You also want to point out what is unique about your proposition and what they stand to lose if they fail to consider your proposal.

Authority

This is the idea that people follow the lead of credible and knowledgeable experts. For example, physical therapists are able to persuade more of their patients to comply with recommended exercise programs if they display their medical diplomas on the walls of their consulting rooms. People are more likely to give change for a parking meter to a complete stranger if that requester wears a uniform rather than casual clothing.

The science is telling us that it's important to signal to others what makes you a credible, knowledgeable authority before you make your influence attempt. Of course, this can present problems. You can hardly go around telling potential customers how brilliant you are, but you can certainly arrange for someone to do it for you. Surprisingly, it doesn't seem to matter if the person introducing you is not only connected to you but is also likely to prosper from the introduction themselves.

One group of real estate agents were able to increase both the number of property appraisals and the number of subsequent contracts they wrote. They did this by arranging for a reception staff who answered customer inquiries to first mention their colleague's credentials and expertise. So customers interested in renting a property were told, "Rentals, let me connect you with Sandra who has over fifteen years of experience in this area."

Customers who wanted more information about selling properties were told, "Speak to Peter, our head of sales. He has over twenty years of experience selling properties. I'll put you through now."

The impact of this expert introduction lead to a 20 percent rise in the number of appointments and a 15 percent increase in the number of signed contracts. Not bad for a small persuasion tweak that was both ethical and costless to implement.

Consistency

People like to be consistent with the things they've previously said and done. Consistency is activated by looking for, and asking for, small initial commitments that can be made.

In one famous set of studies, researchers found (unsurprisingly) that very few people would be willing to erect an unsightly wooden board on their front lawn to support a "drive safely" campaign in their neighborhood. However, in a similar neighborhood close by, four times as many homeowners indicated that they would be willing to erect this unsightly billboard.

Why?

It's because ten days previously, these residents agreed to place a small postcard in the front window of their home that signaled their support for a "drive safely" campaign. That small card was the initial commitment that lead to a 400 percent increase in a much bigger, but still consistent, change.

So when seeking to influence using the consistency principle, the detective of influence looks for voluntary, active, public commitments and ideally gets those commitments in writing.

For example, one study reduced missed appointments at a health center by 18 percent simply by asking the patients, rather than the staff, to write down appointment details on the future appointment card.

Liking

The fifth principle is the concept of liking. People prefer to say "yes" to those that they like. But what causes one person to like another? Persuasion science tells us that there are three important factors. We like people who:

1. Are similar to us
2. Pay us compliments
3. Cooperate with us toward mutual goals

As more and more of the interactions that we are having take place online, it might be worth asking whether these factors can be employed effectively during online negotiations.

In a series of negotiation studies carried out between MBA students of two well- known business schools, some groups were told, "Time is money; get straight down to business." In this group, around 55 percent were able to come to an agreement.

A second group, however, was told, "Before you begin negotiating, exchange some personal information with each other. Identify a similarity you share in common, then begin negotiating." In this group 90 percent of them were able to come to successful, agreeable outcomes that were typically worth 18 percent more to both parties.

So to harness this powerful principle of liking, be sure to look for areas of similarities you share with others and genuine compliments you can give them before you get down to business.

Consensus

This is the final principle. Especially when they are uncertain, people will look to the actions and behaviors of others to determine their own.

You may have noticed that hotels place a small card in bathrooms to persuade guests to reuse their towels and linen. Most do this by drawing a guest's attention to the benefits that reuse can have on environment protection. It turns out that this is a pretty effective strategy leading to around 35 percent compliance. But could there be an even more effective way?

Well, about 75 percent of people who check in to a hotel for four nights or longer will reuse their towels at some point during their stay. So what would happen if we took a lesson from the principle of consensus and simply included that information on the cards, saying, "Did you know that 75 percent of guests reused their towels at some point during their stay? So please do so as well." It turns out that when we do this, towel reuse rises by 26 percent.

Now, imagine the next time you stay in a hotel you see one of these signs, pick it up, and read the following message: "75 percent of people who have stayed in this room have reused their towels." What would you think?

Well, here's what you might think: "I hope they're not the same towels."

Like most people, you probably think this sign will have no influence on your behavior whatsoever. But it turns out that changing just a few words on a sign to honestly point out what comparable previous guests have done was the SINGLE-MOST effective message, leading to a 33 percent increase in towel reuse.

So the science is telling us that rather than relying on our own ability to persuade people, we can point to what others are already doing, especially many similar individuals.

There you have it. Six scientifically validated principles of persuasion that provide for small, practical, often costless changes that can lead to BIG differences in your ability to influence others in an entirely ethical way.

When you master these concepts and implement them in your online marketing efforts, your product sales numbers will dramatically increase.

Action Step: Think of strategic ways that you can fuse the principles of consistency, reciprocity, authority, scarcity, liking, and consensus in your current marketing, communication, and product and/or service promotion.

This includes everything from your product description, the blog posts you write, your email headlines, YouTube videos, paid advertising, sales letters, or any content you create. Everything.

Chapter 11

HOW TO CONDUCT MARKET RESEARCH LIKE A GURU

If you want to do the many things most people can't do,
simply do the few things that most people won't do.
—Frank Kern

O nce you have a great idea for a product or service that you'd like to develop and sell online, it's important to get your hands dirty and do some advanced detective work. This step is where the real money is made.

Conversely, it's also where you can flop if you don't take the time to analyze the market carefully. You need to make sure that:

1. People are looking for information on the topic of your choice
2. There are buyers (not just free-stuff seekers)
3. There are actual products you can sell or become an affiliate of

I've broken this down into six individual components to simplify it: (1) keyword research, (2) reverse engineering your competitors, (3) monetization and commercial viability, (4) what others are saying in the forums and on social media, (5) trending topics, and (6) verticals and related markets.

Keyword Research

This is basically where you compile a list of the words and phrases that people in your selected market are searching for on Google, Bing, Yahoo, etc. Some of these "keywords" will be short, containing only two words, while others may be longer and run between three and seven words.

Ideally, you want to find keywords that have decent search volume but are less competitive to rank for online. For years, I've used a proprietary tool called Market Samurai to accurately uncover profitable words my target markets were using in searches. You can also use Google's keyword planner to discover keywords.

Market Samurai also gives you competitive intelligence data, such as how long a domain has been online; how many links it has pointing to it; the page rank; and whether or not the website has the keywords in the meta title, description, or tags, etc. Furthermore, this program tells you how many people are searching for specific keywords AND it gives you synonyms that you might not have thought of before.

The value of knowing this information is finding out how to rank you website or piece of content (blog post, video, press release, article, Pinterest pin, etc.) for the high-traffic keyword you select. Our goal is obviously to rank #1 and dominate as many keyword phrases as possible.

This process of getting a site ranked high on Google is called search engine optimization (SEO). You can grab a free trial of Market Samurai at:

http://MarketSamurai.com/c/freetrialnow.

Here's something else to note: The next time you do a keyword search on Google, scroll all the way down to the bottom of the first page of search results. Below them, you'll see a "searches related to" section that can also give you more powerful insight into what the market is looking for. That's an easy way to uncover highly searched terms that you might have overlooked otherwise. I'm regularly surprised when I use this method and discover keywords that I had never even considered.

Reverse Engineering Your Competitors

One of the coolest things about Market Samurai is that you can input any keyword and find out who's ranking on the first page of Google. You can then probe deeper and dissect their site's SEO. It's like you're getting an X-ray into their online presence.

For instance, let's say you were thinking of developing a product for German shepherd owners interested in potty training their dog. You could go to Market Samurai and search for "German shepherd potty training" and see the top-ten ranking websites.

When Market Samurai brings back the search results, you can click on each listing, and it will reveal the competitive intelligence info as I just referenced a few seconds ago. It's really that simple. With that information, you will have a good idea what you need to do to overtake them on the search engines.

Monetization and Commercial Viability

Now we need to ensure that the industry or niche we've selected can be properly monetized. Look around. Are there products you can create and sell or simply become an affiliate of within the niche? If not, the niche may be dead, and we should move on to another.

To check and see if a niche is primed to be monetized, we can use the "monetization" module that's available inside Market Samurai. We can also do a Google search and see if any of the top results or sponsored ads (AdWords) displayed on the right have affiliate programs. The more advertisers for any given niche, the more money there usually is to be made. Additionally, checking sites such as Clickbank, Datafeedr, Ebay, Amazon, and Commission Junction can identify further affiliate opportunities.

It's a good idea to have a few products you can sell on your website so that when it's time to build, you know you have an offer for site visitors. Make sure the products you're thinking of creating are a very tight match for the keyword(s) you identified with Market Samurai.

If you identify people as searching for "German shepherd potty training," you don't want try to sell them a dog whistle. Yes, people interested in potty training their dog might be interested in dog whistles, but it's not a perfect message-to-market match. You must have a laser-targeted match from what your prospective customers are searching for and what you're selling to encourage maximum sales.

What Others Are Saying in the Forums and on Social Media

This is where you can get an idea of what others are speaking about in REAL time. Are they looking for specific solutions to their problems? Are they already discussing a potential product you can create?

Checking the social media conversion for a topic serves two purposes:

1. It ensures that people are talking about your niche and/or topic. If there's no discussion going on, you should stop immediately and go into another field. People must be interested enough in the topic to talk about it; otherwise they're probably not buying.

2. It provides you a point of entry to use social media marketing in your outreach campaign. Scouting out the buzz allows you to identify the social media sites, forums, blogs, etc. that are most active within your niche. When it's time to promote and build links, you'll already know the best places people are congregating.

You're going to want to go to each social media site individually and use their search function to see if there are conversations about the subject. These include networks such as Facebook, LinkedIn, Twitter, Pinterest, YouTube, Google+, and Instagram.

On top of using the social networks, you also need to use the service Topsy. com. You simply search for your keyword, and you'll get a look across all kinds of social media platforms where people are sharing images, articles, thoughts, videos, and chatter.

Another place to check is SocialMention. While this service isn't as comprehensive as Topsy, it gives you a look in the sidebar of the reach, passion, positive and negative percentages, and top users talking about your topic.

Another free site to search for conversations around any given topic is Social-Searcher.com.

Just a quick note: DO NOT forget about blogs and forums. They can be a huge source of conversation and potential traffic. To find them, all you need to do is go to Google and type in "(your topic) forums." If you're in the real estate industry and are looking to create a product there, you might Google "real estate forums." From there, you should see hundreds (or potentially thousands) of forums that come back in the search results.

Searching for a list of blog directories? No problem. AllTop.com is one of my favorite free sources I've used for years. Technorati is another good one. You can also just Google "blog search" and see what results populate. You'll see sites like BlogSearchEngine.org and IceRocket.com.

Trending Topics

You don't want to put all your time, energy, and effort into a project if the target market is dying a slow death. Makes sense, right? To avoid this, check with Google Trends/Insights to identify any patterns in your specific niche. Here is the link to search:

http://www.google.com/trends/.

Does it spike at certain times of the year? Is it generally climbing upwards or downwards? Where is it right now in relation to where it's been previously?

Don't be afraid to walk away if you observe a downward trend. You can always find another niche with a longer lifespan.

Verticals and Related Markets

While doing your research, maybe you identified other related markets that might be more profitable or could provide you with other categories, topics, or subtopics for your site. You'll want to investigate those further to ensure you've covered all areas in your keyword research. Just follow the time-tested advice above for any related markets, keywords, niches, or sub-niches you've discovered.

To identify additional related markets, use the following tools:

- Keyword Spy – http://dcincome.com/blog/keywordspy (free trial)
- SEMRush – http://dcincome.com/blog/SEMrush (free trial)

With these two resources, you'll get a good idea of how much your competitors are spending on advertising.

Action Step: Market research is arguably the most important part of starting a highly profitable online business. You MUST do the detective work and use the intelligence tools given to assess if there's a large opportunity in the market you're wanting to service.

Do not shortcut this step! This is where the money is made.

Take a few days to get familiar with the software programs mentioned and the six essential components above. Get organized and either write your discoveries on a notepad or input them on an Excel spreadsheet so you can keep track.

PART II
TRAFFIC GENERATION AND LIST BUILDING

Chapter 12

BUILDING A BLOG YOU CAN QUICKLY MONETIZE

Formal education will make you a living;
self-education will make you a fortune.
—Jim Rohn

B logging has been very lucrative for my companies and me over the years. The recognition, traffic, and sales it's brought my brand is simply staggering. I've had several blog posts go viral and garner mass attention too.

When this first began to happen, I would say I was unconsciously competent. Meaning, I created a great blog post, but I didn't know WHY people thought it was great.

Then, as I began to study my most successful blog posts, I discovered a predictable pattern that ensured they were seen by the masses and shared. That is when I became consciously competent.

You see ... creating content is what you must always be doing, but understand this: CONTENT IS NOT KING! This is probably the opposite of what you've heard from self-proclaimed gurus. A lot of people create amazing content that doesn't see the light of day. It gets buried.

The truth is there's no shortage of great content on the web. So what separates the posts that get liked and shared by the thousands versus the stuff that doesn't? It comes down to two words, "content marketing."

This is what's most important. You've got to know how to get noticed, especially if you're like the average majority who don't have inside connections and aren't "in the club."

Right now, I'd like to share with you my proven formula for starting up a profitable blog that makes you stand out in the crowd even if you're a total newbie.

Here's what you'll discover in this chapter:

- The fastest way to get new customers and sales from your blog without spending money on conventional advertising
- The easiest way to ensure top Google rankings with any blog post
- Insanely simple shortcuts to by-pass most of the technical barriers that prevent most people from getting started (I wish I would've known these when I first began. It would've saved me countless amounts of time and money.)
- The quickest and most "hassle-free" way to get visitors to your blog on a regular and consistent basis—you'll get endless amounts of traffic on virtual autopilot.
- The best platform to use for your blog—if you're not using this one, you definitely should switch ASAP.
- The top blog plug-ins and best extensions to use for maximum traffic, social proof, and exposure
- Simple, effective ways to delegate and outsource most of the "techy" work to get it done efficiently so you can finally focus on building your practice or online business—you'll never get tripped up on these $20 questions again!

- How to position yourself as a leader locally or internationally—you'll get people to actually care about what you have to say, which will help you establish a very large viewing audience.
- What technology you need to get started if you are beginner to the world of blogging
- Strategic marketing tactics that get you an overwhelming amount of traffic to your blog without EVER worrying about a "Google slap" again
- The inner workings of effective new client/customer acquisition strategies with your blog that position you far above anyone else in your area, niche, or specialty
- A cool, free tool that you can easily use to syndicate and propagate your blogs throughout multiple social-networking sites and syndicated networks
- Blog promotional strategies that work like crazy—you could have the best blog in the world, but if you don't know how to market your content, you won't get traffic or sales.
- And much more …

Quick note: In the back of this book is an insightful article I wrote called "How I Got Over 1,800 Likes to One Blog Post." You'll definitely want to read it after you go through this important chapter.

Move the free line

One of my mentors used to always say, "If you want to build a profitable six- to seven-figure business online, you've got to move the free line." It's a simple concept and relatively easy to do. The gains associated can also be tremendous.

"Moving the free line" basically means you're not going to be stingy with the blog posts, videos, or articles you create. Give a wealth of helpful content away at no cost so others can get to know, like, and trust you.

Consumers are VERY skeptical these days, and when you provide free, valuable information that helps them achieve their desired result, you've essentially knocked down a huge psychological barrier. We've already touched on a few important ways to build social proof and calm skepticism in the chapter about positioning. We'll discuss a couple more factors later in this work.

You want to consistently think of ways you can over-deliver value and move the free line. This is a big secret to attracting new customers and sales from your blog while generating dramatically more revenue.

So what is a blog?

In layman's terms, a blog is a journal that's available on the web. It's also called a web log in some circles. The activity of updating and/or posting on a blog is called blogging. Someone who owns a blog is called a blogger. A blog can also be an entire website.

This book you're reading has been responsible for turning thousands of regular people, business owners, and professionals into advanced bloggers.

Blogs are typically posted a few times per week at a minimum. It just depends on how busy you are and if you have a virtual assistant to update the site for you. The cool thing about a blog is that you need very little to no technical background to update and maintain it.

That's the beauty of new technology and evolved content-management systems.

Then and now

In the old days, if you wanted to update your website, you had to know HTML coding, PHP, and a bunch of other complicated computer language. There's no way you could learn it in one short day either. This was a huge barrier for many aspiring entrepreneurs and Internet business owners.

That's completely changed with the introduction of online blogs though. These platforms allow you to update your site fast and efficiently. You no longer have to be a computer geek to make it work for you.

Regarding the structure of a blog, actual blog posts are almost always arranged in chronological order, with the most recent additions featured first. A blog post itself can contain written text, photos, videos, or a combination of all three.

If you've been to my blog at MatthewLoop.com or DCincome.com/blog, you know that I have a variety of content that displays video, audio, text, and picture graphics. It's important for you, as a content creator, to mix it up and consider your audience. Not everyone likes to consume content the same way.

Sometimes you'll want to have all written posts, sometimes you'll want to have videos with a minimal description to spark curiosity, and in other instances you'll want to have professional stock images associated with your text.

There are many different aspects to consider. One of your ultimate goals is to get readers accustomed to the real you. You want them to feel comfortable with your authentic personality and style. We want to build strong relationships, liking, and rapport.

Add elements of authenticity

I'm going to share with you the marketing and promotional side of blogging right now; however, you MUST add your personal flavor (or true voice). Your taste, interest, knowledge, empathy, and expertise is what's going to compel visitors to become blog subscribers.

People are attracted to your message and insight for many different reasons. One of the key reasons others take notice and give you credibility is if they perceive you as being authentic. You know, you seem like a real person and not just a scripted piece of plastic.

Your blog is your home online, so have pictures of your family, experiences, travels, etc. Also, be strategic in how you integrate your interests for the local community or global niche market you're servicing. Personalization, appearing approachable, and having humanizing elements on your blog help build rapport with your audience on a deep level.

Blogs are usually developed by one person (either you or somebody else) and updated regularly. They're often written about a particular topic, or you can post short, value-driven videos on things that interest your market.

If you're a chiropractor, you might write (or record videos) about what it takes to achieve optimal health. Or you could discuss conditions that you treat in your office. Then provide information that will help better the reader's quality of life instantly.

If you're a real estate agent, you could create content about what buyers should look for before investing in a home. Or you could blog about the top mistakes to avoid when selling a house. This is a great way to position your brand as a trusted authority in the marketplace.

Online, you'll find blogs about every topic imaginable. Things like natural medicine, photography, recipes, search engine optimization, basket weaving, weight loss, bodybuilding, dating, personal diaries, and much more.

You can go to Technorati.com and type in any topic or keyword you're looking for more information about. It will then bring back a large list of blogs related to the search term you entered. Technorati is just a huge blog search engine. Google allows you to do the same thing. Just type in a topic or keyword then type "blogs" after it.

You can search for "Natural Medicine blogs." If you live in Atlanta, you can search for "Atlanta blogs." These are a couple of the best ways to find industry-related blogs that you're searching for.

Whole blogging communities have sprung up around many different topics. They put people in contact with other blog owners that they're looking for so they can forge strong relationships, which is something I'm really going to stress ... RELATIONSHIPS.

If you think of blogging and many aspects of Internet promotion, they're not like your traditional direct-response marketing where you can send a postcard out and get five customers the next day. Sometimes, it takes time for others to feel comfortable enough to invest with you.

Don't get me wrong: direct-response marketing should be fused into your overall funnel online. If done right, this is what brings in five-figure (or more) paydays. There are very strategic places to incorporate this style of marketing, as we'll discuss.

The goal is to position you as a trusted center of influence, credible expert, and authority in the market you service. You ideally want to surround the marketplace so that anywhere a prospective client goes online, they see you, your content, or your website.

This is called saturation, and it's a quick way to create immense social proof.

Developing an authority-based blog that Google loves doesn't happen overnight though. However, if you start now and implement the strategies in this book, you're going to be way ahead of competitors and outrank others in your industry for highly searched keywords on Google. Once accomplished, this gets you an avalanche of website traffic from organic keywords.

Why you MUST have a blog

Why is it so important to have a blog, especially this year? Here's the big reason: A blog, if used correctly, is a simple way to virtually connect with perspective new clients and customers; to get them to know, like, and trust you before they ever set foot in your office or do business with you online. It enables you to build a relationship with highly qualified people so they'll eventually buy your product or service and use it to solve the problem they're having.

We're going to discuss the funnel in depth and where I see aspiring entrepreneurs and business owners completely missing out. It's important to have the proper Internet marketing funnel in place because if you don't, everything is going to fall apart. You could drive a tremendous amount of traffic to the site, but if you can't capture those qualified leads and convert them into sales, it doesn't matter at all.

Understand, you're able to build a massive audience and/or fan base if you work your blog strategically and know how to connect with others' wants and needs.

Fans are really great because they want everything that you have. They eagerly want to buy your stuff online. They want to come into your office. They just want to be around you. Fans can also be disciples for your message and share your content with their friends. We want to use our blog to establish a RAVING fan base.

Over-deliver on everything so people can't help but feel compelled to share your content and your message with their peers. That will give your brand a viral surge.

Your home online

Think of a blog as your home base on the Internet. It's a place where you can be yourself and create business or personal content. From there, you can interact with readers through comments on the blog or using Facebook's comment plug-in. Your blog allows people to see your human side and real self.

Presenting yourself professionally is wonderful, but you shouldn't be afraid to kick up your feet and relax. When readers see both sides, they think, He is just like me. He engages with his community and doesn't feel he's too good for them.

You never want to come across as pretentious or "too cool for school."

The great thing is when you begin to post content on your blog, the management is pretty easy. Even a second grader can do it, as opposed to the older, outdated websites where you would need to know complex HTML code. Those sites were just a royal pain in the ass.

An important aspect of your blog is that it's your property. You own it! We don't own Facebook, Google, YouTube, or any other social platform. Furthermore, we have no idea what those social platforms are going to do tomorrow.

Here's what I mean.

So many businesses got burned because they listened to bad advice about how their Facebook fan page was supposed to be their home online. For years, people were paying to build their fans on the social network, then all the sudden the rug was yanked out from under them.

Facebook purposely started to limit distribution and visibility on status updates. Why? It's because they wanted to make more money from their users. They went public and now had an obligation to shareholders. If you're lucky, right now 10 percent of your fans will see your Facebook posts unless you pay to promote.

I warned people for years that this was a bad idea, but very few business owners listened. Those are the ones that got destroyed when Facebook updated their newsfeed algorithm. Those folks never built an email list on a platform they controlled, and their revenue tanked.

All external traffic should lead back to your blog, a squeeze page, or a property that you control. Never forget that.

What's the best blogging platform to use?

This is one of the most common questions I'm asked at seminars and online. As you might already know, there are several services such as TypePad, Blogger, WordPress, and LiveJournal, just to name a few. I use and strongly recommend WordPress above any other platform … hands down.

Google adores WordPress, and when you create your blog like I show you, you'll build authority and "author rank" quickly while creating a nonstop traffic machine you couldn't turn off even if you wanted to.

If you don't have a WordPress blog, get one! But, there's a catch. You need to make sure that the blog is installed on your website.

Pay very close attention here.

The blog should be installed on your current website OR the blog should actually be your website. You can do both with WordPress.

If you don't currently have a website, just make your blog your home site. You can get a domain name from GoDaddy.com.

As an example, let's say you bought AlexPKeaton.com. You could then have a programmer install the WordPress blog directly onto the .com (root URL) of that domain, making your website your blog. Or, if you have a current website like I did before I set up my blog, you can have your WordPress blog installed as an extension on a separate page.

For instance, one of the websites I already owned was DCincome.com. The site had been live for years. I found a freelance programmer on Upwork.com to install the WordPress blog at DCincome.com/blog.

This is very important.

Talk to your webmaster, or whoever created your current website, and see if it's WordPress compatible. If so, have them install the blog at YourSite.com/blog. If your website is not WordPress compatible, I'd recommend switching to an all WordPress site.

NEVER have your blog hosted on a subdomain.

What's a subdomain?

This is basically where you'd go to WordPress.com and sign up for an account directly on WordPress. They're going to give you what's called a subdomain, which just means you're going to have a website and address hosted by WordPress. It's going to look something like www.yoursite.wordpress.com.

Why is this a major mistake? First, your content and/or blog is hosted on the actual WordPress website, which you DO NOT control. If something happened to their website tomorrow, you'd be screwed. Your content would be lost forever. Also, they have rules about what you can and cannot post.

On the other hand, when you have WordPress installed on your personal website, you have ALL the control. You can post what you want, when you want, and you don't have to worry about getting slapped.

Here's another important note.

Subdomains never get ranked as high as regular websites, especially a website that has WordPress installed and consistently updated. You could do all the on-page and off-page search engine optimization (SEO) in the world, but you still wouldn't be able to effectively rank high on Google and compete with other authority sites in your market.

Never get a subdomain for your blog. Got it?

It's always better to have the blog installed directly on your website or just to buy a separate URL/domain name along with a separate hosting account. Then get the blog installed directly there.

As I mentioned previously, contact your current webmaster or whoever manages your website. You want your blog installed on either the website itself at the .com "root URL" or the /blog extension like the example above. Either one is fine.

Outsourcing

If you don't have a webmaster, here's what I want you to do next. Go to Upwork. com. This is my favorite outsourcing website. I use it regularly. They can be your best friends when you fully understand the power of leveraging other people's expertise.

If you're reading this book right now, you're probably an aspiring entrepreneur, coach, online marketer, doctor, entrepreneur, or other professional. You don't have time to get tripped up on these $20 questions or think you need to be a technical whiz. It's all about being resourceful. Strengthen your strengths then delegate your weaknesses.

If you ever have a question, feel free to message me or my support staff on social media and we'll point you in the right direction.

If you know anything about me, checked out my blog, or if you've invested in my other training systems, you understand how much I stress cost-effectively outsourcing to the experts. If it's not your strength, then delegate it. In fact, about 95 percent of all Internet promotion and outreach can be delegated in some way, shape, or form.

If you're feeling overwhelmed, it's because you're not being resourceful. You don't have the strategy in place to acquire professionals in the key positions that keep your online machine going successfully and consistently while you sleep.

For years, I've been teaching entrepreneurs like yourself how to create marketing systems that run on autopilot so you can step away from the business at any time without losing revenue. In fact, most of my private coaching clients generate sales 24/7, even when they're on vacation.

The faster you learn how to be resourceful, the more passive income you'll make, the greater freedom and flexibility you'll have, and the happier you'll be.

You could easily go to Upwork.com and hire a freelance programmer to install your WordPress blog for under $40. They can do a quick install that might take them a few minutes. This saves you A LOT of time and the potential headache of trying to learn this process. If the programmer you hire does good work, keep him/her around on a freelance, per-project basis.

In my business, I have a couple programmers that I can send a quick email to and they take care of what I need. I pull the trigger fast then they implement with speed because THEY are the coding and install experts.

Once the WordPress installation is finished, you're ready to go and log into your administrative panel and start posting content. It's very simple to do. Let your developer take care of the hard, techy stuff.

Note: The best thing I like about Upwork is that you can view each provider's feedback and reviews based on jobs they've completed in the past. You can actually see their portfolio of previous work too. This allows you to be certain that the contractor has experience with WordPress. With Upwork.com, you know exactly what you're getting.

In your job posting, you would also want to mention EXACTLY what you're searching for. The title of the posting might be "Need a WordPress

Expert to Install a Blog." In the job description, you could go into specifics regarding the project.

"I'm looking for somebody who's very knowledgeable and experienced with WordPress. I'd like you to install a blog on this website_____. Here is exactly where I want it, etc."

You can tell the contractor specifically what you want and they'll get it done promptly. Strengthen your strengths and delegate your weaknesses. Hire the programmer on a freelance, per-project basis. That means you pay them by the job. It's the most cost-effective way to get a task completed to your liking.

I don't recommend learning how to program. This is not what makes you money in your business. Your time is best spent working on the business, not in it. Find and hire skilled professionals so you can continuously move forward and grow your Internet empire.

Eventually, you may get to the point in your business where you might want to have somebody on staff part-time or full-time. It's not necessary in the beginning, but keep your options open.

So what else do you need to get started blogging after you get the WordPress blog installed by your webmaster?

Get a custom theme or blog design

You absolutely need a custom theme and professional blog design. I prefer a template with the ability to add pictures and videos to the home page because you want to engage your visitors.

The blog should have personality and be interactive so readers will stay on your site longer. The last thing you want is something boring and dull, which makes people bounce off quickly.

As I mentioned, your blog is your home online, so it should have your style and feel. If you currently have a website with a certain design or template, you might have your webmaster build a congruent blog theme for you. If they cannot, just outsource one. It also needs to have key direct-response marketing and social-proof components. (I touched on this before in a previous chapter.)

In terms of custom blog themes and design, you have a couple options. You can go to Google and search "Free WordPress Blog Themes," "WordPress Blog

Themes," or "Custom Blog Themes." You'll find hundreds of websites that have wonderful themes that you can have your programmer install for you.

Many are aesthetically appealing. They look good and can provide a great first impression as a potential new client or customer visits your website. You can have your webmaster build your own theme or just go to Upwork and hire a programmer.

When I originally had my blog designed, I was searching online through hundreds of blogs. None had what I wanted, only bits and pieces here and there. I wanted it to look great, but it also had to have a direct-response component to get people to take action. I also wanted that WOW factor to make a great first impression.

If you find a professional blog design you absolutely love, you can contact the same person that created the blog you see online. Usually, their contact info is in the lower right corner of the site. However, if they wind up being out of your price range, just go to Upwork and have a developer overseas duplicate the site for you. You'll be able to get all the features that you want for a third of the cost you'd pay someone here in the US.

Theme design tips: Compelling psychological triggers and positioning

We need to assume all the visitors coming to your blog are from cold traffic, meaning they have no idea who you are and weren't referred by a colleague. With this in mind, here are a couple things you can do to create INSTANT credibility on your blog in order to get people to trust you and provide their email.

First, have the Facebook "like" and Google+ buttons at the top of your website above the fold. See an example at my blog: http://MatthewLoop.com. Then, your goal is to get as many likes and +1's as possible.

Think about this. If you went to a website and saw that over 1,000 people had "liked" the website, what would you think? You'd subconsciously give the website or blog some degree of credibility just based on the number of likes. This kind of goes along with the herd mentality.

Use this influence factor to your advantage and make sure you have the Facebook "like" and Google+ buttons displayed at the top for visitors to click.

On top of the number count, when these buttons are clicked, your blog now gets shared with the visitor's friends on Facebook.

Let's delve into the second positioning factor. If you've been featured on major media (FOX, NBC, CNN, ABC, and CBS), display the logos above the fold on your blog. People automatically give you more credibility if you've been showcased on mainstream media outlets.

If you haven't been on TV, have a press release written about an announcement in your business. Then go to PRweb.com and purchase their $250 package. Why? When you do this, PRweb will distribute your press release into the major news outlets.

Many times you'll get picked up on local NBC, CBS, FOX, and ABC affiliates. You can link to those websites from your blog and legitimately say you've been featured on these mainstream channels. This adds yet another important layer of credibility.

Remember, people are incredibly skeptical these days. We're just trying to get them to let their guard down so we can actual help transform their lives for the better. Use the TV logos on your site.

The third way to position yourself as an industry influencer and to capitalize on how people have been conditioned is to have photos of celebrities on your blog. If you recall what I said earlier, I mentioned that celebrity = credibility.

You can have pictures with local or international celebrities. If you go to my blog at http://MatthewLoop.com, you'll see rotating pictures with quite a few mainstream celebs such as Usher, David Copperfield, Def Leppard, Charlie Sheen, Rob Schneider, Michael Gerber, Bob Proctor, Dr. Joe Mercola, and more.

When a visitor comes to your website and sees pictures of you with famous public figures, it's an instant credibility booster and positions you above other people in your market. It's credibility by association and you look cool.

The final influence factor you want to take advantage of and integrate is a Facebook fan page widget on your blog. (See mine right below the rotating images on my website.) This serves as a social-proof builder simply because visitors can now see the thousands upon thousands of other real people that have liked your Facebook fan page.

Think of the Internet as a big popularity contest. If you're perceived as more popular than your competitors, you'll reap the lion's share of the customers and sales.

NEVER, however, let social proof work against you. Always try to stack it in your favor, whether it's fans on Facebook, followers on Twitter, reviews on Google, etc. You want to dwarf your competitors' numbers.

Additional customization tip

If you run a local, brick-and-mortar business, I recommend your phone number be placed in the upper right-hand corner of your blog. You want to make it blatantly obvious and easy for others to contact you.

You have to make it easy for people to call your business. People don't instinctively know what to do. It's the same thing on your blog. You want to guide prospective clients in a step-by-step manner so it takes all the guesswork out and makes it easier for them to do business with you.

Remove as many barriers as you can, and you'll see that your website and/or blog will convert much better. In the end, that's the most important thing. You could have the best website in the world, but if it doesn't get people to take action and buy your products and services, it doesn't matter.

This brings me to another important point. You've got to know your metrics. If you send 100 visitors to the blog, how many actually become sales and/or new customers? Google Analytics can tell you the traffic numbers and how others are finding your site online. You need to calculate these numbers so you can track—and then improve them—to increase your overall conversion.

Include a short, memorable, one-liner slogan

Another thing that you should have on your blog is a short, memorable slogan or three words that really describe what your site is about. If you go to http://MatthewLoop.com right now, you'll see I actually have two.

One in the header image to the left says "social media revenue strategist" and the other just below the header image says "Earn More, Experience More, Give Back."

That sets the tone so when someone visits this page, they know exactly what information they can expect to receive. They know my mission.

If you look to the right on the header graphic, you'll see three bullet points that tell the reader what's in it for them when the subscribe to my email list. Above, you'll see a title that says "Grab My FREE Blogging Success Blueprint."

Something to realize here is that the average Internet surfer typically stays on a website for only a few seconds, so you need to impress quickly and get their attention. That's what my blog is geared to do. Hence, people stay there for several minutes on average.

Your blog must have the WOW factor so you can grab attention and increase your conversion easier. Have your own slogan that's congruent with who you are, your specialty, and your personal mission.

Take some time, investigate, and really put some thought into this because you want to give the best first impression and attract the ideal clients, patients, or customers you're searching for.

What WordPress plug-ins do you need?

A blog plug-in is a very simple extension that allows your WordPress blog to have magical powers, as I like to say. There are ten crucial scripts that you want to have.

You don't need to get caught up in the programming language. Just know that once you find a webmaster or programmer to install the blog, he can also easily add these individual plugins.

The following is a comprehensive list.

- Facebook comments

   This particular plug-in allows Facebook comments to be posted on your blog under each post. Just Google "Facebook comments plug-in" and you'll be able to easily find it. If you want to see an example of how it looks, then visit my blog and find a recent blog post. If you scroll down after the post, you'll see the Facebook comments section.

- Akismet

The Akismet plug-in prevents spam from getting posted on your blog. When your rankings start to rise, when your Google page rank increases, and when the traffic starts to surge, be prepared for spammers. This is one of the plug-ins that can save you A LOT of time, energy, and hassle. Definitely have this, or another spam plug-in, installed:

http://wordpress.org/extend/plugins/akismet/

- Audio Player

The next extension you'll want to have is the audio player. If you do any teleclasses or teleconferences like I frequently do, you'll want to have this audio player plug-in installed.

The audio player allows audio MP3s to play from your blog. It's extremely simple once the script is set up. Here's the link:

http://wordpress.org/extend/plugins/audio-player/

- Google XML Sitemaps

Google XML Sitemaps is a must for your WordPress site. This extension helps Google spider your blog faster and easier. Google likes scripts that are easy, that it can pick up very quickly, and websites that are organized. That's what the XML Sitemaps plug-in does without getting too technical. It just makes it simple for Google to read and crawl your website:

http://wordpress.org/extend/plugins/google-sitemap-generator/

- All in One SEO Pack

The next plug-in that you absolutely must have is the All in One SEO Pack. Remember that SEO stands for search engine optimization, which is basically the process of getting your website ranked at the top of Google.

This script allows you to alter, organize, and create different types of metadata for the website and each individual blog post (meta title, meta description, meta keywords, etc.).

Here's a powerful blog post to check out when you have a couple minutes. The video shows you how to create top-ranking and "SEO friendly" blog posts.

http://dcincome.com/blog/how-to-create-top-ranking-and-seo-friendly-blog-posts/

I'm not going to get too heavy into metadata because it's something that your programmer can help you with. However, if you're going to do market research, you should be familiar with keywords and these concepts already. The site metadata needs to contain the keywords that you want to rank high with on Google.

In a few minutes, I'm going to share with you an awesome tool I use that makes knowing exactly what prospective clients and sales are looking for VERY simple. In the meantime, here's where you can find the All-in-One SEO pack.

http://wordpress.org/extend/plugins/all-in-one-seo-pack/

Yoast SEO is another popular WordPress plug-in that's very similar to All in One. It's another great option.

- Twitter Widget

     The Twitter widget script is another great plug-in. If you visit my blog, you'll see it on the right, just below the Facebook widget. It's the live conversation feed from Twitter so my readers can see what I'm speaking about this second.

     Anytime I post and update from Twitter, it immediately posts that update on my blog. When a new reader visits my blog, they get to see I've recently updated my Twitter status. That tells them I'm actively involved in social media and that I engage with followers.

     Building community is extremely vital, and this little widget shows you're listening to your audience and building relationships. That's critical. Here's the link to the extension:

     http://wordpress.org/extend/plugins/twitter-widget-pro/

- Tweet, Like, Google +1, and Share

     This is another essential plug-in I highly recommend. You can see that on my blog at the bottom of each individual post. When someone clicks these, they can instantly share my blog posts on Twitter, Facebook, or Google+.

Another important thing I'd like to point out here is that this plug-in helps you build social proof. The more that your readers, family, and friends, or subscribers retweet, like, and +1 your blog posts, the better you look. You give the impression your content is popular. Online, whoever appears more popular wins. It sounds kind of childish, but it's true.

The web is a big popularity contest and people typically congregate around whoever is followed the most. It's almost like that mass herd mentality. People are very predictable given certain situations.

You want to do your best to shift the social proof in your favor, and that's what this social plug-in can do. In addition, when a person shares your posts, it gets you more exposure and more traffic to the site.

Make it easy for readers to share your content too. The average Facebook user has over 250 friends. When they click the "like" button, their friends get a chance to see this. This one strategy can bring massive viral traffic to your site.

You can find the plugin at this link:

http://techxt.com/tweet-like-google-1-and-share-plugin-wordpress/

- Pinterest pin-it button

This is basically another share button that allows others to spread your content on the wildly popular image-sharing website Pinterest. You need to make sure you have a high-quality image on each blog post so others can share it.

This widget also gives a numbers count like the Tweet, Like, Google+1 share plug-in referenced above. You can find it at this link:

http://business.pinterest.com/widget-builder/#do_pin_it_button

- Get the Image

This is a highly intuitive script that can grab an image by custom field input, post attachment, or extracting it from the post's content. I'd recommend having a high-quality image inserted in each blog post in case others want to share your content on Pinterest.

- RSS Feed

     You also want to make sure that your programmer installs an RSS feed. Most WordPress templates and themes come with that standard, but just make sure that it is installed. RSS stands for really simple syndication. It allows others to get and receive your updates very quickly.

     The news now finds us. We don't have to search anymore for our interests, hobbies, or news. That's why you want to make sure that you do have the RSS feed on your blog.

     These are the plug-ins I personally use, and I strongly recommend you have them on your blog. They will greatly help your optimization efforts. There's no need to get overwhelmed here because your programmer will get these up and running for you in no time.

Lead-capture system

This is where many bloggers, entrepreneurs, public figures, brands, and professionals completely miss the boat. The majority of business owners I speak with do not have an automated, online follow-up system in place. Nor do they have a solid lead-capture mechanism or ethical bribe.

Here's the deal. Since we know that the average person stays on any given website for only a few seconds, we have a VERY limited window of opportunity to get a qualified email address and name of a prospective client or customer that's interested in our services.

Getting their contact info on that first visit is essential if you want to have a long-term, sustainable, lucrative business.

If you're getting 100 visitors a day to your blog and/or website and you're not building an email list, you're losing A LOT of money.

Why?

The sad reality is that most visitors that go to your website once will bounce off and never come back. When you have a list, you can email them valuable content and periodic direct-response offers that make them take action!

I've said it before. Your email list is the LIFEBLOOD of your Internet business. If set up correctly, it allows you to generate customers and sales while you sleep. You can also generate sales on demand.

I use Aweber as discussed earlier in this work. Should you decide to go with them, you can grab a dollar trial at MyProResponse.com

Other email management services include InfusionSoft, Mail Chimp, Constant Contact, and GetResponse. Some of those services are easy to navigate while others are way more complex.

The money is in the email list and your relationship with subscribers. Remember that.

Some people might click the orange RSS feed to subscribe to my blog, but that's not guaranteed. Email list building is one of my top priorities, and it should be yours, too. Set yourself up for success. ALWAYS be list building!

So, what's the best way to get a name and email from an interested prospect?

Like I've spoken about before, the answer is to have an ethical bribe, such as a free consumer report or free video training series that provides valuable information presented objectively.

Here's an example.

Let's say you're a pain-management doctor and most of your practice is for low back pain or disc-related problems. You can offer a free report called *5 Secrets to Alleviating Low Back Pain without Toxic Drugs or Risky Surgery*, or something along those lines.

Or maybe you're a real estate agent. You could then create a free consumer guide titled 10 Questions You MUST Ask before Choosing a Realtor and Buying a Home.

These reports can be short, between five and ten pages. You'll simply answer (from your experience) some of the top questions people ask and what they should be asking. This positions you as a consumer advocate and above competitors in the marketplace.

In order to be really compelling, you must have a strong title of a report as well as three to five bullet points below it telling them "what's in it for me." Here's an example:

1. Avoid the single-biggest mistake most people make when _____.
2. Discover the #1 secret to _____.
3. Find out the BEST way to _____.

This creates intrigue and curiosity so they'll provide their contact details in order to access this free report.

Focus on delivering real value in the report and don't hold anything back. This is a classic example of "moving the free line." At the end of the document, you can make a call to action for your business.

As mentioned previously, you could also deliver a free video training series. It's totally up to you though. The most important thing that will happen is that you will now be building a list once these systems are in play.

Most people are slow dates these days. They need to get to know, like, and trust you before doing business with you. There's no better way to create this than through consistent email follow-up.

Notice, if you're on my email list, I regularly deliver valuable blog posts and videos. Then I periodically make offers for different products of mine. Much of the content I distribute has been automatically queued to go out on certain days.

You set it and forget it with Aweber. Meaning, I can write twenty email messages and have them in the queue to be sent to anyone that enters their name and email in the lead-capture forms, hence, the term "autoresponder." It's automatic follow-up and allows you to leverage your time, energy, and efforts for your business.

More leverage = greater profits with less work!

The bottom line is you must have a lead-capture form on your website and strong follow-up procedures if you want to MAXIMIZE your customers and sales online.

The email deliverability rate with Aweber is a high 99 percent. This means you can be assured your emails get delivered. They also allow you to track who opened the emails and which subscribers clicked the links within. You can view the numbers or percentages.

For example, if you send an email to 1,000 subscribers, you'll be able to see what percentage opened, actually clicked the link, and went to your blog. You MUST know those metrics so you can consistently strive to improve open rates and click-throughs.

Many email management systems I see out there are mediocre and don't have the statistical capabilities Aweber does. What gets measured gets improved. If you cannot track your stats, it's time to switch email services.

DO NOT leave anything to chance here. You'll get dramatically more traffic, customers, and sales when you implement what I've laid out in this section.

Normally, when I post a new blog, I'll send an email to my list shortly after. This creates a massive SURGE of traffic in addition to training subscribers to click the links in my emails.

This helps to fuel engagement and interaction on blog posts. That, in turn, helps the blog rank better on Google, creates more social shares, and leads to more traffic and sales.

Metadata

We need to touch on the subject of blog "metadata" a little more since it's very important. What I'm referring to is called "on-page" search engine optimization (SEO). This is another aspect of SEO that gets your website ranked higher on Google by altering internal data.

Your website should contain specific information that enables Google to recognize the fact that the blog is relevant to targeted search terms and keywords online.

- Meta Title

    If I'm attempting to rank for the keywords "training your parakeet to talk" on Google, I would want to make sure that the words "training your parakeet to talk" were located in the meta title, meta description, and meta tags of the website. This keyword should also be found written on the home page, too.

    When you install the All in One SEO Pack, you (or your programmer) will be able to enter this data with ease. If you're uncertain here, don't be afraid to delegate to an expert. (Hopefully, you've done your keyword research already so you know what prospective clients, patients, and customers are searching.)

- Meta Description

Your website meta description should have the keywords in it too. Make sure to include compelling copy in your meta description. It's what gets people to click on the actual Google listing. Spark curiosity and interest.

An example might be:

Before training your parakeet to talk, read this first! Here are 5 critical things you MUST do beforehand.

If someone types in "training your parakeet to talk" on Google, they'll see ten listings on the first page. That description you see under the title of each listing is the hook, so make sure you have compelling text there. Give away a free report and allude to it within the meta description.

You can test different description headlines to see which one converts better.

- Meta Tags

The meta tags of your website and/or blog are just like the keyword tags of your videos and articles you might have previously distributed online. Make sure to include the keywords you want to rank #1 on Google that you've thoroughly researched. These should be found in your website meta tags and basically tell Google that your content is relevant to the corresponding area of the search engines.

When you create an individual blog post, you'll also be allowed to enter keyword tags for each post. You don't want to overload this section with unrelated keywords. Make each blog post specific to a topic, niche, or sub-niche. Then, vary the keywords accordingly.

For example, if you're an attorney and you've authored a blog post about slip-and-fall accidents, you wouldn't have keywords related to "intellectual property law" because they have nothing to do with that blog topic.

Remember, your primary keywords and variations of them should be located in the meta tags section. It's a critical on-page SEO component.

If you have questions, speak to your programmer as they are usually fluent regarding this.

Permalinks

Permalinks are the permanent URLs (website addresses) to your individual blog posts, as well as categories and other lists of weblog postings. A permalink is what bloggers use to link posts, or how you might send a link to your story in an email message. The URL to each post should be permanent and keyword-rich.

If you go to your WordPress admin panel and create a new post, first you'll enter the title. If the permalinks are enabled, you'll see a website address appear just below the edited blog title. You may need to click on the white text box below it. A permalink looks like this:

http://dcincome.com/blog/3-ways-to-add-an-extra-100000-in-recurring-income-this-year/

If your permalinks are not enabled, the blog post URL might appear like this:

http://dcincome.com/blog/p122

Have your webmaster double-check that they're active on your blog. This helps with SEO just like having your keywords in the domain name of your website does. The last thing you want to do is write a great blog post and not have keywords in the URL.

How to title a blog post

When you master the art of creating powerful headlines for blog posts, people will be ten times more likely to click on your post compared to your competitors' posts, even if you're not ranked #1 on Google. This is a little-known secret you can use to literally swipe traffic from others for free.

The person that becomes a pro at writing compelling headlines will get more visitors at the #2 or #3 spot on Google than their competitor at #1.

Remember, you can have the best, most helpful content in the world, but if you cannot get people to click-through to see it, it really doesn't matter. Here a couple ways to construct compelling titles:

1. The "before" you do something blog post or article

These always pull clicks like crazy because of the associated consumer friendliness and/or the implied negativity. When people see posts like this, they think they should read this BEFORE doing anything else. Pretty simple stuff, but highly effective at getting your content read. See examples below.

- Before You Visit a Chiropractor, READ THIS FIRST
- Don't Visit an Atlanta Dentist until You Watch This
- Thinking of Weight-Loss Surgery? Read This First

The posts in this category should be written in a nonbiased, consumer-friendly format. You might point out some frequently asked questions or pros and cons associated with the topic. Then, at the end of the post, you can steer them to your solution.

2. How to _____ in (X Number of Days / Hours)

Here's a super simple one that's almost always an instant winner, getting you many more clicks and site visitors. It's simple and easy to write, and it entertains your reader. It plays on our natural curiosity.

- 7 Things You Must Do after a Sports Injury
- 5 Things You Must Do after Every Gym Workout
- 3 Things You Must Do after Publishing a Blog Post

Use either one of these blog title templates to knock out a killer blog post when you're strapped for ideas. To access fourteen more powerful copy-and-paste headline templates that give you an unfair competitive advantage when you create blog posts, visit the following page:

http://dcincome.com/go/1182-2/

What Should I Write About?

One of the most commonly asked questions I get from business owners and entrepreneurs is, "Dr. Matt, what should I blog about?"

My response typically consists of pointing out the fact that since you already have specialized knowledge and expertise in some area, we just want to get those ideas out on paper in little bite-size nuggets.

I'd recommend surveying your market, subscribers, or customers to get an idea of what they really want. You can also start to eavesdrop in some of the online forums related to your industry. See what others are speaking about there. Make notes on some of the burning questions they're asking. In conjunction, create a list of subjects you could deliver value on.

Finding notable online forums is pretty easy, and it's similar to finding blogs. Every industry has special online forums and active communities. Go to Google and key in "(your industry) forums" and see which ones come back. You'll find hundreds that populate in the search results.

If you choose, you can write some blog posts yourself or hire a professional ghostwriter from Upwork.com. Doing this takes advantage of outsourcing and leveraging your time. If writing is not your strong point, delegate it to someone proficient.

By the way, don't limit yourself just to writing. You can shoot simple, two- to three-minute videos, post them on YouTube, then embed the productions on your blog. Should you go the video route, speak to the camera like you're speaking with a close friend. Make sure the lighting is good and that you have a tripod to avoid shaking.

Once the video is completed, you can hire a pro on Upwork to transcribe it for you. This is a good example of strategically repackaging your content.

When possible, always repackage your content because you can mass distribute it to separate social mediums and different directories online. This will boost your traffic and influence in the market even further.

You might want to post one blog per week, or perhaps you want to do one post every other day. It's totally up to you. However, the more value-based, ORIGINAL content you have on your blog, the more Google love you'll get. It's going to help your search ranking, your authority as an author, and your website traffic. This will ultimately lead to more sales.

There are numerous topics you, or the person you hire, can write about. Take an inventory of what you're currently passionate about or talk about what problems your market is facing. Research what solutions people are looking for.

You can write about why you became a _____. Subscribe to other blogs in your industry, and see what hot topics their content focuses on. Interview other influencers in your space. I think you get the idea.

You don't have to write super long posts. They can be 400 to 600 words. Make sure you don't have six sentences per paragraph either as you want to make it easy on the reader's eyes. Don't complicate things.

One marketing strategy I really like is finding local celebrities in your town. You can find famous people in any industry or niche you're involved with.

Think about this, in the natural health field, Dr. Mercola and Dr. Oz are very well known. Let's say you approach one of them by emailing or giving a call to one of their assistants. Then you ask them to write a blog post for you or maybe even do a short video.

You'd be surprised by the people you can get in touch with that would be very happy to donate content to you because it's going to be mutually beneficial. Doing this will get that celebrity more exposure and in front of a new audience, and it's going to gain you more exposure—not to mention that it helps provide credibility by association. That's one of the little-known secrets very few entrepreneurs and professionals are using.

With either local or international celebrities, it's incredible what people think and do sometimes. You don't want to fight the trend. The bottom line is you want to have guest writers for your blog that have more of a presence online than you do.

Again, you don't need to write every post yourself. You can easily find a regular ghostwriter for probably $15–$20 per post, sometimes less. They can work on an hourly rate if you want to bring somebody on part-time or full-time. It's purely up to you. They can give you the amount of content you need—however much you can handle.

Keyword research

I alluded to it before, but you absolutely must do your keyword research before you create a blog post. Find the terms that people are already searching for in your market, and create blog posts around them. That's a very important strategy.

If you're doing a video, say the keywords in the video. Google now has speech-to-text conversion, so that's going to influence video indexing. It's still in the infancy stages, and there is a lot of speculation on how much it weighs, but don't even take the chance. State the keywords within the videos you make, just to be sure.

Look at Google's first page. This is one of the things I really want you to recognize. There are always a variety of listings. There are many different ways that you can sneak into the first page, whether it's with an article, press release, video, image, or blog post.

Blog posts typically get indexed well if your blog has authority. Soon I'm going to talk about how to really increase your blog's authority online. When you do, you're going to post a blog and it will automatically get ranked on the first page. Many times it can be indexed in the top slot because in the local business market, very few people even know how to use this method. It only really gets competitive on a national level.

You want to make sure that you write a title, description, and keyword tags for every post in the All in One SEO Pack. Again, I'm not going to get too technically involved here, but in your WordPress back office you can find some easy video tutorials on YouTube on navigating and how to use WordPress. Go to your back office to get an overview of your dashboard.

Once you actually add a new post, what you're going to find is if you scroll all the way down to the bottom, you'll see the section where you have the All in One SEO Pack. There, you'll be able to add your blog post title, description, and keyword tags. So when your post gets ranked well on Google, that's what people will see. Do your keyword research beforehand.

Market Samurai

One research tool I've used for years is Market Samurai. It's a fairly simple program, and they have easy-to-follow video tutorials that show you the ropes.

If you go to MarketSamurai.com/c/freetrialnow, you can get a limited-time, free trial and demo it for yourself. Market Samurai enables you to assess your competition for certain keywords and SEO, and it has numerous other ninja-like functions.

Let's say you want to rank #1 on Google for "Anchorage chiropractic office." You could plug those words into Market Samurai, and the software will provide insight about your competitors. It tells you exactly how competitors are ranking, how many links they have to their site, their domain age, keyword search volume, metadata, etc. This works for global businesses as well as for small local ones.

This is a very important detective tool, and I don't share it that often. You can know your competitors inside and out with this advanced software. It doesn't matter whether or not you're selling stuff online to an international marketplace or just locally. It's a MUST HAVE for any serious Internet entrepreneur.

You want to rank for as many keywords as possible that people are searching. Depending on the market you're entering, this can be dozens of keywords or more.

It's important to go through each and every one of the keywords you want to rank atop Google for. You're going to create a blog post that has valuable information regarding the topic of your choice. Then you can strategically rank it while getting backlinks to this particular post. (We're going to talk about backlinks shortly and why they're so important.)

Let's say you're a chiropractor and you have a great, informative blog post (that you or a ghostwriter wrote) titled "Chiropractor in Anchorage Helps Locals Alleviate Low Back Pain" in which you discuss what low back pain is, what causes it, and how you can prevent it. In this particular post, "Chiropractor in Anchorage" could be your keywords because you know, based on your research, people are searching for that phrase.

Make a call to action at the end of your blog post too. Tell people exactly what to do next. If their symptoms are not improving, put your phone number down at the bottom. Tell the prospective new patient to call right now or visit your website for more information. This example can be applied to any market or industry.

Guide everyone by the hand and make it extremely easy for them to get in touch with you. Provide value first and start to go down the line with those keywords you've compiled based on your market research.

Just remember, before you publish your blog post, make sure you enter those keyword tags as I mentioned before. This will allow Google to index it online on the relevant page you're seeking. You also want to make sure that the keywords you select are found throughout the description of the blog post, two or three times depending on how long it is. This is important.

The keywords should be in the title, description, and keyword tags of the blog post.

Once that's all completed, you're going to click the "Publish" link in your back office in WordPress. Now your post is going to be live for your local community to see. It's extremely simple. Once that post has been published, the fun part begins. It's time to syndicate your content and really announce it to the world.

One of the things that the All in One SEO Pack does is it helps to ping your site out into that blogosphere. This allows hundreds of other networks to pick up your content, getting more local traffic to your website. This will help you build your authority.

Pingler.com

When I post a new blog post, I submit it to Pingler.com immediately afterward. This site syndicates your post, propagates it, and pushes it out to many other networks that take blog content. Then they distribute it so people can see it online.

This is a must after you publish each blog post. Some blog plug-ins will have this blog distribution feature built-in. That's a question to ask the programmer that develops your blog.

Email list

We talked about accumulating an email list before. Let's say that this is a blog post for your potential new customers. If you have a list of 5,000 email subscribers and/or potential clients, you can immediately send a broadcast with your Aweber account.

You can go ahead and send an email out, or you can put it in your follow-up sequence and deliver it at a later time. Doing this regularly will help you provide consistent value to your audience.

Now you can start to get tremendous amounts of traffic to your blog post from just your email list alone. Again, you're going to build trust and credibility by doing that because people can see that you're out to help and empower them. It's important to be that go-to expert they instinctively turn to as they're going to look favorably at your efforts.

Share on Facebook, Twitter, Pinterest, LinkedIn, Instagram, and Google+

The next thing you can do is share your blog post on Twitter, Pinterest, Google+, LinkedIn, Instagram, and Facebook. You can get your friends, family, email list, and colleagues to share it too.

Look down at the very bottom on many of my blog posts. What do I say? I usually will have a blurb that states, "Like this post? Share it with your friends. Here's the link below." I make it so simple for people to share the content. That's why you can see floods of doctors sharing my links on Facebook and many tweeting my blog posts.

When you do what I just suggested, your traffic grows exponentially. You remove those barriers that would have once held you back from getting your blog content syndicated or bringing traffic to your website.

Backlinks

The next thing I'd like to quickly discuss is linking—more specifically, using what are called backlinks to secure those top spots that you want on Google. The blog post below shows you what Google wants to see in terms of links. Take a few seconds, go to this page, and bookmark it:

http://dcincome.com/blog/3-new-google-link-building-guidelines-post-penguin/

Think of links back to your website (backlinks) as votes. Typically, if you see a website that's ranked #1 online, usually that site has the most authority and high-quality social shares and links to it as opposed to the surrounding competitors. It has the most votes, the most authority links, hence it's ranked #1.

Of course, all links are NOT created equal, but they are arguably the most powerful ranking factor. You want high-quality online properties linking to your website on a consistent basis as it helps your site's positioning, credibility, and trust.

Market Samurai, as I mentioned before, will enable you to assess other factors that are very important, providing an unfair advantage over the competition.

An important factor of SEO is having your keywords in your domain name. The other one is the age of the domain name. But again, when it comes down to it, backlinks are the most important aspect. Social shares do matter, and someday they might even overtake links as the main authority signal. Today, however, links are still king.

That's why you or somebody else should consistently build general, natural-looking links. Sometimes anchor text backlinks can help as well. What is an anchor text backlink? How is it is different from a regular link back to your website?

An anchor text backlink is exactly what it says—text. Let's say that we're on a blog, forum, or any other web property online, and we're trying to rank for "best silicon baking mat." You need more anchor text links that have "best silicon baking mat" linked back to your website than your competitors. There are places in forums where you can add your signature with a link.

Some blogs will allow you to post comments in certain sections. There are even services that will allow you to create blog posts or articles with anchor text links in them, or what are called the resource boxes at the end of the articles. This is your chance to get anchor text real estate. When you create great content, others will share it and then you get a chance to get "earned links." These are weighted the most heavily.

Just to give you an easy example, if you go to Google's home page, in the upper right-hand corner you're going to see some text links. One of those text links is going to say "Gmail" if you have a Gmail account. One of them is going to say "Images," and there are a few other ones up there. Those are actual text links. That's called anchor text, meaning if you click on one of those links, it's going to redirect you to Gmail (or wherever the link is connected).

However, anchor text (as a whole) should be no more than 5 percent of your link profile. Read that again and underline it! Refer to the blog post I recommended above for the proper linking guideline. You can also read more about anchor text here on Wikipedia:

http://en.wikipedia.org/wiki/Anchor_text

Link building is overlooked by many entrepreneurs, brands, and professionals. Unfortunately, they're leaving a bunch of money on the table. A good number of businesses never really get a chance to realize more new sales and customers because they can't rank their blog posts high enough. Make sure that you start to get backlinks in the appropriate ratios to your blog post.

There are numerous ways you can get links like through articles, press releases, blog posts, forums, video sharing sites, etc. Articles give you the opportunity. Some higher-ranking directories like EzineArticles.com give you a chance in the resource box to promote yourself or your business. That's your chance to get much-needed anchor text backlinks from a very high-ranking authority website.

Remember, all backlinks are not created equal.

Blogs, forums, social networks, press release directories, video networks, .gov and .edu sites, and the top article websites are web properties where you can get them. As you produce solid content, other authority websites have the chance to syndicate your posts, which gives you more credibility and authority.

Author rank

Quite simply, author rank is your reputation with Google online. This is dependent on many factors. You must consider this whenever you create content, especially now that Google is placing heavy weight on how trustworthy and credible you are.

The author rank algorithm takes the following questions into consideration:

1. How often is your content shared?
2. How quickly is your content shared?
3. Who shared your content, and did those who shared your videos, articles, press releases, or blog posts have expertise in that topic?
4. Do the same people always share your content?
5. How many comments did your content generate?
6. Who commented on your content?
7. Did those who commented have expertise in this particular topic?
8. Were those comments of high quality or low quality?
9. Were the comments on your content of positive or negative sentiment?
10. How often is your content endorsed; for example, how many times is it "liked" on Facebook, +1 on Google, pinned on Pinterest, tweeted on Twitter, etc.

11. Who endorsed your content?

12. Did those endorsing your articles, press releases, videos, or blog posts have expertise in the topic?

13. Do the same people always endorse your content?

The better your author rank is, the more credible you appear in Google's eyes. Then they start to rank your content high on the search engines when you follow everything laid out in this blogging-success blueprint.

One other quick note, the more original content you have on your website and/or blog, the more it helps your Google ranking. This is not really new, but it does play a factor in your visibility online.

How I got over 1,800 Facebook likes for one blog post

Right now, I'd like to share with you my proven formula for getting attention in a "noisy" world. Among many other accomplishments, this knowledge has enabled me to get over 1,800 Facebook shares to this blog post:

http://dcincome.com/blog/fact-or-fiction-chiropractic-saves-lives/

When you follow these powerful steps, you'll always have a leg up on your competitors.

1. Create a controversial blog post headline.

Most blog post headlines flat-out suck! They're boring. And the headline is one of the most important components to any successful blog post—some would argue that it is the most critical piece. Why?

Because your headline is the initial attention-grabber.

Whether on Google, Facebook, Twitter, etc., the blog post title is seen first. If your title is strong, you can hypnotize people into clicking your link even if you're not in the best line of sight.

With this said, you obviously need to know your market well. What do they want? What solutions are they seeking? What mistakes are they making?

Previously in this blogging section I shared a couple powerful examples of how to title a blog post. Don't forget that I also have fourteen more compelling, copy-and-paste headline templates at this page:

http://dcincome.com/go/1182-2/

2. Deliver value.

Now that you have an eye-popping title, you MUST deliver the goods in the actual content. This should go without saying. It's best to make your content practical so that people can easily implement the information the same day.

Bullet the important points to make it easier for the person reading to consume it.

To deliver phenomenal value, you must understand the market you're servicing. Be authentic and don't be afraid to go against the conventional grain if your intentions are to clear up misconceptions and empower.

Address major concerns your audience is facing and provide facts and analysis. Always ask yourself, "Does this content I'm creating help solve a problem or better my reader's quality of life?"

Also, make sure you have clear, specific action steps you're giving others to fast-track their implementation.

3. Elicit an emotional response.

Don't shy away from controversy or the path less traveled. You need to get readers emotionally involved with your video or written blog posts. Fuse personal stories into the mix to help people connect with you on even more of an intimate level.

Research, find, and include the pain and pleasure points of the audience you're appealing to. Get specific with the small details so you can paint a vivid picture for others.

Furthermore, be direct and give your honest opinion—regardless of popularity.

4. Tell readers what to do next.

You'd be absolutely amazed by just how many business owners and entrepreneurs do not tell readers what to do next. If you want an individual to like and share your post, TELL THEM directly.

Never assume they'll automatically share the piece no matter how great it is. Give people a good, sincere reason why they should tell their friends.

Lastly, you need to make it very simple to share your content. Have the social share buttons on each blog post, just as you've seen on mine.

5. Email subscriber and client lists.

Your email list is your #1 biggest asset online. It's the lifeblood of any brick-and-mortar or Internet business. When you post new content, email your subscribers and clients that are in your inner circle. They'll be more likely to share your stuff because you have a long relationship with them.

In your emails, evoke curiosity and let people know the "secrets" they'll discover by reading the content. Or let them know what mistakes they'll avoid.

You also need to list three to four bullet points in the email stressing what's in it for them.

6. Facebook advertising

Facebook advertising has been my secret weapon since 2008. Nothing has gotten my companies and me more exposure, traffic, and sales than this strategy. We've spent over $500,000 with the social network and managed over a million dollars for clients (and for good reason).

With the ad that was created for the blog post referenced a few paragraphs ago, I was spending an average of twelve cents per click! You can't afford not to run ads with numbers that low. I promoted the blog post on Facebook for three weeks straight. My click-through rate was as high as 5.12 percent at one point as well.

Paid advertising is the FASTEST way to get noticed and overcome critical mass in any market. It's impossible to compete with the sheer volume of targeted traffic Facebook sends.

If you're not using Facebook ads consistently and your competitor is, you're getting crushed and don't even know it. Facebook is an untapped goldmine of exposure if you create, optimize, and run ads like I teach. Success and sales are predictable.

Return on investment has never been higher and ranges from 8:1 all the way to 35:1 on average. That means if you invest one dollar, you get $35 back. I've had private coaching clients get over 100:1 ROIs as well. Strategy is everything!

Here are a few quick tips when running Facebook ads to a blog post:

- Strive for thirty cents per click or less. If you're paying more than that, you're doing something seriously wrong. Contact us and get professional help.
- Click-through rate (CTR) should be 1.5 or above.
- Set a preliminary low budget of $7 per day. We can always scale big once the ad is performing well.
- Let the ad run for a couple days. Sometimes the cost per click (CPC) drops dramatically after the first day.
- Test these two Facebook ad types: "website clicks" and "boost posts." If one performs better, stick with that type.
- Test different images, headlines, and ad descriptions. The image accounts for over 70 percent of the reason why a person clicks the ad. The title comes in at a strong second.
- Always drive traffic to a blog post with a call to action or a squeeze page with an email capture form. YOU MUST DO THIS. You're literally throwing money down the tubes if you're not capturing names and emails from Facebook traffic. Never send visitors to a plain website home page.
- Far too many brands, public figures, and businesses pay for traffic only to let everyone look at their page briefly then bounce off. There should be a blatantly obvious (and irresistible) ethical bribe of sorts at the end of the blog post that clearly tells the visitor what to do next.
- Remember, Facebook traffic is not "search" traffic like you get on Google. They're not searching for specific keywords, so we can't just send them to a sales page. Instead, drive the traffic to a straight squeeze page.

The process I've described here is what enabled me to get over 1,800 Facebook likes to a blog post and has been responsible for countless others going viral. This, in turn, has gotten us countless sales and clients from the exposure.

This formula is reliable and works like crazy.

Do not haphazardly create a blog post then hope the magical unicorns will carry and promote it online for you. Be proactive and commit to being unstoppable! The formula above is guaranteed to get you noticed.

7. Twitter advertising

This is one of my favorite ways to drive super-targeted traffic to content we produce. You can set up your first ad at the link below. (You must have a Twitter account first.)

http://ads.Twitter.com

We're seeing very low costs per engagement, much like on Facebook. Twitter boasts over 200 million users, and the ad targeting is similar to that of the social network. You can target by location, followers of other popular figures, by keyword, and more. Start with a low budget of under $10 per day to get your feet wet.

You are essentially tapping into real-time, live conversations on Twitter. Very few businesses are using this advertising platform, so "get while the gettin's good"—and while the clicks are cheap.

What to do after publishing a blog post

Publishing unique blog posts a couple times a week is a recommended strategy. However, it's important to make sure that content actually gets seen by as many targeted people as possible.

You can have the best content in the world, but if no one knows about it, then it doesn't matter. This is where tactical promotion and outreach come into play. Here's where to distribute the blogs after they are published:

1. Go to Pingler.com to submit the blog post.
2. Email your list (current clients and general subscriber list of prospects).
3. Share the blog on your social profiles (Facebook, Twitter, LinkedIn, Google+, Pinterest, and Instagram).
4. Submit your blog to blog aggregates and directories—AllTop.com and BloggerScope.com.
5. Submit it to Medium.com (repackage the content).
6. Utilize Facebook advertising (with retargeting)—Perfect Audience.
7. Utilize Twitter advertising (if budget allows).
8. Convert your blog post into an audio that you can stream via iTunes, SoundCloud, and Stitcher Radio.

9. Reach out to other bloggers. Send twenty-five personalized emails to the top bloggers and social media influencers in your city or community.

10. Utilize StumbleUpon ads, which are super-low cost per click

11. Utilize JustReTweet (pay for others to retweet).

12. Utilize Triberr (a social sharing community—if you're going to use it, you need to be active).

Other proven ways to monetize your blog

As your blog becomes more popular and your community grows, sponsors may begin to seek you out. You can also be proactive and go looking for them. I know many bloggers that offer banner advertising space right on the blog, and they collect a monthly fee from the advertiser.

I also have some clients that have built relatively large audiences, and they offer product review services. For $500, they'll write an honest review about your product. The benefit is that that it's an easy way for a new product to break into the marketplace while getting in front of the perfect audience. For the blogger, it's a simple out-of-the-box way to add an extra source of income.

Chapter 13

FACEBOOK STRATEGIES THAT MULTIPLY YOUR IMPACT AND INCOME

*It's not what you do that determines your success, impact,
and profitability with social media; it's how you do it.*
—Matthew Loop

F
acebook is one of my favorite social platforms to generate targeted traffic to my squeeze pages and website. The social network boasts over 1.3 BILLION members, and it is a goldmine if you follow the strategies I'm about to share.

I could write an entire book on Facebook; however, I want to share with you only the golden nuggets that are going to get you more recognition, traffic, visibility, influence, and sales—a.k.a. tangible results!

You see, the problem is a lot of marketers and businesses stay "busy" on the social network and mistake that for actual productivity. They get caught up in doing things that don't make them money.

Listen, I like to have fun on Facebook, but I also treat it like a business and guard my time militantly. I have a checklist or an idea of what I need to accomplish, so I'm in and out and then on to the next high-leverage business-growth activity.

Less than 10 percent of all marketing strategies will actually produce new website traffic, customers, and exposure, so I intend to focus on those only. Here's the deal though: If you don't have a Facebook account, open one immediately. Just go to Facebook.com and follow the directions.

On the network, you have only two types of traffic available, free and paid. The no-cost traffic can come in the form of a referral or from "earned" social sharing. For example, any action you take on Facebook will either get shown in the newsfeed or the ticker to the right for your personal friends and fans to see.

Whether you click the "like" button, the "share" button, comment on a status, check-in with a business, post a text status update, share a photo or video, etc., every action has the potential to get seen by thousands of Facebook users.

The beauty of this is that the average Facebook user has over 300 friends connected to their personal profile. So if you post a blog with great content or share something of value on your timeline, your friends may easily click a button and share it with their entire list. Then, if their friends see it, they have the opportunity to share the content. And so on …

Now, multiply this by a few dozen or a hundred friends! There's a massive opportunity for you to get your message to the world if you harness Facebook correctly. Your content can literally spread like a virus. This is the goal.

With that said, there are some important things you MUST know about the world's biggest social network.

Times have changed and so has Facebook. The last thing you want to do is appear outdated with your prospective customers. If you don't have a large presence on this platform, research confirms that consumers trust you less.

It's kind of like twenty years ago when every business was in the yellow pages. If you weren't in that directory, you looked suspect and people were more skeptical in regard to your brand. Why? It's because every reputable business was in there.

The consumer mindset has shifted but the same principle applies to Facebook. There's no use fighting the trend or holding out. You've got to start marketing your business like it's the actual year we live in and have an overwhelming presence on the social network ... period!

Here's what you need to know right now to be most effective.

1. Facebook has hijacked your fans and friends

Did you know that with any given status update, only 7–10 percent of your fans and friends see it? Yes, you read that correctly. All of those people that came to your Facebook business page over the years, who clicked the "like" button, who became fans expecting to see your content regularly are more than likely not getting your updates now.

That will come as a shock to many unsuspecting entrepreneurs.

Facebook is a business and now wants you to pay for newsfeed visibility. Yeah, it's kind of a bummer. However, there's no sense in getting worked up about it. For me, it felt like a bait and switch, but it's their network and they can do what they want.

We must adapt or perish. The gatekeepers have reared their ugly head again. If you want the large reach, you're going to have to pay.

2. Facebook is NOT your home

One of the biggest mistakes so many people have made over the years is that they've used the social network as their central hub of communication online. They've driven much of their traffic in their videos, blogs, press releases, and articles to the social network to get more fans.

The problem with this has always been that you and I don't control what Facebook does tomorrow. Facebook could update their algorithm (like they did) and crush your visibility—and your ability to get your message to your audience—overnight. Less visibility = diminished exposure = decreased website traffic = fewer online sales.

Ideally, you should be building an email list of prospective customers. You do this by offering something of value on your website in exchange for a name and email.

For instance, here are some examples of free report titles:

- 3 Questions You Must Ask before Choosing a Fish Oil Supplement
- 5 DUMB Mistakes Most Bulldog Owners Make When Potty Training Their Puppies
- What Every Woman over 30 Ought to Know about Getting Rid of Ugly Wrinkles

Make the report consumer-friendly and address the commonly asked questions as well as the myths that surround your topic. We do this so we can overcome objections before they consciously arise in the prospective customer's mind.

Giving the prospective customer a free, valuable report will make them more likely to opt-in and provide you with their name and email. We need to build an email list because most people aren't ready to buy from you on the first online interaction.

Why? It's because they hardly know you.

When they're on your email list, you can deliver great informative content, testimonials, and then make an exceptional offer. We have to get people to know, like, and trust us first. The goal is to build a relationship and a strong bond with your email subscribers.

3. Beating Facebook's newsfeed filter

If you're looking to maximize your reach and post distribution on the social network, pay close attention. Of all the engagement factors, comments are the most important! The more comments you get to each status update, the more exposure you get in the newsfeed. Simple.

"Likes" and "shares" are great, but in my experience comments can give your posts the most legs and viral exposure. So how do you create this type of engagement?

Ask open-ended questions. Have image-caption contests. Incorporate fill-in-the-blank or multiple-choice status updates to spark conversation. Not only that, make sure you are commenting on your own threads. As Facebook sees this windfall of engagement, they end up showing the content to more of your friends and fans.

There is also another way to beat the algorithm filter if you have the budget. You can "boost" a status update. Once you post an update, look on the right below the update and you'll see a little blue button that says "boost post."

With that option you can target your business page fans, friends of fans, or a custom national and/or local audience. I would get in the habit of boosting your best content.

Lastly, make sure to upload ALL your recorded videos to your Facebook fan page. There is an option to do this when you click on the "photos" tab below you header graphic. On that next screen you'll see a button that says "add video."

Facebook is showing favoritism to video because they are trying to complete with Google and YouTube. Many times videos will get more impressions and views than other types of content posted on the social network. Use this knowledge to your advantage.

4. Harness the power of Facebook groups

From my experience, Facebook groups are one of the most underutilized communication methods by brands, corporations, small businesses, and entrepreneurs. At the moment, they are still free to use, but there's no telling how long that will last.

One of the MAJOR benefits of using a Facebook group is that your posts and status updates have much more visibility than a post from a personal profile or fan page. This is an enormous advantage!

Groups that you are a member of usually get priority in the newsfeed too. They stay at the top longer. Not to mention the fact that anytime the administrator posts an update in the group, it's like an instant message to all members.

Meaning, that if I have a group with 10,000 people, when I post a topic to discuss in the community, Facebook shows a pop-up in the lower left corner to anyone that's on the social network at that exact moment.

Groups can be set to public or private, and you can use them a few different ways.

- You can use them as a "members only" portal to provide value to current customers. Let's say you create a product and you'll likely to add (as a bonus) a private Facebook group where members can help each other and where you (the expert) can answer questions. I do this. You'll want to as well. Customers LOVE being able to interact in this fashion.

- You can create a public group around a specific keyword or topic. Let's say you release a product on how to potty train a German shepherd. You can also start a group for German shepherd lovers and offer tips, deliver value, raise awareness, talk about current related events, and encourage active discussion. Periodically, you can promote events or products that provide solutions to common problems that members face.

- Remember, you're essentially building a community of like-minded people here. Facebook users are searching for groups around their interests all the time.

- You can use a Facebook group to communicate with your team. As you grow your business and it becomes successful, you might eventually find yourself with quite a few team members. A group can keep everyone on the same page from a project-management standpoint.

- Create a private group solely as a customer-support hub. As your business grows, you might find that it's necessary to bring an employee on full-time to manage support tickets. Having a group like this that answers questions promptly can dramatically reduce product returns and/or chargebacks.

How to create your Facebook fan page

On the social network, you have your personal profile. That's the one you originally create when you sign up for Facebook. Do not confuse that with a Facebook fan page. It's NOT the same thing. Fan pages are for businesses, brands, and entrepreneurs that will be doing promotions.

To set up a fan page, go to the following page and see the instructions: https://www.facebook.com/pages/create.php

You'll need to select what type of business you have. The options Facebook gives are:

- Local Business
- Company or Organization

- Brand or Product
- Public Figure
- Entertainment
- Cause or Community

Once you've followed that process, you can edit the page and put a business description, website address, cover photo, timeline graphic, add your interests, etc.

Here's a quick tip if you own a small business: The title (business name) you give the Facebook fan page will be what appears on Google. I mention this because Facebook fan pages can get indexed well on search engines for specific keywords.

In a local market, this is much easier to use to our advantage. Let me tell you what I did originally when we set up our fan page for our chiropractic office.

I had been in practice for only a couple years, but I knew that no one was searching my personal or business name online. So I made a careful observation that Facebook business pages were getting ranked well on Google.

Instead of titling the fan page with my business name, I titled the page with keywords that I knew prospective patients were searching on the web. The title I chose was "Chiropractor Lilburn GA | Matthew Loop DC."

Not only did I do that, but I also selected my "vanity URL" for the page. Facebook allows you to have your own custom website address for pages. For this page, I selected this:

www.Facebook.com/LilburnChiropractic

You see, Google rewards you with higher rankings if you have your keywords in the title and URL of the business page, just like in the "metadata" of a regular website. Of course, you need to be active on the page, continuously posting content and getting engagement.

The only reason I didn't select ChiropractorLilburn in my Facebook vanity URL was that it was taken. Nonetheless, after a few weeks the page began to rank on the first page of Google when anyone searched "chiropractor Lilburn." That produced foot traffic through our clinic door each month!

Simple and powerful.

So in this instance all I did was capitalize on and piggyback off the credibility of an authority site to get high Google rankings for my Facebook fan page. You can do this with other social media sites like Pinterest and Twitter too.

Updating statuses on your Facebook (a.k.a. posting)

Your Facebook posts should be mix of content that includes regular text, video, content from other websites, content from your personal blog, infographics, images, etc. The majority of what you post should relate to the target market you're servicing. Always strive to deliver value.

Ideally, I recommend posting anywhere from three to five times per day. Your goal is to stimulate engagement from as much of your fan base as possible. I had to learn this years ago when I was initially posting about health-related stuff. Not everyone gives a damn about health, so my engagement hit a plateau!

I'd find the same fans commenting over and over, but I wondered what happened to everyone else. Remember, no two people are the same. Everyone is going to have a slightly different personality, so you want to vary your updates accordingly.

You can ask open-ended questions, do fill-in-the-blank updates, tell stories, post jokes, write inspirational quotes, post educational content, and much more. We want people to view you as the "go-to" source of information in your respective niche. Be creative!

Having trouble thinking of what to post next? No problem. You can access an endless content bank at the following site:

http://AllTop.com

Go there to see popular stories by topic, category, and interest. But shh … keep that resource between us.

Publishing a status update is a simple process, and I've included a screenshot to help you hit the ground running.

Looking at this image, the arrow is pointing to the place where you can type anything you want. If you post a link to a website, Facebook will auto-populate a bold title, image, and description. They pull this from the metadata of the site you're linking to.

Know that the title, image, and description of the auto-populated info can be altered. Meaning, you can click on each of those things before you publish the post and modify them. This becomes important when you're running "page post engagement" ads, a.k.a. boosting posts from your Facebook ads manager.

To add a photo as a status update, just click the photo/video field you see in that image. Next to that, you'll see the offer/event tab, which is self-explanatory.

You can add a location to your post by clicking the location marker in the lower left and entering the name of a business.

The rifle scope in the lower left allows us to target a specific segment of our fans for the post we're about to publish. Once clicked, you can set an audience based on gender, interests, location, relationship status, age, etc.

In the lower right you see the "post" button. This publishes your content live. DO NOT click that until your status update is exactly how you want it.

That little down arrow you see in the same button allows you to time your posts. It's very convenient, especially if you have a busy day ahead. So if you have five Facebook post ideas and you want to queue them up throughout the day, you can easily take a couple minutes and do it.

When you click the "boost post" option, you'll see something like this.

With these quick boosts, you can either target fans that like your page, fans and their friends, or select a custom audience like I've done in the screenshot. You can pay $5 all the way up to hundreds, depending on how many users you want to see your content. You want to boost your best status updates for increased visibility.

Whether you like it or not, Facebook is a business. They have an obligation to shareholders to make money, and they're getting good at nickel-and-diming users. If you're a business, you've got to pay to play. There's no getting around it. Yes, it feels like a bait and switch, but there's not much you can do.

Marketing your Facebook business page to gain fans and mass notoriety

There are four important reasons why you absolutely MUST grow your Facebook fan count on a regular basis. For starters, the web is a big popularity contest. If you have more fans than any other competing brand, you win the social-proof game.

The more popular you appear, the more credibility you'll have in the prospective customer's mind. As childish as it sounds, perceived popularity influences buying habits.

The second reason you need to be growing your fan page numbers is that it's also an indicator of trust. I mean, if 100,000 people like your fan page, you must be great, right? Conversely, if you have just ten fans, then people can look at your brand with skepticism.

The third reason for getting more fans has to do with increased visibility and exposure. The more fans you have, the more people will get to see your Facebook status updates. This creates top-of-mind awareness and familiarity. The more users that see your posts, the more will visit your website, read your content, and see your product offers.

Finally, the more fans, engagement, and content you have, the higher your fan page will rank on Google for your business name and/or page title. In other words, it helps your SEO. It's not uncommon to see a Facebook fan page ranked in the top three slots on Google for a brand name. This can also help with reputation management.

Here are the twelve of the best ways to attract an endless windfall of Facebook fans:

- If you run a local, free-standing business, get customers to check in using the Facebook mobile app on their phones. When they click the "nearby places" link, the social network will populate the businesses in the area. Once they find yours and hit "check-in," it will post directly to that customer's personal profile.

   The benefit of doing this is that the average Facebook user has over 300 friends. Chances are, if you're helping someone that's used your services, they have other local friends.

   You need to make it fun for them though. Have a weekly contest and offer an incentive, whether it's a special bonus or complimentary service. Anytime they visit your business and check in, they get a ticket to the end-of-the-week raffle.

   These check-in numbers can add up quickly. That means easy free exposure for your business, which can generate word-of-mouth referrals hand over fist. I've worked with small business clients that are getting hundreds of check-ins each week. That translates to tens of thousands of FREE impressions.

- Here's another small business strategy to acquire fans rapidly. Put a laptop or tablet in your business and get people to "like" your Facebook fan page when they come in. Unlike when trying to get Google reviews, you don't get penalized for having people login from the same IP address.

   Give customers a reason or two to be connected, whether it's added value, keeping up with recent news, exclusive coupons, etc. You can also run a contest for members of the fan page.

- Use Facebook as your business page. The social network gives you an option to use your business page when commenting, sharing, or liking. I find not enough businesses are doing this, but it's great for getting new fans.

To see what I'm referring to, visit your fan page, look in the upper right corner, then see this screenshot below for the option.

When you use Facebook as your business page, the name of that fan page will be seen when you like, comment, and engage. So if you're adding value, people will click on your profile to become a fan.

Let me give you an example. Let's say your fan page name is "Atlanta Dentist | Dr. John Smith." You've seen a local restaurant running commercials in the area, probably spending tens of thousands on advertising to attract local fans.

Well, what you could do is use Facebook as the fan page above, become a fan of the restaurant's page, then "like" and comment. Any action you take will say that "Atlanta Dentist | Dr. John Smith" has liked this post.

That's easy (and free) exposure. Just be a problem solver and/or add to the discussion. Naturally, you're going to get targeted traffic to your fan page by doing this. You can use this same strategy on a national scale as well.

- Another great way to get fresh qualified likes to your page is to network with other Facebook fan page owners in your industry. See if they're looking for fresh content that you can contribute to their fan page members or website.

If they accept guest blogs, then they'll more than likely share the content on Facebook as well with a link to your page.

- Use Facebook advertising. While I normally don't recommend this medium for just getting fan page likes, it can be done. You can also have a giveaway to incentivize your target market to like your page. For instance, I know business owners that have given away a free iPad to one lucky fan page member after a thirty-day contest.

  When you create an ad, it's the "promote your page" option. Usually, when you advertise your blog posts or squeeze pages, you'll naturally get likes as by-product. We'll talk in-depth about Facebook advertising in the next section.

- Add a Facebook fan page widget (a.k.a. Facebook "like" box) to your business website. Once you start to get an avalanche of traffic to your website by using what you learn in this book, naturally many visitors will see this box and decide to follow you on Facebook.

  To see an example of what this widget looks like, go to MatthewLoop. com, scroll down a little, then look to the right.

- Publish high-value, engaging content on your own fan page. This can be in the form of a blog post, information graphic, video, simple text status update, and an image. Doing this will get you "likes" and "shares," which spread your message virally for free! As a by-product, you'll get more fans.

- Ad your Facebook fan page URL to your email signature block. How many emails do you send out each and every day? If you're like the average American, it's probably anywhere from twenty to fifty! That's easy free exposure you can get just by adding a simple blurb that says, "Like Us on Facebook at Facebook.com/YourFanPageName."

- Promote the fan page on other social networks and media. If you're on Twitter, Instagram, Pinterest, LinkedIn, Google+, etc., you can post links for those followers to like your Facebook fan page and stay connected. If you use major media such as TV, radio, newspaper, or billboards, have your Facebook website address included on them. Make sure you set your "vanity URL" at Facebook.com/username first. We want to make our fan page web address easy for folks to remember.

- If you've already built an email list of targeted subscribers in a specific niche, you can email your tribe and let them know about your fan page. Give them a couple reasons to join or offer exclusive content there they can't get anywhere else.

  Invite your current contacts to like your Facebook fan page. If you have a personal profile on the social network, this option allows you to invite those friends. It also allows you to directly import your email contacts. If you're like me, you might have hundreds or even thousands of contacts! Using this methods helps you gain momentum and hit the ground running.

  Currently, this "suggest page" option is found when you go to your fan page, then click "notifications" at the top left. Realize this location could change, but know that it's available to you. See the following screenshot.

- Measure, track and improve. Use your Facebook insights tab on your fan page to see what times of the day are getting the most impressions to your posts. This will vary market to market; however, tracking this can help you gain maximum visibility to your organic status updates. In turn, you'll get more engagement and new fans all because you've unlocked the perfect times to post.

Facebook paid advertising

Let's talk about Facebook's paid advertising platform for a moment. Some refer to this as Facebook ads, Facebook pay-per-click, or Facebook ppc. Quite honestly, it's my secret weapon when it comes to generating highly qualified leads, mass recognition, floods of website traffic, and new clients and sales.

After personally spending over a half million dollars on Facebook ads and managing close to a million dollars in ads for other companies, I'll encourage you to "get while the gettin's good."

The social network's ads platform is the FASTEST way to reach critical mass in your selected market while shaping public perception. You can flip a switch and turn on an avalanche of targeted traffic. Facebook can deliver as much as you can pay for. We're able to get clicks for pennies in some cases, but we usually average between ten and thirty cents.

Imagine spending just $100 and getting 1,000 clicks to your specific ad! It's the most cost-effective paid advertising medium right now.

Let's put this in perspective.

We used to run television and radio ads to a few different websites. These were direct-response advertisements too. Meaning, once the person landed on the website, they were compelled to take immediate action.

We would pay about $250 for a thirty-second, late-night commercial slot. According to our website analytics, we were getting between 200 and 300 visitors to the site when the commercials aired. So if we break it down, we were paying around a dollar per click for the TV advertising. Compare that to ten cents per click on Facebook!

That's ten times the clicks for the same money spent! Facebook obviously wins by a long shot here. It's very cost-effective, and you get more bang for the buck! It levels the playing field and allows people like us to compete with major brands and corporations—not to mention, your ads on the social network can target according to specific interest, keywords, schools, age, zip code, hobbies, purchase behavior, other popular fan pages, and much more.

Facebook advertising is so much more advanced and specific than a television or radio campaign that blankets a city in a shotgun approach. You can visit the following page to set up your advertising account and learn more:

https://www.facebook.com/business

The page might look something like what you see in the screenshot below. Somewhere on it, you'll see a "create an ad" button. To run ads, you may also need to create a business fan page if you have not done so already.

Facebook helps you reach your business goals

So, why are Facebook ads so effective, and why can they produce such low costs per click? It's because the most powerful (and effective) ads on the social network appear in the newsfeed. Statistics prove this is where the majority of users spend the most time reviewing status updates. Some call this "native" advertising because it's hard for a Facebook user to differentiate it from a regular status update of a friend.

Click-through rates (CTR's) tend to be a lot higher with ads featured in the newsfeed. We've had as high as a 7.1 percent CTR before. You should strive for at least a 1.5 percent CTR though. The higher the CTR and relevancy score, the lower you'll pay per click.

In terms of cost per click (CPC), you'll want to make sure you're getting below thirty cents per click. Anything above that means something is wrong with the ad or that you haven't split-tested enough. You might need to change the title to call out your audience better, alter the description to make a better case as to what's in it for them, or just upload a more curiosity-evoking image.

My best ad I ever ran garnered a staggering six cents per click! So that gives you an idea of what's possible.

Make your daily ad budget $7 per day when you start, and in terms of your cost per lead, strive for one dollar or less. Don't be satisfied with anything over that. In order to achieve stellar numbers like this, your ad needs to be able to make your target audience stop in their tracks. Secondly, your landing page has to do a solid job of compelling prospective clients to give you their name and email.

Always split test your ads with other ads that are slightly different. The cool thing is that you will know within two days max if your ad falls in the target CPC we're looking for.

After you test a few ads and determine which one has the lowest CPC, you can always scale up the budget on that ad. The reality is, Facebook can deliver all the website traffic you can handle or pay for. It's just a matter of how well we convert that traffic into email opt-ins.

That's really important too. We NEVER drive Facebook traffic to a sales page or the home page of our website. That is a very costly mistake most new business owners and marketers make! Why not, you might ask?

It's because users on Facebook aren't looking for products to buy like they'd "search" on Google, for example. They are on the social network to hang out with friends.

So the appropriate way to get them to take action of any sort is to use Facebook ads to drive people to a squeeze page. Then we have an offer that gives them something of value for free in exchange for a name and email.

Once an email is collected, you could make a low-barrier offer (something under $10) on that thank-you page. But regardless of what they decide to do then, we have their contact information, so we can start building a relationship with them.

The two most common Facebook ads I use are "send people to your website" and "boost your posts." When you create your first ad, it might also say "clicks to website" or "page post engagement." It's the same thing.

Here's a screenshot of how it looks at the moment.

Understand that Facebook does update the look of their site periodically; however, the functions and user options usually stay the same. So don't freak out if, when you're reading this, Facebook has slightly altered their advertising interface.

After you select your objective here, Facebook will ask you to enter the website address you want to drive traffic to if you chose "send people to your website." If you selected "boost your posts," then it will bring you to the page where you can get specific about who you want to target.

On that next page, you'll see targeting options such as geographic location, gender, languages, age, interests, behavior, etc. You'll also see a box that says "more demographics." When clicked, that box will show fields like ethnicity, relationship status, financial, work, home, education level, life events, and politics.

Facebook gives you another field called "connections" where you can target those associated with your fan page, your app, or event.

Once you have the parameters set, you can progress to the "campaign and ad set" option where you can select your daily budget and name the campaign accordingly. From there, you'll navigate to the "bidding and pricing" field.

Let Facebook automatically optimize your website click bid for you. Don't worry about manual bidding. If you create a good ad, Facebook will show it often, and your CTR and CPC will be at the acceptable levels mentioned previously.

Now, let's back track for a minute.

If you selected "send people to your website," you'll also see a place where you can create an ad headline and a short text description. Additionally, Facebook allows you to upload a new ad image or graphic from your computer.

If you chose the "boost your posts" option, the headline, description, and image will be pre-populated because you're simply promoting a current status update from your Facebook fan page.

The rest of the targeting criteria I spoke about above will still be available to you for this page post-engagement option. You also have the option to run the ad continuously or on a schedule. That's up to you to test. You'll find this under the "ad scheduling" section.

Let's talk about the ad formatting right now.

The ad headline

This is where you call out your target audience OR create an irresistible post that your audience feels compelled to click.

For example, let's say you're a consultant that helps dentists grow their practices, and you want to target dentists on Facebook with a "clicks to website" ad. A sample headline could be any one of these:

- *Are You a Dentist?*
- *Attention Dentists*
- *For Dentists Only!*

If you're targeting dentists using the "page post engagement," remember, we need to think about the headline when we actually post the status update to our business fan page. This is critical. The great thing is that in these types of posts, we have more characters we're allowed to use in the headline text.

Using the same dental consultant example, here are some headline ideas if we were going to use a page post-engagement ad.

- *5 DUMB Mistakes Dentists Make When Promoting Their Practices*
- *3 Big Mistakes to Avoid When Marketing Your Dental Office Online*
- *Before You Offer a Free Dental Exam, Read This First*
- *What Every Dentist Ought to Know about Starting a Profitable Practice*

Those headlines above could either draw the Facebook traffic to a squeeze page or an informative blog post that delivers value to that particular market. If we're sending them to a blog post, always make a clear call to action at the end.

The main goal is to get people on our email list before we attempt to make the sale.

The ad image

Like I've mentioned previously in this work, your ad image accounts for over 60 percent of the reason a prospective customer will click the ad itself. Some sources will say it's over 75 percent of the reason. Regardless, it's the main attention-grabber! Your images should stand out like no other.

Every market will be a little different in terms of which ones compel the most. Sometimes industry-specific images are good. So if you're targeting dentists, you might use a tooth in the ad because that is something a dentist would connect with fast.

Other times a picture of a beautiful woman will attract a high volume of clicks. Images with red borders can work. Cartoons can pull too. Or just anything that might create curiosity.

The bottom line here is that you need to test different images to see which ones pull the best in your market. There are plenty of stock image sites available online like iStock and ShutterStock.

NEVER just pull an image from Google images. That can land you in hot water fast if the image has been trademarked.

You will also want to test images that overlay text within them. For example, you might have the same text in your image that's in the headline of the Facebook ad.

Remember this though: Facebook will disapprove your ad if the text takes up over 20 percent of the total graphic. They have a tool in their ads manager that helps you measure this.

Lastly, the social network gives you the option of using one image for your ads or using up to six images. You can test this to see which type of ad is pulling better in your market.

The ad description

This is your chance to tell the targeted Facebook user and prospective customer, "What's in it for me?" Why should they click the advertisement? The text in this section has to be benefit-rich and make them very curious.

Going with this previous example of a dental consultant targeting dentists, we might use either one of these:

- *Use this proven blueprint to attract an extra 20 new clients per month WITHOUT spending money on traditional advertising.*
- *Free video shares the #1 secret to serving more patients this year and multiplying your dental practice revenue*

Place one or two sentences in the Facebook ad description box and put a call to action text at the end like "click here."

Here are some Facebook newsfeed ad examples from past campaigns:

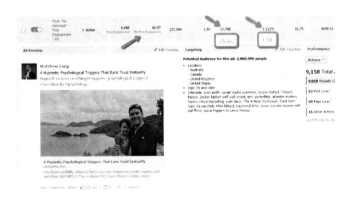

As you can see from the ad above, the cost per engagement is an insanely low seven cents. The CTR is at a high 5.2 percent. When you divide the numbers out, the average cost per website click is just north of ten cents.

So we spent $690.61 and the ad reached 133,004 people. It received 10,795 total clicks, and 9,019 of those were website clicks.

That's AWESOME and we'll run these numbers all day long! We're getting ten highly targeted website clicks from prospective clients for each dollar spent. No other advertising medium at this moment allows you such leverage!

This ad worked well because of several factors. The image was beautiful, a family pic of my son and me with Trunk Bay in the background. It stuck out like a sore thumb.

The title, "4 Hypnotic Psychological Triggers that Earn Trust Instantly," is compelling and catches the attention of the entrepreneurs, marketers, and businesses owners I was targeting.

The description said, "Use these credibility influence factors to calm skepticism, create rapport, and earn trust INSTANTLY. Your website must have these in today's time!"

Lastly, the ad targeting was right on the money.

It was the perfect message to the perfect audience. For that ad, I targeted Facebook fan pages of other known influencers in the social media and entrepreneurial world. You need to know the top influencers in your industry to do this effectively.

In case you're curious about the content, you can watch that video on my blog below:

http://dcincome.com/blog/4-hypnotic-psychological-triggers/

Another great thing about this ad is that it garnered twelve Facebook shares, 375 "likes," and twenty-one comments. You have to remember, anytime a Facebook user takes an action like that, it shows in their newsfeed for their friends to see.

So we got quite a bit of extra free exposure and clicks because of the viral nature of Facebook.

This ad above also performed really well, reaching 266,890 Facebook users, garnering 4,650 website clicks while spending only $583.29. We created this advertisement for website clicks specifically. The CPC stayed at twelve cents, which is fantastic. The CTR was a solid 4.14 percent.

With ads this cheap, you can't afford not to run them. You can bury competitors and overcome critical mass in no time. We directed this one to a blog post. You can read it here:

http://dcincome.com/blog/jk-rowlings-new-book-proof-that-content-is-not-king/

We targeted authors, journalists, and writers guilds. Everyone in that circle knows who JK Rowling is. So the image of her was easily identifiable and jumped out to the right crowd.

The title of the ad was, "JK Rowlings New Book: Proof that Content is NOT King!" That actually goes against conventional wisdom in this market. It made them do a double take.

The description was, "This is the MOST famous example of how you've been lied to. Discover why simply creating content does not lead to success, recognition or sales."

Again, pretty compelling if you're in that market.

Here's another example of a great Facebook ad that we ran for a few months. As you can see from the following screenshot, the likes approximated the number of shares! That's when you know you have a great ad that people love.

We garnered an average of sixteen cents per click on this ad. CTR was a nice 4.89 percent. When everything was all said and done, we had a whopping 1,173 likes and 1,286 shares! We had reached a total of 175,306 people that we targeted via popular business fan pages.

The tile of the ad was, "Before you Start a Business, Watch This FIRST."

The ad description we used was: "Here's how to avoid the #1 MOST common mistake beginners make that keeps them a slave to their business. Not learning this lesson early-on costs many entrepreneurs the freedom and flexibility they so desperately desire."

You can see the blog post we directed the traffic to at this link:

http://dcincome.com/blog/before-you-start-an-online-business-watch-this-first/

This advertisement worked so well because no one wants to make costly mistakes. Remember, people are more likely to take action to avoid pain as opposed to seeking pleasure. It's just how we're wired.

The title of that ad is formatted in a consumer-friendly way that generates awareness. It compels prospective clients to click to learn more. The image I used was an actual close-up screenshot from the video. It gives the appearance that you and I are having a heart-to-heart conversation. Plus, it was unique to the market I was targeting.

IMPORTANT NOTE 1: When setting up a Facebook ad, after the text box in the ad creation section, you'll see an option to incorporate a call-to-action button. I usually don't use one because one of the goals of the ad is to BLEND IN to the newsfeed so it doesn't actually look like an ad.

In our testing, I've discovered this gets us a lower cost per click. If you put a call-to-action button in your ad, Facebook users immediately know it's an advertisement. So many will not click the post. This might vary based on your market, but it's something to consider and split test.

IMPORTANT NOTE 2: There's a blue link below the text box and call-to-action option that says "show advanced options." When clicked, it opens up and gives you another field to populate called "newsfeed link description."

Make sure you fill in this field anytime you create an ad where you're sending clicks to your website. If you don't, then your ad will appear in the newsfeed without a text box description. That's a conversion killer! Don't make that mistake.

Many times we simply will just copy and paste the words from the text box or ad description in there. Other times you may want to add more text since it gives you up to 200 characters.

IMPORTANT NOTE 3: You'll want to periodically review Facebook's advertising guidelines as the social network is getting a bit stricter these days. Sometimes they'll change the terms of service and this can affect how your ads perform. Visit the link below to see what Facebook does and does not like:

https://www.facebook.com/ad_guidelines.php

For more information on increasing website clicks and conversions, visit:

https://www.facebook.com/business/a/online-sales/page-post-link-ads

To get even more help with your ads, go here:

https://www.facebook.com/business/resources

Facebook video ads

How would you like to upload a video to Facebook and use their advertising platform to pay one cent each time a person viewed the video? Pretty silly question. I mean, who in their right mind wouldn't take advantage!

Here's a screenshot of exactly what I mean.

The relevance score on this video ad was 10/10 and the CTR was at a high 5.3 percent! It just goes to show you how little you can pay when you dial a Facebook ad into the right audience.

As you can see, the total view count is a whopping 125,796! That includes "paid for" views (113,362) and views earned from the 502 shares and the 1,370 likes. Even if your marketing is terrible, you're still able to BUY critical mass and fame in a marketplace if you do it right.

To get this much brand exposure on TV or radio would easily cost you tens of thousands of dollars. This many views cost us only $1,370. Who knows how long this window of opportunity will be available too.

The social network is showing a bit of favoritism to video. It's now getting more newsfeed visibility, which translates into more actual views. Facebook is intent on competing with YouTube, and they're trying to incentivize users to upload their videos there.

There are two ways to upload a video. One is through your personal profile or business fan page. Just go to your status update box on Facebook and you'll see a text above that says "photo/video." Once clicked, you can upload a photo or video from your computer.

The other way to do it is to go to the photos section on your Facebook fan page. You'll see a box below your timeline graphic that says "Add Video." It looks like this.

Once the video is uploaded to Facebook, we can go to our ads manager and then create an ad. We'll select the "get video views" option. Targeting is similar to the normal ads we run, so don't worry.

The great thing about this type of ad is that we can use a custom image thumbnail if we don't like the scenery in the video. Remember, your image accounts for the major reason why someone will click the ad. It has to stand out.

You have a text box similar to the description box on normal Facebook ads. It's only ninety characters, so we have to be very concise. This short blurb should entice users and make people very curious about the content of the video.

The social network gives you the option to select a call-to-action button; however, as I recently mentioned, I don't recommend doing this. Remember, we want to blend in natively to the other newsfeed status updates that aren't ads. If you use a call-to-action button, your story looks like an ad, which leads to a drop in your CTR most of the time. This translates to a higher cost per click on the ad!

Start your budget small at seven dollars per day. We can always scale up if we find the video is a winner.

Drive the traffic from the video to a squeeze page, blog post, and sales page. See which one converts the best. Like always, though, it's best to get visitors onto an email list you control so you can communicate and market to them for years to come.

Your video should deliver on the benefit you mention in the description box and be valuable to the viewer. Having done that, we can direct this person to a squeeze page and give them several reasons why they'll want to go there now to instantly access what you have to offer.

Facebook video ads can be used to deliver helpful advice to your market, communicate with current customers, drive prospects to educational blog posts, answer frequently asked questions, or get them to your squeeze page so you can offer them something of value in exchange for a name and email.

I believe this is a HUGE opportunity for business owners and entrepreneurs of all types. We have no way of knowing how long video advertising will be this cheap, so I'd recommend utilizing this medium to your advantage immediately.

Return on investment

With Facebook advertising, you should strive for a minimum of a 5:1 return on investment (ROI). That means for every dollar you invest, you should receive five in return. We've had upwards of a 118:1 ROI before to show you what's possible. That means for every dollar put into advertising, 118 came back! How would you like to replicate that?

What we can measure we can improve. Facebook even allows us to put a "tracking pixel" on our website to measure the conversion. To do this, you'll go to your Facebook ads manager then click the "conversion tracking" link on the vertical navigation bar on the left.

So, go here:

https://www.facebook.com/ads/manage

Then, see this screenshot of the Facebook ads manager menu.

You'll then see something like this:

If you don't know how to place the code Facebook provides on your thank-you page, get your current webmaster to do it. Or you can hire a freelance programmer from Upwork.com.

Two other critically important features that I want to point out are "audiences" and "audience insights." If you look at the previous screenshot, you'll see a link in the menu bar for those.

Under the "audiences" section, you'll see a green "create audience" button in the upper right. Click that and a drop-down menu will appear with the options titled "custom audience," "lookalike audience," and "saved targeted group."

The true beauty here is that we have immense flexibility and laser targeting for our Facebook ads. For instance, as you can see by the previous screenshot, you can use the "customer list" option to upload a data file to Facebook.

So if you're building an email list of subscribers like I've recommended in this book, you can upload your Aweber, InfusionSoft, Constant Contact, Mail Chimp, or Get Response lists into Facebook and then target those specific people with an ad!

The next option for "website traffic" allows you to basically retarget and show Facebook ads to people that have visited your website. You can set up your audience to include everyone who visits your site, or even create separate audiences for people who visit individual pages on your website.

All you need to do is install the custom-audience pixel on your website to start building your follower base automatically. You can also send this code directly to the person who manages your website, and they can make sure it works.

In regards to "app activity," this allows you to build a custom audience to reach people who take specific actions in your app, such as reaching a specific level in a game, adding items to their cart, or rating your app.

Now, progressing to "lookalike audiences," this allows you to reach new people who are similar to an audience you care about. All you do is select a source (your fan page or another one you manage) and a country, then choose an optimization.

See the following screenshot for how it looks:

The cool thing about this is that Facebook does the work for you and scans its network for those that are similar to the fans you currently have. Very few business owners, marketers, and entrepreneurs know about this hack.

Test and use it to your advantage!

Let me briefly talk about the "audience insights" option in the ads manager menu bar. When clicked, it brings you to a page where you can create an audience based on your fan page or from the whole social network.

You'll see options to select from such as demographics, lifestyle, page likes, geographic location, activity, household, purchase behavior, relationships, education level, etc. Facebook charts this stuff out for you so you can easily see precisely how many fit your selected target market.

You can also create and save a list here to make it easier for you. For instance, one list I created targets only affluent people who are connected to specific public figures. Anytime I want to run an ad to this group, it's saved in my preferences. You'll save a tremendous amount of time doing this, especially if you're marketing to the same group over and over again.

Another link you probably noticed in the ads manager menu bar was the Facebook power editor. To learn more about it, visit the page below. It's mostly for advertising agencies that are managing hundreds of accounts.

https://www.facebook.com/help/211683245531881

Have a question about one of the ads you've set up? No problem. Facebook now offers an "advertiser support" option, visible in the ads manager. You can email them and they'll typically get back to you in one business day.

Action Step: This chapter was probably like drinking from a firehose, especially if you're newer to social media business promotion. Read it over a couple times and get familiar with Facebook and its powerful advertising platform.

Although I consider Facebook advertising the "holy grail" of marketing at this stage of the game, it's vital to take a comprehensive approach and incorporate the free, organic strategies outlined here. However, don't think you have to implement everything at once! You don't.

Take one strategy, get it going to where it feels comfortable, and then move on to the next. We want to stack and layer method on top of method. Eventually, the snowball turns into an avalanche!

Follow these steps we've outlined:

1. Create a Facebook fan page if you don't already have one.
2. Start to build your fan base/audience by using the tactics outlined.
3. Get in the habit of posting three to five times per day on your Facebook fan page.
4. Set up a Facebook group around your topic.

5. Set up your first Facebook ad. Once your squeeze page is live, you can build your list, collecting names and emails in exchange for valuable content.

6. Use retargeting in conjunction with your Facebook ads. This is where a cookie gets placed on the computer of anyone that visits your site. Then this person will see your advertisements on different sites they visit.

Imagine this scenario: You're on Facebook, hanging out with friends, and then you decide to click on an ad for a product you find interesting. When you're taken to that product page, you get sidetracked because you hear the dog barking at the mailman. You head over to the window to calm your friend down. However, you totally forget what you were doing and the computer shuts off.

Tomorrow, you wake up and happen to be on CNN watching the news. What do you see? Why, it's a banner reminding you to check out that same product you saw yesterday! How coincidental … or is it?

Not only does this advertisement follow you around online as a reminder, but you see it on very credible websites (ABC, CBS, NBC, etc.). Now it has a whole new layer of credibility. You finally go back to the product page, have a look, and buy!

This is such a powerful, effective strategy because research shows the average consumer will need to hear and/or see your message seven to ten times before they buy. Just like with email marketing, the big money is in the follow-up!

Perfect Audience and Adroll are great retargeting companies to couple with ads.

Always test and fine-tune your ads strategy. Keep testing. Measure and consistently improve your results.

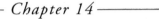

Chapter 14

LUCRATIVE YOUTUBE
MARKETING TACTICS

If you set your goals ridiculously high and it's a failure,
you will fail above everyone else's success.
—James Cameron

I f I had to choose one social media platform that has had the GREATEST impact on my business and life, it would have to be YouTube. In 2006 when this video sharing network launched, it completely revolutionized the Internet. It allowed the average "non-techy" person to broadcast themselves online with ease.

Here are some statistics that will show you just how large YouTube has become and how it's influenced our culture:

- More than one billion unique users visit YouTube each month.
- Over six billion hours of video are watched each month on YouTube— that's almost an hour for every person on Earth.

169

- 100 hours of video are uploaded to YouTube every minute.
- 80 percent of YouTube traffic comes from outside the US.
- YouTube is localized in sixty-one countries and across sixty-one languages.
- According to Nielsen, YouTube reaches more US adults ages eighteen to thirty-four than any cable network.
- Millions of subscriptions happen each day. The number of people subscribing daily is up more than three times since last year, and the number of daily subscriptions is up more than four times since last year.

When it comes to using YouTube and online video, there are four main reasons we're harnessing this incredibly powerful network:

1. To rank our videos atop the first page of Google and YouTube for keywords we've researched—this helps us get highly targeted traffic to our content and website.
2. To build trust, liking, and rapport with prospective and current customers—we want to create a continuously growing community of loyal fans.
3. To deliver immense value—viewers will then feel compelled to share our content.
4. To get a prospective customer take action—we want them to subscribe to our email list and/or buy our product.

Remember these points anytime you make a video. These are our goals.

There are only three types of YouTube marketing strategies we primarily need to focus on. The first is creating a video, optimizing it, then getting it ranked high on Google for any given keyword or phrase. All video content gets ranked on Google if done like I'm going to show you.

The second strategy is using YouTube's sponsored ads platform. This is similar to Google AdWords where you pay per click for ad placement. It's a fast way to flip a switch and get in front of your perfect audience if you have a small budget.

The third method we can use to our advantage is "piggybacking" on trending videos or hot news topics. We'll discuss that more in a bit.

Setting up your YouTube channel

Getting started is easy. The first thing you need to do is go to YouTube.com and open an account if you don't already have one. It takes a few seconds. Accounts are synonymously referred to as "channels."

Once you sign up, they'll send you a confirmation email with an activation link included. Click that link inside the email and you'll be good to go.

Create Your Channel Icon and Art

Your channel icon is basically your profile picture. You can either upload an image from your computer or select a still image from one of your already uploaded videos. If you upload an image (which is what I recommend), upload one that's 800px by 800px.

For your YouTube channel artwork, the network recommends you upload a single 2560px by 1440px image. This gives the best results on all types of screens and devices, including desktops, laptops, smart phones, tablets, and televisions.

Upload a Video Trailer

You can showcase a trailer that plays only when nonsubscribers visit your channel. This short video is your chance to show off your account and encourage viewers to subscribe.

YouTube allows you to choose a trailer from one of your previously uploaded videos, or you can just enter a YouTube video URL.

Add Custom Links and Links to Other Social Media

YouTube provides you the option to overlay one custom link and several social links on top of your channel graphic.

For the social media links, you need to select from YouTube's drop-down menu of social platforms. You won't be able to enter your own links, but there's a variety of social media sites to choose from, including Google+, Twitter, Facebook, Tumblr, etc.

So, what do you need to get started?

At the moment, making videos is pretty simple. You don't need to invest in expensive gadgets, nor do you need to be a "tech geek." You can shoot quick videos from a smart phone, camera, laptop, tablet, or video camera.

These days, you'll find most technology is very good at capturing quality footage. The three most important things that you need to consider (from a technical standpoint) when filming are:

- Lighting
- Camera stillness
- Sound quality

Personally, I find natural light works the best. It just looks better on the skin. Overcast days are great for shooting outside too. I try to stay away from indoor fluorescent lighting because it's not too flattering.

In terms of keeping the camera still, get a tripod and use it religiously! This is the best way to ensure your videos won't look all wobbly and unprofessional. You could have an amazing video that delivers a highly valuable message to your niche market, but if your newbie cameraman can't keep the darn thing still, it's going to distract the viewer.

They won't stick around and watch the whole clip. In fact, they might even get pissed off and click the thumbs-down button! I'm sure you'd agree we'd like to avoid that.

When talking about sound quality, you really want to try to avoid any echo when you're speaking. Echoes can be common if you're indoors, depending on the room you're filming in. To remedy this, you could get an external microphone from Amazon to complement your camera. It's up to you, though.

If you film outside, you usually won't have any echo issues, but you may have to contend with the wind, the neighbor's kids screaming, police sirens, or other external factors.

Where should you film the videos?

Sometimes you'll find me filming videos in the office, at my house, outdoors, in Costa Rica, Paris, etc. I do this to take viewers on a journey with me. When you vary the scenery, it makes you look interesting and like a real person.

So my recommendation is to switch it up. You don't need to be in a fancy studio to shoot videos or have access to a green screen. It doesn't matter where you create your content; just have some pleasant-looking scenery in the background.

Another thing to note: Don't wear the same clothes in each video. Even if you do a couple videos on the same day, switch your shirt.

Camera shy? No problem. Do this.

When you venture on camera for the first time, you probably won't like the way you look, sound, or act. You might just flat-out suck too. It's fairly common, and I can certainly empathize. In 2006, I felt very uncomfortable and was my worst critic.

My first couple videos were terrible. I cringed when I heard my voice and thought, "My God, do I really sound like that?"

However, I knew that YouTube was the way of the future, and I wanted to capitalize on the enormous opportunity at hand. I jumped all in.

One of the many great things that came from me stepping out of my comfort zone and getting on camera was that I observed my excessive hand gestures and that I said "um" sometimes. This experience helped me "decrease the blah" in my communication, which only distracted others from the important message I was trying to convey.

Now, if you're feeling a little timid, here are seven proven, effective ways to overcome camera shyness quickly.

1. *Focus intently on your message.* You have a purpose for doing your videos. You want to deliver value and help as many people as possible achieve a desired result. Once your purpose is stronger than your fear, nothing can stop you.
2. *Relax. You are the expert.* You know exactly what you're talking about. Be confident in your ability to explain the topic of choice. All we're trying

to do is take the knowledge you communicate daily offline and put it in an online video so we can expand our reach and our impact.

3. *Practice beforehand.* Repetition is king and breeds familiarity. The more you practice, the easier it gets. For some, it's difficult to speak to an inanimate object and maintain enthusiasm and focus. That's why you need to do it a couple times before you record.

4. *Speak to the camera like you'd speak to a friend.* Imagine your mom and dad are in front of you and you're carrying on a casual conversation with them. This can help ease your nerves.

5. *Don't use a script.* This might seem counterintuitive, but hear me out. It's okay to have an outline so that your bullet points are in order. However, the last thing you want is to sound scripted. If you talk like a robot reading your lines verbatim, you'll turn people off immediately.

I find that when people who are new to making online videos and try to use a teleprompter, the final product typically doesn't come out as planned. (That's not to say you can't use one in the future as you get more comfortable.)

The thing is we're creating content around a topic that we know very, very well. You probably talk about these things all day long anyway. You just need to have a few bullet points to keep you organized.

For instance, if you're a chiropractor making a helpful video for fibromyalgia sufferers, you might stick a piece of paper on a wall behind the camera that has these words on it.

- Ask a related question to create a pattern interrupt
- Introduce myself
- Talk about my experience treating fibromyalgia
- What is fibromyalgia?
- What does the research say?
- Who does fibromyalgia typically affect?
- Tips that help relieve the pain and discomfort
- Places to visit for more resources

- Here's what to do next (click "like" button and subscribe to my blog)
- Call to action

Keep it simple. You don't want to rant on different tangents or get sidetracked. Stick to the topic and your notes.

6. *Exercise prior to filming.* The more exercise you do, the more oxygen gets into your system. This has a calming effect after you've worked out and had time to sit for a bit.

If all else fails …

7. *Have a glass of wine.* Let's not get carried away on this one … if you know what I mean. But for many, one glass before taping is great for relaxation. Hey, whatever it takes.

What should you talk about?

This is a really good question and it's important to have a clear direction in terms of where you want your videos to go.

Your topics of discussion will revolve around a few different things like the keywords you've researched, commonly asked questions, myths, misconceptions, questions your target market should be asking, and reviews and comparison-style videos.

You should have dozens of keywords that you want to try to rank your videos for on the search engines such as Google, Bing, and Yahoo. In the next section, we'll cover the most important factors for getting your YouTube videos ranked at the top.

I'd also make a list of the top ten or so frequently asked questions people typically have when it comes to the product or service you're selling. If there are myths or misconceptions in the industry, you'll want to create compelling content around those as well.

Do your due diligence and see if there are other competing products in the same space that have major brand recognition. If so, you can do review/comparison videos to show people how you stack up versus the others.

What's the ideal video structure?

I provided a sample video discussion outline with the chiropractor example a minute ago. Here is a quick guideline you can use time and again for the educational "lead generation" videos you produce. I want to make sure this is super easy for you.

- *Ask a question to create a pattern interrupt*
  - ᵒ *For example, "Would you like to learn a simple way to drop ten pounds in just ten days without dangerous diet gimmicks or starving yourself? If you said yes, you're in the right place at the right time."*
- *Introduce yourself*
- *Make the viewer curious about what you'll discuss (state a couple points here)*
  - ᵒ *"In this video, I'm going to share with you the biggest mistake most make when _____."*
  - ᵒ *"I'm also going to reveal the #1 secret to _____."*
- *Deliver the goods! Share the tips that get the viewer closer to the result they desire*
- *Add third-party research for credibility (if applicable)*
- *Make a call to action (*visit a website, click the "like" button, etc.)

Do you need to edit your own videos?

No, you don't. Once you've created the raw video file, it's relatively easy to hire a freelance specialist from Upwork.com and have them do a video intro, outro, or add text and/or effects within the recording. Video editing is not something I normally recommend doing on your own.

Most Mac computers come with iMovie and most PCs come with Windows Movie Maker. Those two are simple editing programs if you wanted to take a stab at editing. Super high-end software like Final Cut Pro and Adobe Premier are very complex to learn. It's better to hire an expert that's already knowledgeable about top-level sophisticated programs.

I would suggest that you definitely incorporate a short five- to ten-second intro and outro in all your videos. It just adds an extra degree professionalism and helps your brand stand out.

If you go to Upwork.com and outsource this overseas, you can get a top-quality intro/outro for under $200. You can then use this on any new video you create. It will benefit you for years to come.

The twelve YouTube video-ranking factors

Here's how to get your videos to rank better on YouTube and Google. We're going to cover twelve specific ranking factors, many of which you have direct control over too. When used correctly, we can lock in a first-page Google ranking with our videos.

This gives us a strong competitive advantage simply because YouTube thumbnail images stick out like a sore thumb in the Google search results. Your eyes naturally gravitate toward images as opposed to traditional text listings.

It's important to create awesome content and then upload that content in a way that is going to put your best foot forward on this massive video-sharing network. Anytime you make a new video, you'll want to review this checklist to make sure all your i's are dotted and t's are crossed.

1. Title of the Video

This is one of the most important ranking factors if you're attempting to rank a video high on YouTube or Google. For many of your videos, you should definitely have the keywords in the title, preferably at the beginning—this has to make sense though.

We don't want to just stuff a bunch of keywords in the title to fill space. The title should also be clever and awesome as we're trying to garner a high click-through rate.

Here's an example title: Atlanta Back Specialist Shares 3 Ways to Instantly Relieve Back Pain.

The keywords in the above title are "Atlanta Back Specialist." If someone in that city is searching for a back specialist, odds are they're in pain. When they see a video title like this, it's a perfect message to market match. That individual will be more inclined to click the video because they're in pain and are seeking advice from a back doctor.

Make sense?

When prospective clients are doing a search on Google or YouTube, you want to have your content in front of them so that they see it and say, "Yes, that's exactly what I'm searching for!"

The title also needs to be congruent with the content of the video for maximum positive impact. If you create a video titled "Easiest German Shepherd Potty Training Trick Ever," it better be the best, easiest, and most useful video ever. If you don't come through on a title like that, you're setting yourself up for poor ratings and comments. Always follow through and deliver on what you say.

Remember, the title of your video is the initial attention-grabber when someone is searching online. You've got to do your keyword research and determine which words and phrases you want to rank for on Google and YouTube.

2. Video Description

The video description is your chance to make the viewer curious about the content of the video. You'll want to have two to three sentences that basically share, "What's in it for me?" Why should they watch the video? What will they learn? What will they miss out on if they don't watch?

Somewhere in the description section, you'll also want to mention the keywords that you have in the title (in order). It should make sense in the description, too.

Secondly, make sure to place your website address (including the http://) or relevant blog post URL in the description box. We do this for a couple reasons: (1) For SEO—a link to your website from YouTube helps your website ranking. YouTube is an authority property online, and when you get links from sites like this, it passes "SEO juice" to your own website and helps to push you up the search engines. (2) Adding a relevant link to the description box is for the ease of the user. If you reference a website in the video, you can tell them to click the link below to check out the content you referenced.

Lastly, you'll want to add a transcription of the video content. We'll discuss this below.

3. Keyword Tags

On YouTube, this is the section that's immediately below the description box when you upload a new video. YouTube brings you to a screen where you see a place for the title, description, and tags.

Using the example I gave a few moments ago, if our main keyword we were trying to rank for on Google was "Atlanta Back Specialist," we'd need to have that keyword phrase in the tags.

Typically, your YouTube video tags will be no more than five to seven words. So if our video title was, *Atlanta Back Specialist Shares 3 Ways to Instantly Relieve Back Pain*, these would be the keyword tags we'd input.

- Atlanta Back Specialist
- Atlanta Back Specialists
- Back Specialist Atlanta
- Back Specialists Atlanta
- Atlanta
- Back
- Specialist

Each of these tags will need to be separated by commas in YouTube.

If you observe what I did above, you'll see I have the main keyword, but I also have it listed in the plural. I have also reversed the keyword order because I know some people search for the condition then city in that sequence.

Lastly, you'll see that I've broken the individual words and placed them separately. One important thing to note is ALL words in the sample tags section above are relevant to the video title, content, and description.

Do not place miscellaneous words in the tags that do not belong. Keep it relevant so you have the best shot at ranking high for the money keywords you've researched.

4. Video View Count

Assuming you have the YouTube title, description, and tags input correctly, video view count is arguably the top factor for a top ranking. Meaning, the more views you have, the higher the video will rank on YouTube and Google. It's pretty simple.

Now, a slight X-factor here is if your video is actually holding people's attention. This goes back to the fact that the video should provide immense value according to what the prospective customer is searching for. If your video doesn't hold attention and people flake off within the first thirty seconds, your video will not rank as high for the keyword you've targeted.

Getting video views is pretty simple once you follow the traffic-generation methods I've outlined in this book. You can email your list to build momentum, use Facebook ads, create a blog post, share it on social media sites, SEO the video, participate in social exchanges, etc.

5. Amount of Time Watched

I spoke briefly about this above. The amount of time a viewer watches the video is important and YouTube favors content that holds attention longer. If the person checking out the video bounces off within a few seconds after seeing it, that tells YouTube the content is not good or relevant. If that's the case, they'll rank the content you created lower.

YouTube has a valuable "insights" tab where you can see when the majority of people are leaving your video. This tool can give you great data, so you should review it regularly.

6. YouTube Channel Authority

This is under your control because you are responsible for the content you create. Google constantly searches for YouTube channels that have authority, and it does play a factor in how your videos rank. If the market is more competitive, it's easier for someone who consistently creates awesome videos to rank for keyword terms versus someone who just uploads a random video.

It is a little controversial, though, in that YouTube also has the power to let any person with a cell phone rank well for a video if they have enough user engagement, which is what we're going to discuss shortly.

However, all else equal, if you have a solid channel where you have great content and good engagement on your other videos, that's going to trickle over into your current video and getting it ranked. So you need to look at all your videos as a whole along with your channel when you're trying to rank well online.

7. Incoming Links to the Video

This might surprise some, but inbound links do influence a YouTube video's ranking. Links are still king online, and you want to get them to your channel and to your videos. When you create an awesome piece of content, people will naturally want to link to it so they can share with friends.

You can expedite this link-building process by sharing your videos on your blog and social media websites such as Twitter, Pinterest, your Facebook fan page, Google+, LinkedIn, etc. It's also a good idea to email your subscriber list to get the momentum rolling.

If you submit press releases or articles, you can include a link to a video in them. Diversification is key. When you proactively build links, you want to get them from different sources and they should look "natural."

There is an informative article I wrote on my blog called "3 New Google Link-Building Guidelines (post Penguin)." You can view it at the page below. The same applies to online videos.

http://dcincome.com/blog/3-new-google-link-building-guidelines-post-penguin/

8. Social Shares

The great thing about YouTube is that it allows you to quickly and easily share your videos on different social media sites such as Twitter, Facebook, Tumblr, Pinterest, Reddit, Google+, and many more.

Google tracks these social shares, and they do affect how the video ranks. As more and more people share what you've created, the higher your video will rank if you've titled and tagged it correctly.

This is one of a few different engagement factors that you must have if you want to get as many views as possible and scale the great wall of Google.

9. Embeds

This refers to those individuals that want to take your video and embed it on their actual website, or if you want to do the same on your site or blog. The more embeds, the better a video will rank. Usually, after I post a video on YouTube,

I'll create a blog post with a few sentences that evoke curiosity, then embed the video on my blog.

To do this, all you need to do is grab the embed code from YouTube. It's located below the video you're watching under the "share" text. When you click that, you'll see the "embed" text. Click that and you'll see the code you can copy and paste.

If you don't know how to embed a video on your site or blog, have your webmaster do it for you.

10. Comments

If you produce valuable content that helps a person achieve their desired benefit, you're going to get people to comment on it. Also, a great way to spark conversation is to ask a question at the end of your videos.

Comments are arguably the number one engagement factor that helps a YouTube video rank well. Something to also consider here is that if someone that comments has strong channel authority, it looks even better.

Make a point to respond to some comments as well. This two-way interaction tells YouTube that active engagement is happening. All things equal, a video with more comments typically gets ranked higher than a video with few comments.

11. Likes and Favorites

Similar to Facebook, YouTube has its own "like" button (otherwise known as the thumbs-up). People can also click the "dislike" button or thumbs-down. Either way, you're getting engagement. Ideally, you'd like a viewer to say, "I really love this video." However, when you put yourself out there, be prepared for those that hate.

If you get a lot of thumbs-down responses, then that might signal to you that you missed the mark with that piece of content. Take the feedback constructively so you can improve next time.

Ratings (either way) can help rankings though. The same holds true if a YouTube user clicks the "favorite" button. If someone likes it enough to place it in their favorites, that's a good sign, and it is definitely helpful in garnering better search engine placement for the video.

12. Transcription

Whenever you record a video, get into the habit of getting it transcribed. You can easily hire a person from Upwork or use one of the resources I've recommended in the Tools and Resources section in the back of this book.

Having the transcription in the YouTube description box does help with ranking. However, some sources report that it's better to have it in the "captions" section. YouTube will try to transcribe your video, but the majority of the time it's not very accurate.

When you're watching one of your own videos on YouTube, look below it and you'll see a gray box with a "cc" inside it. Click that and it will take you to captions and subtitles. From there, you can add/upload new subtitles if you choose. You should be logged in to do this.

This Google support link below shares details about uploading subtitles:

https://support.google.com/youtube/answer/2734698?hl=en&ref_topic=3014331

Creating, optimizing, and ranking a video on Google

We actually discussed this topic when we were talking about the twelve video ranking factors previously. You'll want to review that a couple times and use that list whenever you upload a new video to YouTube.

In order to optimize your video and have the best chance to get indexed on the first page of Google, the keywords need to be in the title, description box, and tags. If you don't do this, your chances of getting ranked high for a relevant search term are slim to none.

For example, let's say you create a video about underwater basket weaving and you want your specific market to see it. You've done your research using Market Samurai and the Google Keyword Planner and found that "underwater basket weaving tips" is a highly searched term.

So you create a video that gives three tips every underwater basket-weaving business should know if they want to be successful. The title of the YouTube video would be *Underwater Basket-Weaving Tips*.

In the video description, you'd have your website address (including the http://) on the first line. Then you'd write a three- to four-sentence description that makes the individual curious enough to want to watch the piece of content.

An important point here is that you should also mention the keywords from the title in the description box. Don't just randomly stuff them in there either. They should make sense.

In the YouTube tags section, here is what you should have: *Underwater basket-weaving tips, underwater basket weaving, basket weaving under water, underwater, basket weaving, tips*

This process is not too difficult at all. You just need to always pay attention when you upload the video the first time. You can always go back and change the title, tag, and description later. However, I've found that doing this is not as good at getting it right the first time.

If you switch the title at a later date, it can take Google weeks to update it in their system, so you have a chance to rank for the keyword you want. Sometimes, it takes even longer.

The power of the video thumbnail image

The thumbnail image is the picture you see either in the YouTube or Google search. Whenever you upload a new video to YouTube, they automatically give you three random still images from the video to choose from. The image you select will be what viewers see publicly when they search or if your content pops up as a related video.

If your account is verified and in good standing, you may have the ability to upload custom thumbnails for your video uploads.

As you might guess, the image that people see from the video should evoke curiosity and compel them to click. We want to make it unique so it stands out from the crowd. A simple way to see what type of images are working well in your niche is to look at competing videos with the most YouTube views and subscribers.

It's also a great idea to view the channels that have the most subscribers to observe what they're doing. Many times you'll find close-up faces; bright, contrasting images; sexy women; and weird stuff or images that make people very curious.

A good thumbnail can be the difference between your video getting hundreds or thousands of free video views per day versus just a couple. No joke. I've seen it happen many times. Don't overlook this important optimization component.

The best way to mass distribute a video after it's been published

One of the things you must realize is that although YouTube is the most popular, it's just one of many video-sharing websites online. The only thing better than having a video on one site is having that video on multiple websites garnering traffic and exposure 24/7.

People would rather watch an educational or instructional video than read a book. But like a blog post, rarely will the content just automatically get shared. We have to actively promote the video to create momentum, which gives it the best chance to go viral.

Here's how to properly distribute your videos in order to get the most eyeballs.

1. Upload it to YouTube. We just talked about this in-depth. Your initial set of videos should be based on certain keywords (some content general, some that are keyword specific). You might have twenty-four videos to make, or you might have sixty. I always create new content via online video because it's easier to deliver it to subscribers.

2. Embed that same YouTube video in a new blog post. The blog post should be a variation of that video title, not the exact same thing. So, if your video is titled "Underwater Basket-Weaving Tips," then your blog post could be titled "3 Underwater Basket-Weaving Tips That Work."

3. Email your subscriber list if the video is relevant. This helps it gain serious momentum depending how large your community is. You should have two lists: one for customers and one for prospective customers.

4. Share the blog/video on social networks such as Facebook, Twitter, Instagram, Google+, LinkedIn, and Pinterest.

5. Upload your video to other hosting services such as DailyMotion, Vimeo, your Facebook Fan Page (video section), Veoh, Viddler, etc. Make the titles slightly different from your YouTube title. There's no need to pay for any subscriptions either. You can find a list of networks here:

http://en.wikipedia.org/wiki/List_of_video_hosting_services

6. Use sites such as Microworkers.com and Mturk.com. This is where you can outsource small tasks (like watching a video) where real people around the world can help you. Note: NEVER USE FIVERR for getting video views.

7. Facebook advertising—this is a simple and cost-effective way to get targeted traffic to your videos. You can either send the visitors to a YouTube video or your blog post with the YouTube embedded in it. I do the latter so I can keep the prospective customers on my website only.

8. Use YouTube in-stream advertising if applicable. This is like Google AdWords but much cheaper. These are the ads you see during the first fifteen seconds of a video. They are highly targeted and take advantage of "search" traffic.

9. StumbleUpon–, Pinterest–, and Twitter–sponsored advertising can also increase video views quickly. You'll want to test each one to see which pulls better for you.

Piggybacking on trending videos and hot topics

This is a really powerful method because you're capitalizing on what's hot in the news media. If you intend to piggyback on breaking topics, you need to be able to pull the trigger and create good content fast—I mean within a couple hours.

Don't be random with this either. Stick to your industry. If you're selling health and beauty products, you're not going to want to piggyback on a YouTube video uploaded by CNN that discusses "presidential election results."

Let's say celebrity Charlie Sheen undergoes a bad plastic-surgery procedure that's extremely evident to try and look younger. Let's also say you have a blog about natural ways to slow the aging process.

If the Charlie Sheen story breaks RIGHT NOW, is all over the news, and CNN uploads the video to YouTube, you have a small window of opportunity to attract a windfall of viewers. The video you create should be uploaded that same day within a couple hours (or less).

If the CNN video is titled "Charlie Sheen Plastic Surgery Fail," then you'd want to title your video almost the same. A sample title would be "Charlie Sheen Plastic Surgery Fail: What They're NOT Telling You."

In your description box, you need to have the keywords and a couple sentences, but you should entice the viewer by things the media is not telling them. This is just an example. As we spoke about before, your title, tags, and description need to have those keywords that CNN is using.

Aside from quickly discussing the hot topic in your video, you might also offer tips and strategies for those that are considering plastic surgery but don't want to go under the knife because of the fear that something could go wrong.

We're not trying to "sell" any product in this video. We just want to give the viewer some great information and then make a call to action at the very end that leads to our free report or other ethical bribe. The possibilities are endless when it comes to this promotional strategy.

We're capitalizing on YouTube's most popular videos to flood our own site with qualified visitors. With this piggyback method, I have personally amassed HUNDREDS OF THOUSANDS of video views without spending one cent on paid advertising.

I've had many clients tell me they've done the same. Use this clever strategy to your advantage as soon as possible.

AdSense for YouTube

This section was taken directly from Google. AdSense is a free, simple way to earn money by displaying targeted ads next to your online content. With AdSense, you can show relevant, engaging ads to your site visitors and even customize the look and feel of ads to match your website.

How it works:

1. You make your website ad spaces available by pasting ad code on your site, and you choose where you want the ads to appear.

2. The highest-paying ads appear on your site. Advertisers bid to show in your ad spaces in a real-time auction. The highest-paying ad will show on your site.

3. You get paid. Google handles the process of billing all advertisers and networks for the ads on your site to make sure you receive your payments.

You can sign up for AdSense at:

http://www.google.com/adsense/

Criteria for YouTube Partnership

Your YouTube channel may be eligible for the YouTube Partner Program if it meets the following criteria:

- The program has launched in your country. (If the program is not available in your country, you will see a notification in your monetization settings.)
- Your account is in good standing and hasn't previously been disabled for monetization.
- You upload original, quality content that is advertiser-friendly.
- Your video content complies with our Terms of Service and Community Guidelines.
- You have reviewed YouTube's copyright education materials.

Set Up Your YouTube Channel and Videos for Monetization

This is where you get paid by linking AdSense to your YouTube account. Becoming a YouTube partner allows you to monetize your videos on your channel and earn money from the revenue earned.

Here's how to enable your YouTube channel for monetization. First, you'll want to check your channel's eligibility. To do this:

1. Visit the "Monetization" tab in your account settings.
2. If your account is in good standing and hasn't been previously disabled for monetization, click "Enable My Account."
3. Follow the steps to accept the YouTube monetization agreement. You may see a different message if your account is not eligible for monetization.

Monetize Your Videos

You may enable eligible videos to earn money from relevant ads after you opt in your channel for monetization. This guide at the link below has more information about how you can enable monetization for specific videos.

https://support.google.com/youtube/topic/24324?rd=1

You also need to associate your YouTube and AdSense accounts in order to begin receiving the revenue you've earned from monetizing your videos.

Approaching popular YouTube users and buying link placement

YouTube has a variety of weekly success stories. We're talking about kids and adults that will create a video that becomes a smash hit within a couple days. Many of these people don't know the first thing about business either. They have no idea they're sitting on a goldmine.

I see very few online entrepreneurs using this tactic I'm about to share, so the opportunity is massive.

Why not approach one of these YouTube channel owners that has hundreds of thousands of subscribers and offer to pay them to put a link in their most popular video? If you offer some high school kid $100 per month to put a link in at the top of his description box and possibly an "annotation" in the actual video, he just might take you up on that because it's free money. (Ideally, we want to strive for relevance here as well.)

Let's say the video you're scouting has over one million views and grows by 20,000 per day too. Maybe it's a video that shows people how to increase their vertical leap by six inches in just a week. It was made by a senior in high school because everyone kept asking him how he jumps so darn high. BOOM! This kid uploaded the home video and it went viral.

We just happen to find it by doing our own search on YouTube. What if you had a product for basketball players that complemented this video content? The product you either developed or are an affiliate with is called, "How to Slam Dunk a Ball in Two Weeks or Less Even if You're Only 5 Feet 7 Inches."

What you have to offer goes perfectly with the video training. If this high school kid accepts your offer and you're now paying $100 per month, you know you need to make that much to break even.

Within a couple months, you'll know if the alliance was a winner. I had a private coaching client do this, and he was averaging a 10:1 return on investment (ROI). Meaning, for every dollar he spent he would get ten in return! Who wouldn't spend $100 to get $1,000? I'd do that all day EVERY day of the week. I'm sure you'd agree.

This is the type of opportunity you have if you work this strategy the right way. There are countless numbers of popular videos on YouTube where the channel owner doesn't have the first clue about how to monetize their following.

YouTube sponsored advertising

This is otherwise known as "AdWords for YouTube" and is flying low under the radar at present. You get charged per video view, but if you do this correctly, you'll pay pennies on the dollar for high-quality search traffic!

Here's what Google has to say about this powerful platform. I've included the transcription below, but you can view the tutorial titled, *How to create an AdWords for Video Campaign*, at this link:

http://youtu.be/Sv7q0ngsHlE

"With AdWords for video, you can introduce your business to billions of viewers on YouTube and beyond.

This video will show you how to:

- *Set up your first AdWords for video campaign.*
- *Create your video ads and choose how they'll appear and*
- *Choose the audience that should see your ads.*

Before you start, we recommend that you link your YouTube and AdWords accounts. You'll need to have the channel's YouTube login credentials or the video owner's permission.

You'll see linked accounts at the bottom of the Linked YouTube accounts page.

When you're ready to create your new video campaign, sign in to your account, choose the Campaigns tab, and then click the New campaign (+CAMPAIGN) button.

Enter a campaign name and your daily budget.

Next, choose the ad networks where you'd like your ads to appear. We recommend leaving all networks selected to expose your video to the largest possible audience.

Now, choose your target locations and languages. Make sure your selected language matches the language spoken in your video.

To create a new video ad, you'll need to tell us which YouTube video you'd like to advertise.

You can search for the name of your video in the box, or enter the YouTube URL here if you know it.

If you have video content you'd like to promote before short or long-form videos on YouTube and the Google Display Network, you can create an in-stream video ad.

Under "in-stream," you'll enter a display URL and destination URL.

If you want, you can add a companion banner, which is simply a box inside of or next to your video ad where you can add a promotional image or other video. Decide if you want to use an auto-generated image from videos in your own channel or upload your own image for the companion banner.

With annotations you can layer text, links, and hotspots over your video to add interactivity and promote engagement. You can show or hide annotations from your ad.

If you want to show a video next to YouTube videos, as part of a YouTube search result, or within other website content across the Google Display Network, you can create an in-display video ad.

Just choose a thumbnail image, and then add a headline and 2-line description for your ad.

Select a squeeze page for your ad.

And then give your ad a name.

You can set custom tracking parameters if you want.

Next, you'll choose how often you want to rotate your ad and set a limit on how frequently your ad will show.

When you're done, click Save and continue.

Next, select how much you want to pay when someone views your video. This is called your "Max cost-per-view, or CPV, bid." This is the most you're willing to pay when someone watches the first 30 seconds of the ad or watches it all the way to the end, whichever comes first.

You can select a default maximum CPV bid for all ads in the campaign or select Customize bids per format to set individual bids.

Your ad traffic estimates will update as you make changes.

You can choose to limit your ad's reach by using demographic targeting, for example, by age, gender, or specific interests.

You might want to keep your default settings to reach all viewers. For example, if you choose to target only men and women aged 55-64, you could significantly limit your ad's exposure.

Once you're done with your targeting settings

Click Save targeting group.

You're all done creating your first video ad and campaign!

Now you know how to create an AdWords for video campaign that shares your story with a whole new audience on YouTube.

For more help with creating a video ad campaign for YouTube, check out the AdWords Help Center."

The #1 sponsored ad to run on YouTube

Of all the ads mentioned above, the "in-stream" ads are arguably the most lucrative and effective. You can use them to raise awareness, drive website traffic, generate leads, and make sales. Some marketers also refer to these as "pre-roll" ads.

Because relatively few businesses know how to use them, these in-stream ads are really cheap too. We've gotten as low as nine cents per view before. I would strive for twenty-five cents per view or below. Anything higher than that means you're doing something wrong.

Successful social media advertising on YouTube depends on how well you target your prospective customer. You've got to do your homework and know your market inside and out. What publications do they read? What TV shows do they watch?

Here are your targeting options for the in-stream ads:

- Geography
- Language
- Demographics
- Topics
- Interests

The first three should be relatively easy, and you might know them off the top of your head. Topics and interests are the primary targeting options though.

They both use a similar set of categories to help you show the ad to the right individuals, but the difference is that "topics" are the type/category of videos that people are watching right now.

The "interests" option is for showing the ads to someone who watches videos of a specific topic even if they're viewing something else at the moment. There are numerous categories and subcategories. You need to go through them with a fine-tooth comb and think, "Is this subcategory one that my ideal customer is likely to watch? We want to get as specific as we can at this stage because we don't want our ad to get shown to those that are not qualified or interested in what we're selling.

There will be occasions that this cannot be avoided. However, an easy way to solve this problem is by calling out your perfect audience AT THE START of the video you create.

For example, if you created a product that helps tennis players serve faster, you might open the video ad by shouting, "Are you a tennis player?" Or you could start the video by saying, "This one simple trick adds an extra twenty miles per hour to tour serve almost instantly!"

You've essentially called out your target market in the first few seconds of the ad, which is what we must do. Questions are great because they create a pattern interrupt, causing the viewer to think and then respond.

The second intro example I gave above is where we've featured a benefit that our audience is looking for. Both are great ways are open a video advertisement.

If we don't grab their attention in the first few seconds, then we're up the creek without a paddle if you know what I mean. We'll end up paying a much higher cost per view.

Be creative and direct. Get to the point fast. You can even be outrageous.

How to create a compelling video for your YouTube in-stream ads

You really have three options at this stage. Videos can be created with you speaking in them, they can be quick testimonials from happy customers, or they can be animated and have simple narration. Regardless, keep your videos between thirty seconds and two minutes maximum.

My strongest suggestion is to use these in-stream ads to get people onto your email list first before you try and sell them. Like I've talked about many times in this book, we want to offer an ethical bribe like a free report or free video training series in exchange for a name and email.

So going with the tennis product example above, we'd have a YouTube in-stream ad that calls out our ideal audience like: "This one simple trick adds an extra twenty miles per hour to tour serve almost instantly!"

We would then say something like, "In this free video you'll also discover _____."

Rattle off an extra two to three persuasive "benefit-rich" bullet points that tell the viewer what result they'll generate by grabbing this information now. Or let them know the biggest mistakes most tennis players are making.

Refer to the previous squeeze-page examples in this book for ideas.

We can also use the prospective customer's pain points to influence their decision making. No one wants to experience more pain. In fact, most people are MORE LIKELY to take action when it's to avoid pain, rather than to seek pleasure.

Finally, at the end of our short video, we tell people exactly what to do next, and we show it on the screen. If you want them to visit your site to grab their free training video, say it and flash the URL on the video.

Here's the great news: Actually creating a good video is a HUGE obstacle for most people. That's arguably been the main reason that the overwhelming majority of businesses have stayed away from YouTube in-stream ads. The creation process stops them dead in their tracks. The barrier of entry is perceivably high. What does this mean for you?

Quite simply, it means very little competition.

Getting your video created for the ad is not as expensive as you might think either. Yes, you could pay a company between $3,000 and $5,000 to get an over-the-top professional one with all the bells and whistles. But that's not what I'd recommend.

You can easily go to Upwork.com and hire a video specialist overseas to do a great job for you at a fraction of the cost you'd normally pay. That's up to you. It doesn't hurt to review all your options.

Here are some powerful tools and resources that help you create high-quality affordable videos:

- *PowToon.com* (they have a free branded version but you'll want to pay for the upgrade)
- *GoAnimate.com* (not free but a more advanced software program)
- *Promoshin.com* (more costly, but very professional)
- *Doodle-Video.com* (done-for-you whiteboard-style sketch videos)

IMPORTANT NOTE: Inevitably, someone is reading this right now and is thinking to themselves, "Why haven't you talked about building your YouTube channel subscriber base?" I mean, you see many of the top YouTube channels always pushing to get subscriptions.

Here's what you need to know: 95 percent of the top YouTube channels that have the most subscribers are not marketers. So they really aren't making that much money from their channels. Do you know where the bulk of their earnings come from?

It comes from the channel owner allowing Google to run ads on their videos. This is AdSense, and we spoke about it in this chapter. Just remember, you have to apply to be a YouTube partner to be able to feature ads on you videos and get paid for it.

I know a couple top YouTubers that have over a million subscribers. They're making between $7,000 and $10,000 per month by allowing YouTube to run ads on their channel. That's NOT a lot compared to what they should be making. Many of these men and women aren't building an email list off YouTube either.

This is plain dumb.

Why?

Well, what happens if YouTube decides to change their terms of service one day and finds that one (or many) of your videos violate their policy guidelines? Sometimes they give you warning notice; other times they'll terminate your account without any correspondence. I know. I've been there.

The goal of using social media platforms such as YouTube, Facebook, Twitter, Instagram, Pinterest, LinkedIn, and Google+ is to get people OFF these networks and onto an email list that you control. This is how a savvy business owner looks at it.

If you're not selling anything and just hanging out with friends, then this doesn't apply to you. However, if you want to create and grow a sustainable (and highly profitable) business that feeds you 24/7 for years to come, you need to think like an Internet millionaire.

The real money is in the email list! Never forget that.

AdSense earnings are just icing on the cake. These top YouTubers I just spoke about would be making five to ten times what they're making if they were knowledgeable about email marketing.

Smart entrepreneurs don't chase subscribers. Subscribers result from creating excellent content on a regular basis. Of course, we should always issue a call to action at the end of the video and tell viewers what to do next. After you direct the viewer to your website to download your free report or video training, tell them to subscribe to your channel.

We can also include an "annotation" in the video that links to our YouTube subscription button. These annotations are little colored pop-up boxes that you can feature at any time in the video. They stick out like a sore thumb and grab attention. Place one in the video when you tell the viewer to subscribe.

Learn more about YouTube annotations here:

https://www.youtube.com/yt/playbook/annotations.html

Yes, we want people to subscribe to our YouTube channels, but it shouldn't be the primary goal. Got it?

Action Step: You'll want to incorporate all the strategies mentioned in this chapter in your marketing and promotional efforts. Online video is something you'll never stop doing. For me, it's MUCH easier and faster to create a simple video than to spend two to three hours writing a single blog post.

I take my camera with me wherever I go, and you should, too. If you become inspired or have an important lesson you want to share, draft a quick outline and then press the record button. Remember, most of your educational videos should be bite-size and under five minutes.

Make a list of keywords you want to rank for on Google, Bing, and/or Yahoo, and then start creating stellar video content around them. You might have a list of a couple dozen keywords initially. That's fine. Commit to doing at least three videos per week. If you can do more, fantastic! Just like with any form of marketing, consistency is key.

Keep your eyes peeled for hot, trending topics where you can add value and piggyback to get massive amounts of free exposure.

Actively seek out YouTube channels that are specific to your industry. Find the ones that are getting hundreds of thousands (or millions) of video views, and then message the channel owner to see if they'd be open to you paying them for ad space.

Test the YouTube in-stream ads regularly to find your sweet spot. Once you hit the optimal cost per view, scale up your budget and see how many sales you're getting out of 1,000 views. If your return on investment is 5:1 or greater, great! If not, test other ads until you hit your goal.

Chapter 15

HOW THE PROS
CASH-IN ON TWITTER

Success is the sum of small efforts, repeated day-in and day-out.
—Robert Collier

O f all the social networks that have come and gone throughout the years, Twitter is probably the MOST misunderstood. It's so much simpler than Facebook, yet for many, it's like drowning in an ocean of endless chatter.

Twitter is what's classified as a "microblogging" platform, which literally means "small blog." You have only 140 characters to work with in your status updates, so you have to be short, sweet, and to the point.

Like Facebook, you're able to upload photos to your status updates as well.

On Twitter, the news finds you quickly! This is a social network that centers around "down-to-the-second" conversation. This is incredibly powerful for many reasons. One of the most easily observed is in politics.

We've seen examples in the last few years where social media has seriously sped up the protesting process in countries such as Egypt, Iran, and the Ukraine. It's also dramatically accelerated the organization of revolutionaries, transmitted their message to the world, and galvanized international support.

Here are some Twitter statistics that might interest you:

- There are 284 million monthly active users.
- 500 million tweets are sent per day (that's 350,000 tweets sent per minute).
- 80% of Twitter's active users are on mobile.

I submit to you today that Twitter is one of the MOST valuable marketing tools ever created. If you have the right message targeted to the right market, it can spread like wildfire!

The first thing you need to do if you haven't done so already is open an account. They'll probably send you an email asking you to verify that it was actually YOU that opened the account. You'll click the link contained in their email.

Once done, you're ready to add your personal info to your profile—including your website. You'll upload an avatar image. This can be a professional picture of you. Then you can upload a custom background image. You want this graphic to be congruent with all your other social networks for branding purposes.

In order to get the party started on Twitter, you'll want to "follow" some people that you know. These can be celebrities, friends, news channels, restaurants, etc.

When you follow someone, you can click the "home" text at the top of the page, and it will direct you to the newsfeed. This is similar to what you see on Facebook, only less cluttered. Anytime you, or a person you follow, updates a status, it's called a "tweet."

As you view tweets from your friends in the newsfeed, you can either reply to them, favorite the tweet, retweet the post, or click the three dots you see in the image below. That brings up more options such as share via email, embed tweet, mute, and block.

To clear up some terminology confusion, let's briefly go over a few words:

- **Reply** – Refers to when you click the arrow pointing to the left. The @ symbol will appear, and you can respond directly to that person. They'll see your reply too.
- **Favorite** – This is basically the same as the Facebook "like" button in that it tells the other person that you liked their tweet/status update. The favorite button is the star-looking icon that has the number 472 next to it, below the image above.
- **Retweet** – This is similar to a Facebook "share." If you see something you'd like to repost and give the original poster credit, you simply click the retweet button. It's the one with the two arrows in a square-like pattern to the left of the number 609.
- **Embed Tweet** – This is where you can get a custom code from Twitter then put the actual tweet on a blog post you're writing.

What to post on Twitter

On Twitter, I like to post links to blog posts I've written, links to other helpful content in my industry, inspirational quotes, videos from YouTube, informative graphics, my thoughts at the moment, pictures, etc. I will generally post more on this medium than I do on Facebook—typically around five times per day.

I also like to search individual keywords related to my industry and see who's talking about specific topics. Then I'll reply to the conversation and add value.

Something to remember, if you're simply replying to a status update on Twitter, it won't show on your profile home page by default. Others coming to your profile will only see your tweets unless they click the "tweets and replies" text as show in the image below.

If you would like your reply to a person to be seen by default and on be on your profile home page, you must add a character before the @ symbol.

So, let's say I'm tweeting to @tonyrobbins and responding to one of his motivational videos. If I just click "reply," type the message, then click "tweet," it will not be featured on my profile page by default. However, if I add something like "Hi @tonyrobbins (insert tweet response)," this update will now be seen by default on my profile home page.

The eight best ways to leverage Twitter

1. Keep in touch with your existing customer base.

This is basically where we encourage clients to follow us for updates related to their membership, new content, seminars, events, etc. We can also maintain top-of-the-mind awareness with current customers.

Customer support also falls into this category. If I ever have an issue with a company or brand, I tweet to them on Twitter. If the company is on the ball, response time is usually under an hour.

2. Acquire new followers in your related market who fit your ideal customer profile.

We can use Twitter's "advanced search" for this purpose (more on that later), or we can use their advertising platform. We're also able to follow others in hopes that they find us interesting and follow us back.

For example, let's say you're trying to become known in the personal-development space. Tony Robbins is on Twitter and is arguably the most famous person in that industry, boasting over 2.5 million followers. It's highly likely those individuals that follow him and subscribe to his updates are interested in self-improvement.

If you have a product related to that, your biography and background profile graphic would reflect this. You'd then follow his followers to target the right market. You'll find a certain percentage will follow you back if you appear interesting enough.

3. Rank high on the first page of Google search.

Twitter profiles rank exceptionally well on Google at this time, so we can strategically use that to our advantage. This won't be applicable in all situations, but it's something to consider. Normally, I'd recommend using your own personal name for the profile name, but you could do something different.

Let me give you an example. Let's say you're a dentist in Phoenix, and you're fairly new to the area. Other doctors have been online for several years, so you know it will take time to compete with them if you're just purely doing SEO on your dental website.

But, you discover that Twitter (like YouTube) ranks really well on Google. So you can essentially piggyback off the authority of the site.

When you create your profile on Twitter, instead of entering your first name, enter the word "Phoenix." Instead of entering your last name, enter "Dentist." So your profile name appears as "Phoenix Dentist."

This strategy comes in handy if you're new to a market. No one is going to be searching for your name because they don't know you. However, prospective clients search for keywords/topics they know all the time.

We're just trying to position our brand in front of where people are already searching so we can capitalize on continuous Google search traffic.

4. Become a trusted, valuable source of industry information.

When you post tweets with great content (either yours or from others) that helps your market achieve the end result they're seeking, you become a trusted authority. You'll attract more followers, and people will start to engage with you.

Remember, consumers do business with those brands they know, like, and trust. We ideally want to be the go-to resource for people in our market. When they think of (insert your specialty), we want them to think of us first!

5. Search for live, up-to-the-second keywords/topics people are discussing.

This is the most powerful feature on Twitter, hands down! You can literally tap into conversation, solve problems, and engage in real time. Now, you could use the regular search at the top of Twitter for this, but the "advanced search" page is better.

You can find it here:

https://twitter.com/search-advanced

You'll be able to search things like words, people, places (location), dates, and other things like positive/negative sentiment. It doesn't matter if you have a local, free-standing, national, or international business; you'll find this search function extremely advantageous!

When you're on the advanced search page, it should look something like what you see below.

Let me show you a quick example that's applicable to any type of business. If you just happen to be a chiropractor in Atlanta and are searching for people that are talking about headaches right this minute, you can use the advanced search.

Here's what came back when I input the data:

As you can see from the screenshot above, seven people in the last minute tweeted about headaches! What you don't see from the screenshot is the fact that as I scrolled down, I counted twenty-two people in the last minute that tweeted about headaches.

Were all of those people qualified for a chiropractor to give some helpful advice? No, they weren't. Some just mentioned the word "headache" but didn't have real pain associated. However, as I counted the numbers, 40 percent of those tweets were qualified. Meaning, these people actually had a headache that a chiropractor could potentially help. Mind you, those numbers were just in the last minute too!

However, keep in mind that the goal here is not to just spam your website links when you reply. You need to enter the conversation and provide value first. Give some tips and/or strategies that will get them closer to the end result they're seeking. In this example, real people are looking to get rid of the splitting pain in their head!

You can do the same thing regardless of whatever niche market you're in. You can search industry specific keywords or potential problems people have.

Your job is then to enter the conversation and be a problem solver. Offer a helping hand. You can bet this individual will see your profile and check out what you do.

Even if they don't respond, you'll still be seen as a value provider because it was nice of you to try to help. This act creates goodwill in the marketplace.

IMPORTANT: As you go about implementing this strategy, make sure your responses are different for each person. You don't want them to appear "canned." It doesn't look authentic on your behalf, and Twitter does not like this. If you send the same exact response to twenty people, Twitter will view that as spam and potentially block your account. That's the last thing you want to happen.

Be original, sincere, and authentic. It will come across in your writing, and prospective clients will be receptive to you because they'll feel you're genuinely there to help.

This insanely powerful method of offering free advice that helps improve the lives of others has gotten me thousands upon thousands of Twitter followers.

Did I know any of these people beforehand?

Nope.

That's okay, though. This is a social network. People are there to be ... guess what? SOCIAL! It's about meeting and connecting with other like-minded people that add value to your life. Don't be shy—just get in the game!

6. Harness the Twitter advertising network and pay per click.

Twitter has its own form of paid native advertising which allows you to promote your account and also promote selected tweets. The great thing about this platform is that you can set a low daily budget you feel comfortable with, and there is no minimum daily spend either.

Twitter allows you to target ads by country, city, gender, language, interests, keywords, usernames (popular accounts), and TV shows. If you have an email list, they allow you to upload it and show ads to that list only (just like Facebook does).

Your cost-per-engagement bids can either be automatic, or you can manually bid. They will give you suggestions on what amount to bid, but I always recommend starting 50 percent lower for a couple days to track how many engagements you'll get.

To get started, visit:

http://ads.twitter.com

Get your account set up and you can start testing some ads. A good cost per engagement to strive for is below thirty-five cents. In terms of engagement rate, strive for above 1 percent.

If you already know who's famous in your target market, you can easily set up ads to target those individuals and their followers! Never has getting your message in front of the right audience been more simplified.

Just like with Facebook advertising, we're not just going to funnel the traffic to a sales page on our website. Why? Because people are not on Twitter to buy things. They're on the network to hang out with friends and to see what's happening in the world.

When promoting a selected tweet, we want to drive Twitter users to a squeeze page that offers an "ethical bribe" or a high-value blog post that has a clear call to action at the end. Think email list building FIRST when advertising on social networks.

If you need a refresher on how to structure the ads, see the Facebook chapter in this book. On Twitter, you just have fewer characters to work with, so your ads need to be more concise. You can still add images to some, but it's not required like on Facebook.

If we were placing ads with Google AdWords, that would be a different story altogether. People are actually searching for keywords on Google like "buy stainless steel cookware" or "(insert product name) coupon code."

Never forget the difference in the type of traffic.

By now after reading this book, you should know that one of the main goals of our marketing is to create a massive spiderweb online. Wherever a prospective client goes, we want them to see our face, our content, our ads, or our website.

We want to be everywhere so that we're the only logical choice for them when they're actually ready to pull out their credit card and buy.

While certain methods I'm sharing are more high leverage than others, we want to utterly blanket and DOMINATE the market. I want you to become the celebrity expert in your industry like what's happened to me. When you reach this tipping point, sales come fast and furious, and you can't turn the traffic machine off even if you want to.

Twitter advertising is just another accelerated way to accomplish this goal. We stack this on all the other layers of marketing, and soon very few (if anyone) will be able to compete with you.

7. Monitor the conversation around you or your brand.

Twitter has its own search bar at the top of the site, and you can plug in your name or your company's name. You'll want to perform a search with and without quotation marks to make sure you're not overlooking anything being said.

If you're a small business or start-up, you'll want to do this once per day. If you're a major brand, you might need to have a dedicated person do this. It just depends on the volume of tweets that mention your company's name.

8. Hold question-and-answer sessions with your audience using hashtags.

I like to engage this way periodically, and you should make this a part of your communication routine as your email subscriber base and social media following grows. You find major celebrities using this method on a regular basis too.

The first thing to do is create a hashtag, which is as simple as thinking of a couple words that describe your conversation. Then, put the number symbol in front of it.

Here's an example. One of my hashtags from a previous question-and-answer session was #AskDrMatthew. People would type a question on Twitter, then include #AskDrMatthew after the question to make sure I saw it. I had a separate browser tab open on Firefox to monitor this hashtag so I could see when others tweeted to me.

You can post a tweet right now on Twitter with a hashtag. Then after the update is published, click on that hashtag and it will bring you to a new screen where you'll be able to see anyone that mentioned that particular tag.

If I have a slow day and want to spark engagement with my tribe, I'll send an email to my list letting them know I'm online RIGHT NOW and they can ask me anything. You can do this spontaneously or let people know a week in advance.

Experiment with both. Obviously, if you plan the event beforehand and give your audience a heads-up, you can expect a bigger turnout to the live chat.

This is not going to be a pitch-fest. You're simply answering questions, helping your target market get closer to the results they desire. Naturally, this positions you as the expert on the topic of discussion.

Action Step: Get your Twitter account going strong, and refine your strategy according to what you learned in this chapter. Make sure you have a professionally created profile background and that your bio is complete before you start following others or interacting.

We want to lead with our best foot forward. As I mentioned previously in this book, the way your market perceives you is critically important to your success and profitability.

Use Twitter's advanced search option as your main method of connecting with prospective customers in your niche market. Become a regular and respond to ten tweets per day to start.

On top of that, I recommend tweeting three to five times per day. If you're interested in seeing the reach of your tweets, you can visit:

http://analytics.Twitter.com

and get an idea of the impressions.

These updates can be about news related to your market, quotations of interest, pictures, and helpful advice that gets your followers closer to the results they seek. You can also create content such as blog posts and videos and then post the links to your Twitter profile. Vary it up.

Chapter 16

THE PINTEREST
TRAFFIC MACHINE

We are what we repeatedly do. Excellence,
therefore, is not an act but a habit.
—Aristotle

W hen you think of Pinterest, think of Facebook without the whining. It's a virtual corkboard where you can post beautiful images about things you love and/or are interested in buying. According to the network itself, "It's a place to discover ideas for all your projects and interests, hand-picked by people like you."

Here are some insightful statistics about Pinterest:

- The photo-sharing network boasts over 70 million users.
- Over 75 percent of its membership is comprised of women.
- 42% of women who are online in the US use Pinterest.

- Pinterest drives more traffic that LinkedIn, YouTube, and Google+ combined.
- 70% of all Pinterest users are there for shopping inspiration.

Pay close attention to that last statistic by BizRate Insights. This is the MAJOR differentiating factor between Pinterest and other social platforms.

People aren't on Facebook to buy stuff. They are there to socialize with friends. When it comes to Pinterest though, users harness this visual-bookmarking tool to get ideas for purchases!

Pinterest functions like a social network, except that the updates that are posted by members are either in picture or video form. Images are the focal point.

To give you an idea of how fast an image can go viral, check this out: Awhile back I posted a stunning image of Venice, Italy, and mentioned in the text box that it was one of the most beautiful cities in the world.

Well, an hour after I "pinned" this image, I went back to my profile and saw that same image had sixty-five re-pins. What that means is that as people saw the image I posted under my "Travel" board, some decided they wanted to pin it to one of their boards too.

Think of a Pinterest pin like an update on Facebook or a tweet on Twitter. It's just Pinterest language for posting something new. Think of a re-pin like a Facebook share or a retweet on Twitter. It's when someone shares the content.

When you pin something on Pinterest, you can either upload an original image or graphic, or you can pin something you found from a website online. In the Venice example I gave, I found that image from another travel website online. I then copied the URL in the browser bar and inserted it on the Pinterest option like you see on the following screenshot.

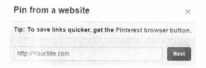

The photo-sharing network automatically populates the image on the website and allows you to write a text description underneath. You'll also see a couple boxes below that you can check in order to automatically share the content on Facebook and Twitter.

In the previous screenshot, do you see the "select a board" option? Well, this is where you can select which of your boards you would like to pin the image to. Think of boards (a.k.a. Pinboards) as categories.

For instance, if you visit

http://Pinterest.com/MatthewLoop

you'll see a collection of boards I've created. Some of them include favorite travel destinations, books I recommend, products that make me money, Facebook marketing, and LMFAO. Inside those Pinboards, you'll see a preview of some of the pictures (individual pins) contained within each board.

Now, let's go back to the Venice image I was talking about. Because that picture I posted (from another individual's website) was getting so many re-pins (shares), it ended up going a bit viral. To date, it has over 500 re-pins!

That's good news for me and GREAT news for the person who owns the website where the image is hosted. My Pinterest profile consistently gets the exposure since I was first to pin the picture of Venice; however, when anyone clicks that image itself, they are taken to the website where it's found. That means that whoever owns that website is getting a boatload of free traffic without lifting one a single finger!

This brings up a valuable point: **every single page of your website and/or blog should be "pin ready."** Meaning, every page should have a high-quality image on it just in case someone goes there, loves the content, and wants to share it on Pinterest.

If you post a great article that delivers a tremendous amount of value, and a prospective client wants to pin it on Pinterest, they won't be able to if the page doesn't have an image. Don't make the mistake of forgetting to add images to your website!

If you need top-quality, royalty-free images, just go to:

http://iStock.com.

Believe me when I say that each image will be a worthwhile investment. Not only does it enable you to get pins, but it generates passive traffic in two other ways.

If you add alt tags to your images, which describe what it is, then you'll get some passive traffic from people searching in Google images. Secondly, if your blog has high-quality images, you'll find that others "ethically swipe" them.

By this I mean they save them to their computer and put them on their own blog. The ethical part is that they give you credit for the image by linking to you. This gives you a valuable backlink and a little bit of passive traffic.

That also reminds me…

After every blog post, you must have the social share buttons that include the Pinterest pin-it plug-in. If you go to the following blog post, just look below the actual video; you'll see the related blog posts and the social share plug-in.

http://dcincome.com/blog/the-2014-social-media-revenue-summit/

Here's an example of what it looks like.

Your webmaster or programmer can install this Pinterest plug-in along with the Facebook "share" and "like," the "tweet," and "Google+" buttons. Remember, we want to make it as simple as possible for visitors to spread our content.

Here's what you need to do right now:

1. Go to Pinterest.com and register an account.
2. Complete your profile in its entirety.
3. Link it to your Facebook and Twitter accounts.
4. Make your website and/or blog pin-ready.
5. Start creating Pinboards and begin pinning images from your site, other people's websites, or from other Pinterest users.

In the following screenshot, you'll see what the profile page looks like. It has your name, location, short bio, links to Facebook/Twitter, user activity, and Pinboards that preview your pins.

When I click on an actual Pinboard, it will take me inside to view individual pins. This is what it currently looks like.

Here are seven tips that will help you create an authority profile:

1. Use a professional headshot.
2. Tell users what you do.
3. Share any credibility-boosting info (news exposure, awards, etc.).
4. Tell users what they'll find on your Pinboards.
5. Include a link to your website.
6. Include a link to your Facebook business page.
7. Get a lot of followers fast. More followers = more credibility.

Now, because Pinterest is mostly women and is full of buyers, we want to take advantage of this in order to flood our website with qualified traffic.

Do you want to know the #1 secret to getting a windfall of traffic from Pinterest?

Here it is.

Create compelling content and images that get you RE-PINS! As demonstrated previously in the Venice, Italy, example … pins can go viral pretty fast without you having to spend one dime. (Remember that re-pins are when another user clicks the "re-pin" button and pins your pin to one of their boards.)

Plus, when someone re-pins your pin, it gets exposed to all their followers, and then if one of their followers re-pins it, it gets exposed to their followers too—all the while the image maintains the original credit (you) and the original link!

Now it's time to start pinning content!

Now that your site is pin ready and you've signed up and completed your profile (self-explanatory), it's time to get active and start pinning. First, you need to create some boards. You should create boards that are relevant to your blog, website, and target market.

For example, if you have a chiropractic blog and are a doctor in Atlanta, you could have one board titled "The Nervous System," another called "Tips to Optimize Your Spinal Health," and one called "Atlanta Chiropractor Testimonials."

If you have a blog about how to potty train a German shepherd, you could have one board titled "German Shepherd Potty Training Tips," another called "Client Success Stories," and one called "German Shepherd Potty Training Problems."

Notice that some of your boards will have your money keyword (or keyword phrase) in the title of the board itself. This is very strategic because we know that Google indexes Pinterest boards and pins very well.

Here's what I mean: You could do a search for some of the most competitive keywords online today. On the first page, don't be surprised if you see a Pinterest Pinboard (or an individual pin) with the exact search phrase in the title. Let me give you a powerful example.

I just did a quick search for the words "Bohemian Leather Bracelets" on Google. This is the search result it brought back.

Out of a WHOPPING 1.53 million results for this keyword search, the #1 organic listing just below the ads comes from Pinterest! It's even ranking higher than Amazon and Etsy.

How insanely cool is that?

If you have a freestanding business in a local market, it's ridiculously simple to piggyback on the authority of Pinterest to achieve first-page Google rankings for any keyword. Similarly, if you're selling stuff online, you can get first-page rankings with time and strategic effort!

Okay, so what does a top Google ranking translate to for your business? It means you'll get the lion's share of the traffic for prospective customers searching that keyword. Not only that, a fraction of those will turn into bankable sales.

As famed ESPN anchor Stuart Scott used to say … "BOOYAH!"

Realize this: There is a direct correlation between the quantity of re-pins your Pinterest pin receives and the rankings boost you'll get in Google. More pins means a higher jump in the Google search results.

The "catch" here is that your keywords need to be mentioned in the text section of the image you're pinning. So if I was trying to rank a Pinterest pin for the keyword "best Miami cosmetic surgeon," I'd want to have a great related image and then that exact keyword phrase in the pin text box.

Remember, the key to making this strategy work is getting others to re-pin this content. You have a few ways to do this.

The first is to rely on the organic traction and sharing that will occur from followers that see this pin. Depending on your audience size, the sharing will be variable. Secondly, we can use the Pinterest advertising platform and pay to promote this pin to a targeted audience. We'll discuss that in depth later on.

The final way to get re-pins and shares quickly is to hire a virtual team to help us. Sites such as Microworkers.com and Mturk.com are fantastic for this. You basically post a task you need completed, and then workers do what you ask for pennies on the dollar. These resources come in handy, especially when you're just starting out and haven't built a large following yet.

Here's something else to keep in mind: There's also a correlation between the competition of the keyword phrase you're attempting to rank for and the amount of boost you'll get from the re-pinning activity. As you probably guessed, the more competitive key phrases need more re-pins to move up in Google's search results. There is no exact number, so you'll have to experiment and see.

Now that you're started on Pinterest, you want to create boards for topics you are interested in and based on the market you service. However, don't create too many boards to start with; you can always add them as you go along. In fact, when you pin an image, you can either add it to an existing board or create a new one.

Now, let's get pinning …

Pin seven to ten images per day, or outsource this task.

Break your pinning into batches to increase your exposure. I recommend you spend five minutes at midday, five minutes in the early evening, and another five minutes late at night populating your boards with high-quality, relevant pins.

Make your pins a mixture of original pins you find after browsing the web, ones that come from your site, and other images you find from other Pinterest users. I suggest a ratio of something like 30 percent original pins, 50 percent re-pins, and 20 percent pins from your own site. Pin only quality images and keep them relevant to the topic of your boards to ensure that people want to follow you.

How to create graphics to upload to Pinterest

There are numerous ways you can create custom images or graphics that can be used for unique pins. For starters, you could simply upload a photo that you've taken. You could also use a program like Photoshop to add text to that image if you want.

Don't have the time to create images? No worries … outsource them! Below, you'll see an image I had created by a freelance graphic designer in India. I simply gave him this photo of me in Providenciales and told him the text I wanted. He did a great job too!

Now, if you know how to quickly edit photos with Photoshop, good for you. You don't need to know how, though. Graphic designers are a dime a dozen and are easy to find. All I did was go to Upwork.com and post a job description of what I needed; then I began getting bids from all over the world. After browsing through the providers, I decided on the one who had great ratings and quite a few similar jobs under his belt.

Guess how much I paid for this 800 x 800 image?

A buck.

I'll pay that any day because I know the value of my time. Even if I was a master at Photoshop or another graphics program, my time is worth much more. Yours is too!

You might say, "Shoot, it only takes me ten minutes to do this on my computer." It doesn't seem like a lot of time. However, if you're editing six images per day, that's an hour devoted to this task. You can pay someone a dollar per image to do this stuff and leverage your time.

Now, there are numerous online websites that have simplified the process of creating simple quote graphics. Some of them include:

- http://PicMonkey.com
- http://PinWords.com
- http://Quozio.com
- http://Pinstamatic.com
- http://canva.com

When just starting out, you can create your own images if you choose. As you grow, this is a task that can easily be delegated on the cheap to a professional.

Okay, as I mentioned before, the real key to getting traffic with Pinterest is to get people to re-pin your images. One of the most effective way to get more re-pins is to have more followers.

If someone chooses to follow you, then they are exposed to each one of your pins. They are interested in what you have to share and are more likely to click through to your website when you pin something from there. They are also more likely to re-pin your pins, which will expose your image and website to their followers, who may also re-pin to their followers, and so and so on.

No matter how many times your original pin is re-pinned, the original credit will always remain with a clickable link to your Pinterest profile and the board you originally pinned it to. If someone clicks on the image, they will be taken to the original source of the image, which would be your site if that is where you pinned it from.

Getting dramatically more followers and re-pins is simply about being active. Here are some ways to grow your follower count quickly.

Follow other users you find interesting

If you see someone pin something that you find interesting, you can start following them (or the board they pinned to). You can follow individual boards rather than entire accounts so you can avoid unnecessary and irrelevant pins.

That means if you follow someone or someone's Pinboard, they get that email notification. A high proportion of people will follow you back. Or they'll click through to your profile where they could re-pin some of your pins.

You can also use the Pinterest search to find and follow others in your targeted community by searching the keyword, topic, city, zip code, etc. Look for images you can re-pin from users in the community your product will service.

Re-pin other Pinterest users' pins

When you re-pin someone's pin, they get an email notification. Chances are, they will click your name, which will take them to your profile where they could start following you, browse through your boards and click through to your site, or re-pin some of your pins.

"Like" pins from other people

If you want to show your appreciation for a pin but you don't have a relevant board to re-pin it to, you can "like" a pin. When you do, the original pinner will get a notification. Again, they may click through to your profile where they may start following you or re-pin some of your stuff.

Be sure to comment on people's pins

This is a very effective way to build a following. If you see a pin where you can add an intelligent comment, then do so. It's a much more personal way to start building relationships on Pinterest.

Add a "Follow us on Pinterest" button or Pinterest icon to your website

You can add this to your blog sidebar to get a few extra followers each day. As Pinterest becomes more and more popular, this button will become more effective. I have the Pinterest icon on my blog at MatthewLoop.com. Just look to the right below the "resources" tab.

Get your pins re-pinned by other users

The best way to increase your exposure and your following is to get your original pins re-pinned far and wide. As I've already explained, when someone re-pins one of your pins, it goes out to their followers, and it includes clickable links back to your profile and the board you originally pinned it to.

The more re-pins you get, the more exposure your profile and board will get and the more followers you'll attract. Therefore pinning really high-quality images is the key to getting more followers, more re-pins, and therefore more traffic.

Fuse your existing social networks

One of the fastest and easiest ways to get more Pinterest followers is by tying your account to your existing Facebook and Twitter profiles. Doing so (and setting up your permissions correctly) means that every new item you pin will be displayed to your followers on these networks. Since you already have established connections with subscribers on these sites, you'll find that many of them elect to follow your Pinterest profile naturally.

Make it easy to pin your content

Integrating Pinterest buttons into your blog posts, product pages, and other areas of your site can help boost the number of times your content is pinned and lead to new followers for your profile.

Because Pinterest is newer than many other social networks, simply having these buttons in place provides a visual reminder for people to subscribe to your profile and engage with your content on this new site.

Pin regularly

As with any social media site, determining how often to pin new content involves finding the ideal balance between posting so little that there's no value in following your profile and posting so often that people get annoyed with your constant updates. For best results, see the sample task list at the end of this chapter.

Name your Pinboards accordingly

Giving each board on your Pinterest profile a fun, unique, but understandable name is a crucial part of attracting new followers.

Because many subscribers elect to follow only the boards that are most relevant to them, it's important that your board names make it immediately apparent what each of your boards is about. Also, use researched keywords in the board titles.

Curate your own pins

If you only ever re-pin content from others, you aren't bringing anything new to the table, which gives Pinterest users even less of an incentive to follow you. Instead, create your own new pins based on content you find on other social networking sites or from resources you're familiar with that haven't yet been featured extensively on Pinterest.

Follow other power pinners

On Pinterest (just like on Twitter, Facebook, and Google+), following other users (especially power users with thousands and thousands of unique subscribers) is a great way to get your content noticed and spread across a much larger network of people.

To find other pinners to follow, search for a few of your industry's general keyword phrases on Pinterest and take note of the users that appear to publish the most content and have the most followers.

Follow these users yourself and re-pin some of their content. Many will return the favor by following you back and sharing your pins with their networks!

Set up a pin exchange

While it's considered inappropriate to pin your own content too frequently, you can always team up with other site owners, friends, or retailers in your industry to organize a "pin exchange" that allows more of your content to be seeded on to Pinterest without your direct involvement.

Greatly expand your Pinboards

It should go without saying, but when you offer plenty of different boards across a wide variety of interests and topics, you're creating more opportunities for people to follow you. While it's a good idea to create boards that are relevant to your website or business, consider creating boards on your personal hobbies and activities as well to reach a larger group of people.

Pin "breaking news" type content

As mentioned previously, if you want to build your number of Pinterest followers, it's important that you be seen as a "thought leader" in your industry, not just someone who re-pins content from other people.

To increase this perception, try to be the first to create pins for news items within your industry. You could even create boards to feature new products and services that are released locally or in your global marketplace, making you the "go-to" pinner serving your field.

Write keyword-rich pins for image captions

One of the ways that people find new Pinterest users to follow is by searching the site for interesting keywords or phrases in order to uncover new pinned content. If your pins don't appear in these searches, you're losing potential followers that could have subscribed to your boards.

For this reason, it's important to integrate relevant keywords into your pin captions. Don't simply stuff your pins full of meaningless keywords, but at the same time, don't use basic captions like, "So funny!" that don't give Pinterest users or the site's search engine any information about what's going on in your pins.

Make sure the pictures you pin are of great quality

Because Pinterest is such a visually focused site, the quality of the images you use in your pins will go a long way toward attracting new followers.

If the Pinterest bookmarker doesn't automatically capture an attractive image (or if there are no good images used on the source content page in the first place), manually create the pin on your own using a high-quality, visually appealing picture from iStock.com.

Which images are the best at pulling traffic?

Unfortunately, there are no rules for which images are going to get shared the most. It's dependent on a number of factors, such as time of day, the description used, and who pinned it.

Of course, beautiful women, stunning scenery, and puppies usually work like a charm, but each market will vary. Your best bet is to take a look through the most popular pins using the "popular" link at the top of Pinterest.com to get an idea of stuff that gets shared.

On the following screenshot, you'll see how to access the most popular posts section. This location could change in the future, but you should know that it's something that Pinterest will more than likely always have. It's in the upper right of the Pinterest interface.

Click the three horizontal lines to the right of the search bar first. Then you'll see the "popular" text link on the dropdown menu.

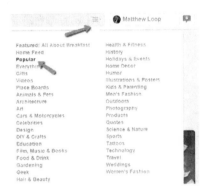

Here are even more powerful ways to incorporate Pinterest into your social media marketing and business-growth strategy:

1. Pin lots of content and do it steadily, instead of in huge bursts. This helps to maximize your exposure and engagement.

2. Think of creative and interesting board names. They get shared whenever you pin something, so make them enticing. Be creative as you need to keep your board names short. There isn't a lot of room for long, descriptive titles.

3. Tag other Pinterest users in your pins by using "@username" in your descriptions. Network with other professionals and businesses in your local community or field by using this feature. Not many people are doing this, so it's a great way to build your following and stand out.

4. "Like" other people's pins to give a thumbs-up when you want to recognize great posts or content. Remember, any action you take on Pinterest sends a notification to that person's email. People still like getting email notifications from Pinterest, unlike Facebook.

5. Pin from many different sources, instead of just from one or two sites. Variety is important on this massive photo-sharing platform.

6. Mix pinning your own unique finds with doing a lot of re-pinning. The person whose image you re-pin gets notified via email, and they also get a credit on your pin, which increases their following

7. You can pin your own blog posts, but don't overpromote. Follow the usual etiquette rules of any other social media site, and don't be "that guy" that just talks about himself.

8. Pin your YouTube videos! Pinterest has a special section just for pinned videos. There are far fewer videos than images on Pinterest at this point, so use them to distinguish yourself. Videos are simple to pin.

9. When you pin an image, add a description under it. Be smart about these descriptions because a good description will stay with an image as it gets re-pinned all over the Pinterest world. If the image is something from your own site, you can use your business name in the description.

10. Use Pinterest's embed option to publish pins as content in your blog posts and website pages.

11. Get the Pinterest iPhone app so that you can re-pin on the go, pin from your camera, and add a location to your pins so others can find your images.

12. Optimize your website content for Pinterest sharing. Use images in every single post you write so that your post can be shared on Pinterest. When you find yourself getting lazy about this, remember—not using an image in your post means no one will pin it.

13. The prettier a picture is, the more it will get pinned. The images that appeal to Pinterest members are powerful and emotive, so keep that in mind when choosing your pictures. That combination tends to work well for your blog readers too.

14. Build seasonal or holiday boards that relate to your product and promotions (e.g., New Year's resolutions, Fourth of July, etc.). Users love these.

15. Go ahead and add a "Follow Me on Pinterest" button to your blog and/or website to advertise that you're an active pinner.

16. Search for new images to pin (or for trends) by using Pinterest's search function. The search bar is in the top left of every Pinterest page.

17. Use keywords in descriptions of pins so pinners can find your images and boards when they do their own Pinterest searches.

18. Add a "Pin It!" button to the footer of each of your blog posts so your readers can quickly and easily share your content on Pinterest.

19. You can add contributors to any of your boards. Use this feature to engage your staff (if you have any) and let them contribute to your Pinterest presence by adding to your company boards. Your staff will love this, and your boards will be richer for it!

20. Add prices to your pins to create your own Pinterest shop. To add a price to a pin, type the $ or £ symbol followed by the item's price in the pin's description. When you add prices to your pins, they may be featured in Pinterest's "Gifts" section.

21. Create a board that tells the story of your practice and communicates your core values. Make this board available to people as part of your marketing process.

22. Consider creating "thank you" boards for current or past customers that send special appreciative messages.

23. If applicable, pin tutorials on your boards. Need to walk a customer through how to use your products or services? Or do you want to create free how-to videos to use as promotional materials?

    Pin your videos and presentations on special "How-To" or "Tutorial" boards. Anything you teach your customers can be made into a tutorial.

24. Be on the lookout for trends. Click on the "popular" link on your Pinterest home page to research what's catching on with pinners, then integrate those trends into your content strategy.

25. Be yourself. Pinterest is all about personal expression, so don't be afraid to pin stuff that represents who you really are.

26. Create a special board to highlight your virtual employees. Use the description under each photo to write a bio of each person.

27. Show behind-the-scenes photos of your business. People love knowing how you make things!

28. Become an information curator for your marketplace. Gather the newest and best resources for your industry on your boards.

29. Establish yourself as a trusted source of information on Pinterest, and your following will grow by leaps and bounds.

30. Integrate your Pinterest account with Facebook so you post content in both places at once.

31. See when you're getting the most re-pins, likes, comments, and referral traffic by regularly analyzing both your Pinterest profile and your site traffic stats. Test out pinning on different days of the week and times of day to maximize traffic and audience engagement.

32. Create moderated boards for your customers to express their support for you. They can add videos, blog posts, and photos from your events.

33. Do you have a number of different ideal customer types? Create a separate board to represent each client persona, then use those boards during your sales cycle and embed them into your website pages so people are clear about the kinds of customers you're trying to attract.

34. Create boards for the classes, teleseminars, and webinars you teach, and use them as supplemental material for your customers. You can use the boards during your class or presentation, or send your customers home with Pinterest boards to explore after class.

    If you're teaching a live class or workshop, include pictures from the actual event.

35. Create boards for referral sources, local small businesses, and strategic partners, and let them add to the boards. Engage with the partners so they know they are included and appreciated.

36. Allow your best clients to join in on certain boards and pin ideas and suggestions about how to get the most out of your product or service.

37. What could be better for showcasing how awesome your company is than creating a dedicated testimonials board? Do it!

38. Use Pinterest boards to tell client stories. Turn boring written case studies into powerful visual stories.

39. Create beautiful, visually interesting coupons, and add them to your boards.

40. Your customers will be blown away if you create special boards just for them that include resources and ideas tailored to their individual situations. This will really make your business shine if done regularly and well.

41. Offer exclusive Pinterest promotions. Create pins that give special promotions for following you on Pinterest.

42. Run a Pinterest contest. Invite your readers to pin links and images from your site that inspire, motivate, move, or entertain them. Then judge the winners by creativity or ingenuity and offer a juicy prize. Offer to promote the winners' Pinterest boards on your site as part of the contest

43. Sign up for Pinterest business and use the "promoted pin" option to get mass market penetration quickly. More on that now.

The power of Pinterest advertising

Pinterest offers a targeted ads platform where you can pay to get more clicks and exposure to your best pins. The great news is that it's ultra-cheap right now. We're averaging between a low eight to twenty-five cents per click!

There is no minimum ad spend either. That means, even if you have only five bucks per day to devote to it, you could run ads to get more likes, comments, re-pins, and website traffic!

My advice is to get while the getting's good. It's hard to predict how long this window of opportunity will be open.

To begin, you need a Pinterest business account. Or you can just convert the current personal Pinterest account you have into one—your choice. Visit this link to get started:

https://business.pinterest.com.

Once on that page, you'll see a link that says "get started." Follow the simple instructions, and you'll be on your way.

Bookmark the following URL since you'll be going there frequently. At the moment, there is a waiting list, but that probably won't be that way for long. Sign up anyway:

https://ads.pinterest.com/ (your Pinterest ads manager).

On this page, you can create new promoted pins, monitor existing ones, track your ad spend, see your cost per click, look at your click-through rate, view your impressions, see how many re-pins the promoted pin received, check your total clicks, and track your conversions. You'll also be able to view all campaigns that are live and running.

To create a new promoted pin, click the red button at the top that says "promote." Pinterest then brings you to a separate page where you can choose from your most popular pins. Select the one you want to advertise.

Finally, you'll be brought to a page where you can choose the targeting criteria. Among them are geographic location, language, devices, gender, and search terms/topics. You then select your daily budget and your maximum cost per click. Always start your maximum cost per click very low at ten cents.

Run the ad for a couple days and see how much traffic Pinterest delivers. If we find that price is not bringing too many visitors, we can bump it up slowly.

Ideally, we should strive for a five percent click-through rate at minimum. If the number of re-pins we get is one quarter (or greater) of the overall clicks we're receiving, that's a great ad!

In terms of return on investment (ROI), you want to shoot for a 5:1 or greater. That means for every dollar you invest, you get five back in profit. Tracking and knowing your numbers is critical anytime you're spending money online.

Remember, Pinterest promoted pins are a form of native social advertising. Our strategy and marketing funnel is similar to that of Facebook. Test these three types of promoted pins.

1. An ad that drives people to a valuable blog post of yours and then has a call to action (or special offer) at the end—whether that's to buy something or download a free report.

2. An ad that drives Pinterest users to a sales page or product checkout page where this person can buy what they're searching for.

3. An ad that sends the traffic to a straight-up squeeze page where we're collecting a name and email in exchange for information they're seeking. Review the squeeze-page section of this book for a refresher.

Here's another website address you'll want to bookmark: https://analytics.pinterest.com/ (your Pinterest analytics center).

On this page we can easily track our statistics from our Pinterest profile, target audience, and paid promotions. We can see which users by country and city are frequenting our pins most. We can also view by language, gender, and interest.

This area of Pinterest is pretty simple to navigate, and it's intuitive to use. The following screenshot gives you a quick summary of profile and audience activity within a selected date range.

Surefire ways to increase your pin engagement

It shouldn't come as a surprise, but great creativity can increase engagement on your promoted pins! The Pinterest research department studied over 100,000 pins and found that text and background are two factors that can affect the number of clicks and re-pins your pins get.

More of these key insights are captured in this guide below, so you can create effective direct-response pins and give pinners a reason to click.

https://pinterest.app.box.com/s/z6ka4sstoca8w4h01awmgistih62o82b.

If you don't want to type in that ugly link, then view some of the "best practices" at the following URL:

https://help.pinterest.com/en/articles/promoted-pin-best-practices.

Once there, you'll see blue clickable text that says "download our creative guide." That will take you to the same document.

Pinterest has also created a board titled "Great Promoted Pins" that makes it easier for you to model successful promotions. DO take advantage of their research. You can access the board here:

https://www.pinterest.com/business/great-promoted-pins/.

Here's a quick picture I thought you'd find valuable that highlights a few important factors that help increase pin engagement.

Action Step: Reread this chapter a couple times and use it as a guide when you're laying your foundation on Pinterest. Incorporate as many strategies as possible so that you set up your traffic pillars like the Parthenon.

In the event one goes down, you still have multiple pillars supporting the structure. There is a sample daily task list you can follow below.

You can do this, or you can delegate it to a virtual assistant or someone in your office. Just make sure it gets done. Doing this consistently will exponentially multiply your website traffic and exposure.

Follow at least twenty targeted people per day.

If you have a local or Internet business, use the Pinterest search to seek out and target individuals based on geography, topics, or keywords. Currently, there are no limits to the number of people you can follow.

"Like" at least twenty images per day.

Preferably from twenty different people you connect with. You can "like" two images on their profiles if you want.

Throw a quick, kind comment on at least ten images per day.

Preferably on ten different profiles.

Re-pin at least ten images per day onto a Pinboard you've already set up.

For example, maybe you set up a board for "Cool People in Lilburn." You can find images to re-pin either from the people you currently follow or by using the Pinterest search.

Pin five to ten new, original images per day.

Make sure only 20 percent of these pins are from your own site.

If you have a local freestanding business already, set up a laptop in the reception area of your office and get other customers that are on Pinterest to log in and follow you.

Remember ... EVERY TIME you take an action on Pinterest, the social network sends an email to the person you've either pinned, liked, followed, or commented on. This is huge and great for free traffic and mass exposure. Notifications are turned on by default.

Set up your first Pinterest ad in order to get automatic targeted traffic to your squeeze page, blog post, or product sales page. Test, refine, and perfect the process until you get your desired ROI.

To conclude, Pinterest is a visually appealing, highly effective content marketing tool that has been sweeping the globe quickly. Use these strategies here to drive more traffic, leads, and customers from the Internet to your business.

I strongly recommend including Pinterest as an integral part of your content marketing plan this year if you want to stay ahead of the curve and gain more traffic and exposure for your online business.

Chapter 17

HOW TO BUILD YOUR
BRAND WITH INSTAGRAM

Think big and kick ass!
—Donald Trump

I f you're new to Instagram, think of it as a fun, creative way to share your life (or business) with friends through a series of pictures. The process is simple. You take a photo with your smart phone and then choose a filter to transform the image into a memory to keep in your Instagram archive for the world to see.

Instagram has become a force in recent years and now boasts a membership of over 320 million active users! There's no sign of that growth slowing down anytime soon either. Given that the overwhelming majority of its users are under the age of thirty, you'll need to see if that's in the age range of your ideal customer.

In 2012, this massive photo-sharing network was purchased by Facebook to the tune of one BILLION dollars! This was before Instagram began to monetize their platform with sponsored ads. Here are some other statistics of interest:

- An estimated 70 million photos are shared each day.
- 41 percent of Instagram users report following brands to get perks and giveaways.
- Instagram's brand engagement rate is the highest of any social platform.
- Over 2 billion "likes" occur daily on this platform.

The great thing about Instagram is that studies have shown users are more likely to be shoppers, unlike other many social networks. Now, I wouldn't classify it in the same realm as Pinterest when it comes to buyers, but it is gaining momentum.

It's also important to realize that Instagram is a fresher platform, so people are still hyperactive when it comes to looking at their photo activity or friends and brands they follow.

Regardless of the kind of business you have, you can benefit from having a strong presence on Instagram. There is no SEO value to this photo-sharing network or "Google ranking love" like on Pinterest; however, mass awareness, exposure, and traffic can be garnered internally.

How to get started

You can take the following steps to make sure your brand takes full advantage of Instagram immediately. Sign up for an account at Instagram.com and select a username that clearly represents your business.

Download the Instagram app for your smart phone because that's where you'll be posting from. Add a professional profile image, a short bio, and a link to your website. Here's what the mobile app looks like.

Link your account to Facebook, Twitter, Tumblr, and other third-party social sites where you have an account. This enables you to share images to those networks, and it lets your Facebook friends find you easily when using Instagram's "Find Friends" tool.

It will also create a news story in Instagram for anyone who follows you on Facebook and has linked their Facebook account to this network.

You're going to want to announce to your Facebook followers that you're now on Instagram. Let them know your username. Do the same thing on any other social platform you might be on (LinkedIn, Pinterest, Google+, Twitter, etc.).

Use the "explore" button on the mobile app and search hashtags to connect with your audience. Remember from the chapter on Twitter, hashtags are simply words with the # sign in front of them. So, an example of this would be if you were updating a post on Instagram and had the word #pizza in the status.

If your posts are set to public, you can add these hashtags to your photos and videos. To tag an image or video, all you need to do is take a photo/video and select a filter. On the screen you see after choosing a filter, type your comment and a hashtag in the caption field (ex: #pizza). (Should you want to tag a post you've already uploaded, include your #hashtag in a comment on your photo.)

After you tag your recent Instagram post with a hashtag, you can tap that same tag to see a page that shows all photos and videos people have uploaded with that specific hashtag.

Here's an example of what a hashtag looks like in a normal Instagram post.

20 likes
matthewloop Have you ever met a #hater doing better than you? Me neither. Never

Keep the following things in mind:

•   When users with private profiles tag posts, they won't publicly appear on hashtag pages.
•   Numbers are allowed in hashtags. However, spaces and special characters, like $ or %, won't work.
•   You can tag only your own posts. You can't tag other people's photos/videos.
•   Instagram lets you use up to thirty tags on a post. If you include more than thirty tags on a single photo/video, your comment won't post.

Adding hashtags to your uploaded images is a proven way to find new followers and share your content with more people. However, tags can be somewhat tricky. Here are a few more tips to consider.

Get very specific

Selecting specific hashtags helps you connect with other like-minded individuals on Instagram. For example, if you post an image of a Rolls Royce, instead of just using the tag #RollsRoyce, we could use #RollsRoycePhantom.

The image will then be added to that highly targeted tag page where other Rolls Royce lovers will be able to find the photo easily (without sorting through photos of unrelated automobiles).

Maintain relevance

The goal is to keep it simple for other like-minded Instagram users to find you by making sure your hashtags describe your photo. When you use very general tags like #photo, you may get a few likes, but with over 500,000 photos tagged #photo, it's not the best way to get your images noticed and to connect with those most like you.

Relevant tags attract new followers who will take a sincere interest in your photos and continue liking and commenting on your photos for years to come.

Pay attention

Be observant in regards to other tags used on images that use the same tag as yours. You just might discover a highly popular hashtag you overlooked. Also, keep an eye out for trending hashtags that may be appropriate to tag your photos with as well as ones that fit your brand.

Trends happen very fast on Instagram. If you time an update right and use a trending hashtag, you'll be able to put yourself in front of a free traffic tidal wave where thousands of users can potentially see your post.

Monitor your brand hashtags

Many consumers use tags to connect with you and/or your company. For reputation management purposes, check your Instagram hashtags (your brand and name) just like you would on other social media sites. You'll want to respond to comments and concerns fast so that you can nourish a strong relationship with customers.

How to get more followers, increase your website traffic, build your influence, and attract a steady stream of paying customers with Instagram

Email your list. If you have an email list of clients and/or prospective clients, email them and give these people a couple reasons to connect with you on Instagram. Tell them what's in it for them. Do you post cool stuff here that you don't anywhere else?

Add your Instagram URL to your email signature. If you send out over a hundred emails per day like I do, this can be a tremendous amount of free exposure. Every email service gives you an option to add an email signature. You can include in your signature: "Follow me on Instagram at http://Instagram.com/MatthewLoop (only insert your brand name)."

Run a contest. More specifically, run a hashtag contest. This allows your fans and followers to upload photos under a specific hashtag you choose. Make sure you give a deadline as well. Once the contest is completed, you then select and publicly announce a winner.

Shine the spotlight on your followers. Share photos from your audience on Instagram and other social media websites. This is a great customer-appreciation strategy because it shows you care and are appreciative.

Everyone likes to be acknowledged, so make sure it's a regular part of your protocol. If you are going to share a photo, get this person's permission first. You can see some big companies using this strategy regularly. Starbucks is a great example. Follow them and learn.

Other ways to shine the spotlight on your followers is to "like" and comment on your followers' photos. This form of engagement is priceless. It shows you're actually listening to what this individual has to say. Most brands talk. Very few listen.

Along the same lines, respond to customers in your Instagram posts by using the @ symbol. For example, let's say John Smith is a customer and has left a question for you in the comments section of your recent post. You would start your sentence off by using @JohnSmith and then answering his question.

Lastly, we can embed images from our followers on our website. If you have a physical product that's being used by a raving fan, we can show it off as a form of gratitude.

@mention celebrities and other famous industry influencers. If you have a picture with a high-profile individual in the industry you service, post it! Tag the celebrity as well. This does a couple important things.

One, it can get you noticed by this famous person. If they like what you posted, there is a possibility they could share it with their followers. I've seen this happen quite a bit. Two, it gets you noticed by their followers since many search that celebrity's account name on Instagram.

Use image-caption posts. This is where you take a photo of your product (or anything) and then ask your followers to write the best caption. If you really want this thing to fly, do a contest and have an incentive.

Make use of fill-in-the-blank updates. This is basically where you share a post and your followers have to choose the missing word.

Let your creative juices flow. Post well thought-out photos and be original. Read up on photography tricks to give you some advanced insight on the best angles, lighting, etc. You can use Photoshop to edit pictures if you need to.

Create videos. On Instagram you have the ability to post fifteen-second videos. Harness this opportunity to share words of wisdom, tips, strategies, breaking news, etc. Video can keep people engaged, plus it mixes the content up. Yes, you can even feature your product in some videos.

Embed Instagram videos or photos. This is a cool feature that you need to take advantage of. You can embed your posts (video or images) on your website or blog. If you have a high-traffic website, many of the visitors will see your Instagram post and elect to follow you.

Facebook advertising. Yes, you could set up a Facebook ad to your target market letting them know to follow you on Instagram. This obviously costs money, but if you have the extra budget and want to accumulate more real followers quickly, this is an option. You can do the same thing with Pinterest and Twitter advertising.

Feature your product or service in an authentic way. You can show photos of real people using your stuff as they would normally.

Gather and post testimonials. You can never have too many people singing your praises. Anytime you get a success story or testimonial, post it so that others see proof that what you're selling works—it delivers the promised result.

Tell your story. How did your brand, product, or service come into being? Get real with your audience here. Don't hold back. People connect with stories, so share yours over a series of photos.

Share a glimpse of your personal life. Take your followers behind the scenes and show them how the magic happens. Post a photo of your family every now and again. You can also pull the curtain back on your business and reveal some facts or share images of employees.

Feature exclusive content. Make your audience feel special by sharing specific photos you don't post on other social media platforms.

Do a product launch on Instagram. Opening a new store? Launching a product? Taking your band on tour? Post it on Instagram first when you have the following. You can even take photos and videos of the process that's going on behind the scenes to make the launch a success.

Strategically partner with other companies on Instagram. These brands, businesses, or public figures should be in your target market where your ideal customer hangs out. This method can be used by small businesses, celebrities, personal brands, or by major corporations. Partner up and get them to post your product; in turn, you can post theirs.

Bring an offline event onto Instagram. If you're hosting a seminar, conference, meet-up, or other live event, give a hashtag for attendees to use so they can post and share photos.

Follow other users. Naturally, a percentage of people you follow on the network will follow you back out of courtesy. This can be a good way to get your foot in the door and build a tribe. Ideally, you want to connect with those who are in the industry you service—your ideal client type.

Pay Instagram power users to post about your brand. One of the smartest things you can do is to connect with other Instagram influencers in your market that already have massive followings. Shoot them an email and ask how much they would charge to feature a post by you with a link to your Instagram account or product.

Popular Instagram apps

Over – This is an Instagram heavyweight and overall favorite whose claim to fame is adding beautiful text to photos. This is what I personally use. With more than two hundred fonts, various stock backgrounds, and a ton of customization options, it's an awesome app.

You can also go to Google and type in "Instagram overlay apps" or "Instagram apps," and the search results will bring back pages of tools you can use.

This brings me to an important point.

If you want to increase conversions on your Instagram photos, sometimes it's good to overlay text on the image itself. That's what the app, Over, helps you do. Placing text on an image ensures people don't miss your message. If you want to run a sale, put the message in the photo.

IconoSquare – This useful tool allows you to access Instagram from your web browser on a desktop or laptop. IconoSquare organizes different sections of your Instagram in a clear fashion but also provides helpful statistics. It's a great free program for marketers and businesses.

How often should you post?

In our research, posting on Instagram two to three times per day is optimal. The big key here being consistent and mixing it up. Realize that you have many different types of personalities following you. Not everyone responds to the same thing. You want to regularly distribute content that engages each individual follower.

Remember, you can post a variety of things like short videos, quote graphics, helpful tips, pictures of your product, pictures of you, infographics, written text on a PowerPoint slide, etc.

Pro tip: Use a crystal-clear call to action in your Instagram post caption. This will increase the effectiveness of your post and deliver an easily understood message to your followers. In case you're unfamiliar, your post caption is the first comment that shows instantly underneath every Instagram post. It's the original comment you write when you're uploading a photo.

Here's the great thing: It doesn't matter how many other comments are added from followers after, your original caption always stays at the top and visible beneath the photo. This is the most valuable text real estate on Instagram.

NEVER leave it blank!

Be as descriptive as you need to be. Don't just repeat the text that's on the image—add to it. You're allowed up to 2,200 characters in your captions; however, keep them at a few hundred characters or less.

The goal of the caption is to get your audience to take the desired action you want them to. If you would like users to visit your website, say it! Point them to the link in your bio section, or include the website address in the comments.

If you have the website address in your main photo caption, the link will not be clickable. Some users choose to consistently change the link in their bio to reflect their most recent Instagram post. This method is good for celebrities and brands that have large followings. However, it's not too practical for the average small business owner that doesn't have a big fan base.

At the end of the day your instructions should be clear. If you want others to check out your store, call you, or send an email … tell them!

To make things most effective, engage your followers with incentives.

Pro tip II: Create or have a graphic designer create images that contain helpful tips on them. The advice you provide will obviously depend on the market you serve. What we're looking to do here is to get our viewer closer to the result they're seeking. We're trying to give tips that better their quality of life.

The following graphic is one that I had created. I bought an image from a royalty-free website called iStock and then hired a graphic designer from Upwork.com. It was insanely cheap to do this too. My designer lives in India.

His turnaround time is very quick. This is one of those tasks that can be easily delegated to someone that's more proficient than you with photo-editing programs. Speed of implementation is key.

In the end, the total cost of creating one image was two dollars. That included the purchase and design! As you can see, this one looks very professional too. It even has my website address in the lower right corner.

Some of the images you post to Instagram should feature helpful advice. When you're about to post it live, incorporate as many relevant hashtags as you can. Definitely include your website on the image in the lower right corner as well.

When you get graphics like this created, you'll probably store them on your computer like I did. Whenever I wanted to use one, I would simply post it to Facebook first (from my computer), then immediately go to the Facebook app on my iPhone.

Once I find the image on the social network, I use my phone's camera to take a picture of the screen. Now, you have the photo saved on your phone. Next, bring up the Instagram application and follow the steps. Easy!

Action Step: If you haven't done so, set up your Instagram account today. Use the strategies you learned in this chapter to become a widely recognized business, brand, or personality in the market you service.

Take one method and implement it seamlessly. Then, stack the next promotional method on top of it. Many of the tasks in this chapter could be outsourced to a virtual assistant. We want to try to systematize and automate as much as possible.

Like I mentioned before, post regularly to Instagram and mix it up. Observe some of the power users on Instagram and see what they're doing to build their brands. You might find some great strategies to model.

Instagram has a great business blog where you can observe how other brands are using this immensely popular photo-sharing network. You can find it at:

http://blog.business.instagram.com/

For any support questions or for further explanation of how certain Instagram functions work, just visit:

https://help.instagram.com

and you'll find the answer.

Something to pay close attention to is the up-and-coming Instagram advertising platform. Currently, it's only available to Fortune 500 brands, but that could change at anytime. Because Facebook owns this social network, expect it to be similar to Facebook ads.

It all revolves around native advertising. This means that the ads look like regular posts. The only difference is that the word "sponsored" appears in the upper right-hand corner so you know it's an advertisement. Sponsored ads are already appearing in the Instagram newsfeed.

As with most social media websites, when the sponsored ads are made available to regular entrepreneurs and small-business owners, the cost per click is usually much cheaper because there's hardly any competition.

Early adopters ALWAYS have the biggest opportunity and make the most money. So keep your eyes open. You can learn more about Instagram advertising at this link:

https://business.instagram.com/advertising/.

Chapter 18

SEARCH ENGINE OPTIMIZATION (SEO) TIPS AND TRICKS

If you want to stand out from the crowd, always do more
than what's expected of you. Over deliver then watch as
amazing things happen to your life and business.
—Matthew Loop

I have this love-hate relationship with Google. Sometimes I loathe the search engine giant like nothing else. Why? It's because they have a history of bullying "the little guy." From banning AdWords accounts of small business owners to updating algorithms that give unfair advantages to large corporations and private interest. Other times, I'm thrilled with all the highly qualified traffic they send our way.

One of the big reasons I love Google is when it comes to search engine optimization (SEO). All that means is getting your website or a piece of content ranked at the top of Google for any keyword phrase.

According to Wikipedia, "search engine optimization" is defined as: *The process of affecting the visibility of a website or a web page in a search engine's unpaid results—often referred to as "natural," "organic," or "earned" results.*

As a general rule, the higher you rank on Google, Bing, Yahoo, or any other search engine for a given keyword or phrase, the more website visitors you'll get from online searchers.

For instance, think of your own personal habits when you search. What do you do? You type in a keyword or phrase and then look at the search results. Be honest ... how many times do you look at the second page of Google?

That's what I thought.

Most people want their information and they want it yesterday! Part of the reason Google rolled out their famous "instant" search results was because of this.

Think about what it's like when you begin to type in your search and before you finish, Google has already brought back the top ten results. The first thing you see are the sponsored ads at the very top. They say "Ad" in yellow next to them.

Below that on the left of the search results page are the "organic" listings. I call this the trustworthy section. Consumers typically look through the top listings there, but they are more inclined to click on the top two websites that come up.

In fact, a fairly recent study from Compete.com said that the top Google listing for any given keyword (or phrase) gets a staggering 53 percent of the overall search clicks!

Visually, that means this:

As you can see, when we type in "how to potty train a German shepherd" on Google, it brings back the results you see in the screenshot. An arrow is pointing to the first listing, which will get the overwhelming majority of clicks from active searchers (much of the time). However, I want you to look below at the YouTube link you see AND the big thumbnail image that sticks out like a sore thumb.

This is something to pay close attention to.

You see, most people would rather watch a video than read an article. Why? It's because most people are lazy. It's how we've been conditioned. If we're able to sneak a video in high on the first page of Google for the keywords we're targeting, this is MONEY!

All things being equal, if a Google searcher has the choice to click on an article or a video to get the information they're looking for, they will click on the video most of the time. What would you do?

Go back through the YouTube section of this book as a refresher on how to rank your videos high on Google without spending money. It's one of the most valuable set of skills you'll learn when it comes to promoting your product and/ or service online.

Let's move on to the dirty, dirty of search engine optimization.

There are two types of SEO methods.

Black hat refers to the use of aggressive search engine optimization strategies, techniques, and tactics that focus only on search engines and not a human audience. This method does not obey search engine guidelines.

Black hat SEO is all about gaming the system and finding a loophole to exploit so you get top rankings fast. It's usually a short-lived strategy because Google is always updating their algorithm, so marketers have a difficult time rigging the system.

Then, on the opposite end of the spectrum, you have white hat SEO. This simply refers to the usage of optimization strategies and tactics that focus on a human audience opposed to search engines. This is where you completely follow search engine rules and policies.

White hat SEO is more of a long-term strategy and ensures you won't have to worry about getting accounts banned or your website slapped by Google. It can take a lot of work but the payoffs can be very lucrative when you get positioned for high-traffic search terms.

Our focus will be on the white hat method since building a multimillion dollar brand is not a fly-by-night proposal. It's not about the latest and greatest trick or gimmick.

You've got to know this though: Even though we play by the rules, sometimes we need to tread the gray area. You follow? The reason for this is that we have no clue what Google will do next and how they'll update their algorithm. Let me give you a good example.

One of Google's updates was called Penguin. Sounds harmless enough, right? You're probably imagining a cuddly black and white emperor penguin waddling slowly along the Antarctic snow.

Well, the update was anything but cute and benign! Picture a wolf in sheep's clothing lunging at you with hideous fangs that are about to penetrate your jugular vein. Yes, that's what Penguin was.

For the longest time, if you wanted to rank #1 on Google, all you had to do was build a lot of high-quality "anchor text" links that pointed back to your website. Anchor text links are just clickable text links.

EVERYONE was doing this. It wasn't just marketers trying to game the system. The average local business owner and mom-and-pop shop many times hires companies to do their marketing. These SEO companies also employed the anchor text linking methods.

Now, there were other factors that weighed in on SEO, but that specific type of link was king for over two decades! Then, all the sudden the Penguin update came along and created an apocalypse for many that sold products online. Rankings plummeted overnight.

This brings up a good point though: If you rely solely on Google SEO, without good rankings you get hardly any qualified traffic. Without traffic, sales dry up. With the Penguin algorithm update, many people were put out of business very fast.

So here's a word of advice: NEVER put all your eggs in one basket! That's why you're learning numerous ways to drive traffic to your squeeze pages, blog posts, and sales pages in this book.

The approach I've discovered (and what you're learning here) makes you "Google-proof" so your business is sustainable for the long term. Diversification is key in today's time.

As I've heard Howie Schwartz say again and again, "Google is NOT your friend!"

How to rank your website #1 on Google

If you're interested in protecting and/or increasing your Google rankings for your business website, then pay close attention. SEO has gone through a radical shift in recent times. It's important to understand what specific factors are most influential these days, along with where your time, energy, and effort should be spent.

Here are nine Google ranking factors that you, as an entrepreneur selling stuff online, should be aware of. Strategic implementation of these SEO triggers position your website on the first page of Google faster.

Page Load Speed

From talking to thousands of business owners over the years, not many understand just how much "page load speed" affects the overall ranking of their website.

This is simply a measure of how fast your pages appear when a prospective customer clicks on your website after finding you online. I'm not going to get all technical about this because you can analyze the speed yourself at this link:

http://gtmetrix.com.

If you receive a failing grade, send the report to your current webmaster and get them to do the necessary updates. You're an entrepreneur, not a programmer. Let the experts do what they're good at.

After your website company fixes the site, you can rerun a page speed report to see the improvement. Your Google rankings will thank you.

Author Rank

This is something I've been warning brands about since 2011. Google places weight on whether you're a recognized and trusted author or not. Do you have a history of publishing great content that gets shared? Not only that, are those that are sharing your content REAL authority figures in a related market?

Yes, that's right.

Not all shares are created equal and your rankings will reflect this. You need to be intimately familiar with "author rank" if you want to have a chance of scaling the great wall of Google nowadays.

Go back and reread the "author rank" section in the blogging chapter of this book. That will give you more insight into all the questions you must ask.

You need to know how to become an authority in Google's eyes, including how to create and distribute your content so it goes viral and gets shared. It's one thing to create a stellar piece of content; it's a whole other ballgame to get eyeballs on it.

This is a big reason why our company has exponentially grown each year. We've been showing business owners and entrepreneurs how to flood their websites/content with targeted traffic.

You can have the greatest site in the world, but if you don't know how to get your perfect audience to it by the truckload, it doesn't matter.

Mobile Friendliness

Google has rolled out an algorithm update that rewards the mobile friendliness of a website. Meaning, if your site is easy to view, load, and interact with on a smart phone or tablet, you'll rank higher on Google.

Conversely, if your website doesn't fit the search engine's mobile ease-of-use criteria, then it doesn't matter how popular you are—your rankings may drop. Not sure how your website ranks in terms of mobile compatibility? Use Google's analyzer tool here:

https://www.google.com/webmasters/tools/mobile-friendly/.

If, according to Google, your site turns out to be a train wreck on mobile, get it updated ASAP! Do not roll the dice and hope this thing will blow over. It's not going to.

Bounce Rate

This is basically the percentage of visitors who traffic your website and then leave (bounce) rather than continuing on to look at other pages within the same site. A page with a low bounce rate indicates that it effectively causes new visitors to view more pages and continue on deeper into the site.

A high bounce rate can mean that the website isn't doing a good job of holding visitors' continued interest. That's not always the case though.

Interpretation of the bounce rate percentage should be relevant to your website's objectives and conversion definition. For instance, certain pages of my website have a high bounce rate because we send thousands of Facebook visitors there monthly via advertising.

Our goal for those squeeze pages is to offer a free PDF report in exchange for a name and email. If you recall, we spoke in detail about this in earlier chapters.

The squeeze pages convert at over 30 percent, so they are a success at getting prospective new customers into our funnel. That's their sole purpose … period. The bounce rate on them is very high though, sometimes over 75 percent. You can see a squeeze page example at:

http://DCincome.com/go/bloggingsuccess/.

Social Shares

Social media has changed the way we communicate and Google recognizes this, which is the reason social activity DOES play a factor on how your business website ranks online. Social shares are things such as tweets, Pinterest pins, Google +1's, Facebook shares and likes, Stumbles, etc.

If your website, blog, or content is good, then others will feel compelled to show their friends. Websites with more quality shares can expect to rank higher on Google.

Remember though, the person sharing your content matters! If they are an industry influencer in Google's eyes, they carry more weight and will benefit you greatly if they take action on your content.

Backlinks

Links are still king online. In a previous blog post, I gave guidelines on how they should now be built. Ignore this advice at your own peril. Backlinks should be a mix of earned, natural-looking, general, and anchor text. Just an FYI ... no more than 5 percent of your overall link profile should be anchor text. Ideally, you want them to come from a variety of online properties like blogs, images, forums, videos, press releases, social bookmarks, articles, etc.

If you recall, links are like votes in the search engines. The more quality links you have, the higher your site will typically rank. The person and/or company linking to you matters a lot as well. Always strive to get high-quality links from relevant authority sites online, as not all links carry the same juice.

Making the links look natural is VERY important. Traditionally speaking, there's a difference between the way a marketer would link to a blog post or website versus the average Joe on the Internet.

If a regular person sees a link they find interesting or would like to feature in a blog post of theirs, they'd use natural backlinks like:

- yourdomain.com
- visit this link
- click here
- www.yourdomain.com
- http://yourdomain.com
- read about it here
- here

There are lot more natural phrases, but I think you get the point.

Google has cracked down on what they call "over-optimization" for keywords. Penguin slapped webmasters that created a disproportionate number of anchor text links. That's why it's important not to solely build exact matches anymore.

The crème de la crème of links are called "earned." This is where you create phenomenal content and others feel compelled to repost, link to, or share it on social media. One earned link from a high-ranked authority property on Google (like the Wall Street Journal, Huffington Post, or industry-leading publication) is better and carries more weight than a hundred self-built links.

Website Meta Data

"On-page" SEO is a big deal, and many online business owners don't have their websites fully optimized from this angle. Ideally the primary keywords you're targeting should be in the meta title and meta keywords of the website. You'll also want to mention those words on the corresponding site pages too.

The meta description should be a compelling headline of sorts that makes other web surfers want to click on your listing. Make it benefit rich; there's no need to stuff the meta description with keywords.

See the following screenshot for how the meta title and meta description of your website appear in the normal Google search. The arrow is pointing to the meta title. The meta description is directly under the www.wikihow.com. You can see it compels people to want to click.

Every page of your website and every blog post should have a meta title, description, and tags associated with it. The data should reflect the content on the corresponding pages too. It won't all be the same thing.

For instance, maybe you've already researched the top twenty high-traffic keywords in your marketplace and want to create website pages for each keyword, as well as individual blog posts. You can and should do that.

While we're on the subject of SEO, I also want to mention that in many cases, having the keywords in your website address (a.k.a. domain name) can also provide a slight competitive advantage. However, if your domain name doesn't have them, it's not the end of the world. If we're strategic with our content marketing, we can overtake competitors regardless.

If you're new to creating products online and are thinking about a domain name to buy, your choice can depend on your keyword research. For instance, if you've developed a product that teaches people how to train their parakeet to talk, then this would be an ideal domain name:

http://TrainYourParakeetToTalk.com.

Granted, that's a tad bit long, but it does have our money keywords in the URL. Usually, your website address should be two to four words, but sometimes we'll make an exception.

Dynamic, Unique, and Diverse Content

The original content you create is supposed to attract people like a magnet, provide value, and maintain interest. If it doesn't accomplish this, then it's failed in its primary purpose. You must think bigger than just your website or blog.

Yes, they can be your home, but you must create consumable content in every medium available to you, such as online video, infographics, press releases, articles, podcasts, etc.

Google wants to see link diversification and THEY FAVOR IT. They also give advantages to websites that consistently churn out unique content. Consistently, we see sites that have mountains of content rank higher than sites that have a little.

You can use a software tool like Market Samurai to see how many pages competing websites have on them along with other important SEO factors. Grab your free trial at:

http://MarketSamurai.com/c/freetrialnow.

Creating and distributing many forms of content through social media is also a way to position your brand in every nook and cranny online. You want to just blanket your market so that anywhere a prospective customer goes, they see you and your content.

It's about setting up multiple streams of traffic that consistently feed your business website.

A Working Site Map

This should be standard on every website, but it isn't. A site map makes it easier for Google to crawl your pages so that they can get indexed on the search engines faster. Look on your site and see if you find one. If not, contact your webmaster and let them install it.

Now, aside from the ranking factors we talked about, I wanted to share with you a Google ranking killer that's causing many websites to sink like the Titanic.

What is it?

Two words.

Canned content.

Duplicate website content is a flagrant foul, and you'll eventually get slapped for it. I've written extensively about this in the past. Also, if you syndicate another person's content on your blog, you MUST give credit to the source or risk being slapped for duplicate content.

Check immediately to see if your website company has published the same content on your site and hundreds of others. CopyScape.com is a great place to quickly run an audit. You might be stunned by what you find! (If you created your website from scratch, you're probably in the clear.)

Be creative and resourceful, but if writing is not your strength, then delegate it by hiring a ghostwriter from Upwork.com or any of the other websites you find in the resources section of this book.

Implementing these SEO factors we just discussed will keep you ahead of the curve while maximizing your organic visibility efforts. You'll be able to continuously rank at the top of Google rather than plummeting like so many business websites have done.

Now, how fast you rank depends on how competitive the market is. In some markets, ranking a piece of content (like a video) on the first page of Google will happen long before your website. That's why we have a content marketing strategy in place too. Consistency is key though. A little bit every day adds up in a major way.

Three additional resources you'll find valuable when learning about SEO and all the factors that influence ranking are the periodic table and guides found at these links:

http://searchengineland.com/seotable

http://searchengineland.com/guide/seo

http://moz.com/beginners-guide-to-seo

If you're interested in keeping up with the latest and greatest SEO news and hacks, I'd recommend you check out these two blogs:

http://SearchEngineLand.com

http://Moz.com/blog

<u>Action Step</u>: SEO is a process and you must be committed to it for the long haul. Very rarely are high website rankings achieved overnight in global markets. You've got to build trust and authority in the eyes of Google, Bing, and Yahoo first.

Once your website is up and running, all your pages need to be optimized for the keywords you want to target and rank well for.

Then you need to start creating valuable content in the form of blog posts, articles, videos, press releases, podcasts, etc. You can massively distribute this content online via the strategies you're learning in this book and include a link back to your primary website.

―――――――― *Chapter 19* ――――――――

GUEST BLOGGING SECRETS

―――――――――――――――――――――――――

If you are not willing to risk the usual,
you will have to settle for the ordinary.
—Jim Rohn

W ant to grow your influence and subscriber list incredibly fast? Are
you looking to build a name in your industry and establish expert
"street cred?" If you answered "yes" to either of these questions,
then you absolutely need to incorporate guest blogging as part of your overall
market domination strategy!

This is arguably one of the most important and underutilized strategies for
growing your tribe.

Think of this powerful method in a light similar to this: Periodically, we see
separate famous musical artists collaborate and do songs together. To give you
a great example, let's travel back in time to 1986—you know, the good ole days
when MTV used to play actual friggin' music!

Remember Run-D.M.C.? I was seven years old when I initially heard them cover Aerosmith's "Walk this Way." In fact, before that, I had no idea who they were. When I saw the music video for the first time though, I thought it was the coolest thing ever. The original Aerosmith version was catchy as hell, but this collaboration took it to the next level.

The sound seemed fresh as they had basically done something unheard of at the time: they fused rap with rock. Music is just another form of unique content, to put it in perspective.

So, how did this landmark collaboration affect Run-D.M.C.?

It launched them into mainstream stardom and has influenced hip-hop ever since. The song paved the way for other known pop artists to introduce elements of hip-hop into their music. It pioneered the trend of rhymed/sung collaborations that is still present today.

Now, let's relate this to us.

If you're able to land a guest post on a high-profile site in your marketplace, it rapidly exposes you to a whole new audience. You can literally become famous overnight if you deliver something unique and needed in the industry.

I've personally seen this happen numerous times.

Guest posting and/or collaboration typically leads to audience expansion and dramatically more sales. However, the level of growth will obviously depend on the popularity of the publication you're featured in.

To further clarify, guest blogging is when you write and publish an article on someone else's blog or website. It's a fantastic way to piggyback on other credible industry influencers. If your post is accepted on their site, it's like they're endorsing you.

I've seen people come out of complete obscurity, guest blog for a guru, then become an instant celebrity in the space. It just depends on the quality of the content and the size of the community you're participating in.

Let's take it to the extreme, shall we?

If you have a product or service in the health space and you submitted it to Dr. Oz's website and got published, your life would change because of all the traffic and referrals (assuming you delivered the highest value and got results).

If you had a product that serviced the business sector and your guest post was picked up and featured in the Wall Street Journal, you'd gain instant fame with that readership.

How do you think that would impact your sales?

It would create serious momentum and credibility. On your website or promo material, you could now also legitimately say you've been featured in the Wall Street Journal.

In the industry you're servicing, you'll typically find hundreds of places where you can submit content to be considered. A few publications will be much larger than others, and sometimes you'll just connect with bloggers in your space. Either way, it presents a solid opportunity to get your content and message in front of new eyeballs.

To review, the top three reasons guest blogging should be a foundational strategy in your business are as follows:

1. It builds relationships.

Webmasters and bloggers usually are searching for great content. When you get a reputation as a solid guest blogger who ads value, you're going to quickly create rapport with other bloggers in the same market.

You definitely want to have A LOT of blogger friends because many have their own active communities online. These are people who also love to share content on sites like Facebook, Twitter, Pinterest, etc., which gets you a tremendous amount of free exposure.

By getting in good with the influencers in your space, you grow your impact, which always leads to more blog and/or email subscribers.

2. It's great for search engines and rankings.

Google, Bing, and Yahoo love fresh, original content. In fact, it's one of the factors that plays into overall website rankings online. If you have a site that's consistently churning out high-quality unique content generated by you and others, search engines like Google reward you.

This is not a big secret at all; however, I need to mention one thing here: The website where you guest post is critically important. Ideally, you need to do your homework and be a little selective.

If you just create and submit content for a spammy site on the Internet, your post won't have legs and you'll get associated with junk sites. Remember, reputation is currency. That's worth repeating.

Google feels the exact same way. They even have a measurement called Author Rank, which we discussed in the blogging section of the book. You'll want to review that chapter again as it's vital to your success.

For each guest post you do, make sure that the host allows you to include a link to your website or ethical bribe. Normally, there's an author bio section at the end of guest blog posts.

What you'll find is that over time, these links back to your website will help your ranking on Google, Bing, Yahoo, etc. Your visibility will exponentially increase, and even more traffic will hit your site pages.

3. It gets your message and content in front of a new crowd.

Arguably the best part of guest blogging is that it gets your foot in the door of communities that are already established. You're able to share your empowering message and deliver value. You get to meet new people and develop relationships.

When you lead with your best stuff, you'll amass more fans, blog readers, and email subscribers. People begin to think, "If they're giving away this type of content for free, then the premium programs must be off the charts!"

On the other hand, if you're always hard selling like a used car salesman, you might acquire a bad reputation in the industry. You want to eventually get famous, but not because of that!

Provide value and help people get what they want. Combine the content marketing with everything else you're learning in this book and you'll be unstoppable, destined for greatness!

Another important thing to consider here is that as you build a large audience, you can recruit others in your marketplace to submit valuable guest posts to your blog. This can be a good way to source new quality content.

Not to mention, as your brand, respect, and fame grow, other guest contributors will start to email their lists since they are featured on your site.

What's the best way to find guest blogging opportunities?

Aside from meeting well-known bloggers face-to-face at live events in your industry, you can find relevant websites and communities online. These are the four questions you need to ask.

1. Is the content of the scouted site actually focused on your niche?
2. Is the audience of the blog the right fit for your content?
3. Does the community engage frequently and share the content on social media?
4. Is the featured website owner or public figure active on social media?

Let's say you're selling lessons on how to potty train your German shepherd. You'd want to find German shepherd–related blogs with an active following of dog owners. This is not too difficult, but you'll need to spend a little time searching and compiling a list.

The easiest way to find other websites that accept guest blog posts is by strategically using Google. Who could've imagined?

Search these terms below with and without quotation marks around the words. Replace the (keyword) text you see with the keywords from your topic/industry.

- "(keyword) guest blog"
- "(keyword) guest post"
- "(keyword) guest post guidelines"
- "(keyword) guest post submission"
- "(keyword) submit guest post"
- "(keyword) submit article"
- "(keyword) guest article"

Let's touch on social media searches for a minute.

The overwhelming majority of bloggers and guest posters typically share their most recent posts on social networks like Facebook, Twitter, LinkedIn, Pinterest, Tumblr, Instagram, and Google+.

In my opinion, Twitter is the easiest and fastest one to search. So when you're on the network, just type in "(keyword) guest post" in the search bar. From there, Twitter will populate the latest tweets about guest blogs in your marketplace. From there, follow the links to see if those sites are accepting any more guest posts.

Here's a valuable resource I wanted to share with you. It was put together by Kim Roach, founder of BuzzBlogger. Her article is titled "500+ Places to Syndicate your Content." You can check it out at the link below.

http://www.buzzblogger.com/500-places-to-syndicate-your-content/

Finally, here's one of many communities online that is made up solely of guest bloggers. It's called My Blog Guest. You can sign up for free at:

http://myblogguest.com/

and search for websites that are accepting guest posts.

Not only that, you can post your own information and let people know that you're interested in writing guest articles on a specific topic. This helps blog owners find you easier!

Things to remember when submitting a guest post

Format your blogs like the other posts on the website.

Pay attention here. Do the other posts use images, headers, bold text, or other types of formatting? If so, your article should be similar.

It's all about the reader.

This is not a blog post about your product or company. We're not advertising here. The goal is to create a valuable piece of content and resource that helps others get the result they're seeking. The "author bio" section is where you add your business info.

Always include a call to action to stimulate engagement.

At the end of your helpful blog post, always include a call to action to spark discussion from the community. The more comments you get, the better.

Include a couple internal links back to their previous posts.

This basically shows the website/blog owner that you're familiar with their content and you're an active reader. You can either go through their blog "category" section on their site (if they have one), or you can do a Google search.

If you search Google, you'll need to do it like this:

site:domain.com intitle:keyword

This brings back their post popular posts for any given keyword so you have them handy if you want to link.

Here's a real-world example: Let's say we wrote an article on the health hazards associated with ingesting the artificial sweetener Aspartame. Since Dr. Mercola has the largest health newsletter online, it would be great to submit this content to his site.

Now, let's say his staff accepted the article and your post was scheduled to be published next week. However, you wanted to link to some other Aspartame-related articles in his site to further prove your case.

Well, in the Google search bar, you'd simply input this:

site:mercola.com intitle:Aspartame

Action Step: Create a separate document like an Excel spreadsheet and scout out a couple dozen websites in your industry where you can start submitting guest blogs. List them from most popular to least popular.

Some publications will want original content while others may accept an article you've written and published on your own. Check with the editor of the site to see the specifics.

Submit at least one guest post weekly to multiple online magazines or popular bloggers in your industry. Keep in mind the article formatting for each website may be different. You'll need to check.

If you're not great at writing, hire a ghostwriter. For under $20, you can get a solid blog post written on any topic you choose. Just give the ghostwriter precise instructions of what to cover.

In the resources section of this book, I list a few places where you can hire experienced freelance writers to create content for you. Upwork.com is one of those places. Place a job listing there, and you'll get bids from people all over the world.

One important thing to consider here: If you're going to outsource content writing, you need to find someone that uses English as their PRIMARY language. This should be obvious.

While the guy in Timbuktu will write for three dollars per article, you will most certainly get a lot of spelling and grammatical errors! Trust me, I've been there. Learn from my mistakes. We don't need that hassle. Hire someone from the US or Canada and you'll be fine. Once you get the article back from them, you can add any additional info or slightly tweak it based on your knowledge of the industry.

There is a time and place to outsource and save money. However, when it comes to writing content for your blog or guest posting, we need to put our BEST foot forward and make sure the article is top-notch.

Chapter 20

MAKING MONEY WITH SOLO ADS

The secret of getting ahead is getting started. The secret of getting started is breaking your complex overwhelming tasks into small manageable tasks, and then starting on the first one.
—Mark Twain

This is one of my top strategies for driving affordable, targeted traffic to my products. In fact, when I created a software program in 2012 to service social media marketers, solo ads were the number one method I used to hit our first five-figure month with that particular product!

Solo ads are simply an email–based advertising arrangement agreed upon by two marketers or business owners. The goal is to reach out to a list of subscribers that are registered to either one of them for a fixed price or performance-based agreement.

The business owner sends an email to their subscribers on behalf of another marketer to display their offer or something of value. The approach is performance driven to reach a large audience at once.

Each email sent is generally a text-based email, like what you'd get from a friend. An important thing to point out here is that whenever you utilize solo ads, ALWAYS have your traffic driven to a squeeze page and never to a sales page!

Why?

Our number one goal is to build our own email list as we discussed previously. You're going to have a tiny fraction of people that might buy your stuff immediately; however, the overwhelming majority need to get to know, like, and trust you first.

So, that's what we need to plan for.

When you acquire a new subscriber via your free giveaway on your squeeze page, you should have emails queued up in your autoresponder sequence. These will go out every few days to build a relationship, establish social proof, deliver content, and to finally make your offer.

Most solo ads are done by fixed price, meaning you pay a specific amount of dollars for another person to email their list for you or get you a predetermined number of clicks.

In my experience, if you average the targeted cost per click of solo ads, it tends to be MUCH less expensive than Google AdWords or many other forms of pay-per-click marketing—not to mention, the traffic is warmer and highly qualified.

The overall performance is measured in terms of goals achieved, which generally include purchase, email subscriptions, referrals, social sharing, and others. Metrics that are typically tracked include conversion, IP address, unique visitors, country, referrer, browser, and timestamp.

The performance of a solo ad campaign is typically determined by the number of unique subscribers to a marketer's list and/or the number of sales made.

If you are serious about tapping into the power of solo ads, then I'd recommend these three quality resources below.

- Udimi – http://udimi.com (world's largest solo ad marketplace)
- Safe Swaps – http://www.safe-swaps.com/ (protected email ad swaps)
- Directory of Ezines – http://dcincome.com/blog/ezines

Now, you can also just go to Google and type "solo ad directories" in the search bar and see what populates. You can find hundreds of providers that are willing to share their list with you.

If you're in a specific industry or niche, you can also key in "solo ads (your industry)" and see what results come back. Depending on how large or small your market is, your contacts might vary a bit.

The good news is pricing tends to be rather economical overall with these types of promotions. However, something to realize here is that you have to have a compelling email with a strong call to action in the body. Your email subject headline should grab the reader's attention too.

Here's a quick example of an email I used for a solo ad that ran last year. Pay attention to the structure. We also included a link to our squeeze page where we could collect their email, not to an actual sales page. The email subject headline is in bold and the body is below it.

New Pinterest Tool Gets You Server CRUSHING Traffic!

Since you're a savvy marketer, you
probably already know that Pinterest drives
more website traffic than Google+, LinkedIn,
Reddit, and YouTube ... COMBINED!!

The numbers are staggering and there's
enormous potential to go viral. This presents
a huge opportunity for your business.

Now, a killer new program has been launched
that's changing the face of marketing. Grab
your free demo at the link below.

http://YourSite.com
Here's what this powerful software will do for you:

1) Get you thousands of followers on
Pinterest quickly on virtual autopilot

2) Make you one of the most popular figures in your industry or niche

3) Get you an avalanche of qualified website traffic, recognition, and exposure

4) Dramatically increase your product sales and profits

5) Create an overwhelming presence on Pinterest, which boosts your social proof and credibility

You MUST check this out right now if you're looking to grow your business at light speed this year.

Get your hands on the demo at no cost. Click the link below now.

http://YourSite.com

To greater online profits,

- Your Name

A couple things you should be aware of regarding this sample email. One is that the paragraphs are short and don't progress to the right margin of the page. Why? It's just much easier on the eyes if you structure your emails this way.

The easier your email is to read, the higher your subscriber response will be.

Another thing to notice is that the email sparks curiosity and lets the reader know "what's in it for me"—as in, what the software program will do for them. I made sure that was bulleted.

I also made sure the reader knew the program I referenced was free. They don't have to pay anything to get access to it.

Lastly, I specifically told the individual to click the link. Always tell people what you want them to do. Never assume they just automatically know.

Think about the flow of the funnel this way: We send an email that directs the lead to a squeeze page. The prospective customer enters their name and email and is immediately redirected to a thank-you page. This thank-you page delivers what you promised on the squeeze page (free report, software trial, videos, etc.). You can see an example of a thank-you page at:

http://dcincome.com/go/1344-3/

The thank you page might also have a one-time offer (OTO) that they'll never see again.

It's important to remember that regardless of what the viewer decides to do, we've given them the valuable information we promised AND we now have them in our email database.

In our companies, we regularly see people that buy our products and services that have been on our list for years! If we would've never built an email list, then there would be no chance to build a relationship with them. That means they never would've been a customer.

Don't leave money on the table. Always build your email list first.

In conclusion, using solo ads is easily one of the FASTEST ways to grow your email list. In fact, for this particular list we built, we garnered close to 17,000 opt-in subscribers our first year!

The beautiful thing about this is that we can build a relationship with them now. This leads to increased sales of our existing offerings as well as the opportunity to present the list with congruent affiliate products from partners in the industry.

If you recall, "affiliate marketing" is great because we are essentially promoting another person's product to our list and then getting paid an agreed-upon commission. There are no products to stock on our end, no inventory to ship, no payments to collect, and no customer support.

We just send the email, then get paid! It's a wonderful thing.

Action Step: This will really depend on your budget, but I recommend scheduling at least one solo ad per week to help grow your email list quickly. This hardly requires any work and is a very high-leverage thing to do for your business.

This should go onto a weekly checklist like the other tasks we're talking about in this book. You, or a virtual assistant, can line these solo ads up weekly. Our goal is to automate the repetitive tasks as much as possible.

Chapter 21

PARTNERING YOUR WAY TO WEALTH AND INFLUENCE

Your network = your net worth

—Anonymous

I f there is one high-leverage strategy that has been the MOST profitable for my companies over the years, it's been joint-venture partnerships. This is where you seek out other members of your community that have large email lists of their own, then start to network with them.

The end goal is obvious: your ability to offer your product to their list, paying this influencer a specific affiliate commission on each sale. Commissions can range from 25 to 50 percent, depending on how you both structure the deal.

The important thing to realize here is that you should be going into these relationships with the attitude, "How can I help you?" Always give first. Don't just ask someone you've never met to promote your stuff. That's bad etiquette, and you probably won't get a reply.

This is where your OWN email list comes into play—or your ability to drive traffic to affiliate offers. When you start making other people money, trust me—they take notice in a big way. It's infinitely easier to strike a deal with a partner when you've already made them money. They consider you an asset now, which changes the dynamic considerably.

I've met some of my joint-venture partners through the Internet and some offline at seminars and events around the country. When these relationships are in place and are leveraged appropriately, it's the easiest, most cost-effective way to send targeted traffic to your products and services. It's usually the most profitable method too.

Imagine meeting a joint-venture partner that has a list of 100,000 subscribers or customers that they've organically acquired over the years. These are people that trust this individual and their recommendations. It's warmed-up referral traffic at its best! We know that referrals are the easiest to sell and typically make the best customers too. It's a win-win.

Imagine making a quick $5,000 just from one affiliate partner in a day or two. It's happened to me on numerous occasions, and it's a wonderful feeling! That's the power of relationships like this when you develop them. Then that opens you up to a possible cross-promotion, where you both are continuously promoting each other's offers throughout the year.

You see, your email list is the ultimate bargaining power. When you have several thousand subscribers on your list (10,000; 50,000; etc.), you can then search out other partners to promote their products, actively helping them in their endeavors. The chances of them helping you dramatically increase.

How to find joint-venture partners

Let's say you're in the golf niche and have created a product to help golfers shave two strokes off their putting. Now, we're not going to go after direct competitors to start. Ideally, we want to find someone else in the golf niche that specializes in something else.

So let's search for "golf driving tips" on Google.

Once your results display, something to observe is who exactly is advertising in the sponsored ad section of Google (at the top and on the right). Many times, business owners that use AdWords are not only trying to acquire a customer, but they're building an email list!

Click on each sponsored advertisement. Then ask yourself, "Is this person driving traffic to a sales page OR a squeeze page where they have a bold headline, what's in it for me bullet points, and where they are capturing names and emails?"

If you see a squeeze page, YOU KNOW this individual is building a list and understands their list is their biggest asset. This person is familiar with effective marketing strategies.

The next step is to look for the contact information of the website owner. Check the bottom of the site and all other pages. If you come across an email and phone number, that's great!

Sometimes you'll actually have to go to DomainTools.com, which is a great website that shows you the "WHOIS" info of the site. You can look up the registrar information, which normally includes the name, physical address, email, and phone number.

I highly recommend you get on the phone with the prospective partner you're trying to connect with. When you call them directly, it says a lot about you.

When I first began marketing my products online, I started to build my name in a few different niches. I had potential affiliate partners call me. What I realized was that I was more likely to do a joint-venture deal with those I spoke with over the phone because it was easier for me to connect with a real voice.

You might not know the individual's list size when you initiate the contact, but you can always get those details over the phone. List size is important; however, the relationship with the list is MUCH more important. If you see the same guy all over Google and Facebook advertising like crazy and driving the traffic to a squeeze page, you can safely assume this person has a big list.

Going back to our previous example, let's say your golf product is about putting better. Putting is separate than driving a golf ball off a tee. So you could find others in the golf driving sub-niche that could be good affiliate partners. If they're not direct competitors and don't have putting products, I would definitely strike up a relationship.

Remember, lead by promoting them. You don't want to be perceived as one that says, "Hey, what can you do for me?" Don't act selfish when approaching others.

That's a BIG reason why I turn down dozens of promotion requests weekly. Rookie marketers approach me for joint ventures and always ask what I can do for them. We'll receive emails like, "Can you blast this out to your list of x-amount of thousands of people?"

That's a quick way to get deleted from my inbox.

You really need to think about the person with whom you're interacting. How can you help them, and how you can deliver maximum value? When you lead with that type of attitude, partners are going to pay attention.

Powerful tip: Here's another cool tip to get noticed by industry heavyweights. I used this when I first began online. Do a video testimonial for that person's product. (This works best if you've actually used their system to get results.)

I don't care how big you or your business gets, when a customer takes the time to capture their raving feedback on camera, you always notice. A brand can NEVER have too many testimonials online.

Immediately, you think, "I need to personally thank this guy." So, naturally, you start researching who they are and what they do.

This works 99 percent of the time.

Action Step: Take a pen and pad and go to Google's Keyword Planner (formerly the Google Keyword Tool). As an example, input "Golf swing tips" in their system. It will then bring back a list of related terms we can search on Google.

We'll also learn about the search volume and how competitive those specific keywords are. From there, we can search all the sponsored listings of businesses that are actually paying for ads.

I could also go on the left side (organic section) of Google as well. Websites on the left side below the sponsored listings naturally rank high for specific search terms. These individual properties could be collecting hundreds or thousands of visitors per day in super-competitive markets.

Then, just click on any one site to see if that person has an email capture form or squeeze page anywhere else. That's the prime indicator that an email list is being built. Visit as many related websites as you can that complement what you're offering. Use DomainTools.com if you cannot find the webmaster contact info on the site.

By doing this, you'll eventually reach a point where you've established dozens of solid affiliate partners. This is where you can exponentially multiply your reach and revenue.

You see, whenever I launch a product, I notify all my best affiliates ahead of time so they can participate in the launch. They will all mail to their lists on the same day. Everyone wins in this scenario, and massive value is delivered to the marketplace—not to mention, partners end up receiving healthy commission checks. This unified front positions you as an authority quickly.

It's all about strategic alliances. As quoted at the beginning of this chapter, "Your network equals your net worth." This is very true, so focus on building great relationships.

Here's one additional thing to keep in mind: Not every business online has advanced Internet marketing knowledge like you and I do. Far from it! You can find some products in your marketplace that have "accidentally" become best sellers. They are the exception to the rule: Right product. Right place. Hungry market. Right time.

This type of luck doesn't happen often, but it does happen. In this case, the webmaster or product developer has a large customer list. They could still be a good joint-venture partner for you even if you don't see a squeeze page or ethical bribe on their site.

Customer lists perform much better for the simple fact that they've already made a purchase. They're not tire-kickers. Studies show when a consumer buys one item from a company, they're much more likely to purchase again.

Lastly, whenever you get the opportunity to attend a live event in your industry, do it! Meeting prospective partners in person trumps everything. As much as I love social media and the Internet, face-to-face interaction is still king.

You're more likely to stand out from the crowd if you can make a great first impression and strike up a conversation about helping their mission or business. This is easy to do at many live events because the atmosphere is relaxed.

Chapter 22 ————

EMAIL MARKETING
STRATEGIES THAT BANK

The best way to predict the future is to create it.
—Peter Drucker

C lose your eyes for a few seconds and imagine this scenario: You're at your computer on a Tuesday evening writing an email to your list of 4,000 people. It's taken you about thirty minutes to craft this email, and it lets your tribe know about your newest product that just went live! You queued the message up for the following morning so it goes out at 6:50 a.m.

In the email you explain to your readers what the product is, the story behind it, and what it will do for them, and you show them exactly what to do next to purchase. Of course, you remove all risk by also offering a money-back guarantee as well.

Maybe you even feature success stories from people who had early access to this product and found it solved their problem quickly.

Wednesday morning arrives and the email goes out as planned. You start to get flooded with PayPal emails saying something to the tune of, "Payment has been received from John Smith." Every time you refresh the screen, you have more sales. It's a very surreal experience to say the least.

This goes on the entire day until you finally get to peek at your final sales totals. You've just made $11,750 in a single day, which is more than you made the last three months COMBINED!

You are totally stunned and think to yourself, "HOLY COW! Did this really happen?"

Immediately, you log in to your PayPal account and initiate a bank transfer for that amount shown because you're afraid that some mysterious force will take the money if you don't act fast.

That, my friend, is a true story and displays the power of building an email list along with a strong relationship with those valued subscribers. This one thing can change your life forever. It certainly has mine and thousands of clients.

I still recall the first time I made a quick cash surge with email. I ran a three-day promotion to a small list of 1,050 email subscribers. Total sales amounted to just over $6,200. I don't know about you, but that's a lot of money where I come from.

In the words of legendary marketer and entrepreneur, John Reese, "Email marketing kicks the crap out of everything else!" As I've spoken about numerous times in this book, the first step and primary goal of any business using the Internet to sell stuff is to build an email list. Your email list is your lifeblood online. It's part of the foundation.

Ask anyone that's built a successful seven-figure (or greater) business on the Internet and they'll tell you the exact same thing.

What you need to understand is that in a normal situation, a visitor to your website will look around and stay less than fifteen seconds. (That's close to average, believe it or not.) Once this visitor is done browsing, nine times out ten they bounce off your site and never return again. The question we must ask though, is "How do we prevent this?"

It's simple.

We offer an ethical bribe (free report, video series, etc.) on the home page of our website, and then we also have an entire page dedicated to this offer. As we spoke about in this book previously, we call that a squeeze page.

Let me provide you with a personal example here. Whenever I run promotions to my email list, I find that AT MINIMUM of 40 percent of those who purchase my products have been on my list for over a year! It never fails either. Why does this occur?

It's because the buying public is very skeptical these days, even if you're a trusted authority figure in your respected space. Many times, subscribers are "slow dates." You must offer them value and build a relationship while getting them to know, like, and trust you. With some people this happens fast, and with others it's a longer process.

Imagine this scenario though. What if I would've never built or nourished my list properly? I would be taking a drastic pay cut. I'd be missing out on 100 percent of those sales that would normally come from our email database. That makes me nauseous just thinking about it! UGH!

Yes, I could still run a special promotion, but the only people that would see it are new website visitors. We call that cold traffic. This type of traffic never converts as well as those with whom you've built a warm relationship.

Email marketing by itself regularly allows my company to have five-figure paydays.

DO NOT make the mistake I made early on in business. I waited a couple years before starting to build my email list. I'd rather not think of how much money we threw out the window. In hindsight, it should've been one of the first things I did.

There are so many email marketing and management systems out there today—everything from Aweber, InfusionSoft, Constant Contact, MailChimp, GetResponse, etc.

As mentioned in the blogging chapter, I've always used Aweber and found it to be one of the easiest programs to learn. Their customer support is excellent, and the software is affordable even if you're on a shoestring budget. When you're ready, you can grab a dollar trial at:

http://MyProResponse.com.

In your email marketing efforts, use this rule of thumb: Offer great content, value, and case studies 80 percent of the time. Make exceptional product offers and/or affiliate joint-venture promotions 20 percent of the time. Also, train prospective customers to start clicking on your links from the very first email.

Treat subscribers like family and talk to them a couple times each week, at minimum. Some reading this right now may cringe at the frequency I just recommended! What I find, though, is the average person with an email list might communicate a couple times per month. That's WAY too infrequent.

How often do you speak to your best friend?

How often do you speak with your mother?

You probably talk with those closest to you a few times per week. Our email list is no different. Take care of them and communicate multiple times per week and they'll take care of you!

There is something else I'd like to mention here in regards to communication. One of the reasons I've been so successful building a strong relationship with my list is that I write to them like I would write to my best friend.

This is where a lot of newbie entrepreneurs fail. Their writing is cold and doesn't sound like they're speaking to an actual friend. This includes the email body itself AND the subject headline.

There's only one of you, and we need your personality and originality to come through in the emails we send to people. The truth is, your style is not going to attract everyone, which is great! Those that you do attract will stick around, get to know you, and become raving fans.

How to get your emails opened

You could have the greatest, most helpful message in the world, but if you can't get people to open your emails, it doesn't matter. Your product or service could be the best thing since sliced bread; however, if it doesn't attract eyeballs, you won't make money or change lives.

What open-rate percentage should you strive for? Make it a goal to try and hit 25 percent. That means that 25 out of 100 will open it. Believe it or not, that's actually good these days.

People are SO BOMBARDED with emails that we have to grab their attention with the headline and become a trusted resource, or else we just blend in with the crowd. We don't want that.

The great thing about Aweber is that it allows you to send an email to those subscribers that didn't open your first one. I do this all the time. Maybe a week later, I'll send the same exact email (with a different subject line) to those who didn't open the initial email.

You'll be surprised how many more followers open that email. Reasons for this could be the time of day you send it, whether or not the subject is more compelling, or maybe that person was just busy with life a few days ago.

Don't take it personally when you don't get a 100 percent email open rate. Our goal is to build a loyal following that, even though they don't open every email, they're still paying attention.

Clients tell me all the time that they have a separate folder for my emails because they don't want to miss one, even though they don't have time to read them all. That tells me that I'm doing something right!

If you want to maximize your open rates, pay close attention to these several proven strategies that work like magic when it comes to getting your content seen.

1. Ask a question to spark curiosity – When you ask a question, it interrupts the reader's routine/pattern. They have to think of the answer. It's just how we're wired. If the person doesn't have the answer, naturally they open the email to find out.

2. Make it sound negative – As a culture, we have been conditioned to pay more attention to bad news than to good news. For instance, every time I send an email with the subject, "Bad News," the open rate goes through the roof.

3. Avoiding pain and/or mistakes – Studies show that people are more likely to take action when it's to avoid pain, as opposed to seeking pleasure. No one wants to experience pain and make mistakes.

4. Personalize the subject – Use the subscriber's first name in the subject headline. Most autoresponder and email marketing services will

allow you to do this. An example would be, "Hey (first name), did you see this?"

5. Make it controversial and/or shocking – Everyone knows controversy sells, so use it to your advantage.

6. Use scarcity and urgency – We know people like to procrastinate, so we can use this type of headline to get them to take action right now. For example, if you're running a promotion, you'd have an email that says "FINAL NOTICE – 4 Hours Left."

7. Use the mainstream-media way – The media likes to create over-the-top, sensationalistic headlines that have ridiculous titles and questions. This is one you'll want to use sparingly, but it can be effective. You can also incorporate buzzwords that are hot in the news media now.

8. Incorporate humor – Most email subject headlines in the average person's inbox are dull and dry. Being funny can help you stick out like a sore thumb.

Another thing I highly recommend is to Google the words "best email subject headlines" so you can find many more great examples of how to write compelling titles that dramatically increase your open rates.

DON'T REINVENT THE WHEEL!

Use headlines and templates that have been proven to work.

As referenced in the blogging section of this book, you can also access sixteen powerful copy-and-paste headline templates. These can be used for blogs or email titles. I originally created it for doctors, but it's applicable to any business. Download the free guide at:

http://dcincome.com/go/1182-2/.

How to get people to click your email links

This is another art unto itself. The main goal of the email is to get the end subscriber to take the desired action you want. Make sense? Emails don't have to be long; they can be short for the most part. If you're telling a story or pre-selling and positioning a sale, you might naturally have a longer email. That's ok.

Here are some things to consider when it comes to increasing your click-through rate and also making sure your subscribers stick around:

HTML vs Text Emails:
- HTML is much better.
- HTML allows you to use anchor text in your links (higher click through).
- HTML allows you to use images, which can produce a higher click through.
- HTML allows you to track your open rate.
- HTML allows you to track click-through rate without "ugly" links.

Videos and Pictures:
- Embedded videos and pictures are more popular than words.
- Make a picture or an image of a video clickable.
- Also have the link directly under the picture.

Personalize Email Content:
- Readers perk up when they see their name, city, or state.
- Use it sparingly. Overuse will make it lose its juice.

NEVER Use Ugly Links:
- People are more willing to click on clean links or text phrases.
- Don't use long, scary affiliate links. Here's an example of an ugly link:
  - http://allpro.clickbank.com/hoplink/273940745037

Be You, Be Authentic:
- Write friendly emails and stop writing "email copy."
- Use conversational language, not corporate speak.
- Use personality and be entertaining.

Short and to the Point:
- Keep content length short and put the first link close to the top.
- Once you write your email, review it and delete as many words as possible without losing the intended message.

Spark Reader Engagement:
- Set expectations for the next email with P.S. teasers.
- Ask for your reader's feedback on what you're promoting.
- Examples:

o "P.S. Watch your inbox tomorrow for the email titled "Super Secrets.""

o "Here it is: (LINK). Let me know if you try it out, and I'll keep you posted on my progress with it as well."

If you want your readers to click on a specific link in the emails you send, get in the habit of making them curious. You need to let people know what's in it for them if they click the link and read the blog or watch the video.

You can do this in a few sentences; it's similar to when you create bullet points on your squeeze page. We're trying to spark curiosity enough so that this individual feels like they have to click on the link or they might miss something.

How often should I build my email list?

Email list building is one of those activities that should be done EVERY single day! We want to use free and paid traffic-generation methods to get visitors to a squeeze page where we have our ethical bribe.

In this book, I'm detailing my best moneymaking traffic strategies. Once the systems are set up, you couldn't turn off the tidal wave of website visitors even if you wanted to.

Understand this: Your audience can never be too big, but it's not just about the size of your list. It's about the relationship you build with them. That's worth repeating (which is why I've repeated it so often in this book)!

Once you begin to get subscribers, you'll want to email them at least twice per week. Add value to their lives, and you'll build trust and rapport quickly.

The great thing about Aweber and other email management systems is that you can create autoresponder sequences. That means you can queue messages to go out when you want after that person has opted-in to your list.

On one of my lists, I have over 100 autoresponder messages queued. I did the work one time, and now these emails will continue to work for me AUTOMATICALLY for years to come. I can also send email broadcasts to my entire list anytime I choose.

Action Step: Get an email management system if you don't have one. There are many good ones out there. I've always used Aweber and have been very pleased by their customer support and ease of use. Even a second grader could use their platform. Try them for a dollar at:

http://MyProResponse.com.

Get your squeeze page set up if it's not already. Remember, this is the page where you have the free report you're giving away in exchange for a name and email.

If you don't know how to build this page, have your programmer create a web form through Aweber and install the code on your squeeze page. Freelance programmers can be found through Upwork.com if you need one.

Begin to implement the traffic-generation tactics found in this book so you can flood your squeeze page with qualified visitors. Some methods (like Facebook advertising) will produce instant traffic while others like SEO might take a while. There's a time and place for both.

Set goals for yourself in terms of email subscribers.

For example, make it your mission to get at least ten targeted subscribers per day.

This is pretty simple given what you're learning throughout this work. I have lists that get dozens of subscribers per day without lifting a finger. This is because we set up systems that consistently feed the website on autopilot. In fact, one of our email lists averages over seventy email opt-ins per day!

Communicate with your list twice per week AT MINIMUM. These don't have to be long emails or blog posts. We want to consistently give them gold nuggets mixed with testimonials from those that have used our products and services.

When someone joins my email list, they usually get four emails the first week The first email goes out instantly after they opt-in so we can deliver what we promised on the same day. The next email goes out the day after, asking them what they thought of the information. We also include a download link to the free giveaway just in case they didn't get it before.

The third email is sent on day three with testimonials and a link to dozens of success stories. The goal is to build a mountain of social proof in order to further knock down any skepticism. Volume matters here. We're never going to stop getting testimonials. The more, the better too.

The fourth email that's sent typically goes out on day five in the sequence. I like to deliver even more value here and share another great tip. Get the prospective customer closer to the result they want to generate. At the end of the blog, video, or email, we can make a soft offer back to the original sales page.

After the initial seven days following an individual's subscription to our list, they can usually count on getting a couple emails per week from us, sometimes more. Many of these emails will be queued autoresponders while others are regular broadcasts. We'll even throw in partner-affiliate promotions now and then.

From there, I fuse great content emails (80 percent of the time) with offers (20 percent of the time).

Clients that are accepted into our private coaching program are given promotional email campaigns to swipe, and we help them craft their email sales messages so that they will convert at a much higher rate.

For example, one of the email marketing campaigns we've perfected is sent four days in a row to an email list. Consistently, this produces an EXTRA five to six figures for clients in just a few days. This is on top of the revenue they're already generating. (You can learn more about private coaching and if you qualify later in this book.)

In some of my emails, the helpful advice is contained within. In others, I evoke their curiosity then send them to my blog to get all the specifics. Some emails are just client success stories and case studies. It's important to train your subscribers to click the links in your emails.

By the way … expect some people to unsubscribe from your list for a variety of reasons—and that's okay. Don't worry about those folks. They weren't going to buy from you anyway. We're interested in creating value, building a culture, and turning those fans into raving fans.

Chapter 23

USING GOOGLE+ AND HANGOUTS TO GROW YOUR AUDIENCE

Even if you're on the right track, you'll get run over if you just sit there.
—Will Rogers

W hen I think of Google+ (also written as Google Plus), I think of mandatory childhood chores. I really didn't want to wash the dishes, cut the grass, shovel the snow, or clean the house when I was thirteen. However, I knew I'd get grounded if things didn't get done.

Google has basically forced people that care about SEO to join Google+. Should you decide not to participate, there's a chance you'll get bent over and spanked in the organic rankings.

At the time Google+ was introduced, the world wasn't really looking for (nor did it really did need) another social network similar to Facebook. I know I don't like to feel strong-armed online. How about you?

Some marketers and tech geeks absolutely rave about the platform, but the average buying public does not. In fact, it can feel like a ghost town much of the time. The active usage is VERY low according to Stone Temple Consulting. They estimate fewer than 1 percent.

Celebrities have been very slow to adopt Google+ as well. The masses would still rather congregate on Instagram, Facebook, Pinterest, Twitter, Periscope, and YouTube. This is what the prominent data shows.

Google doesn't have a track record of doing "social" very well at all. Some of the previous failed attempts have been with platforms like Orkut, DodgeBall, Latitude, Buzz, and Wave. My prediction is that Google+ will eventually go the graveyard.

Right now, the only thing Google+ has going for it (and hands-down its best feature) is the Google Hangout function. This is what we're going to spend time talking about since this can be highly profitable for your business endeavors.

There are plenty of bloggers that have written in depth about Google+, how to use it, and the most relevant functions. Feel free to investigate for yourself; however, we're going to go straight for the jugular.

You can learn everything you've ever wanted to know about Hangouts at these links:

https://support.google.com/hangouts

http://www.google.com/+/learnmore/hangouts/

When Google+ collapses like almost every other attempt at social they've had, I believe this Hangouts feature will still be around.

You need a Google+ account or Gmail account to get started using Hangouts. It takes a minute to get one set up. Do that here:

https://plus.google.com/.

When you have your Google+ account created, go to your personal page. You'll see a drop-down menu in the upper left (this could change) that looks similar to this.

When clicked, that opens up and you'll see an option to choose Hangouts. Realize, this could change at any time. So if you cannot find it, go to the previous links I mentioned and/or Google the phrase "How to do a Google Hangout."

There are two types of Google Hangouts. You have your traditional video Hangouts where you can converse privately with friends, family, coworkers, etc. This function reminds me of the futuristic phones that were shown in the eighties Hanna-Barbera cartoon, The Jetsons.

Secondly, you have "Hangouts On Air" where you can broadcast yourself to the world or to as many subscribers as you can get in one place. You can learn more about those here:

https://www.google.com/+/learnmore/hangouts/onair.html.

With live public Hangouts you can have as many attendees watch as you'd like. The Hangout can also be recorded and immediately uploaded to your YouTube channel in real time. To be able to livestream and simultaneously record is a very powerful feature.

If you intend to use Google Hangouts for your business endeavors, you'll want to download the Internet browser Chrome. You can do that here:

https://www.google.com/chrome/browser/desktop/.

Or, if you use Firefox or Safari, you can download this specific plugin:

https://www.google.com/tools/dlpage/hangoutplugin.

There are many ways in which you can use this type of livestream, but I'm going to assume you're reading this book because you want to start and/or grow a profitable Internet-based business.

If that's the case, we primarily use this platform to deliver value to our existing subscribers. We can answer frequently asked questions, clear up common myths, or we can hold "how-to" style trainings. Alex Mandossian does this very well.

Remember, although we are educating our prospective customers and delivering value, we want to make sure we're pre-framing and offering our products for sale periodically. After all, we trying to change people's lives in a positive way and make a professional income doing it.

So let's say you have a business that shows people how to make money with real estate. In one example of an on-air Hangout, we might do a thirty-minute presentation that describes for our audience the steps on how to find the best foreclosure deals in their city along with giving them a checklist of what to look for, etc.

The next Google Hangout you do might be one where you show people what to do after they've secured the investment property. So, if the house needs cosmetic repairs, you could show them what would add the most value to the home so as to increase the sale price. You might include another checklist with this training to make it simple.

Then, on the third Google Hangout, you could show them more valuable info and make your offer. Maybe your product is a done-for-you solution where you find deals, help your client close them, rehab the property for them, then help them sell it.

This is just an example.

You can either offer a done-for-you product or a comprehensive "do-it-yourself" training. After all, you're covering only one aspect of making money with real estate in those free Google Hangouts.

If you don't have a formal product to sell, you could use this platform to create one as you go. For instance, I know many marketers that will sell a program before it's been created. They're marketed as live training programs with weekly modules.

Picture this: You create a seven-week training course where you do a one- to two-hour Google Hangout each week with clients. This is automatically recorded for customers to access later. You also get the video transcribed for those that would like to read the info.

Next, you find a programmer to strip the audio from the recorded video so your client can listen to the MP3 in their car or on their smart phone. On top of that, you do one question/answer call with freeconferencing.com each week for additional value.

You also create a few additional video trainings using Camtasia Studio where you record the screen and show them how to perform the individual steps.

So, in your online course, you'd offer:

- Seven weekly live Google Hangouts (with recordings)
- PDF transcripts of the trainings

- MP3 audio version
- One group question/answer phone call for seven weeks (also recorded)
- Cheat sheets or checklists that go with the modules
- Access to a private Facebook group for the community for networking, strategizing, and support

Can you see how we established immense value with this program? You could even sweeten the deal by offering other fast action bonuses if the individual takes advantage of what you're selling by a certain date. (Review the chapter in this book on copywriting and sales to know which points you need to cover in your close when selling your product.)

You are paid in proportion to the value you deliver. If we get the prospective customer to easily see the value in the program as well as what the information is certain to do for them, we can essentially name the price we want to charge.

One of the biggest mistakes I see newbie Internet entrepreneurs make is they charge too little. Don't do that! I've seen online courses like this sell for $397 all the way up to $2,997 on the high end. Most likely, your price point will fall between those figures.

Heck, you could even throw in a personal one-on-one call. It's up to you. This strategy session would definitely increase the perceived value of the training. Just know, there's never a shortage of ways that we can stack value.

The process and sample course I just described can also be applied to webinars. I've included a separate chapter in this book about how to bank with webinars. It's solid gold.

The difference with Google Hangouts is that you're speaking to your laptop camera live while it broadcasts your image to the public. On a webinar, you're essentially doing a PowerPoint or Keynote presentation that viewers see.

One question you may have right now is, "How do I get viewers to my Google Hangout?" That's where your email list comes into play and why it's so crucial to get started building one as early as possible. These are people that already know, like, and trust you because of the value you've already given them.

Even if you don't have a list, you can use Facebook advertising to deliver highly qualified and interested prospects to your events. You'd just want to send them to a registration page that collects a name and email and then also share:

- What the event is about
- What the event will do for them (list four to five compelling bullet points)
- What day and time the event takes place
- The number of limited seats available
- Why they don't want to miss this presentation
- What to do next to secure their spot

Take a moment to review the Facebook advertising section of this book so you know the right way to set up, optimize, track, and profit big from your ads.

A simple automated program that helps you put together easy registration pages for Hangouts and traditional webinars is Stealth Seminar. Should you decide to utilize it, I negotiated a low-cost trial for you at: http://StealthSeminarDiscount.com.

Many of the highest-paid coaches and marketers harness this software. I've personally used it since 2012, and the customer support is the fastest in the business. Absolutely wonderful. Here's a sample registration page so you can see.

How to Get an EXTRA 3,000 Facebook Fans in the Next 30 Days!

Now, what you're unable to see in this registration page screenshot is the opt-in box that sits below the italicized paragraph. This is what it looks like though.

There are a couple things to pay attention to on the previous image: One, there is an option to remind the registrant via SMS (text). This is powerful because over 95 percent of text messages are opened within the first thirty minutes of receiving them!

If you want to absolutely make sure someone sees your message, you send them a text. So, this is a nifty little reminder feature.

Next, you can see a privacy policy link below as well as text that talks about safeguarding the registrant's email. That should always be on your registration page.

This registration page style is one of many that Stealth Seminar offers. You can choose from among text pages like this or ones that have video on them—your call. Test a couple out and see which one converts the best.

At the end of the day, if we're going to send traffic to that page, we want it to collect as many names and emails as possible. Strive for at least a 10 percent conversion from cold traffic (people that don't know you). That means if you send 100 visitors there from Facebook advertising, ten of them should register.

That being said, we've had registration pages convert over 35 percent before from cold traffic. If you host a Hangout or webinar to your email list, your registration page conversion will naturally be higher because your subscribers have a relationship with you.

From my years of research, the functionality of Stealth Seminar is unparalleled. It has many simple features for the beginner and advanced ones for the expert marketer. Keep in mind, it's also one of the very few platforms that integrates seamlessly with Google Hangouts.

Action Step: Open a Google+ account if you don't already have one and test your first Hangout. Practice makes perfect. You'll want to check the basics like your sound and speaker quality with a friend before you do a public livestream on air.

Get comfortable with the interface and function available to you. Review the helpful links I've included in this chapter to learn more about the ins and outs of Hangouts.

Lead with value and help your viewers achieve their desired results.

Realize this is one way to touch your list of followers and to humanize yourself. I like to use a combination of emails, videos, blog posts, teleclasses, webinars, and Hangouts to communicate and add value on a regular basis.

I dedicate an entire chapter to teleseminars and webinars in this book. We'll go in depth so you can strategically use them to educate subscribers and sell enormous quantities of products and programs you create.

Chapter 24

BUILDING YOUR "STREET CRED"
WITH FORUMS

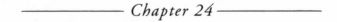

The only place where success comes before work is in the dictionary.
—Vidal Sassoon

When you think of an online forum around your selected topic of interest, think treasure trove. The data and insight these communities can provide you with is astounding! Forums are trustworthy safe havens for many people who just want to go learn and discuss things related to their hobbies.

Depending on the source you reference, 15–20 percent of Americans use forums and message boards to talk about or recommend certain products. If this is new to you, it might surprise you to learn that forums and message boards were around LONG before social media websites. You might even say these platforms were the genesis of social media. There are millions of these communities on the web that contain active users who are opinionated and influential in regards to the tribe's subject matter.

Our goal is to be viewed as a problem solver in communities like this. If done right, we can build relationships, rapport, and goodwill with our target market. It's also easy for us to stand out from the crowd if we deliver solid value.

You've got to be careful, though. If you promote too much, you'll get banned in a heartbeat. All forums have a specific code of conduct you'll need to read through and agree to before engaging. It's usually one of the first threads you see in the community. Go over the guidelines with a fine-tooth comb so you know what's acceptable and what's not. Read everything carefully.

Look for the following stuff. Can you post business-related messages in your signature? Are you allowed to include links in your posts? Are members allowed to promote their businesses? What restrictions do new members have? Can you message other members?

How to find quality forums related to your industry

Use Google! Big surprise, I know. Let's just say you had an interest in real estate investing and you wanted to connect with others that had the same interest. Or perhaps you already developed a real estate investing product and want to get it into the hands of your perfect market.

Here's what you'd do. Go to Google right now and type in "real estate investing forums." It will populate something like this.

As you can see, there are 1.24 million results that come back for that specific search. You could also search "real estate investing forum" in quotation marks to give you more specifics.

The first two listings you see in the screenshot are sponsored ads (Google AdWords). After that, you'll observe ten regular organic listings that are indexed on the first page. For this keyword search, there are over 100,000 pages of listings!

The key is finding the right online forums

Not all of them are going to be worth your time. If you want to be successful, you've got to find the best communities to interact in. Start with those that are the most popular in your target market.

Typically, those that appear on page one though three of Google are the most popular. Also, ask your friends, customers, and Facebook group members which online communities they frequent. On top of that, try searching forum hub websites like BoardReader.com using specific keywords that are targeted to your industry.

After you put your Sherlock Holmes cap on and do some detective work, narrow your list to five to ten active forums that have over 1,500 members and 7,000 posts. In some smaller niche markets this will vary greatly, but you still want to find the most active communities.

Ideally, you want to make sure there's daily activity in the forums you select. Over a dozen new thread posts each day is good. Check to see if the community is filled with spam. If it is, move on to the next on the list since you don't want to waste your time.

If you see a forum created by one of your competitors, it's your call to participate or not. Sometimes competitors can work together; other times not so much. It just depends on how scarcity-minded they are.

Register an account immediately

Membership age is a credibility indicator for many forums. The longer you've been an active participant, the more trust and seniority you have. If you're unable to post new threads or write responses immediately, don't worry. Some communities have a probationary period.

Do NOT think of forums as "one-and-done" marketing opportunities. You're planting roots in them and nourishing relationships, demonstrating your value by answering questions or solving problems.

I've said it many times. Reputation is currency. You only get one shot to build it the right way. Think long term on this.

Choose an easy to remember username and professional avatar

First impressions are everything online as we've discussed. You want to be memorable and taken seriously. Your username and avatar (profile picture) are the first things other people notice.

Your real name could suffice as your username especially if you're branding yourself. Don't make it hard to remember, confusing, or a series of oddball numbers.

For your avatar, use a professional head shot.

Build out your online profile

Make it compelling. This can either make or break your "street cred" in the forum. Give a meaty description of your expertise and life experience. Don't make it too technical. Put it in layman's terms. Humanize yourself by throwing in something personal too.

Introduce yourself to the community

Most forums encourage this practice when you initially join. Don't be surprised if you get welcomed by dozens of members after posting an introductory thread. Tell members why you joined the forum and that you look forward to contributing to the discussion based on your expertise.

Absolutely DO NOT pitch anything in that initial forum post. If you do, you'll get blackballed. People can sense very quickly whether you're genuine or not. Go in with that attitude that you're going to give value first.

Take some time to listen and do research

There's no need for you to start posting new discussions like a madman. Scout around and see how members are interacting and observe the community etiquette. See what people are talking about, what their common challenges are, and what solutions are being offered.

Pay attention to the veterans and who the major influencers are. Keep an eye out for the super active threads and topics that are engaging most of the comments. This gives you good insight for potential products you can create to service the market. Let them tell you what they want!

Contribute value

This is arguably the most critical aspect of using forums in your marketing strategy. Whenever a member asks a question related to your area of expertise or products, wow them with practically useful answers.

Look at each instance like this as an opportunity to create goodwill in the community—not only that, but you get to demonstrate your knowledge. If you give advice, back it up with credible sources. Response time is critical here. Always be prompt.

Do not pitch anything in these conversations. If you appear biased and/or like a used-car salesman, you'll turn people off. The more objective you can be, the more trust you'll gain.

Eventually, members will look at your profile and see your product. You can be sure they will ask you about it, especially if you've consistently delivered value and helped others in the forum.

Place your website address in your forum profile signature section

Practically every forum has a place to include your "signature" in the settings of your personal profile. This is usually written text or a graphic that gets attached to the end of all your posts. Many of these same forums allow website addresses in the signature too.

If you're participating in a forum that does allow clickable links in the signature, make use of it! It's a great way to get targeted traffic to your site as you add value in the discussion threads.

So, let's go back to our real estate investing example for a moment. A short, effective signature might be something like this: Free report shares the *"5 Dumb and Costly Mistakes Most Real Estate Investors Make When Buying a Foreclosure"* – *http://YourSite.com.*

Now, some forums will have a limited number of characters to work with in the signature, so vary your call to action by how much space you have. Ideally, we want to collect a name and email at this stage so we can further build a relationship with the prospective customer. At the same time, we're continuing to give great information off the forum.

Pick your battles carefully

There can be quite a bit of drama on some forums. Avoid as much of it as possible! In some cases, users can get banned by the moderator if things get too heated. If you get into an argument, be professional and respectful. Don't attack the person. That only makes you look bad.

Whatever you do, don't talk about powder-keg, volatile topics like politics or religion. It's okay to agree to disagree from time to time.

With that said, controversy does sell. If there's a controversial topic in the industry you're servicing, you might initiate a discussion about it. The more people that chime in, the longer the post usually stays at the top of the discussion board, which translates into greater exposure for you.

Contact the admin and see if they offer paid advertising

This can be HUGE for your brand if you have a budget. It also ensures your message is seen by a highly qualified group. Some online forums allow sponsored advertising either through the use of banner ads, text ads, or paid discussion threads.

It's in your best interest to contact the admin to see what is offered. Advertising in communities like this is usually much less expensive than many traditional forms.

Offer member discounts if applicable

Once you've developed a solid reputation, you can start to be a little more aggressive with your promotion. All the marketing should be benefit rich though.

Make the members feel like they're VIPs. Have contests, offer discounts, or even give away free samples. Always contact the moderator in advance to ensure you're compliant.

Outsource at your own risk

A daily task like this can be tempting to outsource to a worker over in the Philippines. However, I would proceed with caution. If you want to build a longstanding, reputable brand, you need to hire someone that can replicate your voice.

Way too many times I've seen spammers clutter up forums with promotional stuff. This is short-sighted as most get banned within a few days.

Our goal here is image enhancement. You do that by engaging, adding value, and solving problems. Yes, you can hire a virtual assistant, but you better be darn sure they're on the same page with you. Double-check their content and posts.

Action Step: Do your market research and select the top five to ten forums where you can start to build a presence online. Create and develop compelling profiles on all of them. Be a good listener and look for those instances where you can enrich the community, adding your helpful advice. Keep an eye out for sponsorship opportunities. Always add a signature.

Follow the guidelines in this chapter and you'll set yourself up for success. If you need help, hire someone that knows, or can learn, your industry inside and out.

I have colleagues that spend the majority of their time on forums since that's where the bulk of their sales come from.

It's not about the quantity of traffic coming to your site, it's about the quality. Don't think you need to send thousands upon thousands of people to your website daily to make an extra $5,000 bucks a month. You don't. You just need to send the right kind of traffic there.

Online forums can be very lucrative for your business endeavors because they are targeted places where people congregate around a specific interest. However, you need to put the time in and plant firm roots. Commit to being in it for the long run.

Chapter 25

CREATING BUZZ AND
NOTORIETY VIA NEWS RELEASES

*Opportunity is missed by most people because
it is dressed in overalls and looks like work.*
—Thomas Edison

I n my opinion, press releases are one of the most underutilized promotional
strategies by businesses owners and entrepreneurs. If we harness them
correctly, we can get our name and content indexed by major news outlets
like ABC, CBS, FOX news, and NBC.

The benefit of this is that once you're featured in these major media outlets,
you can legitimately say this on your website. People associate major media with
credibility, so we're able to piggyback on public perception. It also differentiates
you from everyone else in the same marketplace.

Another added benefit of press release distribution is that in some markets
we'll be able to quickly sneak on the first page of Google for competitive keywords.
The end result of that is being able to get more "search" traffic to your website.

Lastly, when we create and promote a press release online, we're able to add a couple links to the content. The benefit of doing this is that Google looks at many news outlets as authority-based websites.

When they pick up your content and you have links to your website in the release, it helps pass "SEO juice" to your site and pulls your ranking up higher on the search engines. It's all about getting quality links from authority properties on the Internet.

So what exactly is a press release?

Quite simply, it's a written news release, media release, or press statement that announces something "newsworthy."

Maybe you've launched a new service or product and you want the world to know about it. Or maybe your company has given a charitable donation and you want to make it public to inspire people. There are many types of things you can announce to the media.

Usually, a press release consists of five to seven paragraphs and ranges from 500 to 600 words in length. According to Wikipedia, the common structural elements include:

Headline – is used to grab the attention of journalists and briefly summarize the news.

Dateline – contains the release date and usually the originating city of the press release. If the date listed is after the date that the information was actually sent to the media, then the sender is requesting a news embargo, which journalists are under no obligation to honor.

Introduction – is the first paragraph in a press release that generally gives basic answers to the questions of who, what, when, where, and why.

Body – is the further explanation, statistics, background, or other details relevant to the news.

Boilerplate – is generally a short "about" section providing independent background on the issuing company, organization, or individual.

Close – in North America, traditionally the symbol "-30-" appears after the boilerplate or body and before the media contact information, indicating to media that the release has ended. A more modern equivalent has been the "###" symbol.

In other countries, other means of indicating the end of the release may be used, such as the text "ends."

Media Contact Information – is the name, phone number, email address, mailing address, or other contact information for the PR or other media relations contact person.

How to get a quality press releases written

Most people truthfully suck at writing press releases, and I typically recommend outsourcing their creation to a skilled writer, either locally or virtually. If you know someone in your immediate area, that's great!

If not, an easy way to find a professional ghostwriter is to go to Upwork. com and place a job posting for exactly what you're looking for. When you post a job on Upwork, allow freelance providers to bid for only three to four days tops. If you let your ad run for the full fourteen days, you'll get dozens of freelance writers contacting you, and it becomes hard to sort through all of them.

Two things you should look for when selecting a ghostwriter via Upwork are:

1. Their experience and reviews. If you can see that they have been on Upwork awhile, have made more than $10,000 on the network, and have over twenty five-star reviews, then chances are this person will do great work on your behalf.
2. Their current online portfolio. The freelance professional you're considering to ghostwrite your content should be able to provide you with samples so you can get an idea of the quality of their work. If they cannot, move along to the next provider.

Press release distribution

After having a skilled writer create content for us, it's time to get it circulated into the major media outlets and on Google, Bing, etc. You can have the best press release in the world, but if nobody knows about it, then it doesn't matter. This is where strategic online distribution comes into play.

Two of my favorite platforms to accomplish this are PRweb.com and PRnewswire.com. These aren't cheap services, by any means. Remember this, though. All we need to do is get picked up in the news outlets one time to legitimately say we've been featured on them.

PRweb is the most cost-effective option for doing this. Their $249 option will typically get you into the well-known media sites.

Here's what happens when you submit your content to them: You'll get a confirmation it's been received, and then you need to keep your eye out for the approval email. This is very important. You want to make sure you've been approved for FULL distribution and not limited.

If they email telling you that you've been approved for limited coverage, you should call them immediately and make the necessary changes so you can get the full circulation you're paying for.

Once PRweb mass distributes the press release online, you'll want to check back every couple days to see where the content has been syndicated and picked up. When you see a major news outlet that has our article on it, such as ABC, CBS, FOX, or NBC, take a screenshot.

I use a free program called Jing (by Techsmith) for my screen captures. Google it and you'll pull the software up quick.

The reason we want to take screenshots of our press release after it's been featured in the news media is that sometimes the content will not stick for very long. These news sites consistently look for fresh stories.

If you want, you can have a page on your website that talks about "news and media" where you can feature videos or screenshots of where you've been seen in the media.

After we achieve the goal of getting placed in major media publications, we can circulate press release content to other less expensive directories and still get a good deal of traffic. Other PR submission websites include:

- *1888PressRelease.com*
- *PRLog.org*

- *i-Newswire.com*
- *24-7PressRelease.com*

Action Step: Find a ghostwriter to consistently write press releases for you. Plan on at least two per month. Brainstorm some possible newsworthy items in your business. Also, make a list of specific keywords you're wanting to rank your website higher for on Google.

Remember, in many markets press releases still get indexed well on Google. Ideally, the keywords you want to target should be in the beginning of the release. For instance, if you developed a "German shepherd obedience lesson" product, you might title a press release "New German Shepherd Obedience Lessons Make Dog Training a Snap."

Each time we create a new press release we would use a different keyword. It's also important to mention this keyword or phrase in the body of the article itself.

For maximum SEO benefit, you'll want to modify the domain name where the release is located too. For example PRweb.com gives you a section where you can alter the website address/URL to incorporate your keywords.

Rather than having a final website address for your press release that looks ugly like this:

www.PRweb.com/12345/release453875630

you can have one that looks like this:

www.PRweb.com/germanshepherd/obediencelessons.

Remember, having the keywords in the domain name helps your SEO and ability to rank high on Google. This holds true when you're trying to rank a regular website or a piece of content like an article, video, blog post, or press release.

Chapter 26

HOW TO MAKE 5 FIGURES IN ONE DAY WITH WEBINARS AND TELESEMINARS

If you want something in life you've never had,
you'll have to do something you've never done.
—Anonymous

What if I told you I discovered a powerful way to flood your business with more clients, sales, and revenue in a few days than what usually trickles in over a whole month? What if I also told you it could be done fast—in the next sixty days or less.

Lastly, what if I said you don't have to be a technology geek to implement this system to realize the highest return on investment and conversions of any other online marketing medium?

Have I sparked your interest yet?

If you're interested in doing this right the first time, then pay close attention to the pearls of wisdom in this chapter. What you're about to learn has completely TRANSFORMED the businesses and lives of thousands around the world.

This proven formula has worked for any type of business you can think of too. It's the exact same blueprint I've personally used to:

1. Sell over $175,000 worth of services and products to a frugal market that supposedly never bought from webinars or teleseminars.

2. Turn prospective customers into paying ones in a matter of hours, not months! I've done this in multiple industries over and over again.

3. Run multiple five-figure teleseminars and webinars that pulled thousands of dollars in sales for everything from information products to coaching to brick-and-mortar business services, all without a lengthy sales letter or without an in-depth launch. This was just by talking on the phone for one hour.

4. Put together a webinar that netted almost $100,000 for a private coaching client.

5. Help other business owners and online entrepreneurs make their marketing (and lives) much easier by using leverage.

One of the most important things to point out here is that you need not be a "guru" to achieve similar, extraordinary results on your own. I certainly wasn't when I began.

Teleseminars and webinars are reliable and work for ANY type of business, brand, or company. It doesn't matter what you're promoting or who you're selling it to either.

The truth is, it makes me happy to see this formula working for so many "average" folks, helping them substantially increase their client base and sales revenue. It works for the little guy just as well as it works for the big-name industry leaders.

Let me tell you a quick story.

The very first teleseminar I did was way back in 2007. Here's how it unfolded. I already had an email list of approximately 1,100 email subscribers, which anyone will tell you is not a lot at all.

I sent out a few carefully scripted emails promoting the call. Once it was go-time, the event lasted about fifty minutes. I was VERY nervous at the beginning of the call, and it probably showed.

The good thing is that I did go over the content a couple times in the days prior. I even wrote a script and had it in front of me while I was on the call. I didn't digress or deviate either.

My palms were sweaty, my heart was racing, and I felt like a total amateur. But believe it or not, 107 participants actually tuned in live. That alone shocked me, but here's the kicker:

When I made my irresistible offer at the end, I ended up collecting a whopping $11,800 on the first call I ever did!

My jaw hit the floor.

Every time I'd refresh the screen, new orders quickly kept popping up. Talk about a total life changer. Even now, I still consider it an amazing payday for the minimal amount of work involved. I mean, that was $11,800 deposited in my bank account the very next day just for spending an hour in my apartment talking on the phone!

If I could make almost $12K practically overnight while fumbling through my first teleseminar, I figured I could make a heck of a lot more if I became more experienced. So, that's what I did.

Through constant repetition, testing, and tweaking over the years, I've conducted dozens of webinars and teleseminars. During this process I've uncovered psychological triggers, persuasion strategies, and marketing tactics that enable you to host enormously profitable webinar/teleseminar events that produce immediate results.

To be fair, I can't take all the credit here.

This is not something I developed out of thin air, nor did I receive a divine stone tablet from the heavens with an exact formula to follow. When I first began, I didn't have a clue about running a highly profitable teleseminar or webinar online.

However, I was smart enough to know there were other marketers and entrepreneurs that had this process mastered. I simply sought them out and learned from them.

I attended their webinars to see exactly what the common denominators were. I paid attention to how these gurus delivered the content, how they positioned their products, and how they closed the audience at the end.

In other words, I walked the talk. You see, I'm not just going to "tell you" to associate with the best to fast-track your profitability and success. I lead by example and regularly DO THIS. You should too! It's the ultimate shortcut to freedom and making the kind of money you want. Ask any wealthy person and they'll say the same thing.

The first marketers I came across that were crushing it with teleseminars were Alex Mandossian and Shawn Casey. The entrepreneur I first noticed who was doing insanely profitable webinars before they became wildly popular was Michael Cage.

Some reading this right now might think a teleseminar is "old school" or outdated. Nothing could be further from the truth though. We still use them in our business and bank every time we do.

Everyone has a phone! More importantly, even the most low-tech people know how to operate one.

When you're just starting out, it's easier to run a teleseminar than a webinar and you're less likely to have hiccups in technology. My recommendation is to do this first to get your feet wet. We'll talk more about that later.

Back to webinars for a minute. They're all the rage these days and for good reason. The average conversion I've seen time and time again is between 10 and 30 percent for those that follow the formula I'm sharing.

That means if you can get 100 people on a webinar, you have a great chance of getting ten to thirty of them to purchase your product at the end. That type of conversion is unmatched. No other marketing medium comes close.

Let me share another true story.

Several years back, I launched a product to a relatively small list of 3,500 subscribers using only a webinar. In total, we had 130 people attend the live event and forty-five additional attended the replay.

Out of the 175 that viewed the presentation, fifty people ended up purchasing a $297 product, which amounted to a nice $14,850 in sales on the front end! Mind you, the webinar lasted just under an hour.

Not too shabby, right?

I could tell you stories from clients and colleagues that completely blow those aforementioned numbers out of the water. Enough build up, though. Let's get into the meat and potatoes so you can model strategies of the world's top marketers in order to maximize your effectiveness.

The best (and most popular) webinar platforms

Let's talk technology for a minute—don't let this scare you though. You'd be surprised just how simple these platforms are to master even for the most inexperienced online entrepreneurs. To save you time, these are the top webinar software providers.

- Stealth Seminar
- Webinar Jam Studio
- Go to Meeting
- Join.me
- Meeting Burner

The top teleconferencing services

- FreeConferencing.com
- FreeConferenceCall.com
- Go to Meeting

I won't be going in depth on how to use these webinar and teleconferencing services, but they are very easy to navigate. Choose one and get familiar with the platform along with how it works. The most important thing is to practice.

When you're comfortable, it will only take you a few minutes to set up an event. Then your marketing machine can be set in motion. Attracting qualified leads into your online funnel is the fun part. There's no shortage of ways we can do that.

In fact, all the powerful traffic strategies you're learning in this book enable you to absolutely FLOOD your events with visitors that are eager to hear what you have to share.

Sample webinar registration email scripts

Before I share with you some email templates you can model, it's important to realize a couple things prior to your first webinar/teleseminar. Hopefully, you've already set up an email marketing system/autoresponder like Aweber.

If not, as mentioned before, you can get a dollar trial at: MyProResponse.com.

A professional autoresponder follow-up system simply allows you the best email delivery rates, specific tracking, the ability to queue email messages to go out when you want, a place to house the list you're building, and the ability to create a lead-capture form.

Other popular email management solutions are Constant Contact, InfusionSoft, MailChimp, and GetResponse. They're all good.

Should you choose to use the webinar platform I personally use and recommend at StealthSeminarDiscount.com, then the email follow-up is automatically built-in. All you need to do is drive people to the webinar registration page.

Here's the protocol I typically use for webinar/teleseminar promotion to my list:

1. Start promoting the event at least ten days out (at minimum). Send one email, then three days later send an email to those that DIDN'T open the first email. Yes, send the exact same email; just make sure to change the subject headline.

   Sending to those that didn't open your first email is a HUGE part of successful marketing and promotion. This is another reason you should have a professional email management system.

2. Send another email to your WHOLE list again approximately three days after sending to those subscribers that didn't open it the first time. This should be more or less a reminder about the important event you're hosting. In fact, you can even title that email "2nd NOTICE" or "IMPORTANT Reminder."

3. Send a FINAL email to your regular subscriber list around 6:00 a.m. on the actual morning of the webinar.

4. Send an email to everyone that actually registered for the event forty-five minutes before you get started. The webinar platform you're using will allow you to send this email.

5. During all of this, you will also want to send emails to your webinar registrants giving them little gems and more bite-size nuggets of what they'll be learning on the webinar. We want them to be excited to join us live.

NOTE: The following registration email samples answer the question, "What's in it for me?" You must give people good reasons to want to take time from their busy schedule to be at your online event.

Everyone is always asking themselves, "Why should I attend and what's in it for me?"

Incorporate highly compelling (and specific) bullet points like you see in the following examples. Don't be general and skip the fine details. If you do, you won't have high attendance at your teleseminar or webinar.

I tried to pull examples from several different industries to show you how similar the scripting is. You'll be able to make this applicable to your business venture too.

• • • • •

Sample email #1

Subject Headline: The #1 Secret to Ending Back Pain FOR GOOD!

Body of email:

Hi, it's (your name),

According to the American Medical Association, over 80% of people will experience back pain at some point in their lives. In fact, it's the #1 reason why employees have to miss work, too.

If you have severe back pain, making it difficult to do daily activities like hold your children, work around the house, etc. ... then I have GREAT news for you.

I'm hosting a FREE webinar that shares the best way to end back pain for good, without invasive surgery, toxic medication, or fly-by-night gimmicks.

Most people overlook this <u>one simple cause</u> and wind up frustrated and helpless, going from doctor to doctor with no permanent relief.

Join me for an exclusive webinar titled _____. This information has helped over 2,500 Atlanta residents lead healthy, pain-free lives and it WILL do the same for you, too!

Register Now at this link (only 97 spots available):

==>   https://insertyourlinkhere.com
Date: 2/5/2012
Time: 2:00 PM EST

Here's what you'll discover on the live webinar:
How to avoid the BIGGEST mistake most make when treating back pain. This one little thing could mean the difference between you getting INSTANT relief or prolonging the pain for an extra 6 months.

The BEST way to eliminate the pain without having to pay thousands of dollars for costly medical treatment.

Stretching and core stabilization exercises that don't cost you a dime to implement. These will help strengthen your spine, making you feel 10x better in the next couple days.

Never before publicly released information and strategies that will help you feel healthier and younger than you have in years.

And much more...

==>   https://insertyourlinkhere.com

Please save the date and time RIGHT NOW. This is a one-time webinar and there won't be a recording. We only have room for 97 spots, too. If history is any indicator, we'll fill up fast.

To your health,

- (Your name)

• • • • •

Sample email #2

Subject Headline: Simple trick gets you a HUGE home office deduction!

Body of email:

Hi Friend,

Even if you claim a home office deduction, chances are you are leaving thousands of dollars on the table every year! Most people don't know what the rules are, nor do they know about all of the amazing deductions that come with having a home office!

Learn how your house is literally a goldmine of tax deductions if you are a business owner!

Join Former IRS Auditor, Tax Attorney, and best-selling author, _____ for an exclusive webinar called:

5 Strategies to maximize your Tax Deductions and Stay out of trouble with the IRS!

Register Now:
==>   https://insertyourlinkhere.com
Date: 12/5/2011
Time: 9:00 PM EST

We will also be covering Strategies like:
How to deduct nearly all your meals and entertainment

How to deduct all your medical expenses (no limits! 100% including vision, dental, braces, and more!)

Tips to dramatically increase your vehicle deductions!

The huge write-offs you get for having a home office!

How income-shifting works (hint: hiring your kids and paying them with pre-tax dollars so they can pay for college, weddings, sports, etc.!)

==> https://insertyourlinkhere.com

If you live in the US or Canada, you do not want to miss this webinar.

Best wishes,
- (Your name)

• • • • •

Sample email #3

Subject Headline: The 5 Best Ways to Monetize iPhone Apps

Body of email:

Hi (insert subscribers name),

I have received almost 30 emails the last few days and they all asked the same question:

"How do I make money from iPhone Apps?"

So, I'm holding a powerful webinar this Tuesday, August 11th at 6pm EST and the topic will be on "Making Money from iPhone Apps."

After attending this webinar, I think your eyes will be opened to the real opportunity that no other people in the history of the world have had.

I want you to think about that last statement I made and ask yourself this one question:

"Am I really going to miss out on the Early Stages of the biggest opportunity ever known to mankind because I was too busy to attend a short webinar that could change the direction of my life?"

Register below

[insert your webinar link]

We will be covering things like:

- AdMob (AdSense for Apps)
- Everwall (Advertising wall within apps)
- AirPush (Paid Push Notices)
- StartApp (Pay per install)
- CPA Offers via Push Notifications
- Etc.

Register at the link below and Join Me on Tuesday, August 11th at 6pm EST:

[insert your webinar link]

Best Wishes,

- (Your name)

P.S. Like every other major opportunity in history, this one will not last. Take advantage while you still can.

• • • • •

Sample email #4

Subject Headline: [Webinar] How to Lose 10 lbs in 10 Days – No Exercise Required

Body of email:

Boy, do I have something special to share with you today!

This coming Tuesday at 7pm EST, you're going to discover something that changed my life and transformed THOUSANDS of people around the nation.

Over half of America is overweight and a large percentage of those individuals are obese.

As you know, this condition causes many to be insecure, to have low self-esteem, have less energy, and just basically become a ticking time bomb.

Being overweight fuels diabetes, heart disease, and cancer and will decrease your lifespan if nothing is done about it.

The good news is, we've uncovered a method that ENSURES safe weight loss in order to restore your health to optimal levels once and for all.

The best part about it is that it doesn't revolve around fad diets, tricks, and is very simple to do.

Curious yet?

I cannot wait to share this proven formula on our new webinar.

Register Now:
==>   https://insertyourlinkhere.com
Date: 1/7/2012
Time: 7:00 PM EST

Here's what you'll discover on the webinar:

1. The #1 secret to losing weight without gimmicks, risky surgery, or dangerous drugs
2. How to have more energy in the next 3 days than you've had in the past 3 years
3. How to lose an EXTRA 10 lbs in 10 days without lifting a finger
4. The BIGGEST myth that can stop you before realizing your weight-loss goals
5. How to face the mirror with a smile every time while looking your best

Register at this link below
http://yourlinkhere.com

See you there,

- Your name

P.S. This will be the FIRST and LAST weight-loss webinar you'll ever attend. Yes, it's that effective and life changing!

Prepare to see a thinner and healthier You in just a few short days!

• • • • •

Webinar replay email script

Here's a sample webinar/teleseminar replay script so you can get an idea of how the email is structured and the formatting. This can easily be adapted to any business. An email should always be sent the day following the event. Send the email to those that were unable to attend the webinar and to your regular list.

It's important to let others know what they missed out on because this typically motivates people to actually listen to the replay. No one likes to be left out in the cold. Also, always add a sense of urgency.

We typically leave replays up online for only twenty-four hours. Tell your people how long they have to listen and get the bonus you gave away on the call. This will help maximize your attendance.

Sample email:

Subject headline - What you Missed on Tuesday's Webinar

Body of email:

"This is genius… Keep it coming!"

Hi … Joseph here. That's what John Smith said on our Facebook page shortly after our first-ever Live webinar Tuesday night.

And in case you didn't get the memo...

Up Close Live is a new members-only service...

Every two weeks, we'll bring on an expert (Tuesday night was master CPA _____) where we'll get into a studio, take questions through live chat, and broadcast it in real time.

Frankly, if you weren't on with us live, you missed out (ask any member who attended!).

Robert, Joe, and I were answering incoming questions from live chat as fast as members were typing them.

Thankfully, we had an entire crew and team to help us out. And fortunately for all, we also taped the entire show and put the replay here.

Here's what we went over Tuesday night...

- What's the best tax structure to hold gold and silver
- A tax-efficient way to use your children
- Why, if your accountant only talks about 401(k)/IRA for saving taxes, you're missing out on 90% of efficient tax planning
- Why you may want to avoid schedule C as a business owner
- Who you should never talk to if you get audited
- Your options if your investment losses were due to theft or fraud
- Two structures you should NEVER hold real estate in
- When two goods make a wrong—avoid this tax shelter mistake
- How to buy real estate with gold and silver without paying taxes
- The proper way to hold real estate for maximum asset protection

Frankly, there were a LOT of amazing tax-saving insights.

I'm probably going to watch the replay of this broadcast two or three more times and take notes.

You can watch the replay along with me too, and take notes—here. (If you're not already logged in, you may have to scroll all the way down to the bottom of the lessons page to find it.)

Hopefully, in two weeks you can join us live instead of watching the replay.

Why? Because the energy on the webinar was electric.

Members got to interact with each other and our staff in live chat. ... We had a customer support line to take calls. ... And best of all, questions were being answered in real time.

Brett Johnson said on Facebook, *"This was a great presentation! This newfound knowledge will save me thousands!"*

"Crystal33" on the webinar live chat said, *"This was an awesome first live event."*

And here are some other live chat comments:

"Dawn" said, *"Great info and great support! Looking forward to the next live webinar!"*

"Vishal" said, *"Robert, Matthew and Joe...this was GREAT. Thanks!"*

"Bryan" said, *"Matthew, thank you for sharing all this powerful information."*

You can watch the replay at this link below (remember to scroll all the way down).

http://yourwebinarreplaylink.com

And once you're done, I'd love to hear your feedback.

We won't know how we're doing, whether you find this valuable or what you like ... unless you tell us!

Your feedback gives us direction on where to take the training series next.

You can post your thoughts on the first webinar of _____ .

Looking forward to hearing from you!

Sincerely,

- Joseph Jones

• • • • •

Registration page examples

Whatever webinar platform you choose to go with, they'll probably have their own set of landing-page templates so you can easily collect registrations. I'm not biased toward any one template. At the end of the day, we just want the most conversions.

You can test a couple registration pages to see which one converts better. Some marketers prefer templates with video on them; others like myself prefer simple text. Here are a couple examples:

This email capture form is what you see at the bottom of this text registration page.

Here's another registration-page example. The video is basically just going to let prospects know what the webinar is about and (more importantly) what it will do for them. You're repeating the compelling bullet points then providing instructions on how to register.

Webinar and teleseminar checklist

Choose one specific topic to cover. Do not go over multiple topics on a webinar. Also, do not overwhelm attendees with information. Keep it simple with three to five important points.

Set the specific time and date of the event and give yourself a deadline. Allow yourself at least ten days of solid promotion so you can attract a large number of attendees to the event.

At least three email reminders should be sent to people after they've registered. Send them every couple days, then a reminder on the day of.

Create a forty- to fifty-minute PowerPoint presentation based on the proven script in The Ultimate Webinar Marketing Blueprint training course. Once you get good at webinars, you can host longer ones.

Grab any presentation images you need from iStock.com or a royalty-free photo site.

Create your irresistible offer and fast-action bonuses for the "close" portion of the presentation.

Select the teleseminar/webinar service you'll be using for the event from the ones provided.

Create a compelling webinar/teleseminar registration page (with "speed" bullet points detailing what you'll discuss). View sample registration pages I've included, or look at examples in Stealth Seminar. Create a short two-minute video detailing everything you'd normally dictate in bullet points.

Address these points in your webinar/teleseminar close:

- Here's what I've got plus "what's in it for me"
- Here's what this product or service will do for you (list bullet points)
- Incorporate real testimonials
- Provide a few fast-action bonuses with value amount attached
- Tell your attendees what to do next
- Guarantee (make the offer risk-free)

Create an actual sales page to direct visitors to after the webinar (this is optional depending on which service you use). Some services such as Stealth Seminar and Webinar Jam Studio let you simply add a checkout link to the webinar so you can put your sales copy in your presentation.

The checkout link should direct to your shopping cart. You can use PayPal or establish a merchant account.

Write all the promotion emails leading up to the event. These should be based on the examples you find here.

Double-check everything for spelling and grammar mistakes. Run through the presentation at least three times so it's familiar and you have it mastered.

Start promoting the free event to your email list at least ten days out. Also, use the traffic-generation strategies you find in this book such as Facebook ads, solo ads, YouTube videos, blogging, joint-venture partnerships, Instagram, etc.

My top three promotion strategies I use to bank are my email list, Facebook advertising, and joint-venture partnerships.

A comprehensive guide to scripting
your webinar and teleseminar presentation

Here's a fast, easy way to plan your next successful teleseminar or webinar. I've discovered a reliable formula that works practically every time to create value, earn trust, build rapport, and attract a windfall of new clients and sales.

I learned this blueprint from studying successful Internet marketer Michael Cage. He was using webinars long before all the Johnny-come-lately teachers and has made an absurdly large amount of money in the process.

In fact, this scripting outline has been responsible for generating for us five-figure paydays from almost every webinar/teleseminar we've ever conducted. Mind you, these events usually last only sixty minutes.

Not bad income for the minimal work involved.

The following formula is broken down into simple questions that you need to answer from the potential customer's perspective.

I'm not necessarily recommending you directly say ask questions during your event. What I do want is for you to use them when you're strategically mapping out what you're going to be discussing.

Understand that for each individual question you've seen in this guide, there could be a few different answers. There's not just one right answer. I want to provide you with the most useful content that quickly produces new clients and sales.

You'll also uncover how to influence attendees with psychological triggers and signals that move them in the direction of your choice. This scripting process is strategic in getting others to take the desired action you want.

IMPORTANT: All the ideas and strategies in this section apply to both teleseminars and webinars even though I most often use the word "webinar."

Introduction

The introduction of your webinar is critically important. It sets the tone for the entire event. You need to grab the viewers' attention. If done right, it's what gets the prospective customer interested and engaged in what you have to say.

Also, the intro should serve to re-excite them, give them the "big idea," and get them to stay with you until the very end of the presentation.

I also need to mention that you must sound enthusiastic here. I mean, if you don't get excited about the content you're sharing, how can you expect others to? The tone of your voice is crucial. If you sound boring and monotone, forget about it. You're toast. No one will stick around!

Why did I make a great decision to be here?

Introduce and humanize yourself by talking about a few small details in your life. Then affirm their great decision to be on the event with you. Reawaken their desire and the reason they tuned in for the webinar by discussing their pain along with the problem.

Engage the attendees' imagination by painting a vivid picture of what life could be like as a result of what you have to offer. Establish social proof by talking about all the states and/or countries that viewers are watching from as well as the number of people present.

Reiterate the bullet points and what they'll discover on the call. Get a commitment by giving them specific directions to follow (like getting out a pen and paper and taking notes when you emphasize important points).

Why should I give you my attention until the end of the event?

Promise your attendees a free bonus (or large benefit) for staying on the entire webinar and listening carefully. It's also important to warn guests about what they'll lose if they don't pay attention or stick around until the finish.

Don't be too specific about when you're going to give it to them either. Participants should be in suspense as to when the reward will come.

Reassure webinar viewers that it will be obvious when the time comes. However, warn them not to take their eyes away from the screen for a minute because you're going to be giving them so much great actionable content that they just might miss it.

Here's another cool thing you can do: You can offer to give them your PowerPoint slides, cheat sheets, or transcripts as resources after the event has ended. Just say you'll provide them with special links later on. Don't say when you'll do it though.

What's the "big idea"?

Every event you host should have one big idea that everything pretty much falls under. Think of it as a container, like Michael Cage talks about. You can let your audience know that all the points you'll discuss during the event will lead back to this idea.

Give your idea context too. Storytelling is a powerful way to do this because it helps people resonate with your content easier. Stories also engage your webinar and teleseminar attendees.

Of all the different types of stories you can tell, it's simple to focus on a problem/solution one. Basically, you're going to reveal a big problem you were having which lead you on a journey to finding the perfect solution.

The body

So, we've gone through our intro and have given our audience a glimpse of the big idea, which is the reason they're on the event. Now attendees are salivating for the information you're about to share. They want it bad.

The next several questions will help you give people exactly what they're seeking in a palatable, digestible form.

What should I not be doing?

In this section, you want to point out the most common mistakes you see most people make and then explain why they make those mistakes. No one likes to shoot themselves in the foot or commit needless errors. You can also use this time to go over popular myths that surround the topic. If you did your market research carefully, you already know what the biggest mistakes and common misconceptions are.

Doing this is a quick way to establish authority in the eyes of those tuning in. When you're perceived as an expert, people feel more comfortable, they trust you, and they are more likely to buy what you're selling.

People have to be shown that what they're currently doing is not going to get them the result that they want. You should have a list of things and explain why those "pseudo-solutions" are not going to cut it and/or why they are just big mistakes.

When it gets down to it, you're basically invalidating every other method but your own. This is vital because it makes your close much easier if you mention what doesn't work and then show attendees what does work.

Why should I believe you understand me and know what I'm going through?

This section is your chance to really shine. If people don't believe you (or believe you know what they're going through), they won't buy … period! You need to practice empathy here. This is where we can fuse another relatable personal story into the presentation.

Tell a story of how you (or a client) was at a very low point and facing nearly impossible challenges. Share your journey of hardship all the way through your discovery and success.

This is very humanizing. It makes your audience think, "He's like me. He gets what I'm going through and has risen up out of the ashes to experience great success (or results). He started at rock bottom, too."

Give attendees hope. You want them to think, "If he can do it, then I can as well."

What's your big promise?

Since we're going to spend a fair amount of time making our audience feel the pain, unhappiness, and frustration of their present circumstances, we also need to future-pace them by painting a clear, promising vision of what their life can be like.

During this process of getting them to imagine and step into their new reality, you're making a promise. The promise is what's possible when they follow your advice and/or do business with you.

Immerse webinar attendees in this new reality right down to the fine details. This experience has to emotionally resonate with them. Give them a snapshot of your life—or a client that's followed your guidance.

For example, when I host teleseminars or webinars, I like to open my audience's minds to the realm of possibility based on my personal—and many of clients'—"rags to riches" story.

I don't just talk about the money and the hundreds of millions of dollars I've helped clients make. Money is not a strong enough motivator for most people. I discuss what money gives you, which is FREEDOM and flexibility—the ability to come and go as you please, when you want.

No reporting to a boss.

No hamster wheel.

No chasing a carrot locked up in a tiny office cubicle for forty hours per week.

No commuting two hours per day in the city traffic.

Money gives you options. For some, it's the ability to spend a Tuesday morning at the park with their one-year-old son who just took his first steps.

For others, it's the ability to be spontaneous and decide to hop a flight to Costa Rica tomorrow and then have dinner at a five-star resort at the bottom of one of the world's largest active volcanos. Can you see what I'm getting at?

You've got to know your core audience—their wants, needs, emotional triggers, and reasons they get out bed in the morning.

Will it really work for me?

Here's something you already know: the buying public is incredibly skeptical these days when purchasing anything online. Some have been burned while others know someone that's been scammed. Needless to say, the BS radar is on high alert.

Many even think their situation is so unique and different that there's no way they could get the result you're promising.

This is where the list of objections you should've made comes into play. The most common objections are things like they don't have enough money, they don't have the time, it's too complex to make it work, etc.

In your presentation, you need to directly call out these objections AND smash them with a hammer. Create a logical discussion that easily overcomes the objections so attendees can see that nothing should be stopping them from acting now.

Testimonials from the kind of people that had similar hesitations can be very compelling at this stage of the game. If you have a video testimonial, just play it during the webinar. That's much more persuasive than a written case study.

You might also relay a story of a client that was skeptical before trying your product or program. Rest assured, there will be skeptics on the webinar. Put yourself in their shoes.

When you address the common objections before they consciously arise in your prospect's mind, this is very powerful. You're more likely to turn that individual into a buyer by the end of your event.

What should I be doing?

This is where you want to give people an overview of everything. Maybe it's even an exact formula. This is precisely what they should be doing, why they should be doing it, and what will happen if they don't.

Be careful not to give away the "how" at this stage. Why not? It's because that's what your product or program will show them.

For instance, let's say you're in the real estate industry and your prospect's biggest desire is to make money by flipping homes in Orlando. You're going to tell the overall formula for success, the pitfalls to watch out for, how to find the best contractors, etc.

You can literally give away the step-by-step process BUT you're not going to reveal the exact contracts you use, how to find the best deals, how to negotiate with sellers, and how to get the highest amount of money at closing.

Why should my search end right here, right now?

You've got to let prospects know that this is where the buck stops. Reinforce the consequences they'll face if they don't do anything. Drive home the point that they don't want to be doing the other options you previously mentioned and describe why not.

Explain to attendees why they have finally found the solution. Doing this provides the perfect transition for the close.

The close

This is the MOST important part of your webinar or teleseminar! You could deliver the best presentation in the world, but if you can't close the sale at the end, it doesn't matter. You'll walk away empty-handed with an upset stomach.

At the end of the day, we know we have a good product that can change lives for the better. We need to do everything in our power to get it in the prospective client's hands.

When you're just starting out, shoot for at least a 15% close rate on your webinar or teleseminar. That means if 100 people attend, then 15 of them will buy. Once you get really good, your close rate can easily double! Practice makes perfect.

Why should I give you permission to sell?

Our primary purpose for doing this is to keep people engaged in our event. If your transition to the close is too abrupt, many attendees will tune out because they know they're about to be sold. That's not what we want. We're not going to force anything on them either.

A great way to get permission is to ask your audience a question. First, though, restate some of the content highlights you discussed during the presentation. You're reminding them of the value and insight they received along with a few points of proof.

Then, state the question. Check the following example:

"You've heard about all the ways that the Standard American Diet (SAD) can destroy your health and make you fat. You've heard how Mike was able to _____ and Matthew was able to _____, and Mary was able to _____.

You've heard about the formulas that I use when I work with clients, in order to see almost immediate weight loss, pain-free living, and dramatic increases in quality of life.

And if you've heard all of that and you know this is what you want for yourself, you've got to be asking yourself one question: 'What's the fastest way to start using this information and protocol, beginning today?'

If you'll permit me, I'm going to tell you the answer to that question."

If your attendees remain on the line, they've basically given you permission to give them the answer to the question you asked. Essentially, this makes for a smooth transition to your close.

After we talk about some of the content highlights and get their permission, we should verbally repeat the problem. This is what actually got them to attend your webinar or teleseminar because they were confident you could help with the solution.

Here's an example:

"You took time out of your busy schedule to attend this event today because you're frustrated, maybe even really fed up with how difficult it is to lose weight on your own.

You're fed up with feeling sick and not having energy. You're tired of people not paying you compliments. You're tired of looking in the mirror and not recognizing the person you've become.

You're tired of people telling you this is how it's going to be and you have to deal with it. Lastly, you're tired of seeing thin supermodels featured in magazines.

Now you're ready for something different in your life. You want a better way of eating and exercising. You want to turn heads when you walk down the street. You want to feel confident, sexy, and healthy again.

The question you're probably asking yourself is, 'How can I start doing that as fast as possible right now?' You heard me talk about some ways to do that today, and I've told you about some of the clients that I've worked with.

I'll try to give you ideas or ways to see how doing what you are doing is not working and that you need another way. I'm going to tell you how to get going as quickly as possible. What I recommend that you do right now is ...."

After this, tell attendees what your mission is.

What brought you in front of them today? Why do you really want to help them get the result they're seeking? You don't want to see your audience continue to struggle and make the same mistakes you did when they have a shortcut in front of them.

Lastly, tell a story of the reluctant viewer if you have one. This is about a person who begged, pleaded, and would not leave you alone because they wanted you to reveal what you've discovered.

See a personal example:

It wasn't my plan to start coaching entrepreneurs how to use social media to start and grow wildly profitable businesses. I was happy being in practice. However, I had so many doctors and professionals asking me how I was attracting new clients from MySpace in 2005.

After all, nobody was teaching social media business growth strategies back then.

I eventually knew I had to get this life-changing information to the masses. I mean, I loved being in practice helping patients, but if I could help other doctors and business owners reach exponentially more people to change more lives, that could create a bigger impact.

Social media had created an incredible "economic stimulus" for my family, and I knew it could do the same for anyone. I was tired of seeing others struggling financially and not living up to their fullest potential. It didn't have to be that way.

With the insight you've just gained in this section, keep in mind that the goal is to smoothly transition from the content portion of the event to the close. We're now trying to get the attendee to take the next step immediately, which is simply to invest in your product.

How can you solve the problem?

At this stage you want to let your audience know that you can definitely help them with their problem. However, the product offer you make has to be uniquely presented so that's it's apparent they cannot get it anywhere else.

You've put this package together only for those that have attended your webinar or teleseminar. In other words, it's exclusive to them and won't be found in another place. Build immense value into the offering in regards to the results they can generate with it and the dollar amount value (which you'll give for a bargain price at the end).

Remember, sales is as simple as:

- Here's what I've got plus "what's in it for me"
- Here's what this product or service will do for you (list bullet points)
- Incorporate real testimonials
- Provide a few fast-action bonuses with value amount attached
- Guarantee (make the offer risk-free)
- Tell your attendees what to do next

As you introduce the solution (your product), go through each component. Tell people the big problem it solves and the end goal it will help them realize. Then it's time to build its value in the prospect's mind.

Talk about why you created the package like this based on your own personal experience.

An example would be, "It helped me go from point A to point B in _____ months, but I wanted to make it more digestible and organized so it could help others achieve results faster in as little as _____ weeks (or days, or instantly). So,

I created (your product name). Here are the details, how it works, and what you get."

Now, you can go through each individual bit. For example, when I'm selling my social media services or training, I list out the individual modules we'll be covering, describe what prospective clients will learn in them, and show people the specific strategies they'll harness when using Facebook.

For each of these components, you'll want to discuss what problem it helps the prospect solve and what goal it will help them achieve.

Then you can attach a value to the specific component. How much is this section of your training or guidance worth? What is the dollar amount? How much will it cost them NOT to have this component (more costly errors or expensive hard knocks)?

You can also fuse client success stories into each individual component to demonstrate that the product works. The more social proof the better.

Immediately after you go through all the components in your product package, building value into each single piece, you close with the entire package overview again. Then you place a dollar value on the package as a whole.

Why should I believe you? Remind me again.

In this section, you're basically reminding your audience that you've already provided them testimonials and case studies from real people like them. You're sharing how many clients you've worked with from all over the world.

Reiterate your experience. Restate your personal journey of self-discovery and tie all that into the product offer you have just presented them.

What's it all going to mean to me at the end of the day?

This goes back to the wants and desire of your event registrants. What do they want more than anything? Keep in mind that the surface benefits are not nearly as important as the emotional, deeper-level benefits.

For instance, the amount of money someone can make with your product is great BUT what does the money allow them to do? Spend more time with their family? Have the freedom they want? Finally break free from debt?

The benefits need to be placed into context too. This is key. Give your audience an example situation they may have encountered and will encounter again. After you do that, let them know what will be different in that situation if they have your product.

Another powerful strategy is to get the webinar or teleseminar attendees to see that your product is really "free." Here's what I mean.

Let's say a salesman at Home Depot is trying to sell you $5,000 worth of solar panels for your house. At the end of his pitch, he says that since you're not using conventional gas or electric utilities, you're going to save an additional $150 per month in bills. On top of that, some companies will actually pay you each month because you'll be producing excess energy to be distributed into the community.

That means that after two years and ten months, the solar panels will have paid for themselves because you will have saved so much on your utility bills. The bottom line here is that if you can find a way for your product to pay for itself, this is the perfect time to tell prospects.

What should I do about it?

Clarity is king right here. It's important to be specific so there are no misunderstandings. You can reiterate what your one-time offer is. Restate what comes with it (what they get), how much it is, and include a risk-free, highly compelling guarantee that makes it a no-brainer.

Something to also add in at this stage is a comparison of the special you're giving attendees on the webinar to any public offer you currently have. Everyone likes a deal—and people like exclusive offers available only for them.

Why should I buy right now and what will I miss out on if I don't?

Whatever product or service you're offering, it's important that attendees know that this deal is available for a very limited time. You can make that special price (with bonuses) available until the end of the webinar, midnight, etc.

Give a strict deadline!

This creates a sense of urgency and scarcity so the prospect is compelled to take action immediately. If you don't do this, your audience will think they can wait. People that wait typically don't buy. Learn from my mistakes!

You can also offer only a limited quantity of your product. When you're sold out, that's the end. They won't see the offer again.

We can also create more urgency and scarcity by using fast-action bonuses. This is a great way to increase sales because up to this point, you've just offered the core product. You've added immense value and it's already an awesome deal by itself.

When you add bonuses, it heavily sways the audience to take action because they can receive those gifts only if they act immediately. It's the icing on the cake. A no-brainer if you will.

It's your call what you decide to offer as bonuses. You could do anything from cheat sheets or e-books, to audios, videos, software, additional complimentary products, etc.

CONVERSION TIP 1: A simple thing you can do to raise your sales conversions is to have instant delivery on your products. People don't like to wait. If there's a way for you to bundle your product into instant-delivery form, do it!

This increases the volume of people that buy your products. It also helps to continue the momentum and excitement you've created during your event.

CONVERSION TIP 2: Discuss and emphasize the consequences of not acting today. Your audience already has a big problem that needs to be solved—that's why they're on your webinar or teleseminar. If they do nothing, they'll have the same problem six months from now, and it will likely get worse. Attendees need to hear this.

You're offering them the opportunity to be in a completely new and better place. You've got a way for them to finally end the pain and frustration.

Couple this strategy with future-pacing. Get them to picture themselves having your product and feeling happy, and how their life will be better days and months from now. We want to immerse them in the vision of their new and improved life. Be as specific as you can.

To recap … when we intensify scarcity and urgency, make our product a very limited commodity, throw in fast-action bonuses, offer instant gratification with a guarantee, remind attendees of the consequences of not taking action today, restate the benefits, and tell them how to order, we set ourselves up for the best possible chance at getting the highest number of sales!

How do I order? Walk me step-by-step. What will happen after the purchase?

Never assume that attendees know what to do next. Tell them specifically what action you want them to take. Repeat this a couple times during your close—not necessarily in sequence though. Here's an example.

"Click the big yellow 'add-to-card' button you see below this video right now. Once on the following page, enter your contact details then click the green submit button you see."

I'm a firm believer in setting expectations.

Let your new customers know what will happen after they've completed the order form. Will they be redirected to a thank-you page with a download link? Will they get an email from support? Will they get a phone call? Be clear.

Dumb and costly webinar and teleseminar mistakes to avoid

Selecting an unspecific and generic title

Not getting this right can be a kiss of death for your live event. It's definitely one of those make-or-break deals. Most people will decide to attend or skip your webinar based on the title alone. You've got one shot here. You need to generate an emotional response from the prospect.

You want them to stop everything that they're doing and think, "There's no way I can miss this."

Let me give you an example. If you're in the weight-loss niche, you could do a webinar titled "How to Drop a Quick 10lbs in Just 10 Days." This is a fairly decent title since you make a promise. It's better than a generic, "How to Drop a Quick 10lbs."

However, great titles have an emotional component to them. Here's an example: "Drop 10lbs in 10 Days: Turn Heads, Gain Confidence, and Feel Sexier Than You Have in Years by Doing this One Thing."

Do you notice the difference?

Too much clutter on the registration and/or squeeze page

We only have one goal for the registration page: to collect a name and an email of an interested (and qualified) prospect. This is the reason the pages are formatted the way they are. DO NOT muck up the page with anything that isn't critically relevant to the event you're promoting.

As mentioned in a previous chapter, include the title of the event, date and time, several compelling bullet points that describe the content and what's in it for the viewer, and a sign-up box. Forget about including anything else because you don't want to distract others from the action you want them to take.

No follow-up between registration and the actual webinar

The stone-cold reality is that most people break commitments all the time! Signing up only gets them over the first hurdle. You still need to remind them a few times and get them excited to attend your event.

If you do a really good job of reminding them, you can expect a 50–60 percent show rate at the time of the event. Sometimes this can be higher. If you don't remind them at all, you'll be lucky if you see a 30 percent attendance.

Face it. Life gets in the way for many folks. They become preoccupied with a hodge-podge of other stuff and forget about you if there's no regular follow-up.

Holding off until the perfect moment

I hate to break it to you, but rarely, if ever, will you have a perfect webinar. Hiccups happen all the time. The more experience you get under your belt, the fewer errors you make. That goes for anything in life.

Imperfect action beats perfect planning any day. Get your first webinar or teleseminar done as soon as you can. Even if you mess things up, you're more than likely going to generate some income from the event.

You'd be amazed at just how many people I've heard say, "I screwed that webinar up." Then, as it turns out, they made decent money. The bottom line is this: Waiting is the worst thing you can do. It will keep you broke.

Every time you do a teleseminar or webinar, you'll get more comfortable. Expect your sales volume to also increase.

Sounding scripted or like a robot

Ideally, you should practice your script at least three times in full before delivering the live event. This is HUGE! Never sound scripted because it instantly makes you boring and annoying. It also makes it seem like you don't really care.

Think about it. How many times have you been on the phone with a big company and you know the rep on the other side is reading from a script? How does it make you feel?

Let me be clear. I'm not saying don't have a script; however, put it in outline form. Or, if it's word for word, you need to go over it several times to ensure you sound like a normal person. Remember, normal people vary their voice tonality and typically have a smooth delivery.

You want to come across as enthusiastic and sharp as a tack!

Going over way too much info

The first time or two it can be very tempting to want to stuff as much as you can into an hour presentation. I mean, the last thing you want to happen is for a prospect to walk away and feel they didn't get the value promised.

I used to feel like that but then I learned simple is better. Cover no more than four to five key points in your initial webinars or teleseminars. People can only process so much information at a time.

If prospective clients develop "information overload," expect them to forget most of what you covered. Learn from my mistakes! This is where a good script comes into play. Do not digress. Stick with the important points you want your audience to know.

Boring attendees to death

We already discussed that you come across as boring when you sound scripted. If you fill the event with dry facts the whole darn time, you risk your audience tuning out due to lack of excitement. Bored attendees do not buy your products either.

You've got to find the perfect mix of education and entertainment. Stories are a great way to jazz things up and enliven the atmosphere.

Having your pitch and close be too apparent

If you're just starting out, it's normal to get a little nervous when the time comes to ask for money. That's why you need to practice beforehand to ensure the deliver remains smooth at the time of the close. Look, you have a great product, and now it's time to make the audience an irresistible offer so it can change their lives.

During your close, do not speed up and/or change the way you speak. Newbies have a tendency to do this. If your attendees sense that you're not as confident or enthusiastic when you're making your product offer, they'll be more apprehensive. If your voice cracks at this stage, you sound weak. That can cripple your sales.

Another important point to mention here is that throughout your live event, you should be sprinkling testimonials here and there so you're actually "closing" the whole time. Your product offering is simply an extension of the webinar/teleseminar.

Being unprepared to answer common questions

If you're an expert, you need to know the answer or be resourceful enough to guide the attendee in the right direction. If you've done your market research, you should know what the most common questions and objections are.

If you don't feel confident on your first event, then give attendees an email either before or during the webinar so they can send questions there. That way, you're able to choose which ones to answer.

If you just open up the lines live and you're unprepared, your credibility can be squashed in an instant. If you lose authority, you lose sales. No one will buy what you're offering.

Make it a point to address (and overcome) the common objections as a part of your webinar. Doing this before the person consciously thinks of an excuse is very powerful and makes them feel more comfortable with you.

Not creating any urgency in your presentation

Let me tell you something you already know. Most people procrastinate. The longer a person holds off on purchasing a product, the less likely they are to purchase. If we host an event, we want people to buy at the end of the event, right when they're the most motivated!

To get most people to act now, they need to understand that taking immediate, decisive action gets them what they want. It also helps them steer clear of what they don't want. That last half is crucial.

We need to consistently remind registrants of the consequences they could potentially suffer for not taking action now. No one likes to miss out on things. People are more likely to act when it's to avoid pain as opposed to seeking pleasure. The fear of loss can be the ultimate motivator.

Providing a vague "what to do next"

Once you've gone through your presentation and you're near the end of your close, you must be crystal clear in your final instructions. If I'm on a webinar, I will literally say this: "Here's what I want you to do next. Click the big orange add-to-cart button below to take advantage of _____."

Never assume attendees know what you want them to do next, even if there's a pink elephant on the screen. If there is one shred of confusion in your ordering instructions, your sales will take a hit. Confused people don't buy. Walk the person by the hand, step-by-step, and be clear.

No follow-up after the event

If you stop your marketing after you do your webinar or teleseminar, you're missing out on a lot of sales. Anywhere from 40–60 percent of those that register for your event will actually show. Some of those attendees don't make it to your sales pitch either. Others need an additional nudge before they buy.

We usually have a replay of the event so that those that didn't attend can access it. Or if a person bounced off early for whatever reason, they get a second chance to view the whole thing.

The marketing that takes place after the live event will capture an extra percentage of prospects and turn them into paying clients. As I've said time and again, the money is in the follow-up. If you don't do anything after the live event, you've essentially garnished your own paycheck.

Disregarding those that didn't purchase

Just because someone didn't buy your product on the first webinar or teleseminar doesn't mean they're not interested. To ignore them is naïve and a mistake. Some individuals need extra contact or more information before they're comfortable enough to spend their money with you.

Not featuring successful case studies or testimonials

In today's time, the buying public is immensely skeptical. We overcome this by stacking and layering on the social proof. Client testimonials are the most powerful way to conquer doubt and substantially increase sales.

We never stop collecting testimonials. This is an ongoing process. I've seen sales pages that have totally sucked from a copy perspective but had dozens of testimonials. This is very persuasive, especially when it comes to asking a prospect for money.

How do you get testimonials? Simply ask. Then offer a special gift for those who are kind enough to give you feedback on your product. This can be a discount, an extra product for free, an additional training, etc.

Not emailing a highlight reel to your list

Our goal here is simple. We want those that didn't attend our event to feel the pain of what they missed out on. Talk about the incredible content that was shared or go into detail about the life-transforming info attendees received that they did not.

You can even include short testimonials from happy attendees. Doing all of this will cause many that missed the event to regret their decision not to attend. Rest assured, the next time you host a webinar or teleseminar, more people will be on because they don't want to miss out.

Not having an automated system in place

The last thing you want to do is to conduct the same event over and over again manually. That's not high leverage. We want to automate the money-getting process as much as possible. This is where programs like Stealth Seminar and Webinar Jam Studio come into play.

If you have a webinar that's converting like gangbusters, the goal is to automate it so that this event can work for you 24/7.

The most common buying objections you must handle

When you study human behavior and buyer psychology, you consistently find that it's best to handle the common objections before they consciously arise in a prospective customer's mind. This is what we also want to do on our webinars/ teleseminars.

Regardless of what product you have and industry you're selling to, most consumers have the same set of mental blocks that you need to overcome. The following are the most common objections.

"I can't afford it."

The reality is, most people can afford it. You either haven't established value in their minds or your product isn't a top priority. If you truly want something (even if you don't have the money), you'll find a way to get it. (If no one is saying this about your product, there's a good probability that your price point is way too low.)

During your webinar or teleseminar, you can plant seeds throughout regarding the cost of working directly one-on-one with you. This exclusivity and personal interaction should obviously be MUCH higher than the cost of the product.

Toward the end of the presentation, when you reveal the price of your program, the amount of money they invest will pale in comparison to working with you privately. We also stack on added fast-action bonuses and attach the real value of those to make it a no-brainer to buy.

So not only are they getting the original product you offered, but they're getting so much more for the same low price.

"I don't believe what you're telling me."

People are so skeptical of buying anything online these days. Some have been burned while others have heard horror stories of people getting scammed. The number one reason people don't buy from you is that they don't believe you.

There's also a cold, hard reality attached to this. The average person doesn't implement what they're taught. They complain about the results they didn't get from the work they didn't do. It's easier to blame the teacher for not delivering, and skepticism increases that much more.

The best way to overcome this is with testimonials and case studies of those that have successfully used your product to generate the results you promise. This is called social proof. The more of it the better.

I've seen sales pages where there's literally fifty testimonials. That's all. We can never have too many people singing our praises. The more testimonials you have, the less skepticism prospective customers will have.

"It looks too difficult."

Face the facts. People like things fast and easy. They want quick fixes and magic pills without having to do any work. It's just how the public has been conditioned. You and I are smart enough to know rarely do things like that exist though.

However, in our sales copy and presentation we need to explain the ease of use as well as demonstrate that anyone can achieve similar results with your product regardless of their skill level.

Show attendees how quickly they can get things to work and just how little time it actually takes. Testimonials can help serve this purpose and make it believable. You want the prospective customer to think to themselves, "If she can do it, then I can too."

"This product won't work for me."

This is one of the very first objections that people usually offer. They either think your product won't work at all or it won't work for them personally. How do you overcome this? With lots of testimonials and stories that people can relate to.

You need to really know your audience and the different types of folks that attend your events. For example, whenever I host a teleseminar or webinar, there are usually three types of entrepreneurs that come to these events.

One, the person that's never used social media strategically to build their business.

Two, the individual that's used social media and has garnered some results. However, they know they haven't even come close to maximizing their effectiveness. They're eager to take it to the master level and multiply their impact and sales revenue.

Three, experienced professionals who are already getting good results with social media marketing but know they're capable of more. They want to learn from someone that's achieved the financial success they want.

So I will tailor my message to these three types of business owners and show them that regardless of where they are, my systems can multiply their income quickly.

Address this objection directly. On your webinar, you can even say, "Even if you think this won't work for you, it absolutely will. Here's why ...."

"I'm not that bad off."

Even when a person knows they need your product and/or service to improve their quality of life, sometimes they convince themselves that they can wait. Or they believe things are still tolerable. They really need to feel the pain of their current situation. As I've mentioned before, prospective customers are more likely to take action when it's to avoid pain as opposed to seeking pleasure.

So it's your job as the presenter to convince event attendees that they cannot afford to wait or remain in their current situation. Incorporate the following points into your teleseminars and webinars.

- If you're not moving ahead, you're falling behind.
- The definition of insanity is doing the same thing over and over and expecting a different result.
- Future-pace them by asking a question like, "If you don't do anything this minute, or five months from now, how do you think your life will be? If you're honest with yourself, you'll probably have the same challenges. They might even be worse."
- Offer testimonials from others that didn't take action immediately and how much they lost by not doing so.
- We can also inject real scarcity and urgency into the mix. Is this a one-time offer? Are only limited quantities available? Are the fast-action bonuses good for today only? Does the price increase tomorrow?
- Reiterate everything the attendees are getting right now. Lay it out bullet by bullet.
- Also, make sure they know what they're missing out on should they decide not to take action today. What are the consequences (emotional, financial, physical, etc.) of them not investing in your product at that moment?

Action Step: Plan to get your first webinar or teleseminar going as soon as possible. As you can see by the depth of this chapter, your events need to be calculated and well thought-out. Always go off a script BUT never sound scripted. Practice the content a few times before your live event.

Give yourself at least ten days to promote the event. Facebook ads, your email list, and joint ventures are the fastest ways to get qualified registrants.

I want to point something else out. If you're doing a webinar, you don't want to have lines and lines of text on each PowerPoint slide. That's a no-no and can put your audience to sleep fast. Your presentation should be a combination of images, stories, and a few words on each slide.

I've even done webinars where I'll have only three to five words on each slide and pretty much read them enthusiastically. I've found this creates anticipation for attendees.

Webinars and teleseminars should be a regular part of your communication, sales, and marketing strategy. If done the right way like I've shared, you can dramatically increase your impact, influence, and income in a short amount of time.

Chapter 27

IS GOOGLE ADWORDS
RIGHT FOR YOU?

Show me someone who has done something worthwhile,
and I'll show you someone who has overcome adversity.
—Lou Holtz

F irst of all, I'd like to say screw Google! (More on that in a minute.) In this chapter, we're going to briefly discuss the search engine's sponsored advertising platform. It's known commonly as Google AdWords.

Anytime you do a search online, you'll see that the first three listings that come back are usually the sponsored ads like what you observe in the following screenshot. You may also view small ads on the right-hand side of the search.

The number of advertisements that are shown will depend on how competitive the market is. The more ads you see, the more competitive the market. Right below the sponsored ads, you have the regular organic listings.

Google has both a search and display network for their ads platform.

The search is pretty self-explanatory. A prospective customer searches a term on Google, and you (as a business) can pay to show up at the top of the search. This is what's referred to as pay per click (PPC) because anytime someone clicks your advertisement, you get charged. Search ads are all text ads too.

The display network allows you to create all types of ads like text, image, and video. Those ads get placed on those websites that are relevant to what you're selling. Cost per click is usually substantially less on the display network.

The average cost per click for search traffic will depend on each market. Should you choose to use Google AdWords, expect to pay at least one dollar per click. That's being very kind too. For some keywords you target, you'll most likely pay between two and five dollars per click.

In some markets, I've seen a staggering $20 PER CLICK!

This is one of the things that really pisses me off about AdWords. Google is predatory in this regard and doesn't really give a crap about the small business owner. In fact, because the cost per click is so astronomical in many places, they squeeze the average mom-and-pop shop out completely.

AdWords has become a platform that favors major brands and advertisers who have tens of thousands (or hundreds of thousands) of dollars to spend each month.

Yes, a small business owner can still break in, especially in a local market, but when it comes to advertising nationally or internationally, it gets harder if you don't have deep pockets.

It's not just about the money though.

Google has quality scores based on keywords that you're advertising for. If you have a low quality score, they will either jack up the amount you pay per click, or they won't show your ads at all. You can learn more about the quality score, how to set up an account, AdWords basics, and managing ads at this link: https://support.google.com/adwords.

Can you run highly profitable campaigns on AdWords?

Absolutely.

But it depends on what you're comfortable spending to acquire a customer. Like I've spoken about before in this work, if I'm going to spend money on ads, I want a bare minimum of a 5:1 ROI.

I'd advise you shoot for the same. Comparing the ROI of AdWords to Facebook advertising, there is no comparison. If you're not getting at least an 8:1 ROI on Facebook, you're doing something seriously wrong.

Across the board, AdWords ROI isn't as high as it used to be either. This is due to click costs ballooning out of control for many niche markets.

Several years ago, Google started to ban AdWords accounts left and right without warning. Some of the banning was a good thing because it got rid of spammer affiliates. However, the dark side of this carnage was that the average small business owner was caught up in the mess.

You see, the typical local dentist doesn't usually know too much about promoting their practice online. This is the same with most small businesses. Many have heard you can advertise on Google though.

So, what do they do? The dentist sets up a sponsored ad because she wants to get the message out to the community about her services. Well, not long after, her AdWords account gets shut down.

POOF! All gone.

The dentist is stunned and left wondering what the heck happened. Once you're banned, you're banned for life. Unless you can find a unicorn tear, you won't be able to effectively appeal either.

No warning. No chance to correct a beginner mistake. Nothing.

I've had hundreds of professionals email me over the years with the same story. These brick-and-mortar business owners were not black-hat spammers trying to game the system either. They were goodhearted people that just wanted to use AdWords to help more people.

I've seen Google bully the little guy often. I don't agree with it, hence the reason for my endearing intro in this chapter.

I'm fortunate to consult with both small business owners and big brands, and I can tell you that if you're spending over $20,000 per month on ads with them, you get preferential treatment. You can make the same mistake as a small business owner and only get a tap on the wrist.

At the end of the day, you have to understand that Google is not your friend. You play by their rules knowing that they can change them at any minute. That's why all our marketing efforts need to be focused on building our email list.

This is the one thing Google cannot take away.

I used AdWords several years ago for a time, and it was profitable because I was promoting products that paid commissions each month for the life of the customer. They were subscription-based software programs.

With that said, I've been able to build my online empire without AdWords being an integral part of the system, so it won't be a focal point of this book. That's not to say you shouldn't dabble to see if it can produce sales in your business.

You can either hire an AdWords manager or partner or learn sponsored advertising yourself. Here are some resources regardless of what you decide to do:

- https://www.google.com/partners/
- http://www.amkhan.com/
- http://www.perrymarshall.com/adwords/

Chapter 28

GETTING PAID TO PROMOTE OTHER PEOPLE'S PRODUCTS

*The more you lose yourself in something bigger
than yourself, the more energy you will have.*
—Normal Vincent Peale

B y many people's standards, affiliate marketing is considered the
ULTIMATE online business. In fact, it's estimated to be more than a
$7 billion industry and it continues to grow every year. Some of the
largest companies in the world, such as Amazon, Walmart, Home Depot, Best
Buy, EBay, and Target, rely on affiliate marketing to fuel their e-commerce sales.

There are even tens of thousands of small to mid-sized businesses that use
affiliate marketing every single day to drive their online sales.

What is affiliate marketing?
To simplify, it's where a merchant (such as an online toy store) will pay a sales
commission for any sales that are referred to its website. This referral process

348

is managed using specially coded links that precisely track who referred the sale to the website. The person (or marketer) who referred the sale is known as the affiliate.

Generating a part-time or full-time income from your own affiliate marketing endeavors has many powerful benefits. The following are just a few reasons why many consider it the perfect Internet business.

It's extremely flexible

You can make money from promoting products and services in any niche market or industry that you can think of. From thousands upon thousands of available affiliate programs, you can promote toys this week, gardening tools next week, televisions the week after, and so on. You can promote any time type of product that you're interested in and make serious commissions each and every month!

Run the business from anywhere

Because this type of business is based 100 percent online, you can truly run it from anywhere. Whether you're on vacation or in another part of the world, if you can get access to the Internet, you'll be able to operate this business.

Very low start-up cost

An affiliate marketing venture can be started for less than $100. Unlike many business opportunities that you may have been exposed to, there are no start-up fees or application fees for becoming an affiliate.

You can work part-time or full-time

If you currently have a job that you'd like to replace with your Internet-based business, you can work and build your affiliate marketing venture in your spare time. If you're able to dedicate a full-time schedule to it, you can certainly do that.

The bottom line is that you can work as much or as little as you want and grow a profitable affiliate marketing business.

There's no inventory to stock

Because you'll be making money promoting products and services that other companies sell, you don't have to worry about stocking any inventory.

No products to ship

Because you're not actually selling something to an end consumer, you don't have to deal with shipping hassles associated with getting the product to the customer.

No payments to collect

Again, because you're not selling a product or service to the end consumer, you don't have to be able to take credit cards.

No customer support

Because you're not dealing directly with customers and taking their money, you don't have to deal with complaints, user problems, and all kinds of other hassles that go along with customer support.

No selling

You've probably heard this one before when subscribing to other business opportunities, but when it comes to affiliate marketing, this is completely TRUE! The merchant's website (where you'll send people) is already set up with great marketing to sell the products and services you'll be promoting.

No website required

Because we just covered that the merchant's website is already set up to do the selling for you, you really don't have to have your own website. However, there are some advantages if you want to set up your own website, and you've learned many throughout this book.

Regardless, you don't have to have your own website to make money in the affiliate marketing business world.

No sales quotas

Most affiliate programs are set up so that you'll get paid your commission EVEN IF you only make one sale in a given month. In fact, if you make higher sales, many times you'll get a raise if you can generate more volume.

No recruiting

Unlike other business opportunities that you've probably been exposed to before, you don't need to build a downline or recruit others underneath you. Affiliate marketing doesn't work like that.

It's simple. You generate commissions and make money by promoting products and services directly to people that want to buy them. That's it. You refer them, they buy something, YOU GET PAID!

Enormous potential

Even with all the incredible benefits you've just heard that make affiliate marketing arguably the best online business, it has huge potential. There are affiliates right now that are making millions of dollars per year in income from their affiliate marketing business—not to mention the tens of thousands of others making a great living this way.

When I started online, this was how I made my first dollar. Eventually, that took on a life of its own, and I began to generate five figures per month just in affiliate commissions.

Check this ... one of the products I initially started to promote in 2006 was a software program. They charged the customer a monthly fee to use it too. So anytime I'd make a sale, I'd get a 33 percent commission for the LIFE of the customer.

From that one affiliate program alone I was averaging over $5,000 per month in commissions! Periodically, they would launch a new program and I'd also get paid on those sales. Several times I recall my checks being over $10,000 in a month from this one program.

So when you start promoting others' products, you want to see if they're just one-time purchases or if they're monthly subscriptions. Also, ask the affiliate manager if you get paid a percentage for the life of the customer.

Physical or digital products: which ones are better to promote?

There is no right or wrong answer to this question. It just depends on your personal taste. From experience, I will tell you that when you promote information products or software, the commission percentages are much higher.

Why is this?

It's because they are digitally delivered online. There are no shipping costs, handling charges, or credit card fees. This creates a bigger profit margin. On average, products, services, or programs that are digitally downloaded will pay between 25 and 50 percent commissions!

On the other hand, if you like the idea of selling flat-screen TVs from Best Buy or Target, you'll get paid anywhere from 2 to 5 percent per sale. Some companies like Amazon reward affiliates around 8 percent for high volume; however, you've got to be very seasoned to do this.

Like other forms of marketing, we need to know what we can spend to acquire a customer. I remember when I was promoting the software program I was just telling you about in 2006, I'd spend $30 via Google AdWords to acquire one customer.

That number was just shy of the commission I'd make in the first month per sale. (I made $33 per sale.) If you recall, though, this program paid recurring commissions for the life of the customer.

Their average "stick rate" was seven months. So essentially I would spend $30 to make $231. That's just over a 7:1 return on investment. Every dollar I spent would give me seven back in return! I was totally fine with that.

Like we spoke about earlier in this book, at minimum we should strive for a 5:1 ROI.

How does the process work?

There are only a few steps to being an affiliate. Here they are in order:

1. Sign up for an affiliate program.
2. Promote and advertise the link you get to the right audience.
3. Track your statistics through your affiliate back office.
4. Receive commissions on whomever purchases.
5. Watch the money roll into your bank account.

Aside from individual companies that have affiliate programs, there are entire networks devoted to connecting retailers with affiliates. The top ones are:

- Rakuten Linkshare – http://linkshare.com
- CJ (commission junction) – http://cj.com
- ClickBank – http://clickbank.com
- ShareASale – http://shareasale.com
- JVZoo – http://JVZoo.com

These websites have thousands of products (digital and physical) to select from. You basically just go there, create an account, then choose which product you'd like to promote first.

Types of affiliate programs

Pay per sale – This means you get a commission on anyone that purchases a product through your unique affiliate link. You get paid a percentage of the sale.

Cost per action (CPA) – This means you get a commission on anyone that takes a desired action, whether it be to enter their name and email, take a survey, or just click a link.

Typically, the affiliate program sign-up page will let you know whether they have a pay-per-sale or CPA platform.

Selecting and promoting a product

As you're learning throughout this book, your focus should be around an industry you know exceptionally well. It's much easier to sell and promote products when you have intimate knowledge of the marketplace.

"The Simple Product Creation Formula" and "Market Research" chapters of this work provide ideas that are highly applicable to affiliate marketing. You need to consider many of the same questions when selling other people's stuff. Furthermore, all the traffic-generation methods in this book can be applied to an affiliate marketing business.

With that said, we still want to build a long-term, recognized, and trustworthy brand. This isn't a one-and-done proposal.

We can make affiliate sales by doing joint-venture partnerships where we email our list, doing SEO to rank our pages at the top of Google, doing review/comparison YouTube videos for searched keywords, marketing on forums, using Facebook ads, harnessing solo ads, etc.

Let me give you one of my earliest examples.

In 2008 when gas prices were soaring out of control here in the US, people were in a panic and getting REALLY pissed off. They were desperately looking for solutions to bring their gasoline costs down.

So I began to do my homework to try to find a solution for the average American. Turns out, there were a couple programs online that were teaching people how to convert their cars into fuel-efficient hybrids.

The great thing was, this could be accomplished for under $200. I wouldn't have believed it myself except for the fact that my mechanic friend ordered the manual and converted his car. The best part of it was, it actually did save him money on gas.

That's when my eyes got big. I did some more detective work, and it turned out that this particular product was on the affiliate network Clickbank! Commissions on the manual were 50 percent.

So what did I do?

I created one YouTube video using a screen-capture program called Camtasia Studio. In the first part of the video, I discussed the problem and referenced major media outlets, research, and articles in the news. This lent irrefutable proof and credibility to what I was saying. I was also bringing up what was causing the pain—sky-high gas prices and how it was affecting the average person.

In the second half of the vid, I let the viewers know what I had discovered while showing the testimonials. Finally, I directed folks to the product website to check it out so they could decide for themselves.

Instead of sending people to the ugly Clickbank URL though, I bought a simple .com domain name from GoDaddy and then just directed the Clickbank affiliate link there. That way, I could give people an easy-to-remember website address.

That's pretty simple to do. You just need to call GoDaddy and tell them you want to "forward" a specific domain name to a .com you recently purchased. They can walk you through it.

YouTube allowed me to upload a custom thumbnail image, so I inserted one that showed a road sign at a gas station. On the sign it said, "arm," "leg," and "first born" in the place where "unleaded," "premium," and "super" would normally be.

People got a kick out of the image, and it made them curious. I titled the video something controversial too. I labeled it "Are High Gas Prices a Scam?"

Long story short, that video took off and went viral. I had 200,000 views in a span of just sixty days! It was crazy. That translated into just over $5,000 in sales each month.

As you can imagine, I was floored!

That's when I finally understood how powerful YouTube could be for affiliate marketing. The interesting thing was, that was just one video!

I still have YouTube content that was created years ago, all the way back to 2007, that periodically makes new affiliate sales for us. I call it pennies from heaven. This is just one way to marketing your affiliate products.

Another way to do it is via email marketing. This is where you mail your list with a special offer from another product developer. You decide on a commission beforehand. Then they may or may not provide swipe copy.

People approach me all the time, asking me to send an email to my list for them. I reject 95 percent of the products, but I will accept a small few for consideration. I've had five-figure paydays from simple affiliate products I emailed to my list.

The best part about it is that my team doesn't have to do any customer support or collect payments. It's easy cash. Just be sure if you elect to promote something to your list that it actually works and is congruent with your philosophy. Your reputation is on the line. Never promote crap!

Reference this book for dozens of other traffic strategies to drive awareness and affiliate sales.

Three approaches to affiliate marketing

1. Drive traffic to the product sales page directly

Some affiliates elect to just drive traffic to the affiliate sales page to try to make money. This can work, but it does take quite a bit of testing. All traffic is not created equal though.

If you send visitors from Google (free or paid), it is search traffic. This means people are actually searching for a solution or product, so initially they're more qualified.

If you send traffic from Facebook advertising, these people are qualified, but they're not searching for your product. So they are not as eager to buy in that moment. That's really important to understand.

That doesn't mean Facebook advertising traffic won't buy; they just have to be approached a little differently. I like to get them onto an email list first before I make them a product offer. That way, I can communicate with these individuals regularly and build trust.

2. Drive traffic to a squeeze page to build an email list

This is the smart thing to do. We can always sell prospective customers later. This is more of a long-term strategy as well. We offer something of value for free (report, video, cheat sheet, software, etc.) in exchange for a name and email.

Some of these prospects will buy now, but those that don't will now be on our list so we can deliver value, educate them, and make exceptional offers. We are trying to build an active, engaged subscriber base here.

3. Drive traffic to a regular WordPress website

Affiliate marketing has changed over the years. I still remember when you could just slap a one-page website up and rank it high on Google for any given search term.

I remember when I had a one-pager based around a specific female product. All the site did was review and compare five different types of products. It gave consumers educational information so they could make the best decision for themselves.

The cool thing was, no matter what choice the visitor made, I was an affiliate partner for each product. I got paid on every sale! The only traffic I was sending to this site was in the form of YouTube videos too.

Those glory days are long gone.

Yes, you can still have a review/comparison page, but it has to be attached to a regular website that's consistently churning out fresh, original content. As stated earlier in this book, I recommend WordPress because Google adores this platform.

So you'll need to hire a freelance programmer from a site like Upwork. com and have them build you a website. If you outsource overseas, you can get something good for under $500.

You'll just have to buy a domain name and website hosting and then have the programmer install a WordPress theme. You can go online and Google "custom WordPress themes" or "premium WordPress themes" and find something suitable so you don't have to create something from scratch.

To be even more specific, Google "WordPress themes for affiliate marketers" so you can see what other templates affiliates are successfully using. Ideally, we still want to capture names and emails with this site too.

Aside from selling other people's products on your website, you can even feature AdSense ads by Google. These are either text or banner placements that can be coded into your site. Anytime someone clicks them, you get a percentage of what Google charges the advertiser per click. You can sign up at Google.com/AdSense and then have your programmer install the necessary code on your site to feature these advertisements if you choose.

Where should you place affiliate ads?

The real money is made within the content. Google AdSense even suggests you place ads within your content because they tend to perform the best.

Your content needs to be top-notch on this type of affiliate website. It must lead first with IMMENSE value. Great content is the main ingredient in the sales process.

You can do product demos on how to use a product and then talk about the results you got. From there, you can send them to a review and comparison page where this prospective customer can make an educated decision on what to purchase.

Action Step: Go to Clickbank or one of the other affiliate networks. Select your first product that you'd like to promote. Here's a hint. The higher the "gravity" of a product on Clickbank, the more affiliates are promoting it.

That usually means that people are making money with that product. The sales page is compelling, and it converts well. Don't let a little competition scare you either.

It's better to search Clickbank for products with the highest gravity so you automatically know the big winners. Once you laser in on one, grab your affiliate link and then start sending quality traffic to the sales page.

I'd recommend really planting firmly within the niche you're wanting to service. This means getting a site built and offering great content on a regular basis. The goal is to establish your brand as an authority in the marketplace.

———— Chapter 29 ————

PODCASTING FOR MAXIMUM IMPACT AND PROFITABILITY

If you think you are too small to make a
difference, try sleeping with a mosquito.
—Dalai Lama

A s of 2015, Apple reports having a staggering 800 MILLION iTunes accounts registered, which also means the company has the same number of credit cards on file! Let that sink in for a minute before we discuss the skyrocketing popularity of podcasting and audio content consumption.

As you probably know, podcasting is nothing new. It's just audio broadcasting over the Internet. In fact, it's been around for more than a decade. Podcasts can deliver breaking news, be major sources of fresh information, provide entertainment, and allow you to keep tabs on topics of interest. Check these eye-opening stats though:

- iTunes houses over 250,000 podcasts.
- *Edison Research* reports that 15 percent of Americans consistently listen to podcasts.
- They also found that 33 percent of Americans aged twelve or older have listened to at least one podcast.
- *Pew Research* says that overall awareness of podcasting is increasing at a modest pace, with roughly half (49 percent) of Americans ages twelve and up aware of podcasting.

For many, this audio content plays an important role in education, motivation, political discussion, and amusement. It's convenient for people to listen to their favorite personalities while commuting to work, when in the gym exercising, or on a plane traveling.

When iTunes decided to add this medium to their platform in 2006, an enormous tipping point occurred. This led to a dramatic surge of new podcasts and the introduction of millions of new consumers.

The growth potential is MASSIVE, especially when you compare it to the hundreds of millions of people that have started blogs or the millions of hours of YouTube videos uploaded each month.

My prediction is the podcast explosion is going to rapidly expand in the coming years. Let's talk about why people love them though.

First of all, they're free! There's no financial barrier to access the educational information, news, or personalities you want.

Next is the mobile convenience factor. Wherever you go, the podcast can go with you because you can listen in on your smart phone. iTunes is in 119 countries, so you can access your audios almost anywhere in the world!

The third reason people have taken an affinity to podcasting is that they can listen and multitask at the same time. These audio downloads are on-demand; this allows you to consume the content during regular daily activities like washing the dishes, running in the park, etc. As you know, it's hard to multitask when watching a video or reading an article.

The final reason why I believe so many people love podcasts is that they can come directly to you, straight into your podcast phone app. When new episodes from your favorite channels are live, you can be instantly notified via the RSS feed.

Here's why the future of podcasting is so bright

The demand is rising rapidly as documented by major research. The barrier of entry for content producers (you and me) is very low. Anyone with a computer, laptop, microphone, and free audio editing software can get in the game.

Once published, the podcast has the potential to reach thousands of people worldwide in a relatively short amount of time, sometimes exponentially more.

There is a plethora of high-quality training available online to help you jumpstart your podcast endeavors. I look at it like this: If you're going to put yourself out there, you want to do it in a professional and polished light. This is your brand. It's your image. You want to make the best first impression possible!

More top-notch podcasters are sharing their expertise, techniques, and tips online. Sometimes this training is free; sometimes it comes at a price. Here are two people that are doing it really well and who give immense value away for free.

Pat Flynn

www.smartpassiveincome.com/how-to-start-a-podcast-podcasting-tutorial/

Cliff Ravenscraft

www.podcastanswerman.com/learn-how-to-podcast/

Another reason the future of podcasting is so promising is that the quality standard is consistently being increased. The bar is rising. Now you have many professional radio producers that have created new podcasts so they can repurpose radio content.

Furthermore, the average content producer is starting to think about monetization. In fact, many podcasters are already making money, but not in the way you might think. Because the audio downloads are free, more producers are acquiring show sponsors.

Brand mentions and thirty-second commercial slots are becoming commonplace. Some content producers report getting $20 per thousand impressions, which is calculated based on show downloads.

Most podcasters are still not monetizing their channels; however, buzz is spreading quickly throughout the digital world. Fortune 500 brands are paying attention because of the lead-generation capability and potential to boost sales using this medium.

You can bet on this: The more revenue generated by podcasts, the more companies and entrepreneurs will take notice and flock to harness this tool for business growth. It's inevitable.

As competition rises, the average players will need to step up their game to the master level or be forced out. Amateur hour doesn't usually last for too long, so the time to capitalize on the opportunity is now! The more you practice, the better you'll become.

The last reason I believe the future is going to be explosive for podcasting is that Apple and Google are in the process of working out deals to get Apple CarPlay and Android Auto integrated into future automobiles.

This one thing will completely revolutionize podcast distribution and accessibility, bringing streaming audio to millions upon millions of new listeners. Talk about a game changer!

Equipment you need to get started

Microphone – There are plenty of podcast mics to choose from. You can Google "best podcast microphone" and dozens of options will populate. I will say that many of the top podcasters I come across use the HEIL PR40 because of the excellent sound quality.

Microphone accessories – You need a pop filter (foam or screen you place in front of the mic), a stand to hold the mic and to position it where you want it, and a shock mount so that vibrations on your desk don't affect the sound quality.

Another accessory is a mic flag, which you can use for branding purposes if you're doing video or photographs of your setup. HEIL also makes a sound c-clamp that can help provide extra stability if you need it. That's optional.

Digital Mixer – The mic connects to this, and it improves the audio quality. A mixer also won't crash like computers can. The Behringer Xenyx 1002 comes highly recommended, but you can Google other equivalent options as well.

Audio editing software – Two of the most common programs are Audacity for PC and Garage Band for Mac. These programs allow you to record, edit, and export the files in MP3 format.

Sometimes you might decide to interview people on Skype.

Unfortunately, Skype doesn't have a built-in audio or screen recorder. In this case you must use a third-party software to do the job. Call Recorder made by Ecamm is an option for Mac. Pamela for Skype is a widely used program for Windows or PC.

Things to think about before recording your first episode

The title of your podcast on iTunes

This can either be your brand name, a highly searched keyword in your marketplace, or both. iTunes is a search engine similar to Google. So people go on there every day and look for podcasts, videos, games, etc. related to their interests.

Don't clutter your title, but you might have one or two keyword phrases mixed in. For example, let's say you're a real estate specialist helping investors buy and/or sell foreclosures.

The title of your show might be, *The Real Estate and Foreclosure Power Hour Podcast or The Real Estate Training Podcast: Buying and Selling For Profit or The Real Estate Marketing Tips Podcast.*

The more downloads and reviews your podcast gets, the higher you'll rank in the iTunes search engine.

Your personal name and tag line

This should be your name, but we can also add a keyword here as well in order to help us rank a little higher in the iTunes search. This also helps potential subscribers better identify who you are. Going with our previous example, something like this would be appropriate: Julie Smith: Real Estate Marketing Expert.

The subtitle of your podcast

Think of this like the meta-description of your website. It's your place to entice others to want to listen to your show. Have a short description of the podcast and make it benefit-rich, as in what the information will do for the subscriber.

The summary/description of your podcast

Don't confuse this with the previous subtitle. This is the primary description for your podcast. Make this section engaging and benefit-rich. We want them to feel like subscribing to your podcast is a no-brainer. Don't forget to place a few keywords in this description because that will help you optimize your podcast in the iTunes search.

Your graphic design

Every podcaster in iTunes needs a piece of artwork to represent their show. For many, this graphic will serve as the first impression for people as they search through podcast directories. We would ideally like this to stand out from the crowd.

Here's something else to remember: Your podcast artwork is what others will see when they play your episodes on their tablets, phones, and computers. It can help to further cement your brand in the minds of the listener.

Artwork is something you can easily outsource to a graphic designer you find on Upwork. You can get more info regarding the specifications at this link: www.apple.com/itunes/podcasts/specs.html

After you've brainstormed and written down these items, now it's time for some fun! The next step is to get your podcast going.

Tips to help you look more professional

Here are some valuable tips that will help you produce higher quality podcasts. If we're going to jump in full throttle, we want to do it the right way. What you're about to discover is the difference between appearing amateur versus being perceived as a professional.

Keep your mouth the same distance from the microphone throughout the entire podcast.

Create this good habit early on. If you tend to drift forward and back while you're talking during the episode, your sound quality will suffer. An easy way to be consistent is to have the tip of your lips barely touch the pop filter the entire time you're speaking.

Check and maintain optimal sound levels

You'll notice these green and yellow lines when you're recording the podcast. I want to point out here that you should never go in the red! Go as close as close as you can in the yellow, but stay out of the red. When editing, we can always bump up the volume if it's too low.

The ideal podcast length

There really is no right or wrong answer to this one. When you're just starting out, my advice is to keep it between fifteen and thirty minutes. It all comes down to how interesting the subject matter is and how you constantly hook your audience. As time goes by, you'll get better at interviewing guests. The important thing is to have fun, make it entertaining, and deliver immense value to listeners.

Have an introduction

Tell listeners what they're going to discover and what to expect on this podcast episode. You can even tease the audience with special surprises. Typically, a show might start with, *"This is (your podcast name) with John L. Smith. Session number ___."*

Then, a little intro might start playing. After that, you can further elaborate on what the show is about and then talk about the guest you're having on. Just a note, your intro music should be "royalty free" to avoid any problems. Google "royalty free" music if you don't know where to look.

If you go to Upwork.com, you'll be able to find a freelance audio editor that can create a professional intro/outro for you. Or you can just Google "custom podcast intro creation" and search through the listings.

Another resource available to you is Music Radio Creative. They specialize in premium audio creation on demand, voiceovers, intro jingles, etc. Here's their site:

www.musicradiocreative.com

Have an outro with a clear call to action

Never assume that listeners automatically know what to do next at the end of your show. Tell people what action you'd like them to take. Do you want them to subscribe on iTunes? Do you want them to rate this podcast? Do you want them to visit your website? Be specific.

Direct listeners to your blog from your podcast

This is a MUST. I'd recommend doing this multiple times throughout your show, especially during the outro. A simple way to get people to visit your blog is to let them know they can find the show notes, audio transcript, and resources mentioned during the podcast.

To see an example of this, check out Pat Flynn's podcast page below and then scroll down and click on any individual episode image. You'll see how nicely formatted everything is.

www.smartpassiveincome.com/category/podcast/

If you use WordPress for your website, there's a plug-in called Pretty Link. I've used it for years. Pretty Link enables you to shorten ugly links using your own domain name (as opposed to using tinyurl.com, bit.ly, or any other link shrinking service).

So, instead of telling podcast listeners to go to:

www.YourSite.com/podcast/epidode1/329585,

you can tell them to go to:

www.YourSite.com/listen.

The plug-in essentially turns long links into short memorable ones.

On top of creating clean links, Pretty Link tracks each hit on your URL and provides a full, detailed report of where the visitor came from, the browser, operating system, and host.

A plug-in like this is useful if you want to clean up affiliate links, track clicks from emails, and links on Twitter, forums, other blogs, etc. If your website isn't built on WordPress, then just Google "Pretty Link alternative."

Another reason we want to direct podcast traffic back to our blog is so that we can build our email list! We want to give them our ethical bribe (information they're already seeking) in exchange for a name and email.

Break up your episodes into different segments

If your episodes are longer, you definitely want to do this so you can create a pattern interrupt. Breaking the podcast up into chunks keeps listeners engaged. You can have music in between each section like you might hear on the radio.

The best way for you to get ideas on how to do this is to start listening to popular podcasts on iTunes. Observe the flow of their shows and what segments they're fusing in.

Get to the point and stay away from BS filler

Don't waste time talking about nonsense that doesn't matter. This will vary audience to audience. People are tuning in for the great content, so we need to get to the point quickly. Now that doesn't mean you can't tell personal stories to humanize yourself because you should. Just keep things on point and relate it to the topic of the day.

Decrease the blah …

"Ums" and "ahhs" just don't cut it. They distract from the main message you're trying to convey and cause the audience to tune out. That's the antithesis of what we want. Our goal is to enhance communication, not hinder it. Better to pause than to use one of those words. Think of it from the listener's perspective. It's annoying to hear gibberish when you expect clear communication.

Enjoy the show!

Look, if you're not excited and enthusiastic about your podcast, how can you expect others to be? Have fun. Bring energy to the show and really get listeners amped up for the episode.

How to conduct a great Podcast interview

Relax. Be yourself. Don't suck. There you go. As simple as that sounds, let me provide a little structure and set the tone for the interview process. I don't want to overcomplicate things because you want to speak with your guest like you're speaking to an old friend.

The conversation should be effortless and natural. You're going to be like a river bank, directing the flow of the conversation based on the value you want to deliver to people who are listening. In order to do this, you first need a guest!

The number one way we get well-known individuals to come on our show is to ask! We ideally want famous people in our industry to participate in many shows because it adds value for the listener, giving them a trusted name they know, plus it gives us credibility by association.

I will say this, though: You wouldn't approach Arnold Schwarzenegger for an interview unless you had a track record of interviewing famous guests in the bodybuilding industry. Get some history behind you and build your subscriber base first.

That doesn't mean other famous people won't be happy to participate. You'll never know unless you ask. Look for celebs that are launching new products and lead with how big your audience is.

Along this same line, you can use your current network to generate referrals. The more connected you are, the easier it will be to get big-named guests to appear. That's why it's critical for you to start attending the popular events in your space.

Some podcasts can be you alone, educating and entertaining your audience. If you can't access an A-player for an interview, go after a semi-famous person. In an ideal scenario, you'd have them email their list about their interview with you.

Your audience is priority #1

Focus on them! You should have a very firm understanding of what their needs and wants are. Put yourself in your listeners' shoes. Give them what they're looking for step-by-step. You, or the person being interviewed, can also provide real-world examples. We want the audience to be able to replicate the method we discuss.

Start with a background story

Whoever you're interviewing probably has a unique and interesting story that lead them to the level where they are today. Our audience should know this person's background so they can relate and identify better.

Ask your guest to take us back in time to the beginning and then bring us up to speed with what's happening now. See if they had any major struggles along the way and ask them to elaborate.

Some simple questions to begin with during the initial phase of the interview are:

- Where were you born?
- Did you have any formal education or training?
- What obstacles or challenges have you faced along the way?
- How did you develop (the skill they are famous for)?

Unravel the secret to their success

Once you provide a little background, history, and context to the listener, you can progress to the main reason you asked your guest to join you today. This is the part where you find out the exact secrets that made this individual successful and widely recognized.

Our goal here is to extract as much of the step-by-step process as possible for our listeners. We want the solid-gold nuggets along with practical strategies anyone can implement. How much of a mindset shift was involved?

Conclude the interview and summarize

Once you've detailed the whole process your guest went through to achieve a certain result along with lessons learned, you can then transition into the close. Depending on the interview time you're shooting for, keep your eye on the clock to track progress.

If you need, you can use the remainder of your time together to create more clarity for the audience. If applicable, pick out something that was important but wasn't fully explained.

Whatever industry you're servicing, think of any major challenges you've personally experienced. When these points arise during the interview, ask your guest to talk about how they successfully dealt with the problem.

At the interview finale, it's good to reflect back and do a quick summary. There are a few reasons for doing this. One, it further clarifies the most important points for your listeners. Two, it might trigger more insightful questions to ask your guest. Lastly, it provides closure so you can move on.

End your guest interview by asking the guest to share their website or resources they have. You can even ask them what new projects they're working on or if they have any additional gems they want to reveal to help the listener get the results they're seeking.

Additional interview tips

Remember, this segment isn't about you. It's about the guest you've invited to join you. It's also about the audience getting value out of the podcast. Know when to shut up! Stay focused on the right things and the popularity of your podcast will grow.

Prepare accordingly. Research your guests in detail before bringing them onto the show. Have a list of questions written down just to make sure you cover all the fine points you want during the interview. Failing to plan is planning to fail.

Ask "How?" if you're unclear about something. The word "how" opens doors. It gives the guest the chance to drill down into greater specifics.

Technical tasks you can outsource

The purpose of this book is not to confuse or overwhelm you with technical details of exporting the audio, tagging it, using web/media hosting, setting up your feed, etc. It's your choice to do that or to delegate the task to someone with experience.

Some podcasters prefer to do the editing and exporting. Honestly, it's a good idea to walk through it a couple times so you know what to do. Pat Flynn and others have made several step-by-step podcast trainings that are easy to follow. Search for them on YouTube.

Once you've been through the process, you can easily outsource to a professional that can do this fast and on the cheap.

After your podcast is published to iTunes, now what?

That's when the marketing and outreach begins! Just from being in the iTunes store, you'll get your fair share of downloads. However, we want to market our podcast just like we'd promote any other piece of content.

The first place you'd start is with your current email list. Let your subscribers know about the new podcast or episode and let them know what it will do for them.

I have one colleague that consistently gets featured in the noteworthy section on iTunes because his email list is so large and he's built a great relationship with them. Anytime he sends an email regarding a new episode, tens of thousands of people go there and download it.

Regardless of how large your email list is right now, it's the first stage in promoting your content because your subscribers know, like, and trust you. However, there's absolutely no shortage of ways to drive traffic to your podcasts.

You can (and should) apply many strategies in this book to do so, such as joint-venture partnerships, Facebook organic sharing, Facebook advertising, blogging, YouTube videos, online forum marketing, Instagram, SEO, press release distribution, etc.

Action Step: Commit to starting your own podcast on iTunes as soon as you can. Set a deadline in the near future and just do it! Your show should revolve around your current business model and what you're most passionate about. Take some time to really think about what value you want to deliver to the audience on weekly episodes.

Have a running list of topics you want to discuss. Some shows can be solo with only you; others can be with guests that you hand select. Follow the interview guide and other tips I've included in this chapter to hit the ground running.

Most seasoned podcasters will tell you that the most important success factor is consistency, just like with any other online marketing medium. It might surprise you that many of the top podcasts on iTunes feature only one episode per week. You can do the same thing.

Don't worry about monetizing the podcast with outside advertisements just yet. The sponsors will come when your audience dramatically grows. This takes a little time. We can still have a large impact and make money by always building our email list along with getting prospective clients into our funnel. Then we can plug our trainings or related affiliate products.

Build a community around the podcast and create engagement by regularly asking for feedback. Pose a question at the end of your episodes and tell listeners to leave their answers on the blog post in the comments.

Ask your listeners to share the podcast if they found value from the show and to rate it on iTunes. This helps you spread the word and get your message out there much faster.

More ratings equates to greater visibility on iTunes. Greater visibility means more downloads! More downloads equals increased awareness, surges in website traffic, growing influence, helping more people better their quality of life, and more money in your bank account.

Chapter 30

OUTSOURCING LIKE AN
INTERNET MILLIONAIRE

I've been blessed to find people who are smarter than
I am, and they help me to execute the vision I have.
—Russell Simmons

rguably the most important lesson you'll ever learn when starting and/
or scaling an Internet business is that you don't have to do everything
yourself! Outsourcing and delegation is critical to your success since
there are only so many hours in a day.

With that said, let me be clear. You need to get your hands dirty in the
beginning just to see how certain strategies are used and implemented. Experience
is a great teacher and gives you insight regarding how to effectively measure and
track your results.

One of the BIGGEST mistakes many brands, entrepreneurs, and businesses
make is that they delegate tasks right from the start before they know what
they're doing. An Internet entrepreneur might have an idea that they need to be

doing Facebook advertising (for example), but they don't want to learn how to set up, optimize, and manage the campaign. So they hire an outside company in an attempt to fill the void.

I see this all the time. Then, a few months go by and the business owner wonders why they are not getting the results they think they should get. The problem here is that not everyone who says they "do" Facebook advertising does it the right way.

Apply that last statement to any traffic-generation method mentioned in this book. You MUST know the exact strategies that make you money (and how to implement them) when the time comes to delegate a specific task.

Don't just outsource for the sake of outsourcing. You need to know what works in your business first. Create a proven system or model one from a successful company. Then you can start the delegation process.

Drive traffic to your website. Find out what strategies produce the most leads and sales. Then, once you know what works, systemize those processes into step-by-step tasks and outsource the repetitive stuff.

Your time is very valuable. Once a task is mastered, delegate fast.

One mistake I made early on in my online career was that I kept writing and submitting articles to online directories when that could've easily been outsourced to a full-time ghostwriter. I knew I needed to "let go," but I was a control freak!

This mindset certainly didn't serve me, and it caused more frustration and misery as I stayed up late burning both ends of the candle performing grunt work.

As an Internet entrepreneur, it can be really stressful if you do everything yourself. Most people learn the hard way that being "busy" doesn't necessarily equate to being productive or earning more money! Don't get confused.

Having the right outsourcing strategy in place allows you to:

- Experience more freedom so you can work on the business instead of in it.
- Save money. You can find overseas workers for a third of the price you'd pay an American.

- Increase efficiency. You get exponentially more work done in less time.
- Multiply your monthly revenue through leverage and scalability.
- Prevent frustration, feeling overwhelmed, and burnout.

In the "tools and resources" section in the back of this book, I've included an extensive list of my best tools, resources, and websites that have enabled me to sell multiple seven figures online. The amount of money that section will save you is well into the tens of thousands—not to mention all the time, energy, and effort you won't have to waste on useless gimmicks.

It took me going to the school of hard knocks to seek out and painstakingly find the best companies, software, and websites for growing a lucrative Internet business.

By investing in this book, you've basically allowed me to be your coach, which means you understand the value of mentoring and the massive shortcut it brings. Your learning curve is reduced by years. You don't have to spend a fortune like I did to acquire my knowledge base.

There are very few marketers who would reveal their very best resources. However, I'm a strong believer in abundance, and I enjoy helping those that take action and help themselves.

Remember this:

It's not the lack of resources that stops most people from building a successful business from the Internet; it's their lack of resourcefulness—not knowing where to go. I've solved that problem for you.

So, what tasks can you outsource?

- Writing articles, blog posts, or press releases
- Setting up WordPress
- Installing plug-ins and scripts
- Project management
- Link building
- Building your following on social networks
- Shopping cart setup
- E-book cover design

- Professional logo creation
- Customized Facebook fan page and Twitter backgrounds
- Market research
- Facebook business page setup
- Transcription
- Keyword research
- Social bookmarking
- Voiceovers
- Posting to online forums
- Google analytics installation
- PPC campaign management
- Audio intros/jingles
- Podcast and audio editing
- Video editing
- Article submission
- Press release distribution
- Online video submission
- E-book and product creation
- Software development
- Customer support
- Graphic design
- Blog design and/or WordPress customization
- Product fulfillment and drop shipping
- Event planning
- And more …

In the "tools and resources" section of this book, I show you where to go to outsource all of those tasks and many more. Personally, I don't like to do a lot of guesswork when it comes to delegating in my businesses.

For this reason, I've come up with a simple formula that enables me to find the very best people to perform any task that needs to get done. I've laid it out for you in the ten simple steps that follow.

1. Get clear

You need to define what you're currently doing, what you don't like to do, what you're not great at, what you want to do more of, and what you want to delegate. To do this, take a minute, grab a piece of paper, and draw five columns with the headings I mentioned in the last sentence.

You might be totally shocked when you see how much you're actually doing on a daily basis. Chances are, you may also be surprised by how much stuff you're doing that you're not good at or don't want to do!

This activity is important simply because it helps you understand where you are currently, where you'd ideally like to be, and what's holding you back. Our goal is to free up our time so we can focus on bigger things that will grow the business fast.

Don't play it safe on the "delegate" column. If you think you can delegate the task, do it! You might think that some things have to have your input or knowledge to be run successfully. Don't worry at this stage though. Just put as many jobs as you can in the delegation section.

2. Make a decision

Quickly prioritize the top three things that need to be delegated first. You have a couple options here. One, you can write out specifically what you need done for these tasks. Create a simple outline with action steps and your process. This should be step-by-step and easy to follow so that anyone could look at the paper and plug and play.

The second option available to you is to shoot a quick screen-capture video of the process. The program I use to accomplish this is called Camtasia Studio—a great time saver. You record a video one time, and you now have a system in place that can be used for years to come.

Take the viewer by the hand and explain what you're doing.

3. Identify your ideal freelancer or employee

The more specific you can be in this step, the higher the quality of applicants you'll attract. It will also make the interview process easier. A few questions you must consider are:

- What skill are you searching for?
- How much experience should they have?

- How fluent in English does this person have to be?
- How many hours do you anticipate needing?
- What qualities or attributes are you looking for?
- What's your budget for this project?

4. Post your job online

Once you have a clear picture of what you need outsourced, the task outline, and the type of person you're looking for, it's time to create your first job posting. My favorite outsourcing websites to find skilled professionals are:

- Upwork.com
- Freelancer.com

The true beauty about Upwork and Freelancer is that after your job has been posted, you will get bids from contractors from all over the world. You can then see how much money these individuals have made on the network, the total number of ratings/reviews (good or bad) they've received, how much experience they have, previous employer comments, and peek inside their work portfolio at previous work.

Your job posting is going to be pretty much a summary of the questions you just answered and the outline you put together. What type of professional are you looking for? What experience should they have? etc.

I typically let my job postings run for seven days or less. You also need to know if you're going to hire someone hourly or on a per-project basis. Understand that whatever their initial quote is, many times there's wiggle room. Don't be afraid to negotiate a better price!

Here's another tip.

All your communication with the provider should go through the message board on Upwork or Freelancer; that way you have a record of everything. This protects you as these websites monitor communication.

A couple other great websites I've used that are solely outsourcers from the Philippines are:

- 123Employee.com
- OnlineJobs.ph

123Employee is actually an American–managed company where the Filipino workers go into an office and are supervised. This ensures you're getting the work that you pay for.

OnlineJobs.ph is a portal where you can interview individual freelance Filipino workers and hire them on the spot. Average salaries can be from $200 to $550 per month for full-time work. Yes, you read that correctly!

Believe it or not, that's pretty good money for them as well. Most jobs in the Philippines do not pay that much. In my personal experience, they're some of the most humble, loyal, and hardest workers as well.

The last company I want to share with you is a real gem. They're called Workaholics For Hire (WFH). They have teams based in the US and Canada. We use them for customer support and project management solutions. You can find them at:

Workaholics4hire.com.

As you build your business, you might find that you don't have the time to "manage" the team of freelance contractors you have. I found myself in this predicament and began to get VERY stressed out because all my time was now devoted to monitoring the team.

Do yourself a favor and learn from my mistake! After months of suffering, I saw a friend at an Internet marketing seminar here in Atlanta and told him my situation. He laughed and instantly knew I needed a project manager. That's when I got the referral for W4H.

A great project manager can swoop to the rescue so you can have more freedom and less stress. They thoroughly manage the workers to ensure weekly tasks get completed. They can even hire and train more staff members if need be.

Project managers command a higher price, but the investment is worth it when you reach that stage in your business.

5. Proactively look for candidates

Once you've posted your job on Freelancer or Upwork, you can browse through top-rated providers and invite them to bid on your project. Usually, the contractors with the best ratings will have a higher hourly rate, but don't let that deter you.

At the end of the day, we want quality. There's a time and place to save a dollar, but even if we do select a very cheap outsourcer, we have to be confident they can give us what we're looking for. That's why investigating their portfolio is so important.

6. Sort and filter the bids

As the bids for your project trickle in, providers will also send you a message with information regarding their experience. Depending on how many freelancers are applying for this job, you'll want to pick the top five applicants to start interviewing.

In the initial application or message the contractor sends, you might see a resume, links to previous projects, answers to the questions you asked, or an attachment with more details. Take all of this into consideration as you go into the interview process.

7. Interview your applicants

I don't have to tell you how important this component is for finding the perfect new member of your team. Here are some quick tips that will help you conduct a good interview so you have the best shot at finding a superstar.

Prepare a list of your interview questions in advance. Create your ideal candidate avatar and base them off that. Do the interview on Skype.

Get specific. The questions you ask need to drill down into the fine details. For example, if you're interviewing a programmer, you might ask him how experienced he is with WordPress on scale of 1–10.

If you're hiring for a project that requires you to look at the contractor's portfolio of previous work, ask them about their role on those projects. Just because you see a website in their portfolio doesn't mean this person built that site. They might have only designed the graphics. Who knows? Get specific.

Work experience is a big deal, so ask your applicant about their experience. Get an idea of what they do really well and what they've potentially struggled with in the past.

If you're inclined, test their knowledge during the interview. Prepare a couple technical questions for them to answer. That will give you an indicator of their current skill level.

On your Skype chat you can use the messenger or you can speak to them live with your computer microphone. Most of my conversations are via messenger, but that's your choice. If you feel better speaking one on one, then do it.

Don't hire the person after the first interview even if you really like them. Just let the contractor know you'll get back to them in a couple days. After all, you have a few more applicants to talk with.

On the other hand, if you know a person is not a good fit for your company, let them know immediately. Don't waste your time or theirs. Thank them for the interview and wish them good luck in future endeavors.

8. Test them out

As the old saying goes, "The proof is in the pudding!" Now that you have a few applicants, go ahead and give them a sample task with clear instructions. Pay attention to how well the freelancer does the job, the time it takes them to complete it, the volume of questions they ask, and how comfortable they appear.

Don't be intimidating. This is their first time working with you, so they probably won't be 100 percent. However, pay attention to the fine details and how well they follow instructions.

You should feel very confident in the contractor's ability. Based on the application, the interview, and the sample task, they're either a good fit for your company or not.

If they cannot perform the task you've given them, try to provide better instructions (or a training video). If you still have problems, then they are probably underqualified and not a good fit. That's when you need to let them go.

If you're having a tough time deciding who the best applicant is, go with your gut. Just make a decision; however, keep the other applicants' contact info for the future. As you scale your Internet business bigger, you'll certainly need more help.

9. Get your new hire trained

We need to get your new outsourcer organized and trained promptly. Help them hit the ground running right away so they can be a valuable asset for your business. The following are several tips that will make your life easier:

From the start, have standard communication systems. Schedule one or two Skype sessions to speak weekly. Then you can message back and forth in the meantime.

If you use a project management software like BaseCamp, you can place your tasks in there and assign them. This helps you drastically cut down on email. Whichever communication protocol and frequency you choose, stick with it.

If an outsourcer is handling specific social media accounts, use an Excel or Google Docs spreadsheet for the account name, log-in address, username, password, and any additional notes.

Use Jing (made by Techsmith) to create video tutorials and screenshots. This is a free piece of software that allows you to write on any screenshots you take. You can also record videos up to five minutes in length. If you need more time with your instructional videos, Camtasia Studio is a great option made by the same company.

Get your new contractor in the habit of sending DAILY progress reports and work summaries after their shift is completed. This creates accountability. You'll check these reports to make sure your new hire is on track and doing the task correctly and in a time-efficient manner.

Have a system in place to track the hours worked. It's your call as to how you want to do it. Google Docs, QuickBooks, and other project management systems do this with ease.

Once you hire the new contractor, send a welcome email congratulating them. Set expectations early and go over the common procedures and communication details. You can even include a little bio of your company.

10. Don't be a micromanager

You've got to know when to let go. It's all about systems. If you create a good system and protocols, your worker's productivity will be high. Yes, you (or a project manager) need to check in and make sure things are going great; however, don't forget that you're getting more done with less personal time used.

If you outsource right, you'll spend a lot less money and be able to spend more of your time doing what you do best and enjoying life!

I realize that hiring someone to help you in the business may be way out of your comfort zone. You might even feel like you should just continue to do everything yourself. Remember this though: every successful Internet entrepreneur uses leverage.

The sooner you get into the habit of outsourcing, the better. You'll have greater freedom, earn more money, and dramatically increase your impact in the world.

Eventually, you'll grow to the point where you'll hire a project manager to supervise all your contractors. This takes you out of the equation so you can focus on more important things like creating and expanding! The beauty is, if you utilize Workaholics for Hire, you can hire this specialist by the hour.

A project manager is quite possibly the most essential role for aggressively scaling a business online to the seven-figure mark. They should have their finger on the pulse of what is going on day to day in your business. You'll hit a ceiling on your income if you don't find a good project manager.

The first contractors you'll want to hire on a "per-project" basis when your online business takes off are the following:

Website programmer

They can install scripts on your site and make changes to the design or coding. It's always a good idea to delegate programming to the experts. This is not a high-leverage activity you should learn. I found my programmers on Upwork, and they've been with me for years.

Ghostwriter

These professionals can write expert blog posts, press releases, and articles for you. This is what they do for a living. You'll be amazed by how great their content turns out. They can also make your products and services look like the best thing since sliced bread.

Now, this should go without saying: NEVER hire a ghostwriter that doesn't use English as their primary language! There is a time and place to get tasks done on the cheap, but this is not one of them as the writing quality is a reflection of your brand.

Transcriptionist

They can transcribe your videos and podcasts for you so you can repackage your content and use it on another platform. Sometimes we also include the transcriptions in the YouTube videos too.

Video editor

You don't need to master Sony Vegas, Final Cut Pro, or Adobe Premiere. The best video editing programs usually have a steep learning curve associated with them. Find an affordable specialist who can quickly edit your videos so you can stand out from the crowd.

Graphic design artist

This is another easy task to outsource in order to save a boatload of time. Whether it's graphics for your website, Pinterest pins, Instagram images, or Facebook quote graphics, you can have a professional quickly design anything you want. Just tell them the idea.

Your handyman or woman

This is a virtual assistant trained to properly distribute the content you create, such as videos, articles, press releases, and blog posts. They can also handle your customer support side of things or manage your paid advertising.

You might even train them to do keyword research. The bottom line is they're like your clone and can step in seamlessly to do what you need.

It's good to have these six types of professionals "on call" so that when you need something done, you can pull the trigger quickly without losing momentum. You don't need a big budget since they won't be working hourly.

Let the outsourcers handle the dirty, more technical work so you can focus on growing the business.

Action Step: Use the valuable information in this chapter to find your first virtual team member. After you go through the process once, you'll feel more comfortable. You're going to be amazed by just how many tasks you can effectively (and cheaply) outsource to highly skilled professionals.

The goal is to replicate yourself over and over.

Create training videos that show your workers what to do and exactly how to do it. You do the work one time and now have a system that any new hire can follow. Get daily reports sent to you to track progress and make use of the trusted outsourcing websites I recommended.

PART III

ADDITIONAL WAYS TO MONETIZE YOUR EXPERTISE

Chapter 31

SELLING PRIVATE LABEL
PRODUCTS ON AMAZON

You miss 100% of the shots you don't take.
—Wayne Gretsky

Harnessing Amazon for business can result in what I refer to as "Oh shit" money! Software also can sometimes fall into this lovely category. You're probably curious what the heck I'm talking about, so let me elaborate.

When you get your foundation and systems set up the right way as an Amazon seller, sales can start pouring in fast and furious!

Why?

It's the BIGGEST online retailer in the United States. That's why.

Now, in case you've been living under a rock, Amazon is an international e-commerce company offering online retail, computing services, consumer electronics, and digital content, as well as other local services such as daily deals and groceries. The majority of the company's revenues are generated through the sale of electronics and other products, followed by media and other activities.

Of all the ways that we can do business on Amazon, in this chapter we're going to focus on the most lucrative method. It also just happens to have the fewest hassles too. I'm talking about selling "private labeling" products.

Amazon boasts over 270 million users as of the writing of this book, and it's only going to grow. What makes this so beautiful is the level of trust they already have with consumers. So we get the benefit of piggybacking on a credible name brand that's known for great customer support.

This helps us a lot because consumers are very skeptical when buying products on the Internet. Whether their skepticism is from a previous bad purchase experience or not, it is what it is.

Scams happen every day; however, Amazon provides a safety net. Due to their global scope/reach, it is also considered one of the most valuable brands in the world.

It's also critical to realize that when people are searching on Amazon, they're looking to BUY. This is very different from Facebook or other social traffic. Yes, we can get social media users to purchase, but the process is not nearly as easy.

Here are some notable stats about Amazon:

1. They have over 200 million credit cards on file.
2. Over 68 percent of smart phone users have the Amazon app.
3. Amazon has sellers in over 100 different countries.
4. Amazon's net sales in 2014 eclipsed $88 billion.
5. To help ease the burden on its warehouse workers, Amazon now uses robots to assist in retrieving items.

Here are the steps to take:

I'd like to try to simplify this whole "selling on Amazon" process for you right now. It's really not as complicated as one would think. When you break it down to its simplest form, we have only a few steps we need to take.

The first step is to create an account on Amazon Seller Central. This is mandatory if you want to sell physical products on Amazon. Here's where you need to go:

http://sellercentral.amazon.com.

Second, you'll want to do your research and find a product on Amazon that's selling like hotcakes. High competition markets are better to get into because there's more money to be made in them.

I would start with something that's related to your hobbies or interests, something you might even be "irrationally passionate" about. Think about all the items you've purchased in the last four weeks or so. Ask store managers what their best-selling products are too. To find a current list of the top 100 Amazon best-selling products, visit this link:

http://www.amazon.com/Best-Sellers/zgbs

On that page, all the categories are listed on the left-hand side. Click on a category that interests you, and you'll be able to see the top 100 best-selling products in that category. This can give you a jump-start and some great insight as to what you might be able to private label yourself.

A very powerful tool that many Amazon sellers use to find opportunities is Jungle Scout. You can literally save hours uncovering product ideas and sales information using this. Learn more about it at this link:

http://dcincome.com/blog/junglescout

This software integrates into your Google Chrome browser and streamlines product research. You can easily extract the best-seller rank, sales volume, estimated revenue, and more without ever exiting your browser or entering an Amazon product page.

Once we find a product that has a low Amazon best-seller rank (preferably under 1,500), we then look to see if other similar (and competing) products are getting bought up equally as well. If so, that's a great sign.

The screenshot below shows how to find the best-seller rank of any product. I went to Amazon then typed in "iPhone 6 case" as an example. It brought back popular search results, and I clicked on one of the listings.

You can do the same thing. Once on a product page, just scroll down until you see a section titled "product details." That's where you'll find the "best seller rank."

It's important to also assess the number of reviews for the primary product you selected and for similar competing products. More on that in a little bit.

The next step is to see if you can find that same product (or something similar) either overseas or from a supplier here in the US. Alibaba.com is probably the most famous website for suppliers all over the world.

Once you've found the product and manufacturer you want to source from, you need to get your unique labeling and packaging designed. If you go through a vendor you find on Alibaba, many times the product manufacturer can handle the design for you. If they can't, then just go to Upwork.com and hire a freelance graphic designer.

When you've found the supplier you're going to be doing business with, hire a professional to do a product inspection or factory audit at their facility first. I use a company called RichForth at InspectGoods.com.

Let's face it, there are a lot of scammers out there. While I've never been "taken" on Alibaba, some people have. A factory inspection/audit ensures the overseas company is REAL and they deliver what they promise.

This inspection should be done before you place your first inventory order with your supplier! The good news is that RichForth is pretty affordable, costing only $103 USD for a professional to travel to the supplier and do a comprehensive evaluation.

From there, you can add your product listing to Amazon Seller Central and then buy some inventory from the supplier. The minimum order quantity (MOQ) will be different, depending on where you go.

There are three components to a best-selling product listing. They are your title, description, and images. When describing your product on Amazon, do the following:

- Include a strong and compelling headline at the beginning. That will capture people's attention and make them want to read your full product description.
- Include benefits, a guarantee, and a call to action. You can list these as bullet points in the listing to make it easier on the eyes.
- Focus on the end consumer. What do they want and what are they looking for?
- Research competitor reviews for ideas. This will be a great source as you can read what people did and did not like about their product. If you see objections on the competitor's product, address those objections in your own product description.

When it comes to the title of your product listing, use the main keyword you want to rank #1 for on Amazon at the beginning of the title. This is the most important thing. Also, add at least one product feature afterward, preferably one that differentiates you from competitors. Lastly, add the guarantee.

Next, we utilize the Fulfillment by Amazon (FBA) service and get our supplier to ship the inventory to one of Amazon's warehouses. Google "FBA Label Requirements" to learn the appropriate (and compliant) way to do this.

Finally, launch and promote the heck out of your product!

A few words of advice:

Do yourself a BIG favor. Focus and apply all your energy and attention to one product and really get that ramped up. Do not spread yourself thin. That's the kiss of death in this business.

Sell a product that's under $50 and above $10. These are optimal price ranges that will prevent you from spending an arm and a leg on inventory each month. Conversely, if the product is too cheap, your shipping costs are going to eat up your profit margin.

Strive for at least a 50 percent profit margin. That means if you sell a product for $20 on Amazon, your net (in-your-pocket) profit after all expenses should be $10.

Sell your product on the high side of what competitors are charging. If we show the value well in our product description, consumers will pay the premium. Obviously, this gives us a bigger profit margin, which leads me to my next point.

Differentiate your product from all the others out there! That could be something as simple as the packaging, the listing title, product images, description, the guarantee you have, a free bonus gift you're offering, etc.

How to calculate your profit per unit sold

This is a CRITICALLY important number that you must know if you're going to sell anything on Amazon. We need to have a good idea of what our net profit will be. These are all the things you must consider in this calculation:

- Product Selling Price (what you intend to price it at)
- Product Category (selling fees will vary by category)
- Amazon Selling Fee (plan on 2 percent of your product selling price)
- Variable Closing Fee (plan on $1 or so)
- Cost of Goods Sold (wholesale cost per unit)
- Cost of Goods Sold – Packaging/Labeling (plan on $1 or so)
- FBA Labeling Service ($0.20 per item fee)
- Inbound Shipping Cost Per Unit (will vary)
- Product Weight in Pounds (will vary)
- FBA Fulfillment Fees (plan on 1.5 percent)

When we add all of those variables up, we'll get our "net profit per unit sold" number. We can then divide that out by the product selling price to determine our "net profit margin."

The secret to getting ranked high on Amazon

Aside from having your main keyword(s) found in the title of your product listing, what you're about to read is arguably the holy grail of the ranking factors!

The key to ranking on the first page of Amazon is to get people buying your product after they've searched for the keyword you want to rank #1 for.

So if you ask your family or friends to purchase your product, you want to make sure that they search the keyword you want to rank for, sort through the pages to find your product listing, and buy the product when they find it.

When a sale happens this way, think of it like a vote. The more people who buy in this way, the higher your listing will rank initially because Amazon is receiving feedback that your product is relevant to that specific search.

IMPORTANT: When your product goes live, don't just give people a direct link to your listing on Amazon. Why not, you might say? It's because a purchase this way will not help you in the rankings.

This is most critical especially when your item is initially launched. Once your product becomes established, the power of the keyword search does drop. At that point sales volume and conversion become paramount ranking factors.

Let's not forget about the power of customer reviews though. Positive feedback (and lots of it) is essential for your success with this type of business.

Face it … whenever someone searches Amazon for an item of interest, what do they do first? They scroll down to read what others have said about the actual product!

Our goal is to stack social proof in our favor so that we're the only logical choice when someone searches for our type of product on Amazon. To do this, we need an ENORMOUS number of positive reviews.

In fact, your goal should be to DOUBLE the number of reviews that your largest competitor has. In some markets, this will be very difficult to do. In others not so much. I want to encourage you to think big though.

The bottom line is this.

The product with the most reviews on the first page of an Amazon keyword search will get the overwhelming majority of new sales and customers. End of story.

As the old saying goes, "The proof is in the pudding." Look at your own habits when you shop on Amazon. I guarantee you're reading the reviews. More reviews equals more social proof and that social proof persuades people to choose your product above all others.

Just in case you're wondering, the reviews you get for your Amazon product listing need to be REAL reviews left by family, friends, and others that have used the product you're promoting.

DO NOT use a website like Fiverr to get fake reviews.

You risk getting your account banned if you get caught. Plus, the reviews from a network like that won't appear believable.

The following is a simple email script you can send to people you know that have tried your product.

Subject line: I need your help!

Hey (friend's first name),

I just started a new business where I'm selling (product name) on Amazon. I really need help gaining some momentum on the site.

So if it's okay, I'd like to give you this product for free in exchange for an honest review on Amazon. It doesn't have to be long at all.

Please tell me where I should send your free (product name) so you can try it out. After you get it, put it to use and write your review at this link (your Amazon product listing URL).

It's pretty simple to do.

Just scroll down until you see the "customer reviews" section and click the "write a review" button.

Thanks for help!

- (your name)

When your friend or family member gets the product, give them a couple days to check it out. Then follow up with them via email or phone. Sometimes people will tell you they're going to give you feedback but life gets in the way. We've all had this happen before.

I find people usually have the best of intentions and want to help you out, but they typically need a friendly reminder. Also, let them know how much it means to you and how grateful you are.

Getting traffic to your Amazon product listing

Most of the book you're reading RIGHT NOW is about getting targeted visitors to your website and/or products. You can apply many of these same concepts to marketing a product on Amazon: Facebook advertising, targeted Facebook groups, Google AdWords, press releases, joint ventures, Facebook groups, online forums, guest blogging, YouTube marketing, Pinterest, Instagram, email marketing, etc.

Another VERY powerful form of traffic generation is Amazon advertising. You'll see an advertising tab in your seller central account when you have a product live. You can learn more about it now following the link below.

http://services.amazon.com/product-ads-on-amazon/how-it-works.htm

This is very similar to Google sponsored advertising where you're putting your product in front of active searchers.

Want to know the best thing about Amazon?

People frequent this massive e-commerce site to BUY stuff! It's a network chock-full of active buyers. So, when you run Amazon advertising the right way, your conversions will be much higher than other promotional mediums.

Remember, Amazon stores credit cards on file, so it's ridiculously simple to buy a product with a couple clicks of the mouse. This is a business owner's dream.

With Amazon sponsored ads, we can pay pennies on the dollar in many cases and get our new products on the first page of keyword searches instantly! We're in the game from the start. Observe how other top competing ads are presenting themselves and model what you see.

You may need to test different ads to ensure you're getting the highest conversion possible. Amazon rewards high-converting products with more visibility. Never forget that.

This platform is much simpler than Google AdWords. In fact, Amazon advertises your product listing, so you don't have to create new headlines, descriptions, or images.

Deal and coupon sites

The following sites can produce a quick surge of sales for your product. Some of the major coupon/deal sites include DealsPlus, RetailMeNot, SlickDeals, FatWallet, and Woot. Just make sure you follow their community guidelines before posting.

You can even send free samples of your product to popular bloggers so they can potentially write a review about it. Many bloggers have audiences numbering in the tens of thousands. This is an easy way to get your product in front of the right crowd.

Tomoson.com is a well-known marketplace where you can give products to bloggers in the industry you're targeting so they can review it and help you generate buzz.

Amazon top reviewer profiles

This is a biggie. You're able to tap into an audience that absolutely LOVES to write reviews on products. It's almost as if they compete amongst themselves to see how many products they can review per week.

Send a complimentary product to them. If you want to really crush it, you're going to have to spend a little money to make A LOT of money. Initially, we need to build momentum and this is a great way to do it.

You can find a large list of the top Amazon reviewers at this link:

https://www.amazon.com/review/top-reviewers

Action Step: Selling products on Amazon is a great way to diversify your online income. Do your product research and market analysis based on the guidelines I provided. Search for suppliers either here or overseas using Alibaba.

Get samples sent to you so you can judge the quality for yourself. See if they do their own custom packaging. Know all your expenses. Launch and market your product like crazy using all the strategies mentioned and others you discover in this book.

Chapter 32

GETTING RICH FROM SPEAKING

Too many of us are not living our dreams because we are living our fears.
—Less Brown

I n 2006, my life changed forever in a few different ways. My name was getting around in different circles and a network marketing company got a hold of me, requesting I speak to their company CEO about marketing their brand on Myspace and YouTube.

At that time, I was new to public speaking. They asked me what my fee was to present for an hour. "Umm ...," I thought to myself. Then I just blurted out, "$1,500 plus airfare and accommodations." The next thing that came out of this dude's mouth was, "Can we meet this Tuesday in Houston?"

I was floored.

That's when I got a taste of how lucrative speaking could be.

I ended up flying there and presenting for an hour and a half. I got back home in Atlanta around 5:00 p.m. that day and sat in front of my computer for about an hour wondering what the heck just happened!

I stared at the check. Couldn't friggin' believe it ....

Since that time, I've performed countless speaking engagements, and I get paid at least a $5,000 honorarium almost every time. Mind you, this is for one hour of speaking.

The bottom line is that, today, the acquisition of knowledge is VERY important. It doesn't matter what business you have. You have information and experience that others simply don't!

There's no reason you can't earn an extra $5,000 per month just from speaking.

This could be on the front end where you're charging a fee for companies to have you come in and talk. Or it could be on the "back end" where you're allowed to pitch any products you have from stage at the end of your session.

I was recently in San Antonio for an event at the JW Marriott where I got to sell my programs from stage after I delivered an hour of valuable content. Guess how much money we made from stage that day?

If you guessed $16,531, you'd be correct! That's a lot of green where I come from. Would you be willing to get on stage and speak for just one hour for this kind of cash? Pretty silly question, isn't it?

Imagine how that would change your life. It takes most people years to save enough money to buy a new car. With that paycheck above, I could've bought a brand-new car in one day ... in cash!

If you have any desire whatsoever to turn your annual income into your monthly (or even daily) income, then you're going to need to add public speaking to your repertoire immediately.

Read that last sentence again.

Live events are quite possibly the best place to meet prospective customers who are ready to buy your stuff now! Here are just a few reasons why:

- Seminar attendees are obviously interested in the topic.
- They're motivated and clearly have some problem they're trying to eliminate.

- They're likely action takers, otherwise why would they spend their time and money being there? (They bought a ticket, traveled out of their way, reserved a hotel, etc.)
- They're potentially losing money by being away from their business.
- The seminar organizer has probably spent a small fortune getting people to come.
- The people in the audience have responded to advertising and marketing.
- The higher price the event, the higher quality the prospect is—just an FYI. In my personal research and experience, I've found that the more expensive the event is to attend, the higher quality people it attracts.

If you go to MatthewLoop.com you'll see I have a "media and speaking" tab at the top of the site. If you click that link, you'll see sample speaking topics, videos from events, what the information presented will do for attendees, and other related content.

I make sure this is front and center whenever a new person comes to my website because it's a lucrative and fun way to share my expertise.

Once you begin to build a trustworthy brand and are known for a great product (or getting people the results they're seeking), you're going to get asked to share your knowledge from stage. Plan for this now.

You don't have to do public talks, especially if you're terrified by getting up in front of a couple hundred people on stage. I would, however, strongly encourage you to get way out of your comfort zone and speak.

Aside from the enormous paydays for such little work, speaking from stage positions you as an expert like nothing else. You also get to be associated with well-known names in your industry if they talk at the same event.

Check out this added bonus: I've been at conferences where the organizers have hired professional photographers to snap pictures of presenters. Normally, this would've cost me several hundred dollars to get prime shots in a position of power. But it was free because I was a speaker. They sent me all the pro pics after the seminar. I still use one of those professional headshots to this day because it's so good.

On top of that, I got to sell my products from stage at the end of the talk. When I'm able to make an offer from stage, I know it's going to be a five-figure payday. That's pretty exciting. Plus, it's always fun to interact with attendees after. You're the instant authority in their eyes.

In the YouTube chapter of this book, I discuss ways to overcome camera shyness quickly. You'll want to apply those same strategies to overcome any stage fright you might be experiencing.

Regardless of whether you plan on speaking or not, it's a good idea to have a media/speaking tab on your website. If nothing else, it positions you very well in the market and differentiates your brand from most other competitors.

There are two programs that I'm going to recommend if you decide you want to become the very best at speaking from stage. These two guys are the best in the industry. You can look at every guru you probably already know that does public speaking. More than likely, they've been to one of these events or have been influenced by their work:

Big Money Speaker Boot Camp by James Malinchak
http://bigmoneyspeakerbootcamp.com/
Profit Point by Joel Bauer
http://www.joelbauerseminar.com/

When you venture on stage, you want to be memorable … period. Yes, you want to give amazing, practical content that the audience can apply immediately to see results. However, I recommend fusing that with a bit of fun.

If you've ever been to one of my speaking gigs, you know I like to get the crowd involved. Some even call it a bit outrageous. What am I doing that's so unforgettable?

I'll typically have a large green dollar sign appear on one of my introductory slides. Then I have an intimate talk with the audience. I let them know I believe in prosperity and abundance and that there's a law in the universe that says, "The more you give, the more you get."

I further go on to let the crowd know that if I have to ethically bribe them to pay attention, I will. The information I'm sharing changes lives.

Right about that time, I take a golden egg from my pocket and place a crisp $100 bill inside it. I'll then get everyone's permission to launch it into the crowd.

But, there's one condition.

I then say, "When I was younger, I used to watch a lot of professional wrestling. I was a huge fan of entertainers like The Macho Man, Hulk Hogan, Mr. Perfect, etc.

"But, there was one wrestler who had the catchiest of sayings. His name was Ric Flair, also known as The Nature Boy. So what I need you to do on the count of three is give me a big WOOOO!!"

The crowd usually loves this. They get involved and scream, "WOOO!!"

That's when I toss the golden egg into a sea of outstretched arms. Hands go flying up and people rise up out of their chairs (some even lunge) as the egg descends. Many folks can't believe I just gave away a hundred bucks like that.

Well, that's not the end of it! I usually fling golden eggs into the crowd multiple times throughout my presentations. I do this to give back, keep people focused, and to create a fun experience.

I usually make a disclaimer beforehand though. I had a guy break his finger at an event I guest spoke at in Las Vegas. His finger hit another guy's wrist, then crack!

The bottom line is that you need to create a presentation that does a good job of disrupting people's daily routines. This is known as a pattern interrupt. Make your talk so good they won't be able to forget the experience.

10 ways to land speaking gigs

You can apply almost all the strategies you've learned in this book to secure speaking engagements. Naturally, when you are seen everywhere in the marketplace, you will start to get calls about speaking. However, here are some proactive ways to accelerate the booking process.

Facebook advertising – I spoke about this strategy in this book. You can create ads and target by city, interest, job, gender, school, purchase behavior, etc. It's very simple to get in front of your target market with these sponsored ads.

Facebook groups/events – You can do a quick search for groups and events that have congregated around your topic of expertise. Depending on your industry, you might find hundreds of possible opportunities. You don't have to limit yourself to local groups either. Get involved with the group and contact the admin to see if they are in need of presenters.

Get yourself on video – Like I do, you should have a media/speaking tab on your website. This is your profile for all to see. On that page, there should also be videos of you speaking because it enhances your credibility. It shows you have experience.

Give away some freebies – When just starting out, you might need to do events for free in exchange for testimonials. Don't sweat it, as this will help you immensely in the long run.

Look for local opportunities – Let's harness the network we currently have. You might speak at the chamber of commerce or go to MeetUp.com to see if there are any local groups that could be a good fit. Check with them to see if they're accepting speakers.

Colleges and universities – If you live close to a college, university, or technical school, this could be a great way to get your foot in the door. Team up with a department head or actual professor to hold a talk on a subject relevant to the class.

Get listed in speaker directories – These are basically matchmaking services that will list you for a fee. Sometimes the fee is up front; other times they take a slice of what's collected should you get booked.

Your existing clients – This is an overlooked way to land speaking gigs. If you spoke for them, chances are they have a network of similar people or organizations that are looking for a professional speaker. See what groups they are a member of and if they accept new speakers.

Do a Google search – It's very easy to use search engines online to find speaking gigs. You can even search for competitors that are popular and see where they've spoken in the past.

Get an agent – Once you're established, you can seek out an agent who has an incentive to promote you. They get a piece of the action, usually a percentage of your speaking fee.

Okay, you've got the gig ... now what?

After you've landed the gig, you need to deliver the goods! That's typically the easy part though, since you probably speak every day to people about what you know.

You can create a simple PowerPoint presentation or have someone do it for you. The overwhelming majority of my speaking engagements are done with the help of a slideshow. A PowerPoint keeps me on topic so I don't digress.

If you've created your own products like a DVD training, book, coaching program, consulting service, etc., you've got to know how to sell it at the end. You can refer to the chapter in this book titled, "The Art of Copywriting and Sales" for a refresher. Remember, your close is everything and the key to making money with speaking.

By "close" I mean your ability to sell the audience at the end of the talk. If you know your product changes lives for the better, it's your duty to get it in their hands through certainty, conviction, and a good sales pitch.

Many times you don't get paid an honorarium to speak, but if you're able to back-end the presentation with a product offer, then you can help a lot of people and make a fortune doing so!

Remember, sales is as simple as letting your audience know:

1. Here's what I've got.
2. Here's what it's going to do for you.
3. Here are the answers to the most common objections and questions.
4. Here is the guarantee and why there's no risk.
5. Here's what other clients had to say.
6. Here are extra added bonuses for today to sweeten the deal.
7. Here's exactly what to do next.

This goes without saying, but you should practice your PowerPoint all the way through at least five times. You want to be flawless in your delivery. The close is the most important part and you want to OWN it.

A few other things to consider:

Dress for success

You don't have to spend a million bucks to look like a million bucks on stage. However, you want to put on your best threads or buy new ones. First impressions are EVERYTHING. If you look successful, people have a tendency to assume you're successful.

In their minds, you're walking the talk, and it makes you appear more credible. If you don't have the right image, it can detract others from buying your product.

Now there are always exceptions to the rule. I know guys that can speak in a T-shirt and torn jeans and still knock down a five-figure payday. I don't recommend the average person do this though.

Visualize your entire talk before stepping on stage

I do this every single time and you should too. All the pros do this. I will usually get in the seminar room before the event begins and walk around everywhere the audience will be sitting. I'll also go on stage so I can preview how things look.

I like to close my eyes and visualize the talk: me being comfortable on stage, delivering value, engaging with the crowd, getting cheers, and imagining good things happening.

I usually couple this practice with positive affirmations I repeat to myself. I find this helps to build confidence and certainty before stepping on stage.

Have order forms ready if you're selling something at the end of your talk

Make sure that you're on the same page as whoever will be handing them out. They should be distributed at the start of your close. To make things even easier at the end, in terms of accepting payment, you can use a credit card swiper that plugs in to your cell phone.

I use PayPal Here, but there are many apps out there that can accomplish the same thing. Square is another popular one. Why is it better to get the client to swipe on the spot? Well, you don't have to worry about their writing being legible when you enter the payment info at home later than night.

NOTHING is more frustrating than when you have someone that wants to buy your service but you can't process the payment! Don't put yourself in that position. Learn from my mistakes!

Get seminar attendees on your email list

As you already know, this is a big one. If we get attendees on our email list, we'll convert exponentially more prospects into buyers in the long run. DO NOT overlook this step.

Normally, what I do is offer an ethical bribe at the start of my presentation. I let them know I have a free thirty-nine–page blogging success blueprint they can access instantly. I also tell the audience what's in it for them and the benefits of having the info.

I'm basically repeating many of the bullet points of my squeeze page. Then I verbally instruct them to take out their smart phones "right now" and go to: http://DCincome.com/go/bloggingsuccess/.

Lastly, I tell attendees to put their name and email in the box they see to the right so I know where to send the report. I'm walking them step-by-step, telling people exactly what to do. I strongly recommend you do the same.

<u>Action Step</u>: Make a decision now to incorporate public speaking into you product offerings. As you've discovered, it can be a very lucrative and fun way to help people with your knowledge, passion, or expertise.

Get a media/speaking page on your website so it gets visibility as your traffic and influence grow. This positions you as a serious professional.

Use the strategies in this chapter to proactively land speaking gigs. Make it a goal to get on stage at least twice per month.

Practice your presentation(s) multiple times before going on stage.

Get comfortable with the content you'll be delivering. Know it inside and out. You are the authority, so let your expertise shine through.

Get your close down to a science. Develop unshakeable certainty! Follow other known speakers to see how they're packaging themselves and their knowledge from stage. Model the greats and never stop learning!

———————— *Chapter 33* ————————

HOW TO MAKE A FORTUNE
FROM CONSULTING

I find that the harder I work, the more luck I seem to have.
—Thomas Jefferson

A s you apply what you've learned in this book to become an industry authority figure, you'll find that certain people would like more private and/or frequent access to you. It is my strongest recommendation that you offer some type of consulting in your business model.

Aside from making a tremendous amount of money from charging a premium, you typically work with more committed customers.

Here's what I mean.

When I first began privately coaching clients, I noticed something interesting. These people followed my advice better, made the best case studies, provided no hassle, referred the most people, and got the best results!

A big reason why this happens is that this type of client is heavily invested in themselves. Meaning, they've got a bunch of "skin in the game." If an individual invests several thousand dollars in something, they will usually follow through.

I really wish I would've learned this lesson MUCH earlier in my online career. Guess how many refunds I've had to give coaching clients?

Zero.

This is due to a couple factors.

One, I get results when I choose to accept a person into one of my high-level programs. If I don't feel I can help them, I won't accept their application. Two, customers that pay a premium are more likely to follow your advice and get results.

Here are some consulting services you can offer:

- Phone consulting (one on one or in a group setting)
- Skype coaching
- Lunch and learns
- Live immersion day (one on one with you for a day)

As you can imagine, depending on how close and how much access a prospective client wants, that will dictate the amount you charge. An in-person meeting is more time intensive and exclusive than a phone call.

If you visit MatthewLoop.com, you'll see I have different levels of private training and access. ALL of these are application based. I highly recommend yours be the same way.

There's something very powerful about having a person complete an application to work with you. It says your time is valuable and that they're not guaranteed acceptance. In fact, one of the fields in my coaching application is "Convince me why I should work with you."

As your business grows, you'll eventually develop a waiting list. This is powerful because it says you're in high demand. It's similar to a popular restaurant or nightclub. When you see a line around the block to get in, what do you instinctively think? It must be a great place, right? Why else would so many people be waiting to get in?

When we have an application process and eventually a waiting list, this same psychological principle is at work.

In my business, I have a three-month waiting list for coaching at present. If you review the tabs on my website, here are the high-end consulting programs you'll find:

- Private one-on-one phone coaching
- Lunch and learn
- Total Immersion Day
- Private Jet Mastermind™

Mind you, these are separate and aside from the digitally downloadable products we sell every day. The goal is to take your expertise and package it so that the information can be consumed in different formats.

This diversification approach enables us to create many sources of income in our business. Some people will want only your inexpensive e-book while others are going to want to be closely associated with you in a top-tier program.

The point is to give people different options!

If you're doing calls, here's a tip: record them to give the client even more value. You can utilize free conference-call lines to do this. FreeConferencing.com is one that I've used for years. Clients call into a number, then I record the calls and have my assistant send the recordings to clients that same day.

The service doesn't cost any money either!

Eventually, we'd like to move those that download our free information or purchase our low-barrier offer up the ladder to our premium programs.

Here are some simple steps to get started integrating your own consulting:

Step 1

Decide which type of consulting program(s) you'd like to provide. You don't have to do in-person meetings if you don't want to. It's your choice. I suggest offering something though. It enhances your credibility.

Step 2

Get the consulting programs listed on your website. Think about what you want to offer and be as detailed as possible. Tell people what you have, what they get as a member, what the coaching will do for them, then what to do next.

If you need an example, visit MatthewLoop.com and have a look at the different options that are featured in the navigation bar tabs.

Just put yourself out there!

Before I ever had anyone sign up for our private total immersion day, I had to get the courage to feature the event on my site. That was a challenge because I knew what the service was worth based on previous client results, but actually asking for that price was WAY out of my comfort zone several years ago.

Here's something you already know: if you don't ask, you don't get!

It's interesting what you find. Certain people want different levels of access to you, so give them options no matter how crazy it might sound.

Anywhere you mention your products or services, you should have a consulting option close by, whether it's on your website or you're speaking live at a seminar. Let people know about your core offerings.

Step 3

Determine a fair price to charge. What is your professional guidance worth? Think of an hourly rate right now. Got it? Now, double it! Most people charge way too low for consulting. Don't be one of them.

Do NOT base what you charge by looking at other perceived competitors in the marketplace. The last thing we want to do is compete on is price. I'd rather compete on value and results than just be rendered a commodity.

When you position yourself correctly like we discussed, people will pay whatever fee you ask if the value is there AND if you can demonstrate your advice works. That's why it's important to always ask for, and never stop accumulating, testimonials from satisfied clients.

When you are known as the celebrity expert in the space and have the social proof to back it up, you stand out from the pack. Again, you decide your own price point for coaching.

I'd recommend your coaching fees be the most expensive in your respective field. There's good psychology behind this too. People associate the most expensive with the best.

Don't believe me?

If you're a woman and are shopping for a new handbag, you have many options to choose from. Two of those brands are Walmart and Chanel.

Which one is better?

Why?

Now let's be honest. Is the leather quality one hundred times better in a Chanel bag than one you could get at Walmart? Allow me to emphatically say, "Hell no!"

Is it better leather? Yes, it is. However, I think we can agree it's not a hundred times better. If you think so, you're delusional.

The reason why many women salivate at the thought of having their own Chanel handbag is because of the exclusive reputation the brand carries. It's known as the best, and a big reason why it's known as the best is because of the high price of acquisition.

Chanel bags are also very scarce. You can't get them just anywhere.

It's very clever marketing and strategic positioning. As with many luxury brands, having access is a sign of social status. Most people yearn to elevate their social status.

The bottom line is that when you're the highest priced in the marketplace, buzz starts to circulate. Prospective clients AUTOMATICALLY consider you better than your competitors on a subconscious level.

The public has been conditioned to believe that if a product is more expensive, it must be better. You and I know this isn't always true, but don't fight the prevailing mass perception.

Step 4

Promote and drive traffic to this page like you would a normal blog post or product. Use the proven social media marketing strategies in this book to gain notoriety fast. As you scale people up the product chain, expect some to want more intimate access to you.

It's also a good idea to offer this program as an upsell to an existing product you offer. So let's say you're selling a digitally downloaded training full of video tutorials and PDF manuals. On that sales page, you could have a "platinum" option right below the standard package. This could be a private consulting upgrade.

I actually do this with my Social Media Elite training program. You know what? A small fraction of people will naturally select the high-end program.

Here are the common reasons why people typically select consulting:

- They want or need extra hand-holding.
- They desire accountability, which ensures follow-through. Weekly coaching holds the person's feet to the fire. Many times we let ourselves down, but it's much harder to let down another person, especially when you've made a commitment.
- They want to work closely with the best of the best in the market.
- They want to delegate and have you train their staff member or team.
- They want a shortcut so they can achieve their desired outcome faster.

If we never offered the one-on-one option alongside one of our normal training products, we would be missing out on hundreds of thousands of dollars in revenue. Again, you're going to find customers that want different access to you. Give them options!

Action Step: Integrate private consulting into your business model immediately. Choose which types you're comfortable with and then put it on your site for the world to see. Follow the advice in this chapter and you'll see that it's not that difficult at all.

I recommend scouting the top players in the market you're servicing. See exactly how they're fusing consulting into their existing business model. Review their coaching pages to get ideas. Pay attention to how they're demonstrating the value of what they're offering.

Have a consulting contract in place as well. The customer should sign this agreement at the same time they submit the application. This document is primarily for setting expectations. You let them know EXACTLY what they're going to receive and what the terms of the consulting program are. Spell it out very clearly.

If the contract states that the coaching is for twelve calls, then the client cannot come back to you and say they "thought it was for fifteen calls." If they did, you'd simply show them proof via the agreement they initially signed.

When we set expectations from the get-go, it enables us to follow through on what we say. Many times I will over deliver though. That means I'll give them a little extra service. However, it's not expected because we laid out what they were going to receive at the beginning.

Google "sample consulting contracts" or "sample confidentiality agreements" and you'll pull back a slew of examples that will help you as you piece your contract together. You can also speak with an attorney who specializes in this type of law.

Chapter 34

TURNING AN IPHONE APP
INTO YOUR OWN ATM

―――――――――――――――――――――

It's not the lack of resources, it's your lack of resourcefulness that stops you.
—Tony Robbins

L et's turn our attention to the easiest and fastest way to make a smart phone app on a shoestring budget! The best part about this is that you don't need to know one lick of programming to make this work. Right now, as it stands:

- According to Statista.com, Apple sold over 168 MILLION iPhones in the 2014 fiscal year! That translates to a whopping 46,000 units sold per day! The first quarter of 2015, Apple has sold 74 million phones and looks to crush 2014's stellar sales.
- 67 million iPads were sold in 2014.
- The vast majority of people who are making apps are programmers, not professionals that have marketing experience, like you or me.

You, reading this book right now, have substantially more marketing knowledge, and you're already way ahead of the game.

- If you review iTunes regularly, you'll see that the top spot in the app store can easily gross over $100,000 per day!
- Apps racked up over 10 billion in sales globally in 2014.

As you can clearly see, the app opportunity is enormous! We haven't even touched on Google's Android market, which is the top dog. According to ComScore, it owns just over 51 percent of the market share, whereas Apple is just over 42 percent. Blackberry and Microsoft fill in the rest.

It seems like every so often in the news, analysts project the market to double in a few years. So what would that mean? I'll use an exaggerated example you might be able to relate to. Let's say you own the only Italian restaurant in the city of New York. As you know, NYC boasts around nine million people.

Now, there are tens of thousands of people searching online every day for either pizza, chicken parmesan, scaloppini, etc. You obviously cannot meet the demand yourself, not even close. Now picture that market DOUBLING in the next few years—like what it's on pace to do. I know this is an exaggerated example, but it should put things into perspective.

It's very hard to wrap your mind around some of these numbers, but the app market and opportunity is huge. It's why I'm sharing with you how I personally created my iPhone application, how easy it was, and how you're going to be able to do the exact same thing.

Step 1 – Decide what kind of app you want to build

This doesn't have to be hard. Get very clear on what you want an app developer to create. You should ask yourself the following questions:

Do you just want to make something for your local business or are you thinking on a much larger scale? Do you want to make a gaming app? An educational app? Travel app? Photography?

Do you have a market in mind, a group of people that you're looking to target? Or do you want to focus on what's currently making money?

Have you been to the iTunes store and looked at some of the most popular applications?

The bottom line here is that you need to be very specific.

Obviously, we know Angry Birds made ungodly amounts of money and still does well. Also, silly little games like Fruit Ninja or Doodle Jump do millions each year.

The amount of income some of these entrepreneurs are making is crazy. Games could be an option for you, but they're not for everyone.

I chose a gaming app for my first application, but there are so many categories to select from. Games tend to be the most lucrative because of the "in-app purchases" that customers make.

It's a super competitive market though. You don't just create an app and make money. You have to promote it well. Don't let competition scare you though. That just means there's plenty of income to be generated.

Start your first app simple and pick something you're passionate about. Make an app about what you'll enjoy working on because if you don't, you'll be miserable in the creation process. Don't just go where you think the money is if you're not going to have fun working on it.

Step 2 - Define the purpose of your smart phone app

Clearly map out the purpose of the iPhone app you want to have built. What are you specifically going to do? What functions is it going to have, in terms of how customers are going to use it? Is it going to be free or paid? What is the desired outcome of the app? Are you going to have ads within the app? Are you going to offer upgrades or in-app purchases?

If you can think of it, a programmer can code it into the application.

Step 3 - Create something that's unique in the marketplace

This is self-explanatory. Don't directly copy an existing app. If something is popular, that's great, but you don't want to have an Angry Donkeys game to try to compete with Angry Birds. Not going to happen.

Be original. It's okay to have some familiarity, but you can't really clone another application simply because people won't be as motivated to download a knock-off. The public has already seen Angry Birds.

Try to look at what's working well. Do your market research in terms of competitive analysis. Check the top-grossing apps by category in iTunes. See which features they have. Reverse engineer their websites.

Don't overcomplicate things! This is one of the big mistakes people make. Do one thing and do it exceptionally well. You can always add additional features and upgrades to the application later on. This doesn't have to be perfect. Just get it out on the market.

Let me reiterate here. Don't feel like you have to make an iPhone game. As I mentioned previously, there are plenty of categories, so if you want to break into something else, by all means, go ahead and do so. There are so many popular apps out there.

Step 4 - Getting the app made

This is actually pretty easy. Even though the development process sounds very confusing, it's simple and I want to break it down right now.

A website that you can use to find a developer for your iPhone application is Upwork.com. This platform is easy to navigate and the process basically goes like this.

- You open an account.
- You place a job posting on their network.
- Freelancers and contractors from all over the world bid on your project.
- You review/interview them and select the best candidate.
- Your iPhone app construction begins.
- When your project is completed, you give feedback.

I outsource much of my stuff on Upwork. Here's why. When you hire a programmer or developer on Upwork, the company actually takes a screenshot of the contractor's computer every fifteen minutes. It ensures that they're working on your application and really not just screwing off.

You don't want to get ripped off when you create your own iPhone application, so I would strongly recommend using an outsourcing website like Upwork so you can monitor the progress. It's good to know exactly what you're getting.

You don't have to know all the fancy programming stuff. That's why you hire a developer to do it for you. You just have to have the ideas. Then the expert turns your idea into reality.

If you've followed me for the last several years with my social media courses, you know that even though I teach so much great content, very RARELY do I recommend doing it all yourself. I'm all about being resourceful and delegating.

Why?

It's because you need to work predominantly on the business, not in it. The more you delegate, the more income you make through leveraging other people's time and effort.

You should spend your time creating these ideas because, as entrepreneurs, we tend to be innovators. Our time, energy, and effort are best focused on doing those things that harness our strengths.

Programming is certainly not my strength. Programming is not your strength either, so you shouldn't be doing it. Outsource it to an expert!

You can find programmers from all over the world on Upwork. That's the true beauty of this. The cool thing is you're not looking to ghostwrite an article. We're not talking about a job where we need grammatically correct English here.

We're referring to a programmer that can do a high-quality job in another part of the world just like someone you would hire here in the US.

One of the things I will strongly recommend is that you outsource your app development. What I mean is when you search for a developer on Upwork, make sure you go overseas. Some people might be shocked I would say that.

The main reason I recommend this (especially for your first app) is that you don't want to spend $5,000 like I did on my first mobile application. If you have an app built here in the United States, you'll spend at minimum $5,000. I know. I've checked: $5000 … $10,000 … $15,000. That's common practice because developers in the US are three times more expensive. That doesn't necessarily mean that the quality is three times better though.

In many cases, I would definitely say the more you pay for a service, the higher quality it typically is, but in this situation, I've found some phenomenal talent overseas for much less. It's just how you screen the talent that is really important.

Upwork allows you to look at the developer and their previous work. You're allowed to review their portfolio and check previous client feedback. You can download iPhone applications they've already built. This is great because you can see their quality of work, which is something you definitely need to know before hiring a programmer.

Test their other apps. Make sure they have a long history and experience. Check to see if they have great user ratings.

Most first-time app entrepreneurs that have problems with outsourcing usually don't screen the candidates well enough. Their primary concern is cost, and while you can get cheap labor, that's not the number one thing you should be looking for.

You must make sure the quality is also there. This is your name and brand on the line. Do your due diligence.

When I originally hired my programmer, I was going to make a super simple version of my gaming app. The goal was to keep it cheap. I had no plans to make it look cool like it does now, spending thousands and thousands of dollars.

However, he personally told me that I would have a much better chance if I made better characters and different things in the application.

Your programmer will have a lot of knowledge on the programming side, which can give you tremendous insight. You don't have to know everything. Give them the list of features you want in your app.

Be sure they fit your standards, in terms of their ratings and reviews. Look through their portfolios and observe their previous work. Download and play their apps.

I wanted to make sure my programmer knew how to upload apps into the iTunes store because that can be a separate pain in the ass if you're not careful. I didn't want to go through that, so I chose to have him do the entire thing for me.

Three mistakes to avoid when getting your app built

Hiring a "team" of developers

My advice is that you don't hire a team to build your first application. Hire an individual programmer instead. If you hire a team, sometimes you get lost in the mix. This is because teams typically have many people, which leads to more hands in the mix.

It's easy to get lost in the shuffle and not get the service you want. I've personally had back luck with teams. Hire an individual developer.

Being too specific in the initial job posting

When you post your initial job description on Upwork, Freelancer, etc., I'd recommend being a bit vague in that posting. Once you start getting bids, tell the individual developer to contact you privately for more information.

This allows you to converse with them a little beforehand to see if you're a good fit. You never want to give away your ideas (or your application) up front because there are some unethical people who will attempt steal what you have.

Once you finally select the best provider for the job, you'll have them sign a Nondisclosure Agreement (NDA) before proceeding. This adds a layer of protection for your ideas.

Look at all the contractor's previous work as I mentioned before, as well as their ratings, written feedback, and earnings, and then test their existing applications.

In my personal experience, I knew my developer was the best choice for me because his previous work was polished. It was easy for me to get a good feel for everything he had done.

Talk to your prospective hire on Skype. This is important. Most programmers will give you their information so you can chat back and forth. You don't need to speak with them directly on the phone. Use the instant messenger.

As you already know, if you hire a programmer from the US, your cost will be two to three times more for app development. Experience is the most important factor at the end of the day. We can find highly seasoned professionals overseas just like you can here.

Not being clear on expectations

Setting and being crystal clear on expectations is critical right from the start of the project. You should have agreed-upon milestones along the way. You both should determine a start date and an estimated time of completion.

You want to know if the developer can also create graphics for you. If not, you will need to get them outsourced somewhere else.

Get all your ideas out of your head and onto paper. Really think your app through. If you start adding stuff during development, it's going to cost more. Beforehand, you should've already agreed on a fair price.

Some programmers will want to bill you hourly while others may quote you the total cost up front. Let them know your budget for the app and the maximum you are willing to spend. You don't want this to be an issue later on.

Monetizing your mobile app

The most successful apps online are making money through "in-app purchases." Look at the top-grossing apps in the iTunes store, and you'll see what I'm referring to.

Take the gaming category, for example. Many times, they'll offer you a free trial of the game, and then you pay to upgrade to the whole version. Once you have the whole version, they then will try to sell you in-app purchases.

Paper Toss is a great example of this. Download it to see what I mean. In fact, whatever category you're considering for your app, you'll want to download the top-grossing apps to see how they're making most of their money.

Your app developer can build whatever you want into the app itself. You just need to have a clear picture of what that looks like based on other popular apps. You should definitely have in-app purchases enabled.

Which reminds me …

One of the more common questions I get is, "Should my mobile app be free or paid?" The answer is BOTH! Have a free version to let people try. Free apps get way more downloads than paid apps for obvious reasons. When a user tries the app and likes it, they'll want to upgrade.

Get more engagement with push notifications

Push notifications are a powerful way to send important info to app users so you can have them revisit your app, view new stuff that they might like, see a special offer, or view a cross-promotion.

Be careful with this feature. You don't want to abuse it or annoy users.

A few options are available to help you get this function integrated. You can build your own push-notification platform. Of course, that can be expensive. Or you can just utilize a third-party provider like Urban Airship, PushWoosh, or Parse.

A couple in-app analytics programs like Localytics and Appboy also let you do that. The most important thing is to review these services yourself and see which one fits best into your budget.

Do you need a website?

Initially, you don't need a website for your application, but you'll eventually want to have one. I'm not talking about a full-blown site either. A simple two- to three-pager will suffice. Here's a popular WordPress template that's available online:

http://templatic.com/cms-themes/iphone-app.

In actuality, there are tons of website templates out there. They're very simple too. This is not like setting up a sales page. You don't need to set up a big, long sales letter to sell your application online.

Do yourself a favor and search for popular apps and their websites. That will give you additional ideas of how the most successful apps are positioning themselves.

How to market your iPhone or Android app

This is where it gets fun. It's one thing to have a great application. It's another thing to get it into the hands of the masses. Don't make the mistake of thinking that just because you have an app created and up on iTunes, it's automatically going to sell. It won't.

Remember too that each app is different, so the marketing will not be entirely the same.

The first thing you need to be concerned with is what's called "app store optimization." This is similar to on-page SEO for a regular website. Making sure you have this covered will help you maximize your downloads.

The factors include:

- Choosing the right application name and associated keywords
- Creating a memorable app icon that's congruent with your app design
- Selecting your best screenshots (consider using text captions to explain them)
- Writing a compelling app description that makes people want to try it now
- Getting great app ratings (and a lot of them)

Plain and simple, we want our application to appear in the app store when people search specific keywords. Optimizing your app with the factors above makes the likelihood greater that you'll appear higher on the keyword searches.

If you appear higher in the keyword searches, you'll get even more downloads. All things being equal for you and your competitors, whoever has the most downloads will rank higher.

Need help choosing the best keywords? Check these sites:

http://www.mobiledevhq.com/

https://searchman.com/

https://www.apptweak.com/

https://sensortower.com/

Aside from all the promotional strategies you're learning in this book, you can incorporate these to get your app out there.

App review websites

There are hundreds of websites out there that have their own tight-knit communities where all the owner does is review apps for their audience. You can go to Google right now and type in "app review websites" and find many of them. Here's a site that has 160 places to submit your app:

https://maniacdev.com/2012/05/ios-app-review-sites.

You can get even more specific by typing in "iPhone app review sites" or "Android app review sites."

Cross-promoting your app

This is a biggie. If you plan to make multiple apps and your target audience is the same, you have an ENORMOUS opportunity for cross-promotion.

You have the option to cross-promote on your mobile app's website, on your normal blog, to your email list, within your other apps, by sending push notifications, on social media outlets, and more. Just make sure the message you're sending is relevant to the audience receiving it.

If you're just beginning and have only one smart phone app, you can reach out to other developers with apps who are in the same niche and approach them with a partnership offer. Start small, maybe with Facebook posts, tweets, videos, in-app messages, etc. and see where that goes.

Find popular bloggers in your industry

Bloggers have their own engaging communities online. Sometimes they will review products they find interesting. You can submit your application to them.

Advertising platforms for mobile apps

If you have the extra budget, you can pay to get more exposure for your new app. Some companies charge you per download while others charge by the number of impressions your advertisement receives.

Nonetheless, this is a great way to gain momentum so you get fresh downloads. Google "mobile advertising platforms" so you can see an extensive list. This link below has the top ten companies, including ones like AdMob, ChartBoost, iAd, and Millenial Media.

http://venturebeat.com/2013/06/12/the-top-10-mobile-advertising-companies/

Realize that marketing is not a one-time proposition. It needs to be done every day. This applies to mobile apps as well as ANYTHING you market and sell online. The best strategy is to combine the above methods with everything else in this powerful book.

Rarely is there one magic bullet that's going to create a gushing faucet of income. If we hit the market from multiple angles though, we're much more likely to have success.

Chapter 35

IN CONCLUSION

You, me, or nobody is gonna hit as hard as life. But it ain't about how hard
you hit. It's about how hard you can get hit and keep moving forward.
How much you can take and keep moving forward. That's how winning is
done! Now if you know what you're worth then go out and get what you're
worth. But ya gotta be willing to take the hits, and not pointing fingers
saying you ain't where you wanna be because of him, or her, or anybody!
—Rocky Balboa

Congratulations, you've made it to the finish line! Now the real fun can begin. It's time to roll your sleeves up and get your hands dirty. I realize your head might be spinning right now. That's okay though. When I discovered this information for the first time, I couldn't sleep for two weeks!

I got the big picture and could see how it all fit together. Ideas were flying left and right. It was as if a bright light bulb began to glow in my mind, but I have to be honest—I felt like I was drinking from a firehose!

Can you relate? Have you ever felt that way?

As you can see, I held nothing back from you. I exposed what the world's highest-paid Internet entrepreneurs, coaches, celebrities, marketers, and consultants are using to grow wildly profitable Internet empires that can be run from a laptop anywhere in the world.

There's absolutely no reason why YOU can't take the information presented—the foundational principles, social media outreach strategies, and marketing tactics you've learned here—and create a lucrative six- or seven-figure business around a passion, hobby, or interest.

I've said it before and I'll say it again: The Internet is the ULTIMATE equalizer. It doesn't care who your parents are or where you came from. If certain things are done in this certain way I've described, success is predictable.

Look at me. I wasn't born into a wealthy family. I didn't have insider connections. I received more cold shoulders than you can imagine. In fact, I even lacked computer savvy when I began. The chips weren't stacked in my favor, and for all means and purposes, I was an underdog.

Through passion, preparation, and persistence I climbed my way to the top. No elevators, just step by step, the old-fashioned way, learning from mentors who were where I wanted to be. I knew my family and I deserved better. You deserve better too!

Don't let current circumstances define you. Everyone fails at one time or another. You are not your past. Discard limiting beliefs and open yourself up to what's really possible in life. Make no mistake about it—the Internet is creating millionaires every day.

Why can't you be one of them? That's the question. I could show you inspirational success stories of people that experienced much more hardship than you or me, yet they defied the odds and came out on top.

I'm here to let you know that you can create the business of your dreams around a topic, interest, or hobby you love. I want you to know that you can get RICH!

Even if you did a small fraction of what I've described is possible—maybe an extra $5,000 to $10,000 per month—think about how that could completely transform your life. I was where you are and observed others firsthand that were making incredible money from the web.

They weren't the smartest guys in the room either. I thought to myself, "What do they have that I don't?" As it turns out, they stumbled upon the same formula you have now learned.

Furthermore, I caught myself thinking, "If this person can do those kinds of numbers, surely I can do at least a quarter of that."

I believe this is a great attitude to have because it helps you venture into the realm of possibility. It also gets the wheels turning inside your head so the natural next step is to ask yourself "how" it can be done.

Know that where you are right now in life is the result of past thinking. When you change your thinking and take action based upon what you discovered in this blueprint, you'll dramatically enhance your results.

Will success and riches happen tomorrow? Of course not.

There's always a ramp up time since we're building a real, sustainable business. However, having this book and access to the information I've shared throughout has given you a tremendous competitive advantage so you can hit the ground running.

You don't have to fumble and folly around late at night wasting precious hours like most beginners do, trying to figure out what really works versus what's just hype. You chose to invest in yourself and now you have a proven shortcut.

That being said, as you get this online machine in motion, you'll still need to split test. Once you start getting some results, you will need to adjust and tweak so you can consistently improve.

The knowledge contained in this book enables you to shave years off your learning curve while preventing needless frustration and costly mistakes. I wish I would've had these tools, resources, and insights when I first began my online career. It would've made things so much easier.

This brings me to another important point. Before you can make a million dollars from the Internet, you must first make one dollar. Don't get your priorities mixed up. That initial sale gives you a jolt of confidence and really sets the stage for everything else.

I still recall my first sale online. The excitement and sense of accomplishment was off the charts! My heart still races when I think about it today. In fact, I remember that moment more than any subsequent five-figure day I've had.

But let's forget about the money for a second. Money is simply a by-product of the value we deliver to the marketplace.

If your goal is to get your message out to the world, to stand out from the crowd, help a lot of people, experience more out of life, take care of your family at a higher level, impact the masses, and leave a meaningful legacy you can be proud of, you owe it to yourself to master the art of social media outreach.

Everyone has different priorities and reasons why they want to have a successful business. At the end of the day though, it comes down to freedom—being able to come and go as you please on your terms, not having to report to a boss, not feeling guilty about taking a vacation because you're not working, being able to financially contribute to the causes closest to your heart, etc.

Using social media to start and grow a business around an interest, passion, or hobby can give you OPTIONS.

It's not the exotic vacations we regularly enjoy that remind me of this either. It's the times when I get to take my son to the park at eleven on a Tuesday morning that I can truly appreciate the "Internet lifestyle."

Or when we go grocery shopping and get to select the best quality organic food without being concerned what it's going to cost at the checkout. The ability to have choices that I didn't have before is something I'm grateful for and never take for granted.

I don't have to be at a full-time corporate job working for someone else making them rich. Neither do you! You've seen there is a better, more fulfilling way.

Now that you've discovered arguably the most important skill set that enables you to create the life you want and deserve, it's time to charge like a rhino in order to MAKE IT HAPPEN! Combined with your current ability, knowledge, and talent, you can extract the wisdom in this book in order to create a business and life you love.

Be sure to join our Facebook group so you can meet and interact with other like-minded entrepreneurs who are dedicated to creating a positive impact in the world. This community will help you keep the momentum moving forward. Just enter "Social Media Made Me Rich" in the search bar and you'll see it.

Connect with me on the following social networks as well. I will personally answer your questions, help you overcome your biggest challenges, and keep you up-to-date on the newest social media strategies that multiply your influence and income.

- Instagram.com/MatthewLoop
- Twitter.com/MatthewLoop
- Facebook.com/MatthewJLoop

Furthermore, visit www.MatthewLoop.com and get on my email list immediately. You'll see a form in the upper right-hand corner of the site. I share powerful social media business growth tips and insight there that I don't share anywhere else. Email subscribers also get first priority access to free giveaways, new video trainings, and special interviews.

• • • • •

At this stage, I find there are four categories that most entrepreneurs, brands, and companies can be grouped into who are reading this.

The first are those that have read this book and won't do anything with the information. Hopefully, that's not you, but I've been around long enough to know there will be plenty of people like this. Many will not make money or move the needle simply because they won't take any action.

Can you imagine that? To those individuals I say, don't be upset by the results you didn't get from the work you didn't do.

The second category you may fall into is that you're doing zero to minimal social media outreach, but you know in today's ever-evolving economic landscape, it must be done. After all, this is how the new generation communicates. You might not have a product or service yet, but you either have an idea or want to get started generating income from the Internet.

The third category you, your company, or brand may fall under is that you're doing social media marketing and getting decent results, but you know you're capable of so much more. You're scratching only the tip of a giant iceberg. You want guidance from a seasoned professional so you can exponentially grow your impact, influence, and income to meet your goals.

The fourth category you might fall under is that you just want everything done for you. You're interested in delegating many of the tasks that go into a wildly profitable social media marketing campaign.

You might even have, or be a part of, a company that's currently not maximizing its effectiveness on social media. I'm specifically referring to revenue generation. So many brands and businesses are using Facebook, YouTube, Instagram, etc., yet they're not getting an immediate return on their investment.

Awareness, branding, engagement, likes, and Facebook fans don't necessarily equate to dollars. Many companies are finding this out the hard way after years of wasting their money and listening to supposed gurus.

There's a time for a long-term payoff, but that has to be coupled with direct-response strategies that create revenue, influence, and impact immediately.

If you're in categories 2–4, we can definitely help you have the most profitable year you've ever had. See the back of this book for information on our advanced trainings programs.

Now I'd like to ask you to be totally honest with yourself based on your own personal history. If you're going to let this information sit on a shelf and watch as the excitement and momentum fizzle out, you might want to consider applying for one of our exclusive trainings listed in the following pages.

Currently there's a waiting list, but applications can be submitted anytime.

Private weekly coaching ensures you're held accountable and increases your follow-through. Letting ourselves down is often easy; however, letting another person down is an entirely different situation. It's much harder to break your word. This is especially true if you have invested skin in the game.

Consulting and mentorship are also great if you're the type of individual that already knows the value of having an experienced coach on board to help propel you to a RECORD year financially.

Rich people understand how important it is to find mentors who have already developed effective systems and mastered certain areas of business. This is the ultimate success shortcut. After all, time is money. It's also the one thing you can never get back, so you need to spend it wisely.

Your best shot at living the good life you've always dreamed about, and attracting everything you want, is to model what the world's wealthiest Internet entrepreneurs are doing. Don't attempt to reinvent the wheel. That can take years.

These moguls have taken the hard knocks, spent ridiculous amounts of money, and figured out the complex systems that work so you don't have to. I've exposed their carefully guarded strategies throughout this book.

What you decide to do with this newfound knowledge is ultimately up to you.

Find a problem. Fix it. Make bank. Enjoy the freedom that comes with it. Experience more in the world. Start a movement. Give back to those less fortunate. I wish you prosperity and abundance in all areas of your life.

PART IV

ADVANCED TRAINING
CUSTOMIZED TO YOUR NEEDS

Chapter 36

DO YOU QUALIFY
FOR PRIVATE COACHING?

There is no good economy. There is no
bad economy. There's just YOUR economy.

—**Grant Cardone**

Our personalized coaching sessions are designed with one thing in mind: getting you RECORD results fast! This is an application-based program, so you must qualify and be accepted.

Don't know where to start?

Do you have challenges with market research, keyword selection, squeeze pages, traffic generation, list building, conversions, Twitter, Facebook marketing, SEO, Google AdWords, Google+ Local/Maps, outsourcing, product creation, blogging, video marketing, Instagram, leveraging automated systems, or just getting an idea out of your head?

I'm going to customize the most effective plan of action based on your current strengths and work with you to achieve your new client and/or online income goals faster than ever.

I've made it easy to access effective and "experience-based" business building expertise.

Why should you apply for this program?

You must meet the following criteria in order to apply for this exclusive training. Here are some situations you might be in now that make you a perfect candidate to gain the most from private coaching with me.

1. Help getting your own product or business off the ground quickly

In my physical business and Internet ventures, I've made the most money pulling the trigger and getting ideas off the ground fast. We're talking about hundreds of thousands of dollars generated in a relatively short time.

Although Internet sales and new customers can come quickly in a short period, there's A LOT you have to get right the first time to enjoy this result. As someone who has been through this process several times, I'm very familiar with what needs to be done right (and systematically) to get maximum results.

Here's a quick list of some of the aspects I can help you with:

- Planning your overall marketing strategy, including a timeline and road map to follow
- Finding and eliminating weaknesses before they stop you in your tracks
- Determining what, if any, technical systems you should have
- Getting your sales page, video, and/or checkout done to a deadline
- Reviewing email marketing copy
- Help crafting a lead resource that ensures viral distribution
- Someone to call on during your initial stages to deal with unforeseen challenges

I'll help you avoid any drama and bring to market a smooth, profitable product without the stress and fear of what you don't know. I've been there and done that a number of times, so you can leverage my experience for your own personal success.

2. Help taking your business to the NEXT level of success

Maybe you're already doing well in your business, but you know that there's MUCH more room for growth. Private coaching is not just about fixing problems or removing obstacles. It's about creating new possibilities, giving you better strategy, and improving what you're already doing.

That's worth reading again.

It's also about having strong accountability and being able to "shortcut" your learning curve by years so you can achieve your goals fast.

For example, if you're a small-business owner like a chiropractor and want to generate an EXTRA twenty new patients (or more) from the web, you need to find someone that has the experience of doing it and follow them!

If you're an Internet entrepreneur and are looking to generate five or six figures monthly, you MUST latch on to a coach who already is where you envision yourself.

3. Strategically map out, create, and sell information products

If you're an information publisher or you want to become one, I'll walk you step-by-step through the process so you'll know how to create and sell membership sites, e-books, audios, video courses, mobile apps, software, or any form of training or educational content.

Since 2005 I've been an information marketer/publisher and currently make the biggest portion of my income from selling training products. I absolutely adore this business model because up-front costs are VERY low.

You can distribute as much product as you can sell, you can fully automate the sales and delivery processes, and your intellectual property is unique to everything else on the market. Proper positioning is essential though.

I'm going to show you how to:

- Select and then implement a differentiation strategy so you're perceived as a real expert
- Develop your marketing funnel so you have a continuous stream of income and are not solely dependent on just one product

- Choose a pricing structure that meets the needs of your market and maximizes your profits
- Build proven systems so your products sell themselves
- Shortcut the technical systems required to roll out new products with ease
- Create a marketing plan that matches your skills and available resources so you have buyers 24/7

4. Building, branding, marketing, and monetizing a blog

I won't go into super detail for this one, but needless to say, if you need help with any aspect of your blog, I'm one of the most qualified information marketers to advise you.

My blogging-success blueprint went viral and was downloaded over 40,000 times. I'm one of only a handful of experienced leaders that blogs about Internet marketing and social media.

I've taught thousands of entrepreneurs, small-business owners, and coaches and have successful case studies from previous students. I have lived and breathed social media since its embryonic stage.

If you want to start a blog, add one to your existing business, grow your current blog and make more money from it, I can help.

5. Any and ALL important aspects of Internet outreach and marketing

The truth is, Internet marketing is a complex, vast subject. If it was easy, everyone would be doing it successfully. That's far from the case as the average majority fail miserably.

Not only am I a full-time social media revenue and growth strategist, but I stay in the trenches because it's my passion. The end result of this total immersion means I have a strong knowledge base about this subject.

Beyond that, I have years of "real-world" experience and have personally sold millions' worth of services and products from the World Wide Web.

Internet marketing topics I can help you with include (but are not limited to):

- Market research
- Getting an idea out of your head

- Product creation
- Keyword selection
- Squeeze pages
- Website creation
- Traffic generation
- List building
- Increasing conversions
- Twitter marketing
- Facebook marketing
- Facebook advertising (ppc)
- Pinterest marketing and paid advertising
- Selling products on Amazon
- Instagram marketing
- Search engine optimization (SEO)
- Google AdWords
- Google+ Local/Maps
- Outsourcing the right way
- Blogging
- YouTube video marketing
- Article marketing
- Affiliate marketing
- Payment processing
- Shopping cart management
- Product fulfillment
- Leveraging automated systems

I'll guide you step-by-step toward making the correct decisions or in the direction of the best resources so you can make the BEST decisions.

6. Systematic business automation and long-term planning

Many have labeled me as strategic and someone who thinks through things completely. I'm good at generating big ideas and seeing the long-term picture and all the little pieces that come together to make it happen.

Strategic business planning and automation can help in the following areas:

- Sales Funnel Development – If you really want a successful Internet business, you're going to need a converting sales funnel, including several products at different prices. I'm familiar with how this model applies to an information marketing business because I've studied and implemented it for many years.

- Email Marketing – Your email sequence is one of the MOST powerful automation tools you have access to. Email marketing is where the money is, so this is definitely an area we have to work on in your brick-and-mortar or online business.

- Technical Programming and Design – Listen, I'm not a tech geek! I just know what types of technology are required to get things done effectively and efficiently. I focus on simplicity in design and programming for my business. Keeping it simple will help you generate more income.

- Business Model Enhancement – I can help you transform a labor-intensive service-delivery business (e.g., a consultancy) to one that is focused on a digital product and utilizes a much less labor-intensive sales funnel model. If you're currently a talented individual trapped in a business that requires you trade your time for money, I can help you finally break free. This will result in substantially more time for you, and no ceiling on your earnings potential.

- 80/20 Leverage Areas – Only a handful of variables in your business account for the majority of your results. Right now you're spending time on activities that don't help your business gain true leverage, but you may not be able to "see" the points of leverage you should focus on. I can do an 80/20 assessment of your business and your life to determine what you should spend your time on for maximum results.

This is not a conclusive list of challenges we face as business owners or online entrepreneurs, but they are some of the more common roadblocks that surface. Many people think they have a tactical problem when they really have a problem with strategy. I'll identify and show you where your real obstacles are.

7. Lifestyle design and personal growth

This is a critically important topic I can help you with. Initially, I expect you'll sign up with a desire to exponentially multiply your income, an area I'll definitely help you with. However, you'll find that your growth and personal development with the right coach can be far and above that.

Lifestyle design is about creating a life you enjoy living every day. We can look at every area to find harmony.

Every millionaire and successful entrepreneur I've spoken with agrees that mindset is THE KEY to success in business and in life! So this is an area I can help you work on. My current mindset is the number one reason I'm successful.

Like most, I didn't have the best mindset when I began. As I evolved and grew, my mindset transformed, and my income exploded.

8. If you need your hand held step-by-step

I'm including this final point based on experience talking to members of my programs. Too many times, the biggest challenge is simply that there are too many options! There are way too many things to do and countless directions you "could" take.

Simplification and having someone highlight a direct path to your immediate desire is the best form of coaching. I will bring laser focus into your life quickly. I also hold you accountable, which fuels consistent action and rapid business growth.

With a little background into what you want to dramatically grow your business and improve your life, we'll work together to find the right path for you. Not only will we do that, we'll uncover the fastest, most intelligent path for you to take

This is something that's unique to everyone and takes time to refine. Private one-on-one coaching is the only way to isolate what you really want.

What this program will do for you

- Make you more efficient and systematic in your business or online marketing
- Show you how to be more resourceful, which gives you more flexibility in your schedule

- Teach you how to work less and make DRAMATICALLY more, maximizing points of leverage in your practice/business
- Get you more customers faster when you implement the proven marketing strategies
- Show you how to generate the professional income you deserve, which allows you more freedom to spend life the way you want
- Eliminate any and all barriers that are keeping you from the level of success you envision
- Teach you a set of skills that will enable you to generate passive income from the Internet for LIFE

To be clear, there is work to do

I've outlined the specific areas I believe are most relevant to today's Internet entrepreneur and what you most likely need help with. Every point may not apply to you, and perhaps I've not gone over the area you need coaching in.

That may mean we're not a good fit, or it could be that you just need to ask me whether I can help before applying for private one-on-one coaching.

One thing that I need to make crystal clear to you is that no matter what you want to change in your business or life, it's going to take work. There are no quick-fix "magic bullets," and I'm not here to do things for you. This is a path you ultimately walk. I simply provide guidance based on what has worked exceptionally well for me.

If you want to create similar things in your life that I currently have, and you're prepared to take the committed steps that I give you to get there, then we will work well together.

I want to be totally transparent with you so you don't have any unrealistic expectations about how this works. You let me inside your business situation, and I then offer a plan of action. After, you need to go out there and get the job done.

We'll clone the process again and again until you reach your desired outcome. We'll work together to adjust the steps as we go, incorporate new resources as we need them, and get you to where you want to be financially at a highly accelerated pace.

Why am I doing this?

You might be wondering why I'm offering you this exclusive opportunity to work directly with me and learn all my BEST success secrets and systems.

The answer is easy.

I'm on a mission to help business owners and entrepreneurs (like yourself) earn more and experience more so they can have the freedom and flexibility they desire. Everyone deserves an incredible life.

This could be as simple as having more family time, taking exotic vacations whenever you choose, or just enjoying an overall better quality of life.

Coaching also allows me a chance to learn more about what colleagues are struggling with, which helps me become a better teacher and mentor. On top of that, it's really fun working with like-minded, motivated people in an industry I enjoy.

My major goal with this private coaching program is to find the rock stars. I want to connect with unique influencers who bring passion to the world and share my belief that in that by helping others, you help yourself.

I'm focused on transforming lives for the better and making sure everyone has a chance to reach their fullest potential.

Does this sound good to you so far?

Okay, great! Here's what to do next if what I mentioned appeals to you. Visit the private-coaching link below to get more specifics and qualification requirements:

http://DCincome.com/blog/coaching

Chapter 37

SPEND A LIFE-CHANGING DAY WITH ME

Follow your bliss and the universe will
open doors where there were only walls.
—Joseph Campbell

This is a top-tier protégé program designed to help you build a five- to six-figure per month PASSIVE income machine around doing what you love.

The Total Immersion Day experience is also for brands, business owners, and celebrities who want to profitably integrate social/information marketing into their existing business model, product, or service.

I'll personally help you map out the exact strategies (fully customized) as well as an EASY-TO-FOLLOW plan of action to ensure you start making more money quickly.

This exclusive opportunity isn't for everyone though.

It's only for those who are serious about DOUBLING or tripling their income quickly while building more freedom into their lives.

If you implement just a couple (of the dozens) of strategies and plans I help you create, you're guaranteed to get back MUCH more than you invest for the day. In fact, my average Total Immersion Day client recoups their investment within the first thirty days.

The one-on-one live Total Immersion Day provides you with the "fast-track blueprint" to mastering and monetizing social media marketing for your company or brand. You'll also discover how to become a celebrity in your industry and a trusted center of influence.

With these time-tested strategies and foundational marketing principles, I've been able to start from scratch and personally sell millions' worth of products and services on the Internet in just a few short years.

More importantly, I've helped private clients generate over $135 million in extra sales combined.

Here's what this experience does for you

- Provide you with much-needed clarity regarding EXACTLY what to do in your business for maximum exposure, leverage, traffic, and revenue. The guesswork is completely removed from the equation because you'll get to look over my shoulder as I walk you through.
- Give you a simple, PROVEN, step-by-step action plan to execute. This is highly customized to your goals, wants, and needs. Everyone is different, so there's no one-size-fits-all approach. It's important to do what you love and to also make great money doing it!
- Help you discover how to be resourceful and save TREMENDOUS amounts of time so you can do more with family and friends. Time is the one thing you cannot get back, so mastering activity management is critical. We'll design your work around your dream lifestyle, as opposed to the other way around.
- Help you learn how to position yourself as the leader and center of influence in your marketplace. You'll learn how to build credibility fast, become a known celebrity, and build a strong audience in any industry.

- Help you discover how to make a GREAT living (and a five- to six-figure per month passive income stream) doing what you love, taking advantage of what you're passionate about. I'm a firm believer in creating a strong legacy that you can be proud of.

- Help you discover how to MAXIMIZE your business profits and shortcut your way to exponential growth and success.

How the day works

You'll begin with a private strategy session

A few days before your Total Immersion Day you'll have an in-depth, thirty-minute conference call with me personally. We'll start your strategy planning on this call and continue it in person.

You arrive in Atlanta no later than the evening prior. We can provide you a list of recommended hotels if needed. Plan on staying at least two nights. (Of course you can stay longer and experience all Atlanta has to offer.)

Starting time is at 8:00 a.m. EST

Usually, we spend the first couple hours of the day getting all your ideas out on the table. I'll ask you a bunch of clarifying questions. The whole time I'm strategically linking all the different aspects of your business: your market, your offerings, your goals, and your ideal lifestyle.

Almost always by the time we break for lunch, it's fairly obvious what your lowest-hanging fruit is.

I see your entire plan mapped out in front of you ... and it's the optimum way for you to leverage your passion along with what your market will pay for.

I take you to lunch at one of my favorite hot spots

Atlanta is filled with an eclectic mix of incredible restaurants. It's one of my favorite things about living here. Over lunch you'll relax so you can rest your excited brain (because you're going to get SUPER energized by what we've mapped out to this point).

The second portion of the day – your complete success BLUEPRINT

Alright, after you've had some wonderful food and fresh air, it's back to the lab. The second half of the day is typically when we go deep within the specifics of your business success blueprint. I work with you to map out all the details of your profit and growth strategy.

This typically encompasses:

- Detailed goals and projects broken down for the next six months
- Your entire website sales funnel (traffic, list building, conversion, sales, etc.)
- Who your ideal client really is (and what they most what to buy)
- All your product and service offerings (we'll identify all your products and/or services for all price points appropriate for your business)
- How to maximize profits (we plan the easiest ways for you to boost your income, including upsells, rate increases, increasing the frequency people buy from you, and much more)
- And much more

Once things are wrapped up, it's time for a fun night on the town

I work with you that day as long as you need. Typically, we'll wrap up by 7:00 p.m. EST. Then we'll go and have a memorable night on the town and let everything we covered marinate.

Work hard. Play harder.

Follow up and continued support

A week after the Total Immersion Day, we'll get on the phone to go over any questions and perfect your plan. I'm also available for emails and short phone calls as you need them in the following months.

This helps quite a bit because as you start to take action on your plan, questions will definitely come up. If you encounter an obstacle, rest assured I've already been there and can keep you moving forward quickly.

A Total Immersion Day isn't right for everybody. Because I spend an ENTIRE DAY with you, you must meet a few requirements. You can get all the specifics at this link:

http://DCincome.com/blog/total-immersion-day/.

Chapter 38

FOR CELEBRITIES, PROFESSIONAL ATHLETES, ENTERTAINERS, AND PUBLIC FIGURES

*Never give up on a dream just because
of the time it will take to accomplish.
The time will pass anyway.*
—**Earl Nightingale**

I f leveraged correctly, social media has the ability to provide you, as a celebrity, ongoing recurring revenue while creating sustainable top-of-the-mind awareness for the long term. On top of that, nothing turns fans into RAVING fans like strategic use of social media.

The creation of a digitally delivered product line enables you to extend your brand equity beyond existing entertainment platforms by offering fans fresh, authentic interactions and experiences.

Through my Atlanta office and supported by our partners worldwide, we provide celebrity and expert talent with a unique, strategic approach to social media revenue generation that no agency in the world offers.

This proven method can easily increase your brand revenue by $1 million per year (or more) quickly. The best part is, the time and work involved are minimal, and everything can be done from the comfort of your own home.

For this reason, a nondisclosure agreement (NDA) must be signed beforehand so specific details can be provided during the initial phone consult.

Our experienced team works with celebrity brands to execute continuity programs that match their core values, allowing for a natural extension of a client's personality and expertise to be showcased using social media.

From music to film to fashion, we create a direct connection between a personality and the fan that extends way beyond the pages of a magazine or movie screen. The result is more liking, trust, and dramatic increases in revenue.

What this customized program is NOT

This is NOT "social media management." Managers manage; they don't generate your brand additional revenue. This is one of the big mistakes public figures initially make and learn the hard way.

This is NOT about licensing merchandise like T-shirts and other antiquated and unprofessional items.

This is NOT about doing public appearances where you must travel and leave your family.

This is NOT about creating a "job" for you or trading time for money.

This is NOT an untested fly-by-night revenue strategy. This has been proven and tested in multiple markets. I've used this strategy to come from out of nowhere and generate millions.

In today's social media dominated world, consumers crave insider information and accessibility to their favorite personalities. We simply help give them what they want, which turns simple fans into RAVING fans that pay you month after month.

Through the launch of relevant and compelling online products and services, social media revenue strategy creates an organic, one-on-one experience between you and your audience.

Imagine that you have five million fans around the world. What if just a half of one percent of those individuals were involved in one of your online programs that cost a low $9.97 per month? Let's do the math.

25,000 x 9.97 = $249,250 per month in recurring brand revenue ON TOP of everything else. That's an additional $2.991 million each year. This is a very conservative estimate based on previous clients too.

Let's use a real-life example.

Jerry Seinfeld is one of my all-time favorite entertainers and is a hero to countless aspiring comedians. Wouldn't it be cool if Jerry offered an online course that taught you everything you needed to know to be a successful comedian?

I mean, Jerry obviously knows what it takes since he's one of the most famous comedians of all time. If you're just starting out in comedy (or any field), you should learn from and model the best in the game, right?

Jerry could offer many aspects of the training in his new online course—everything from talking about how to craft jokes, the creation process, how to get comfortable in front of a live audience, how to ensure the best timing and punchline delivery, mistakes to avoid, the best ways to make connections, etc.

Do you think some aspiring comedians would pay for access to Jerry's training? You bet your ass they would!

What I described here is just the tip of the iceberg as there are many more types of trainings and/or programs that can be offered to your fans. This helps you maximize your impact in the marketplace as well as brand revenue.

Something very important to understand is that the programs we help you build are completely different from traditional boring fan clubs!
The size of your estimated fan base will dictate the amount of revenue you can generate. Let's do some more math with conservative numbers.

If you have ten million fans and just a half of one percent (50,000) subscribed to an "out-of-the-box" monthly membership program at $9.97, you would make an extra $498,500 per month. That's an additional $5.982 million per year WITHOUT having to leave your home!

Here's another example.

Let's say you have twenty million fans and just a half of one percent (100,000) subscribed to a monthly membership program at $9.97, you'd bank an extra $997,000 per month. That's an additional $11.964 million per year without having to fly all over and do public appearances.

Many celebrities and public figures usually ask us, "How much time is involved?"

The answer is not much. Plan on two to five hours per month. We are building stronger relationships with your fans and giving them a whole new level of perceived exclusivity. Can you devote more time if you want? Absolutely. It's up to you.

For more information and to see if you qualify, email VIP@DCincome.com and put "Celebrity Social Media" in the subject headline.

Expect a response in one to two business days to set up an initial phone interview. Not all applicants are accepted.

Chapter 39

WANT ME TO SPEAK AT
YOUR NEXT LIVE EVENT?

I always tried to align myself with strategic partners,
friends, and information to help me with the things
that I did not know, and ultimately, I made it.
—Daymond John

Y ou've made a great decision and I would be happy to speak at your next
big event if it's a good fit. As you can imagine, my schedule fills up very
quickly, so reservations must be made well in advance.

I have a very unique personal story of triumph, and I'm widely regarded
as a pioneer in the social media industry. Way ahead of the curve, I began
harnessing this powerful medium for recognition, traffic, and sales in its infant
stages in 2005.

I've helped tens of thousands over the years and am the highest-paid
social media revenue strategist in North America. My client list includes

everyone from celebrities, global brands, authors, and coaches to small-business owners.

If your event is approved, expect me to engage attendees in a fun and outrageous way. I'm known for showering audiences with golden eggs stuffed with crisp $100 bills.

Here are the various types of speaking/training I am best at and most passionate about.

Sample speaking topics:

- Facebook Fame in 30 Days: More Sales, Traffic, and Recognition than You Can Handle
- How to Get Customers from Social Media without Spending Money on Advertising
- The Ultimate Guide to Making Money with YouTube
- Increase Company Revenue by 30–50% in the next 4 Months or Less
- The Social Media Monetization Blueprint
- The Twitter Referral Machine
- How to Turn Your Passion into Profit: Make Money Online Doing What You Love
- The Ultimate Blogging Success Formula
- And many more …

I currently live in Atlanta and regularly do paid speaking engagements. Honorarium fees range from $5,000 to $25,000 depending on duration, complexity, attendee count, and proximity of the event.

I also speak on stages where I can make a special product offer.

Here's what the information does for you

- Get you exponentially more customers/sales from the Internet each month
- Reveal the BIGGEST, most costly, and counterproductive mistakes to avoid when using social media
- Make your company the most recognized in your industry

- Show you how to be more resourceful and what the best high-leverage growth strategies are
- Show you how to blanket/dominate Google and Bing for money keywords
- Enable your business to become an UNSTOPPABLE public relations machine so that anywhere and everywhere prospective new customers go, they see your site or content
- Get your business measurable and exponential increases in website traffic
- Teach you a set of skills that will generate sales and customers FOR LIFE
- Get your brand message in front of the right qualified prospective clients
- Make lead generation faster, easier, and less expensive
- Enable you to finally have more freedom and flexibility to do what you love anytime
- Give your company the ultimate UNFAIR competitive advantage (locally or nationally)
- Provide you with a proven, reliable Internet marketing strategy

Here's what to do next

To view my speaking reel, sample talks, more specifics, and to see if your company qualifies, visit my media page at:

http://DCincome.com/blog/media-speaking/.

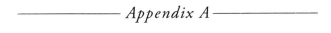

Appendix A

TOOLS AND RESOURCES FOR STARTING A BUSINESS ONLINE

I f you've found your way to this page right now, one of two things has occurred.

The person who referred you must REALLY like you a lot. Or you were reading this book and were curious what tools the world's highest-paid entrepreneurs, brands, authors, coaches, speakers, and trainers use in their businesses.

Previously, this information was available only to those that invested a healthy amount of money in one of my top-tier coaching programs.

Why?

It's really simple.

Those that pay a large amount of money have more of an incentive to implement the tactics because they have a great deal of skin in the game. And ... the hard reality is that those who take massive, consistent, strategic action are the ones who become prosperous.

The last thing I want to do is give away my best resources and tools that have helped me generate multiple seven figures online, and then have only a tiny fraction of entrepreneurs use them.

DO NOT just go through this information and let it go to waste. This is one of the most valuable pieces of information I've ever shared! It has a handful of my best resources and contacts for everything under the sun in terms of profitable social media marketing.

The amount of money these next few pages will save you is well into the tens of thousands, not to mention all the time, energy, and effort you won't have to waste on useless gimmicks.

It took me going to the school of hard knocks to seek out and painstakingly find the best companies, software, and websites on the planet for starting and growing a lucrative Internet business.

The truth is, it's not the lack of resources that stops most people from building a successful business online; it's their lack of resourcefulness, of not knowing where to go.

I've solved that problem for you now.

Hosting and domain names

Bluehost: Every business online MUST have a website address and hosting. This is your cornerstone on the web. The overwhelming majority of my websites are hosted on Bluehost. Their platform is reliable and ridiculously cheap. They offer 24/7 customer support too.

Bluehost is easy to use even if you aren't a computer geek. They also offer a free domain with hosting and one-click automatic WordPress installation. I STRONGLY RECOMMEND Bluehost for your website hosting.

I negotiated a very low rate for my blog subscribers at:
DCincome.com/blog/Bluehost.

Website creation and blogging

WordPress: The top blogging platform online ... and it's free! It features easy content management and customization, even for beginners. Every one of my blogs was built on the WordPress framework.

Get WordPress actually installed on your Bluehost hosting account/domain.

WordPress Themes: A theme is basically your site design or template. It should be professional, not cookie-cutter like most businesses owners have. My blog design was custom built. You'll want to do the same.

Email info@DCincome.com for top-notch programmer recommendations.

The Ultimate Blogging Success Blueprint: My #1 recommendation for starting a highly profitable blog. This guide shows you how to attract a steady flow of new clients and sales from blogging without spending money on advertising.

To grab your free copy of this thirty-nine–page blueprint, just tell us where to send it. Enter your name and email in the submission form found at the top right of MatthewLoop.com, and then click the orange "get access" button.

Shopping carts for product distribution

1ShoppingCart: This is my #1 shopping-cart solution. I've used them for years. If you intend to sell products online, you need a shopping cart to seamlessly automate, track, and organize your orders.

This platform is compatible with most payment gateways and merchant accounts. It also comes with an easy-to-implement affiliate program.

Grab a free one-month trial of 1ShoppingCart at: DCincome.com/blog/1ShoppingCart.

ClickFunnels: (http://DCincome.com/blog/clickfunnels)

Shopify.com

Payment processing

PayPal: I use PayPal for most of my products because it's super simple to set up, and they have a much lower processing fee. You can also sign up for Website Payments Pro, which allows you to accept payments via PayPal and by credit card.

Visit Paypal.com to view their solutions.

PowerPay: You can also accept credit cards by setting up a merchant account. One of the most trusted merchant account companies online is PowerPay. I like this one in particular because they understand online businesses—and information marketing in particular.

Visit Powerpay.biz to view their solutions.

Clickbank: An excellent all-in-one Solution that allows you to accept payments (via credit card and PayPal), and it has a built-in affiliate program.

One of the best parts about Clickbank is they will pay your affiliates every two weeks so you don't have to worry about sending out checks or doing mass PayPal payments.

On the down side though, Clickbank does have a rather high processing fee. Visit Clickbank.com to view their solutions.

Email marketing software

Aweber: The best email marketing tool in the business. Your email list is your #1 asset online. If you don't have a list, the truth is you don't have a real, sustainable business.

Aweber is what I use to collect emails, queue autoresponder messages, create lead-capture forms, grow my audience and then send them weekly newsletters.

Their phone and email support is excellent. Get a $1 trial of this powerful marketing system at MyProResponse.com.

Infusionsoft.com

ConstantContact.com

MailChimp.com

Squeeze pages, landing pages, and sales-letter creation

OptimizePress: Hands down, the best tool for easily building professional, high-converting squeeze pages. They have over thirty templates available. OptimizePress also makes sales-page creation and formatting incredibly simple, and it's WordPress compatible.

Grab your discounted copy at:

DCincome.com/blog/OptimizePress

Keyword research

Market Samurai: The marketing industry's top software program for uncovering high-traffic, profitable keyword phrases online. Market Samurai also allows you to spy on competitors and reverse engineer their presence on the web.

Most businesses fail in their online efforts because they don't have the tools to appropriately research the market.

Grab a free trial of Market Samurai at:

MarketSamurai.com/c/freetrialnow

Webinar technology

<u>Stealth Seminar</u>: Easy, affordable, live, and automated webinar service. I use this platform for real-time events and recorded webinars. The great thing is that there's no complicated software to install and no coding you have to learn.

It's hassle-free, and the customer-service response time is usually under four minutes. I'm not kidding. If you're planning on using webinars in your business, grab the Stealth Seminar discount at:

StealthSeminarDiscount.com

Competitive intelligence

<u>Keyword Spy</u>: (http://DCincome.com/blog/keywordspy) Find out which keywords your competitors are bidding on.

<u>Market Samurai</u>: (http://MarketSamurai.com/c/freetrialnow) Find profitable niches/keywords online and target them with devastatingly accurate SEO.

<u>Trellian</u>: (http://ci.trellian.com) Find out which sites are responsible for sending traffic to your competitors' pages. Extremely Powerful!!

<u>T3Report</u>: (http://t3report.com) Find out who your competitors' top affiliates are.

<u>WhosMailingWhat.com</u>: A vast library of direct mail data, which allows you to learn from their tests and direct mail controls!

<u>Copernic Tracker</u>: (http://www.copernic.com/en/products/tracker/) Monitor website changes. Find out when your competitors are split-testing or changing their websites.

<u>Website Watcher</u>: (http://aignes.com) Similar to above. Monitor websites for updates and changes

<u>WayBack Machine</u>: (http://www.archive.org/index.php) This is an excellent tool for seeing what your competitors' websites looked like in the past in order

to find out how they have changed their website over time. You can then use this data to increase the conversion rate of your own websites.

DomainTools.com: Allows you to find out who owns a particular domain along with what other websites they own.

Graphic design

Killer Covers: Professional, elegant designs for your e-books, CDs, DVDs, e-zines, reports, software boxes, etc. Check them out at:

DCincome.com/blog/ecovers.

99Designs: 99Designs has revolutionized the design process. Multiple graphic artists compete against each other to win your bid. So you can have dozens of different designers creating multiple designs for you. Then you only pay for the one you like best.

Visit their website at:

99Designs.com.

Buying and selling websites

Flippa.com: The top marketplace for buying and selling websites

Web and programmers

Upwork.com (formerly Elance and Odesk): The most popular place to find, hire, manage, and collaborate with online freelancers. Find the help you need to take care of business. Dip into their impressive pool of talented professionals to tackle virtually any project on your timeline and terms.

Freelancer.com.com: (formerly known as RentACoder and vWorker)

InterBerry.com: A top-notch team of programmers

Hiring a virtual assistant

Workaholics4Hire.com

OnlineJobs.ph: World's largest workplace for finding Filipino freelance workers. You can find a virtual assistant to work forty hours per week for just $200–$500 per month on average. You can also hire part-time.

<u>123Employee.com</u>: Offshore dedicated virtual assistants and virtual staffing from American-managed offices in the Philippines.

Transcription

<u>Speechpad.com</u>: Provides guaranteed quality transcription services at a low cost. It's easy to use and they have a fast turnaround time.

<u>Upwork.com</u>: Find a freelance transcription person and hire them on a per-project basis.

<u>Verbalink.com</u>

Productivity tools

<u>LastPass.com</u>: LastPass is a password manager that makes web browsing easier and more secure.

<u>Dropbox.com</u>: One of the easiest ways to store, sync, and share files online.

<u>Evernote.com</u>: This is one of my favorite tools online. I use it every day. Evernote makes it easy to capture and organize your life online. It allows you to take notes, save URLs, web clips, files, images and entire webpages.

I use it to create my online swipe file, mark down ideas for new products, and to keep a running list of article ideas, subject lines, and more.

<u>FreeMind</u>: (http://freemind.sourceforge.net/wiki/index.php/Main_Page) My favorite free mind-mapping software. I use mind maps to outline articles, new products, and business ideas.

<u>RememberTheMilk.com</u>: Website that helps you keep organized. It lets you make lists and will send you email reminders when things are due. It also integrates with Google calendar.

<u>FocusBoosterApp.com</u>: A free application that will allow you to get things done faster by setting a time for each task.

<u>Enounce.com</u>: Change the playback speed of Flash videos for faster learning or easier understanding. From YouTube to educational and training videos, you'll enjoy a more dynamic experience with the variable-speed "slider bar" that gives you the power to change the playback rate from one third to five times normal speed!

TimeTrade.com: (aka TimeDriver) Take the headache out of going back and forth trying to coordinate a meeting with all your partners. Let them schedule based on your availability.

Tungle.me: Online scheduling made easy, no need to send emails back and forth and convert time zones to meet with someone. Free accounts available, but you can also customize your platform to keep your personal branding.

TeuxDeux.com: Online app that allows you to manage your weekly to-do list. If you like making to-do lists as much as I do, you will love TeuxDeux. It's an intuitive platform that allows you to create to-do lists, check off items, delete items, and move tasks around.

The Action Machine: One of my favorite productivity tools that lets you organize your day and complete tasks so that you stay on track. Simply enter your tasks and set a time limit for each one. This software will turn you into an action machine!

InternetDownloadManager.com: A cool tool that will increase your download speeds by up to five times.

Product fulfillment

Disk.com: (I personally use them along with many major online marketers. Speak to Victoria Van Jacobs and tell her that Dr. Matthew Loop referred you.)

Kunaki.com: Print and ship on demand.

Copywriters

Writing sales-page copy is really hard work. However, you won't make sales without it, so it's CRITICAL to your success. These resources can create the copy for a written sales page or video sales letter:

http://john-carlton.com – John Carlton

http://www.DCincome.com/blog/copywriting – Yanik Silver

http://www.rayedwards.com – Ray Edwards

http://www.michelfortin.com – Michel Fortin

http://www.montellomarketing.com – Vin Montello

http://www.mikejezek.com/ – Mike Jezek

Ghostwriters

ContentDivas.com

Upwork.com

Writesyntax.com

Articlez.com

Writeraccess.com

Getarticlesdone.com

Do a Google search for "ghostwriters"

Voiceovers

Voices.com: Voices.com is the industry-leading website for voice talent.

Voice123.com: Another top-notch site for voice-over talent.

Product creation

eBooks Created: (Done-for-you product creation)

http://www.ebookscreated.com/services.html

Have your complete product done for you with EbooksCreated.com. For just $999 you can get a fifty-page e-book, complete minisite design, and an effective sales page ready to go.

The Product Machine:

http://www.theproductmachine.com

Another top-notch product creation service. They also have additional packages that include follow-up emails, squeeze page, short report, affiliate page, and affiliate tools.

PPC campaign management

Upwork.com: Find a certified Google AdWords specialist to set up, optimize, and manage your campaigns.

RocketClicks.com: Run by Glenn Livingston

Amkhan.com: Run by AM Khan

Helpful online forums

Learn anything and everything related to online marketing—tips, tools, resources, and the ability to ask questions while getting answers from seasoned veterans.

Forums.digitalpoint.com

WarriorForum.com

Appendix B

HELPFUL CONTENT
ARCHIVE

THE 12 COMMON DENOMINATORS
OF INTERNET MILLIONAIRES

Have you ever wondered how certain individuals are able to break out and make millions from the Internet? Are you curious what really separates them from the average majority?

What if I told you that 99 percent of rich online entrepreneurs had twelve things in common AND that if you modeled them, your path to seven figures was inevitable? Do I have your attention yet?

Good. … You're going to find this chapter incredibly revealing.

When I began my Internet entrepreneurial journey in late 2005, I wish I would've known these hidden gems I'm going to share with you right now. It would've saved me countless months of frustration.

Without delay, here are the twelve common denominators of Internet millionaires:

1. They're crystal clear on what they want.

Most millionaires I've become friends with mapped out their ideal life LONG before it ever came to be. They didn't write down and set goals for what they "thought" they could get either. They put down on paper what they really wanted in life. This encompassed all areas (business, material, health, relationships, spiritual, etc.). Specificity is king.

Just saying "I want to make more" doesn't do anything to attract your ideal life. Why? It's unattainable. There's no defined, exact figure. It can't be reverse engineered.

How much do you really want to make? How much does it cost to live the life you've always imagined?

Seriously, make a chart, get specific, and map out everything you want for you and the family. Also, include how much it costs. Then when you have a monthly grand total, you NOW have a clear picture.

2. They start an online business around their passion.

To make a cool seven figures from the Internet, you need to absolutely love what you do. I mean, you have to be freakin' IRRATIONALLY passionate about the business!

When you're just starting out, don't be surprised to find that you're putting in ten- to twelve-hour days.

In order to do this day-in and day-out, you must love what you do. In fact, even though you're getting things accomplished, it might not even feel like work.

ALL the Internet millionaires I've met started businesses around things they were passionate about. They found solutions to problems that other people faced. That set the stage for vast prosperity and abundance.

3. They network with other Internet millionaires.

Every seven-figure earner I know is in a high-level mastermind group where they interact with other millionaires. They have coaches because they're always searching to improve their results and make a greater impact.

Seasoned millionaires can provide objective feedback and find overlooked holes or additional profit centers. They give PROVEN advice that's worked in their own business.

Of course, these mastermind groups are not cheap, and some are by invitation only. However, the investment you make can come back tenfold or more in a few weeks. I'm living proof.

When you network with other A-players and top earners, fast business growth is inevitable. These guys don't think like everyone else—that's why they're in the top 1 percent!

Networking with and modeling millionaires, in addition to heeding their advice, can TRANSFORM your life for obvious reasons.

4. They hire their weaknesses.

Wealthy Internet entrepreneurs hire people SMARTER than they are to execute their visions. They know what they're good at, and they delegate everything else. You'll never see them trying to learn everything, attempting to be a jack-of-all-trades.

Millionaires also know that TIME is the one thing you can never get back. Time is more valuable than money, so they hire people for things they're not good at or for things that aren't a productive use of their time, such as household chores.

Work ON the business, become resourceful, and be the creative driver. Don't work "in" the business.

5. They take massive, focused action daily.

I've never met a lazy Internet millionaire, even though you don't have to look too far online to find folks that try to sell this idea. Seven-figure earners make a list of goals and tasks to accomplish each day. Then they work hard and stay focused for the allotted time frame.

They don't expect someone will save them (government, lucky star, lottery, etc.). They also don't get stuck in analysis paralysis or waiting for the "perfect" time.

The action millionaires take is massive, consistent, and unrelenting.

6. They understand it's NOT about the tactics.

It always blows my mind how many Internet entrepreneurs trade their job in corporate America only to become a slave to their online business. Here's what I mean: There's no shortage of marketing tactics or busy stuff you "could be doing" on the web. God knows many social media gurus love to teach the latest and greatest strategy, giving you more shit to do.

The reality is, there's no one magic bullet to getting all the traffic and sales you can handle. If you don't have a solid foundation and if your website doesn't convert traffic into sales, you'll continue to struggle for peanuts.

At the end of the day, sales conversion is the metric of all metrics. This is what gets you paid like a rock star.

7. They know their email list is their biggest asset.

Ask any Internet marketer that's sold millions of dollars' worth of products and services what their most valuable business asset is. Don't be shocked when they tell you it's their email list(s) that they've built from scratch.

You won't hear them talking too much about Facebook fans, YouTube subscribers, LinkedIn connections, etc. They understand social media is just one of many mediums to get qualified, prospective customers onto their email list.

Your email list is the one thing that Google or Facebook cannot take away from you. There are so many ways to deliver value and monetize it as well. The money is in the list. It's your lifeblood online.

8. They know how to sell.

This one single skill set is what separates the Internet elite from the average majority. Mastering the art of selling can add another zero (or two) to your bottom line. Why is this? Here's the deal.

You could have the best product or service in the world, but if you can't actually get someone to take their credit card out and invest in what you're offering ... it doesn't matter.

Let's be clear.

When I refer to selling, I'm talking about educating an already interested person in such a way that they take the next step immediately. You elicit a direct response.

The consumer sees the value, they get the benefits, they understand the product, and they believe it will get them the result they're seeking. This compels them to buy now.

9. They educate themselves on how to be more successful.

Right now, if you were to walk into an Internet millionaire's home, you'd probably find an extensive library of books regarding personal growth, development, and biographies.

Wealthy people are always learning from others that have had great success (in all areas of life). You won't find tabloids, entertainment magazines, and novels sitting on the table like what the average person reads—nor will you find them spending hours on end in front of the Tel-Lie-Vision.

10. They're not afraid to take risks.

Most individuals are incredibly afraid of failure and rejection. They avoid situations that make them uncomfortable or uncertain at all costs. The majority prefer to be in their safe house, which is a big reason why they live a mediocre life, never realizing what they're truly capable of.

Internet millionaires don't mind uncertainty or unknown territory. In fact, they're always pushing themselves out of their comfort zones. They understand this is how personal growth and dramatic life breakthroughs happen.

The upper class look at risk differently too. They live without regrets and don't let the "what if (something negative) happens" scare them. Risk is a part of life. It's far riskier to remain static, never fulfilling your maximum potential.

11. They're always paying it forward.

Internet millionaires have a burning desire to contribute, make a difference, and leave a strong legacy. This is what motivates and drives most, not the money.

What's interesting here is their habit of giving usually begins long before material wealth is accumulated. It's almost as if the universe rewards massive giving with more prosperity and abundance.

The best feeling in the world comes when you're on purpose and paying it forward.

12. They create multiple streams of passive income.

Every single millionaire I've become friends with, interviewed, or met at a seminar has multiple sources of passive income. This is money that gets deposited in the bank without them having to even think about it or do additional work.

The top 1 percent build their Internet empire like the Parthenon. If one pillar goes down, there are several other pillars supporting the main structure. They've set their businesses up in such a way that they couldn't stop the money pouring in even if they tried.

This concept is critical to understand and implement.

In the information publishing business (the biz we're in), there are several ways to establish consistent flows of recurring, effortless revenue—everything from e-books, DVD trainings, coaching programs, software, membership sites, consulting, speaking, iPhone apps, and more.

If you seriously want to create multiple streams of passive income or if you already have one but are not seeing the results you know you're capable of, I have great news.

You have the opportunity to work one-on-one with me and get my most complete training on all aspects of creating a seven-figure Internet empire. Two application-based options are available.

JK ROWLING PROVES
CONTENT IS NOT KING

Unless you live in a cave, you've probably heard the name Harry Potter mentioned a time or two. JK Rowling is the creative genius and author behind these best-selling fantasy novels. The books chronicle the adventures of the young wizard and his close friends. If you haven't read or watched the Harry Potter series, I highly recommend you check it out.

With that said, did you know that JK Rowling published a crime novel under a pseudonym? Going by the name Robert Galbraith, *The Cuckoo's Calling* was released in April 2013.

So, why did JK write using a pen name when she had already scaled the great wall of publishing and success? Sources report it was simply because she wanted honest feedback on her new book. She knew anonymity would guarantee this.

Let's face it: when you become one of the most famous authors in history, you develop RAVING fans. And while they love your work, it's much more difficult to get objective, unbiased opinions.

The Cuckoo's Calling was critically acclaimed when it launched, but according to Nielsen Bookscan, it had sold only 473 copies before the Harry Potter author was unmasked. In fact, just forty-three copies were sold the previous week.

After Rowling's identity was revealed on July 14, 2013, the book surged from 4,709th to the number one best-selling novel on Amazon. Stats also show 17,662 hardback copies were sold within the first SEVEN DAYS after the leak.

So, what does this have to do with anything?

Contrary to the myth many information publishers, marketers, and business owners have been led to believe, content is NOT king, nor is it the key to success! The release of *The Cuckoo's Calling* illustrates this point perfectly.

Even though the book garnered rave reviews and was written by one of the highest-grossing authors in history, the sales were slow. Why? I mean, the novel and writing style were top-tier by a seasoned author.

The real reason the booked gained little traction while JK remained anonymous was that there was little content distribution, promotion, and marketing. And that is what's really king.

We see this online frequently with information publishing. There's SO MUCH great content online, but it gets easily lost in the shuffle. What's the main reason for this?

It's because the authors don't know how to promote the content effectively to reach the critical mass. Or they just don't have an experienced professional team to help.

You could have the greatest blog post in the world, but if no one reads it, it doesn't matter. You won't get attention, recognition, traffic, or sales.

You see, unlike what the "gurus" have told you, simply creating content is not what leads to success. Yes, you have to deliver top-of-the-line material; however, understanding how to propagate it for the world to see is paramount.

Very few eyeballs = even fewer sales.

This JK Rowling example is also a fantastic demonstration of the divide between the big names in publishing and the rest. They have the tools, resources, finances, and connections to mass distribute content very rapidly.

If you're not "in the club," your chances of mainstream success are dramatically reduced. The same holds true for online entrepreneurs and marketers. I've blogged about this before. It all comes back to tools, resources, finances, and connections.

Do you have them? This book provides you with a massive jump-start that most online entrepreneurs never get.

The gap is widening, and the gatekeepers have come back in full swing. You're going to have to pay if you want to play these days—unless you are in the 1 percent that get picked up by a major publisher.

Distribution is getting more difficult for most because the financial barrier keeps increasing. Also, as the old saying goes, "It's not about what you know, it's about WHO you know."

SIDE NOTE: Can you imagine how the publishers that turned down "Robert Galbraith's" new detective novel must feel? Yes, they didn't know it was JK, but man, they MUST be kicking themselves.

HOW I GOT OVER 1,800 FACEBOOK LIKES TO ONE BLOG POST

B logging has been VERY good to me over the years. The recognition, traffic, and sales it's brought has been simply staggering. I've had several blog posts go viral and garner mass attention too.

When this first began to happen, I would say I was unconsciously competent. Meaning, I created a great blog post, but I didn't know WHY people thought it was great.

Then, as I began to study my most successful blogs, I discovered a predictable pattern that ensured they were seen by the masses and shared. That is when I became consciously competent.

You see ... creating content is what you must always be doing, but understand this: CONTENT IS NOT KING! This is probably the opposite of what you've heard from self-proclaimed gurus.

A lot of professionals create amazing content that doesn't see the light of day. It gets buried. There's no shortage of great content on the web.

So what separates the posts that get liked and shared by thousands versus the stuff that doesn't? It comes down to two words, "content marketing." This is what's most important.

You've got to know how to get noticed, especially if you're like the average majority who don't have connections and aren't "in the club."

Right now, I'd like to share with you my proven formula for getting attention in a "noisy" world. Among many accomplishments, this knowledge has enabled me to get over 1,800 Facebook shares to this blog post:

http://dcincome.com/blog/fact-or-fiction-chiropractic-saves-lives/.

When you follow these powerful steps, you'll always have a leg up on competitors in your industry.

1. Create a controversial blog post headline.

Most blog post headlines flat-out suck! They're boring. Yet the headline is one of the most important components to any successful blog post. Some would argue that it is the most critical piece.

Why?

Because your headline is the initial attention-grabber.

Whether on Google, Facebook, Twitter, etc. … the blog post title is what is seen first. If your title is strong, you can almost hypnotize people into clicking your link even if you're not in the best line of sight.

With this said, you obviously need to know your market well. What do they want? What solutions are they seeking? What mistakes are they making?

In my famous *Blogging Success Blueprint,* I share two powerful examples of how to title a blog post. If you currently don't have a copy of that PDF, just place your name and email in the form you see on the upper-right corner of the blog I included above so we can send it to you for free.

I also have fifteen more compelling, copy-and-paste headline templates you'll find in *The Ultimate Content Marketing Blueprint* training program.

2. Deliver value.

Now that you have an eye-popping title, you MUST deliver the goods in the actual content. This goes without saying. It's best to make your content practical so that people can use and easily implement the information the same day.

Bullet the important points to make it easier to consume for the person reading.

To deliver phenomenal value, you must understand the market you're servicing. Be authentic and don't be afraid to go against the conventional grain if your intentions are to clear up misconceptions and empower.

Address major concerns your audience is facing and provide facts and analysis. Always ask yourself, "Does this content I'm creating help solve a problem or better my reader's quality of life?"

Also, make sure you have clear, specific action steps you're giving others to fast-track their implementation.

3. Elicit an emotional response.

Don't shy away from controversy or the path less traveled. You need to get readers emotionally involved with your video or written blog posts. Fuse personal stories into the mix to help people connect with you on an even more intimate level.

Research, find, and include the pain and pleasure points of the audience you're appealing to. Get specific. Go into the small details so you can paint a vivid picture for others.

Furthermore, be direct and give your honest opinion regardless of popularity.

4. Tell readers what to do next.

You'd be absolutely amazed by just how many business owners and entrepreneurs do not tell readers what to do next. If you want an individual to like and share your post, TELL THEM directly to do that.

Never assume they'll automatically share the piece no matter how great it is. Give people a good, sincere reason why they should tell their friends too.

Lastly, you need to make it very simple to share your content. Have the social share buttons on each blog post like what you see at the bottom of mine.

5. Email subscriber and client lists.

Your email list is your #1 biggest asset online. It's the lifeblood of any brick-and-mortar or Internet business. When you post new content, email your subscribers and clients that are in your inner circle. They'll be more likely to share your stuff because you have a long relationship with them.

In your emails, evoke curiosity and let people know the "secrets" they'll discover by reading the content. Or let them know what mistakes they'll avoid.

List three to four bullet points in the email stressing what's in it for them.

6. Facebook advertising

Facebook advertising has been my secret weapon since 2008. Nothing has gotten my companies and me more exposure, traffic, and sales than this strategy. We've spent over $500,000 with the social network (and for good reason).

With the ad that was created for the blog post referenced a few paragraphs ago, I was spending an average of twelve cents per click! My click-through rate was as high as 5.12 percent at one point as well. You can't afford not to run ads with numbers that low. I promoted the blog post on Facebook for three weeks straight.

Paid advertising is the FASTEST way to get noticed and overcome critical mass in any market. It's impossible to compete with the sheer volume of targeted traffic Facebook sends. If you're not using Facebook ads consistently and your competitor is, you're getting crushed and don't even know it.

Facebook is an untapped goldmine of exposure if you create, optimize, and run ads like I teach in my private coaching programs. Success and sales are predictable. Return on investment has never been higher and ranges from 8:1 all the way to 11:1 on average.

The process I've described here is what enabled me to get over 1,800 Facebook likes to a blog post, and it has been responsible for countless others going viral. This is reliable and works like crazy.

Do not haphazardly create a blog post then hope the magical unicorns will carry and promote it online for you. Be proactive and commit to being unstoppable! The formula above is guaranteed to get you noticed.

BEFORE YOU USE THE PERISCOPE APP, READ THIS FIRST

With over one million users joining this platform in the first ten days of its launch, the Periscope app has turned out to be a communication juggernaut! According to the Wall Street Journal, Twitter quietly purchased Periscope for just under $100 million a few weeks before it was live on iTunes.

Think of Periscope as a live streaming app. That means, with the simple push of a button from your mobile phone, you can broadcast video live to anywhere in the world. Live streaming is nothing new; however, the ability to be able to do it from an app is a total game changer!

Influencers, brands, and celebrities are starting to recognize this, which is a huge reason for Periscope's lightning-fast rise to fame. The great thing is that anyone can use it with ease.

The first thing you need to do is download the application from either iTunes or the Android app store so it's on your phone. Once you do that, you can start playing around with Periscope's features. You'll see it's fairly simple.

The navigation bar has only a few options, and it's located at the bottom of the app. When you're ready to start a live broadcast, simply click the camera icon; it will then pull up another screen asking you to enable your microphone, phone camera, and location. Once you've done that, you're good to go! You can then live stream.

Some things to consider as you start to use Periscope are time of day to broadcast, the title of your live stream, and comment responses.

It's always a good idea to check your Twitter stats at www.analytics.Twitter.com so you can get an idea of what time of day your followers are most active. It's a good idea to do your live broadcast at that time unless you're going to email your list ahead of time so they can plan to attend.

Realize that every time you starting shooting a video, your Twitter followers get a notification about your show being live on Periscope. On top of that, the mobile live streaming network sends a pop-up notification to your Periscope followers! This is awesome because it's kind of like a text message.

This one single feature makes it easy to create a surge of viewers when you build your following on Periscope! Expect your engagement to skyrocket as you acquire more quality followers.

Even if many of your followers miss the show, Periscope saves the videos for twenty-four hours so people can catch the replay. If you're really happy with the live stream after it's completed, you also have the ability to save it to your phone.

Now we need to talk about the title of your video. Think of this as your "unique selling proposition." It's what differentiates your content from the rest of the pack. This is seen in the "featured" or "recent" streams section of the app.

In this book and in the resources provided, you learned how to create compelling, benefit-rich titles that make people want to click. Periscope is a platform where you need to use those newly acquired skills!

Titles can be "How to _____," "3 Mistakes to Avoid When_____," "Breaking News: _____," "The #1 Secret to _____," "What questions did you have about _____?" etc. Refer to the many examples given in this book.

Lastly, let's touch on comments and responses. This is one of the best features of Periscope. Anyone that's watching your broadcast live can "like" the video.

When done, a heart shows up. Other watchers can see the number of hearts you get as well as comments from others.

When you acknowledge or respond to fan comments aloud, this shows you're paying attention to the feedback and makes viewers want to engage even more. Always make a point to have the conversation flow both ways.

Just an FYI ... the quantity of hearts you get helps your channel get ranked in the "Popular People to Follow" section of Periscope. Secondly, there's also a section called "Most Loved" that's for those live streams with the most hearts.

To get lots of views to the broadcast, make sure to email your list and share the link on Twitter, Facebook, and other social media outlets. Also, turn on the location tagging option in Periscope. That gets you even more visibility. You can use many of the strategies you've learned in this book to pull extra traffic too.

Here's how you can profitably integrate Periscope in your business:

Below, you'll find several different ways that you can use live streaming in your lead generation, customer support, or sales process.

Question/Answer Sessions

If you have a product, you can hold a members only Q&A strategy mastermind where you're answering any questions your customers have. You can also use this method to build rapport with prospective clients like you would during a live Google Hangout.

The feedback from viewers is instant. Realize you can do sessions like this on the fly or plan them out a few days in advance. It's up to you. You'd be surprised by just how close some prospects are to buying what you have to offer. One simple live Q&A session can round up many that are on the fence.

Run a Contest

Just like what you'd do on Facebook to stimulate fan growth, you can do the same thing with Periscope. Have a contest that's specific to anyone who follows you on this live stream platform. Alert your email list and update your social profiles days in advance to promote this giveaway.

Product Launch

Doing a new product launch? Fantastic! Use Periscope to reveal it to the world. Create buzz with a series of short content-rich videos. You can even interview others that have used or are currently using your product.

Show a Behind-the-Scenes View

People like to get a glimpse of what happens behind the curtain, so give them what they want. Use Periscope to give an office tour or to interview your team. This helps others develop a personal connection with your brand or business.

Influencer Endorsements

This could be from a major celebrity or a local weatherman that's on TV all the time. Either way, it gets your company noticed and creates credibility by association. We've seen major brands start doing this by having famous entertainers take over their Periscope accounts and surprise the audience. That's a surefire path to high engagement.

Share Stories

Stories connect us on a deeper level. Consumers like to do business with brands, business owners, and entrepreneurs who they feel are like them. They want to know you understand their problems and that you can relate. Personal stories of hardship, success, reluctant heroes, rags to riches, etc. help bridge this connection.

Presentations

Do you do like to do white-board or other types of presentations? Great. You can use Periscope to broadcast them live and get instant feedback! As questions come in, you can further tailor your content to the needs of your audience. This helps you build authority in the eyes of your viewers. It's also convenient for them because they can view your presentation at home, in the car, etc.

Other similar platforms to consider

Other mobile apps you should definitely be aware of that have live stream capability are Meerkat, MyEye, and Live for Facebook mentions. Facebook has only made live mentions available for verified pages (those with the blue checkmark on them). I suspect that will change in the near future and that it will be rolled out to everyone.

All of these competing platforms function pretty much the same. Periscope is the leader in the marketplace though. Plus, it's a favorite for celebrities and public figures.

Live streaming from mobile is NOT just some fad that's going to come and go. It's here to stay, so it should be integrated into your overall outreach and brand promotion strategy. The earlier you get in, the better off you'll be. Early adopters are the ones that gain the biggest influence and reap the most profits when new communication tools arise.

SHOULD I TELL MY FAMILY I'M
STARTING AN ONLINE BUSINESS?

Aspiring Internet entrepreneurs ask me this question all the time, so I wanted to address it here. When starting an online business, DO NOT tell your family and friends immediately! They will tend to think you're batshit crazy (in other words, certifiably nuts).

Listen ... I get it.

You're excited and you want to share your enthusiasm with your inner circle. However, those closest to you almost always do not totally understand your vision nor have they seen the potential and case studies you've witnessed. Heck, I still have friends and family that probably think I sell drugs.

Seriously!?

Making money online is an ALTERNATE universe for most people. The average person has been conditioned to exchange time for money, and it's not easy for them to think outside the conventional box. Also, the conversation can get a little tricky as you start generating A LOT of income from the Internet.

I distinctly remember the conversation I had with one friend. He asked me what my highest-grossing day was. I told him, and he became real quiet. His posture started to sink not long after. It's not easy for some people to know that you've earned in a DAY what they've made in an entire month of working hard.

On the other hand, a few will be inspired to learn more. I know I certainly was the first time I met a seven-figure Internet marketer. My eyes were opened to a new world of possibility. Then, once I got my first sale I was totally hooked.

When you're just starting out on the Internet, you need to MINIMIZE resistance and surround yourself with other encouraging entrepreneurs that are already making money online.

In most cases, telling your family at the beginning will only lead to more headaches. Once they see those fat bank deposits when you're up and running, that's a different story.

I cannot stress enough how critical this is to your confidence and overall attitude.

IS PHILANTHROPY PART OF
YOUR SOCIAL MEDIA STRATEGY?

As a business owner and entrepreneur, when you experience great success in life, I believe it comes with even greater responsibility. The power to impact and transform typically amplifies when you've been blessed with prosperity and abundance. You're simply able to reach and serve more beyond your physical means.

This being said, are YOU committed to leaving a legacy that makes a positive difference in the world through contribution and philanthropy? This is a powerful question many successful entrepreneurs don't think about early in their careers.

Why?

Well, because it's easy to get preoccupied with toys, trinkets, lifestyle, and other material things initially.

Then, something interesting happens.

Eventually you realize that while it's cool to have nice possessions, the acquisition of "stuff" is not what leads to happiness and life fulfillment.

The simple act of GIVING does.

When I reflect on some of the most incredible moments of my life, I remember instances when I was on purpose giving freely without expecting anything in return. I'm talking about activities like donating my time, empowering someone with life-changing knowledge, giving away money, sharing a meal, offering a gift, etc. All of those brought (and still bring) such wonderful feelings and real meaning.

Besides providing greater fulfillment, you also begin to evoke a natural law of the universe. You know, the one that says, "The more you give the more you get." It's so true.

When you come from a mindset of abundance, you're positioning yourself to receive abundance. On this important note, let's talk about what you can do TODAY to make philanthropy a regular part of your life and social media strategy.

Step 1: Find a charity you're passionate about that aligns with your attitudes, values, and beliefs.

If you cannot find one, create your own nonprofit. The organization you select should be congruent with who you are on a deeper level so you can genuinely be committed to helping the cause.

Don't just choose a nonprofit because it's trendy or what everyone is doing. Do your research and due diligence based on what key issues are important to you.

In order to start giving back or making a difference, you don't need a charity though. Help your neighbor. Just get involved and do something!

Step 2: Interview the charity and know where the donations go and in what percentages.

It's important to know how much money actually goes to the cause versus how much goes to administration costs.

You'd be absolutely shocked to know that the overwhelming majority of contributions for many well-known nonprofits, organizations, and charities goes to keeping the executives with fat pockets.

We see this A LOT in health care. Know as much as you can about the organization you're connecting with. Since you're going to be making donations regularly, you might even request to see the books.

Step 3: Commit to a monthly contribution.

When you've finally decided on the right charity for you, take a percentage of your gross revenue each month and give it away freely to the organization you're supporting. Or lend precious time to the cause. As you know, contribution doesn't always have to be about donating money.

Just make a goal to help in some way. It's important to create an empowering habit of giving though. It serves you and the people you come in contact with in all walks of life.

Step 4: Give credit and recognition where it's due.

Be a force for good and let family, friends, email subscribers, blog readers, and business customers know about the charity you support. This brings them more recognition and can help enlist other people to champion your cause.

Don't be shy about edifying the organization you're proud to be associated with either. Chances are, they're seeking to positively impact as many lives as possible. Getting them attention and spotlight recognition first by being a powerful voice.

Step 5: Publicize this act of kindness.

In today's time, people like to do business with others that have a strong "why." Here's what I mean: The public loves heartfelt stories, and many want to be part of something bigger, a movement if you will. They want to know there's a noble purpose behind what you do.

When you come across as sincere, authentic, and committed to making an impact, you'll have others who want to join the cause and associate with you. This one act alone is a HUGE differentiator from the rest of the businesses in your space. Look around in your market; you might be stunned at just how few incorporate philanthropy.

When people see and understand your motivations are deeper and not just about the money, it resonates on an intimate level with them. The price of your product or service almost becomes irrelevant.

If you articulate why you do what you do and then back it up with actions, you become a magnet for your perfect audience. You'll earn their respect, and they'll want to be part of the movement.

Not to mention, when your company announces philanthropic donations via the media, it also helps attract more attention to the charity you've aligned with. It reflects great on both of you.

So in a nutshell, making charitable contributions is just a wonderful habit to get into.

You get to lend a helping hand to those in need, which creates goodwill and fulfillment. It creates an empowering habit that serves you and others, and it shows your audience you're committed to an important cause bigger than yourself.

Philanthropy also leads to good PR and notoriety for your business, which then creates more growth and contribution.

Incorporate what you've read here today into your social media strategy and watch the impact you make greatly expand. You'll also experience more prosperity and abundance as a result.

Leave a legacy you and your family can be proud of. Start now!

Important Note: Each "for-profit" product, training, and service featured on the website (MatthewLoop.com) is tied to a nonprofit initiative. This is done because my companies and I are committed to paying it forward. It's just the right thing to do.

When you invest in your success through our programs, you're not only helping yourself, but you're also helping support entrepreneurs in developing nations, wounded soldiers, and more.

3 WAYS TO ADD AN EXTRA $100,000 IN RECURRING INCOME THIS YEAR

H ave you set and solidified your goals for this year yet? If so, I would imagine that one of them is to earn more money, right? Well, this article is going to reveal three powerful, PROVEN ways to generate an extra six figures in recurring income this year.

I've done it many times over, and so have quite a few of my personal coaching clients.

I'm sure you'd agree that having a small business (brick and mortar or online) can be tough at times, especially in this uncertain day and age. However, when you have additional, reliable streams of revenue rolling in, it affords you the ability to create your own year-round prosperous economy.

So what are the best ways to create an extra six figures ON TOP of your current business? Here they are in no particular order:

Personal coaching/consulting

This is a revenue steam that I've been blessed in ABUNDANCE with. It still blows my mind that people are willing to pay such a premium for experience-based advice. But I get it. It's what I personally do in many areas of my life.

If I need information that I know will add more income to my business, I seek out a master in that specific area. It's much cheaper for me to "buy speed" from an expert than to mess around learning for weeks, months, or more. This is one reason the rich get richer. The top 1 percent always know the value of their time and are interested in speed of implementation. Time is money.

In my business, I offer private phone coaching or a live, in-person, total immersion day. Both are application-based programs.

I get to work with professionals I want to work with, and they pay a premium for my Internet moneymaking knowledge. Most clients make their investment back in the first forty-five days or less too.

It turns out that those that pay high prices for a service value it more, are less hassle to me, implement what I say, and then get the best results and make the greatest case studies. It really doesn't get any better than that.

Start doing speaking gigs

In 2006, my life changed forever in a few different ways. My name was getting around in different circles, and a network marketing company got a hold of me, wanting to speak to their company CEO about Myspace and YouTube marketing.

I was kind of new to speaking at that time, and they asked me what my fee was to present for an hour. "Umm …," I thought to myself. Then I just blurted out, "$1,500 plus airfare and accommodations."

The next thing that came out of this guy's mouth was, "Can we meet this Tuesday in Houston?"

I was floored.

That's when I got a taste of how lucrative speaking could be. I ended up flying there and speaking for around an hour and a half. I got home back in Atlanta around 5:00 p.m. that day and sat in front of my computer for about an hour wondering what the heck just happened!

Since that time, I've performed countless speaking engagements, and I get paid at least a $5,000 honorarium almost every time. Mind you, this is for one hour of speaking.

The bottom line is that the acquisition of knowledge is VERY important in today's time. It doesn't matter what business you have. You have information and experience that others simply don't!

There's absolutely no reason you can't earn an extra $5,000 per month just from speaking—not to mention that most of the time you get to offer your product or service when you're finished, which leads to way more back-end sales and income.

Master information product development and marketing

In a separate blog post, I outlined how my "secondary" source of income became my primary, overtaking my practice. I accomplished this through profitable marketing of video trainings, e-books, and teleseminar audio courses. They simply solved a HUGE problem that the market was facing.

These products are able to be sold 24/7, which enables you to break away from the "exchanging time for money" hamster wheel. Imagine having sales pour into your bank account while you sleep. It's a total game changer and never gets old, trust me.

I'm going to group affiliate marketing into this category as well since it's where you take a digital product that someone else has created and promote it. This is where I actually got my feet wet in Internet marketing in 2005.

The first affiliate commission I made changed my life. It opened my eyes to the fact that making real money online was not only possible, but it could be used to grow a six- and seven-figure business.

As I built email lists in different industries, the commissions came easier and faster!

As an affiliate, you don't have to stock any inventory; there's no recruiting others; there are no products to ship and no handling payments; the start-up cost is low; and you have huge flexibility to promote how you want. It's one of the easiest ways to generate income from the web.

As my business grew and technology progressed, I went on to develop other things like premium webinar trainings and iPhone apps.

Now, everything I touch turns to gold. Meaning, it's easy for me to go into any market and create a passive source of income from scratch. Here's an example: http://DCincome.com/blog/how-i-created-an-extra-2163-month-passive-revenue-stream/.

IMPORTANT: If you are seriously thinking about adding one of these proven recurring, passive income methods or if you already have one but are not seeing the results you know that you want, I have great news.

You have the opportunity to get my most complete and detailed training on all aspects of information marketing.

Two options are available at the links below. Find out if you qualify for private one-on-one coaching or the Total Immersion experience today.

http://DCincome.com/blog/coaching

http://DCincome.com/blog/total-immersion-day

HOW TO CREATE A FREE
REPORT (7 EASY STEPS)

In the world of Internet entrepreneurship, an organically acquired email list is the backbone and foundation of your business. It doesn't matter if you're an online business owner or have a brick-and-mortar company either.

You MUST build a list if you're serious about maximizing your effectiveness, reaching the most customers, and growing your business to extraordinary levels.

Here's a reality check.

No matter how aesthetically appealing your site is, the overwhelming majority of people that go to any given small business website stay there for less than thirty seconds. Studies show that once the visitor is gone, they rarely return.

Knowing this, it's critically important to "capture" as many names and emails as possible in order to *follow up* with them so prospective customers get to know, like, and trust you.

You've got one shot to do this. Internet surfers are highly skeptical these days, and most are "slow dates."

Around 1–2 percent (on average) will actually go to your website, pick up the phone, and call you immediately or place an instant order. This holds true if you own a physical or online business.

One of the numerous benefits of building a list is that your conversion numbers skyrocket in the short and long run if you're sending follow-up emails on a regular basis. Conversion numbers can jump into the 15–20 percent range.

I'm sure you'd agree that's a huge difference from not building a list. This alone can add an EXTRA zero to you income this year if you nourish the email list properly.

Here are the questions you have to ask yourself before we dig in:

Do you want more clients/customers without having to do more hard work? And would you like to dramatically increase the percentage of web visitors that call or buy your products or services?

If you answered YES to those questions, pay close attention and follow this professional advice.

The real secret to increasing the number of walk-in referrals you get from the Internet is to have a "consumer awareness" oriented free report or giveaway on your website. That's our "ethical bribe."

You're providing someone with essential information they're ALREADY seeking in exchange for their name and email address so you know where to send the report.

The following are seven simple steps that will help you create a valuable free report that positions you as a trusted authority in the eyes of your potential new client:

1. Think of a compelling, consumer-friendly name for the report. The title will make or break you and could be the difference between you getting a trickle and a flood of new clients/customers.

Some examples include:

- *Before Visiting a Divorce Attorney, Read This Consumer Report*
- *5 Mistakes MOST People Make When Choosing a Chiropractor*

- *10 Questions You MUST Ask Before Visiting a Cosmetic Surgeon*
- *Before Considering Risky Back Surgery or Dangerous Pain Meds, Read This*

2. List the top ten to fifteen frequently asked questions you get on a sheet of paper. You could probably answer these in your sleep as they come up so often. Also, list a few questions that people "should be" asking you about your service or specialty. Make sure that common objections are in there as well.

Your goal here is to answer questions before they consciously arise in your potential customer's mind. This builds trust and rapport quickly.

Open an account on FreeConferenceCall.com. This service doesn't cost you anything, and it has an option to let you to record your conversation. Call in to the specific number they give you with a friend, spouse, or family member who will be the one asking you the questions you wrote down.

3. Open up with a simple introduction about why the report was created. Remember, this is not about you. It's all about providing valuable information to the end consumer that will be reading the report.

Have the other person on the phone ask you the questions you wrote down in interview style. Naturally, you're steering them to your service as the only logical choice by the way you answer the questions.

This powerful technique helps you rise above the perception of being just another commodity. This enables you to charge what you're worth instead of competing on price alone.

At the end of the call, make a professional call to action that is available for only a limited time to those that "qualify."

4. After you download the MP3 file at freeconferencecall.com, hire a transcription specialist from Upwork.com or SpeechPad.com to transcribe the audio recording you created. Our goal is efficiency here.

They can even edit and format the document for you per your instructions. Turnaround time can be as little as a few hours to a couple days depending on how fast you need it.

5. Get an e-book cover designed at eCoverArt.com or Fiverr.com. This is the image that you will place on your website next to the lead-capture boxes. You can get a very nice, clean cover design very affordably.

You ideally want a cover designed because it elevates the perceived value of the report the consumer is receiving. It looks real and tangible.

6. Get an Aweber account. This is what you'll use to place lead-capture (a.k.a. opt-in) boxes on your website.

It also helps you to manage your collected email database, queue autoresponder messages, send email broadcasts, and track statistics (like email deliverability, open rates, clicks, etc.).

You can get a $1 trial of Aweber email marketing software at:

MyProResponse.com.

It's the system that I personally use, so you know it's the best.

7. Download the free PDF converter a DoPDF.com to turn your transcribed word document into a professional-looking downloadable PDF.

Your programmer or webmaster can handle the duty of placing the free report image and Aweber code on your website. Let them do what they're best at. Ideally, you want this ethical bribe and offer on the right side of your site above the fold.

This is the simplest way to generate a custom, free report you can give away to collect names and emails in order to build your list! Not to mention, it requires MINIMAL effort on your part since you now know how to be more resourceful.

The real power comes in when you develop a large email list (into the thousands) from all the traffic that's visited your website. Now you can literally push the email send button and initiate an avalanche of new customers and fresh passive revenue if you have the right campaign.

This is the ULTIMATE form of online leverage!

14 DUMB SOCIAL MEDIA MISTAKES YOU MIGHT BE MAKING

H ere are the common (and all too costly) social media promotion mistakes that brands, entrepreneurs, and business must avoid making in order to multiply monthly sales volume and revenue.

1. Thinking that having a website constitutes marketing online

The same holds true for a Facebook fan page. Having those are great; however, you MUST know how to be able to send a flood of qualified traffic to the site (and be able to convert them) if you ever hope to get new customers.

You could have the best product and website in the world, but if people don't know about it, you're screwed. Having a website is not the same as proactive Internet promotion. It's only the start.

2. Assuming that all website traffic is created equal and having unrealistic expectations

An example of this would be Google search traffic versus Facebook advertising traffic. While both can be extremely effective for generating new sales hand over fist, realize the marketing, ad creation, and destination pages have to be structured differently. There is a certain (and predictable) way to ensure success with any traffic source.

3. Subscribing to the notion that social media marketing is unprofessional

This perception is hurting A LOT of brands and entrepreneurs right now and has prevented them from harnessing this highly powerful business growth platform. Professionalism is dependent on how well you position yourself online in your marketplace.

There are a number of factors that determine this, and I went over many in this book.

Many brands are still on the sidelines while customers are leaving them behind. Conventional advertising is all but dead. Just know that people want to get to know their brand and see that there are real people behind the curtain.

If done right, no other outreach medium showcases this better than social media.

4. Expecting Facebook page "fans" to automatically convert to paying customers

The truth is, you must build relationships with most prospective clients first before they'll ever do business with you. Now, there are direct-response methods that you can use to dramatically accelerate this process, but the majority of entrepreneurs and brands don't use them.

On this same note, the number of fans you have is not directly proportional to the paying customers you can expect. Too many "gurus" have pushed this nonsense for years.

5. Searching for the "magic bullet" tactic that will get you all the sales you want

There are dozens of strategies to combine when using social media marketing effectively. There is no quick fix. Anyone that has built a business or large brand from the web (including myself) never hit it big overnight. Social media can change your life, but it takes work and commitment.

6. Going ALL-IN without a well-structured, systematic, daily/weekly task list

Without a plan, social media promotion can be a HUGE nonproductive time suck. This is where many business owners go off the cliff. Because some of the marketing can be done without spending money on traditional advertising, a lot of brands assume that it must be simple. The truth is, it's not.

7. Not tracking your website analytics AND how well your site is actually converting online visitors into sales

What gets measured gets improved. You must have a baseline to compare your stats to. It's important to know how many visitors are coming to your site, how long they're staying there, where they're coming from, what pages they're frequenting, the site bounce rate, etc.

8. Getting caught up in the latest "shiny object" promotion tactic and not focusing on core fundamentals

Certain social media strategies have worked like magic for years and will continue to work. Traffic generation and building relationships hasn't changed as much as fly-by-night consultants want you to believe.

If you're not getting the results you want, it's probably not because you're missing the latest and greatest tactic. Focus on the foundational principles.

9. Becoming overly preoccupied with Google and minimizing all other aspects of social media marketing

Google is just one aspect, yet many brands look at a #1 Google ranking as the pinnacle of Internet success. This is not smart and certainly doesn't guarantee new customers and sales.

10. Inconsistent communication, outreach, and promotion

This is the kiss of death. When you stop and start, you lose traction. If you're a business, this makes you vulnerable to your competitors. If you're a celebrity, long absences come across as if you don't really care too much about your social media fan base.

There are proven ways to seamlessly delegate in-office without spending a lot of time, money, and effort. Remember though: "busy work" does not necessarily constitute strategic outreach.

11. Updating in the third person

This point is specifically for celebrities and public figures. It's in very bad taste to have another person update your Twitter, Facebook, Instagram, etc. Fans expect you to interact with them. Even the busiest entertainers and artists are personally updating their accounts daily. It takes a couple seconds.

The only exception to this is if you have a team member posting an update with an image, video, or link to a public appearance, current project, etc. For the most part, though, it should be your voice to maintain authenticity. You need to personally update the accounts.

12. Thinking social media is optional for your brand or business

Would you believe there are still major companies, small businesses, and entrepreneurs that are hardly (sometimes not even at all) doing social media! It's 100 percent necessary now. If you don't use social media and have an OVERWHELMING presence online, potential clients look at you as suspect. Translation ... they trust you less. Research has proven this time and time again.

This year and beyond, you MUST master the art of social media outreach or you're in for a rude awakening as times change. Each day that passes is an opportunity missed. Act fast, act now!

13. Hiring a social media manager and expecting growth

This should be painfully obvious, but many fall into this trap. A manager manages. It's unreasonable to expect a manager to have the mind of an entrepreneur in order to grow your brand or company. Managers have never built million-dollar companies from scratch with social media.

You need strategies that develop relationships, grow your influence, make an impact, create buzz, generate goodwill, and multiply revenue. There's a time and place for a manager once you have proven yourself and bankable promotion methods are in place.

As a social media revenue strategist, I help brands, businesses, and public figures uncover hidden profit centers so they can reach, serve, and earn more. I also teach them the tactics, tools, and resources that are working now to produce massive growth.

14. Thinking you can do everything alone without professional guidance

You're an entrepreneur and/or business owner, not an experienced social media expert. Know your limitations and when to get help. This can save you headaches, frustration, and wasted time and money.

If Internet promotion were easy, every brand would have a BOOMING bottom line. If you look around, you'll see in short order this is not the case. The window of opportunity is shrinking as the web evolves.

The question is, are you evolving with it? If you're ready to get serious in regards to attracting an avalanche of new fans, customers, sales, greater brand visibility, and more recognition from social media, we need to connect.

34 RULES FOR MAVERICK
ENTREPRENEURS

Yanik Silver redefines how businesses is played in the twenty-first century as the intersection of more profits, more fun, and more impact. Starting with his first million-dollar idea at three o'clock in the morning, he has bootstrapped seven other products and services to the seven-figure mark from scratch without funding, taking on debt, or even having a real business plan.

Yanik's story and businesses have been featured in *WIRED, TIME.com, USA Today, SmartMoney.com, MSN Money, Entrepreneur, Fox Business News, WORTH. com,* and the *Wall Street Journal* among others.

He is the author of several best-selling marketing books and tools including *Maverick Startup, Instant Sales Letters*® and *34 Rules for Maverick Entrepreneurs.* Yanik is the host of the annual Underground Online Seminar®, a noted "Top-10 Event for Entrepreneurs" by Forbes.

His latest venture is Maverick1000, a private, invitation-only global network of top entrepreneurs and industry leaders. This group periodically assembles for breakthrough retreats, rejuvenating experiences, and "giving forward" opportunities with participating icons such as Sir Richard Branson, Tony Hawk,

Chris Blackwell, John Paul DeJoria, CEO of Zappos.com Tony Hsieh, Russell Simmons, and Tim Ferriss.

Yanik's lifetime goal is to connect evolved entrepreneurs to catalyze innovative business models and new ideas for solving 100 of the world's most impactful issues by the year 2100. Leveraging business as a multiplier for good … co-creating something great.

As a self-described "adventure junkie," Yanik has found that his own life-changing experiences—such as running with the bulls, flying MiG jets, HALO skydiving, exotic car rallies, and zero-gravity flights—have not only expanded his limits but also led to breakthroughs in ideas, focus, and business thinking. In between checking off items on his "Ultimate Big Life List," he calls Potomac, Maryland, home with his wife, Missy, and two mini maverick adventurers in the making, Zack and Zoe.

I've been a fan of Yanik's work for years. He's the epitome of a man living the "Internet lifestyle" and someone I've modeled closely in many aspects of business.

Here are Yanik's 34 rules for maverick entrepreneurs:

1. It's got to be a BIG idea that you, your team, and your customers can "get" in seconds.
2. Strive to create ten to a hundred times in value for any price you charge. Your rewards are always proportionate to the value you provide.
3. You must charge a premium price so you have a large margin to provide an extraordinary value and experience.
4. Provide a "Reason Why" customers should do business with you and pay you a premium.
5. Get paid before you deliver your product or service. And when possible figure out how to create recurring revenue from transactions.
6. You get to make the rules for your business. Don't let industry norms dictate how you'll work or who you'll work with.
7. Create your business around your life instead of settling for your life around your business.

8. Consistently and constantly force yourself to focus on the "critically few" proactive activities that produce exponential results. Don't get caught up in minutia and bullshit.

9. Seek to minimize start-up risk but have maximum upside potential.

10. Get your idea out there as fast as possible, even if it's not quite ready, by setting must-hit deadlines. Let the market tell you if you have a winner or not. If not, move on and fail forward fast! If it's got potential, you can make it better.

11. Find partners and team members who are strong where you are weak and appreciate being paid on results.

12. Your reputation always counts. Honor your obligations and agreements.

13. Never, ever get paid based on hours worked.

14. Leverage your marketing activities exponentially by using direct-response methods and testing.

15. Measure and track your marketing so you know what's working and what's not.

16. Bootstrap. Having too much capital leads to incredible waste and doing things using conventional means.

17. Your partners' and employees' actions are their true core—not what they tell you.

18. Keep asking the right questions to come up with innovative solutions. "How?", "What?", "Where?", "Who else?" and "Why?" open up possibilities.

19. You'll never have a perfect business, and you'll never be totally "done." Deal with it.

20. Focus most of your time on your core strengths and less time working in areas where you suck.

21. Make it easier for customers to buy by taking away the risk of the transaction by guaranteeing what you do in a meaningful way.

22. Always have something else to sell (via upsell, cross-sell, follow-up offer, etc.) whenever a transaction takes place. The hottest buyer in the world is one who just gave you money.

23. Always go back to your existing customers with exceptional offers and reasons they should give you more money. It's five times less expensive to sell to happy customers than go find new ones.

24. However, the flip side is this: fire your most annoying customers. They'll be replaced with the right ones.

25. The marketplace and competitors are always trying to beat you down to a commodity. Don't let that happen.

26. Develop and build your business's personality that stands out. People want to buy from people.

27. Create your own category so you can be first in the consumer's mind.

28. Go the opposite direction competitors are headed—you'll stand out.

29. Mastermind and collaborate with other smart entrepreneurs if they have futures that are even bigger than their present.

30. Celebrate your victories. It's too easy to simply move on to your next goal without acknowledging and appreciating the "win."

31. Make your business AND doing business with you FUN!

32. Do the unexpected before and after anything goes wrong so customers are compelled to "share your story."

33. Get a life! Business and making money are important, but your life is the sum total of your experiences. Go out and create experiences and adventures so you can come back renewed and inspired for your next big thing.

34. Give back! Commit to taking a percentage of your company's sales and make a difference. It this becomes a habit like brushing your teeth, pretty soon the big checks with lots of zeros won't be scary to write. If you think you can't donate a percentage of your sales, simply raise your price.

RECOMMENDED READINGS

The 10x Rule – Grant Cardone

The 7 Habits of Highly Effective People – Steven Covey

Atlas Shrugged – Ayn Rand

Awaken the Giant Within – Anthony Robbins

The Brand Within – Daymond John

The Credibility Code – Cara Hale Alter

DotComSecrets: The Underground Playbook – Russell Brunson

The E-Myth – Michael E. Gerber

The Four Hour Workweek – Tim Ferriss

How to Win Friends and Influence People – Dale Carnegie

Influence: The Psychology of Persuasion – Robert Cialdini

Launch – Jeff Walker

The Law of Success in Sixteen Lessons – Napoleon Hill

Lead the Field – Earl Nightingale

Magic Words That Bring You Riches – Ted Nicholas

Maverick Startup – Yanik Silver

Pitch Anything – Oren Klaff

Predictably Irrational, the Forces that Shape Our Decisions - Dan Ariely

Rhinoceros Success – Scott Alexander

Rich Dad: Poor Dad – Robert Kiyosaki

The Sandler Rules: 49 Timeless Selling Principles – David Mattson

The Science of Getting Rich – Wallace Wattles

Screw Business As Usual – Richard Branson

Success Principles – Jack Canfield

Think and Grow Rich – Napoleon Hill

The Ultimate Sales Letter – Dan Kennedy

The Ultimate Sales Machine – Chet Holmes

Winning Through Intimidation – Robert Ringer

You Were Born Rich – Bob Proctor

CPSIA information can be obtained at www.ICGtesting.com
Printed in the USA
LVOW11s1146110216

474536LV00032B/247/P